The
Adena
People

The Adena People

BY WILLIAM S. WEBB AND CHARLES E. SNOW

with a Chapter on Adena Pottery
and a Foreword to the New Edition by

JAMES B. GRIFFIN

THE UNIVERSITY
OF TENNESSEE PRESS

Library of Congress Cataloging in Publication Data

Webb, William Snyder, 1882–1964.
  The Adena people.
  Reprint of the 1945 ed. published by the University
of Kentucky, Lexington, which was issued as v. 6 of its
Dept. of Anthropology and Archaeology Reports in anthro-
pology and archaeology.
  Bibliography: p.
  1. Adena culture. I. Snow, Charles Ernest,
1910–   joint author. II. Title. III. Series:
Kentucky. University. Dept. of Anthropology. Reports
in anthropology, v. 6.
E78.04W38 1974   970.4'7   74-10598
ISBN O-87049-159-8

FOREWORD TO THE NEW EDITION

The Adena People by William S. Webb and Charles E. Snow was one of the major publications on eastern United States archaeology in the first half of this century. The result of a long-standing collaboration between two faculty members of the University of Kentucky, the book has been widely praised and still remains a standard reference work on this prehistoric Ohio Valley occupation. *The Adena People* has historical interest because the study gives a clear view of American archaeology as practiced in the 1930s and 1940s. It was a time of intensive excavation and taxonomy; field techniques that seem crude beside the sophisticated skills of today, and a willingness to speculate, led archaeologists to postulate a variety of taxonomic relationships, many of which—including much of the interpretation in *The Adena People*—would be immediately discarded by modern researchers. The emphasis on excavation, on the other hand, meant that a great deal of data was recovered, and, although today we might wish it had been handled more fastidiously, much of that data was reported only in works of synthesis like *The Adena People*.

The authors of this treatise were representative of the archaeologists of the day. William Snyder Webb was born, raised, and educated in the Lexington, Kentucky, area and lived most of his life there. He had a number of careers, of which archaeology was perhaps the most important during the latter part of his life. His professional training was in physics; he was appointed an assistant professor at the University of Kentucky in 1908 and became head of the Physics department in 1919. In 1929, Webb was also appointed head of the Department of Anthropology and Archaeology and, along with W. D. Funkhouser, constituted the department. Funkhouser at that time was head of the Department of Zoology, and the two men combined to produce a number of archaeological reports, establishing the remarkable University of Kentucky series in archaeology and anthropology.

Because of the associations Webb had built up with professional archaeologists, in 1934 he was asked to take charge of the Tennessee Valley Authority archaeological program; he headed this program until the emergency of the Second World War forced its temporary curtailment. Thomas M. N. Lewis of the University of Tennessee worked under Webb initially in eastern Tennessee; David I. DeJarnette was the University of Alabama representative in northern Alabama. Over a period of years there was gathered in the TVA area a group of young field and laboratory archaeologists who had received training at a variety of schools and who were the primary contributors to the development of field and laboratory techniques under Webb's general direction. In 1936–37, when it became possible to initiate a WPA archaeological program in Kentucky, Webb took some of his best young men from the Tennessee Valley operation and put them to work on Archaic, Fort Ancient, and Adena sites in Kentucky.

The Adena sites, and the Adena complex, stirred Webb's imagination. *The Adena People* is typical of Webb, not only in its conception and format, but also in its expression of distinct opinions about prehistory. Webb was a man of very strong opinions, both personal and professional; having once made up his mind that a given research path or idea was correct, he followed it with drive and determination. He was able to develop or accept a new notion, work on it, worry over it, and finally convince himself that it must be true. Thereafter, no amount of argument or contrary evidence was likely to sway him.

Webb died in 1964 at the age of eighty-two. An obituary was published by William G. Haag (1965) and an assessment of his contribution to southeastern archaeology was prepared by Douglas W. Schwartz (1967), both former students and associates of Webb.

Charles Ernest Snow, co-author of *The Adena People*, reached the University of Kentucky by a quite different route. He was born in Boulder, Colorado, and received his training in physical anthropology at Harvard University under Professor Ernest A. Hooton. When Snow finished his doctorate in 1938 he was hired by Webb as a physical anthropologist for the TVA Archaeological Project in Birmingham, Alabama, and Snow contributed to the studies published on the work in northern Alabama. When World War II shut down the TVA program, Webb was able to get Snow an appointment at the University of Kentucky in 1942 as an instructor. By 1946 he was a full professor, and from 1952 to 1957 he was chairman of the Department of Anthropology. Like Webb, Snow received the University of Kentucky Distinguished Professor Award, and in 1960 he received the first Distinguished Teacher Award. He was a match for Webb in enthusiasm; it was Snow who persuaded Webb that "the Adena people" must have come into the Ohio Valley from "down Mexico way." Charles E. Snow died in 1967; his obituary, written by William M. Bass, appeared in the *American Journal of Physical Anthropology* (Vol. 28, No. 3).

Adena was the name given to the farm of Thomas Worthington,

one of the first senators and the sixth governor of Ohio. The large mound on his property north of Chillicothe, Ohio, was excavated in 1901 by W. C. Mills of the Ohio State Museum. The materials from this mound and the structural features formed the ideal Adena mound that Emerson F. Greenman used in 1932 when his *An Analysis of the Adena Culture* was published. Greenman's method was simple:

> In the following study, sixty mounds are classed as Adena in type which have not heretofore been included in that culture. In this process the zoological method of identifying a species is used as far as it is possible to do so. . . . the first specimen of the type to be found and described is the type specimen. While the Grave Creek Mound, number 55 herein, was partially excavated in 1938, the Adena Mound, number 1, was the first one belonging to the culture-type to be completely excavated and described, and it is therefore the type specimen, a fact already recognized by Shetrone in *Culture Problem in Ohio* (p. 161). The inclusion of other mounds under the specific term *Adena* is made herein upon the basis of the characteristics exhibited by the Adena Mound.

In other words, any mound which contained two or more traits of the thirty-three Greenman listed for the Adena Mound was regarded by him as belonging to the Adena culture. This was particularly true if the mound did not contain Hopewell or Fort Ancient material. Such a method allowed Greenman to expand the number of Adena mounds considerably and to enlarge the list of traits from thirty-three to fifty-nine. By working with this method in the center of the Ohio Valley he was reasonably successful in identifying probable Adena mounds, but his mound number 53 in Illinois is an Illinois Valley Hopewell mound, and number 70, the Bat Creek Mound in East Tennessee, is definitely not Adena.

Greenman very clearly demonstrated by his trait list and analyses that all the mounds classified as Adena shared only one major cultural feature—the building of mounds into which burials were placed. They held in common very little in the way of burial practices or grave goods. Furthermore, only the Adena Mound had as many as 33 of the 59 generalized Adena traits; Beech Bottom Mound in West Virginia evidenced 29; one mound had 18; two mounds each had 17. In fact, 57 of the 70 mounds that Greenman called Adena had 10 or fewer traits identified by him as Adena.

Greenman recognized a close cultural connection between Adena and Hopewell when he wrote that "it is a different numerical predominance of the same or similar traits which constitutes the difference between Adena and Hopewell" (Greenman 1932:493). He could not decide on the relative ages of Hopewell and Adena because he accepted a number of historic associations as valid in mounds he believed to be Adena. He also was writing in a period when Adena was believed to be not very remote in time from the historic tribes. He became involved in his study in identifying the type of archaeological remains the Cherokees were thought to have left in the Ohio Valley, and ended by assigning the Cherokees to Adena.

It should be noted that Webb's writing, like Greenman's, reflects the influence of the "direct historical approach," or the attempt to identify various prehistoric complexes as direct antecedents to historic tribes. Since the extreme time depth in the eastern United States was not known at this time, many prehistoric cultures now known to be early were thought to be late, and many archaeologists felt it was possible to relate them to historically known groups.

The Adena People by Webb and Snow was an effort to synthesize the data from a series of Kentucky Adena mounds excavated under the general direction of Webb and to include as part of the interpretation a study of Adena and Hopewell skeletal material. An analysis of the relationship between Adena and Hopewell was also to be a major part of this monograph. Webb, of course, did the analysis and interpretation of the archaeological data. He added twenty new Kentucky sites to Greenman's list and added the traits included in them to the Adena trait list, so that "on the basis of this new trait list many mounds explored by early investigators may now be shown to belong to Adena. Such a list has been prepared, the mounds being numbered from 91 to 173 and designated *Supplemental Adena Mounds*" (Webb and Snow 1945:14). For the 173 mounds Webb listed some 218 traits. He rearranged the trait list and provided annotations on some of them which are valuable and sometimes reveal arguments which are typical of him as he pressed to show connections where they could hardly be supported.

The last two Ohio mounds listed by Webb—numbers 146 and 147 —were regarded as Adena on information provided by me from a collection I had obtained on loan from the American Museum of Natural History. This collection was prepared for publication by Barbara Herman (1947) and returned to New York without my having taken a single photograph of the specimens. The mound listed as Adena number 127 was the platform mound on the Baum site in Ross County, which I had included as Fort Ancient. While both of us could be wrong, it is not likely that both of us are correct.

Webb followed a similar but not identical methodology to that of Greenman. It had nothing to do with the Midwest Taxonomic Classification, even though some of Webb's shortcomings have been blamed on that system. While Greenman prepared tables showing the frequency of the traits of the Adena Mound in other mounds—and the specific traits in each of the seventy mounds—Webb made no attempt to indicate the degree of homogeneity or lack of it in burial practices and grave goods within the 173 mounds or within some smaller regional group versus another group. Neither did he attempt to provide a chronology by analyzing differences within mounds from bottom to top as they had been constructed, nor to compare the material from different locations within such single sites as Mt. Horeb in Kentucky, nor to attempt to find a sequence in an area as might have been done with the group of mounds near Athens, Ohio. Webb attempted to base a chronology on the presence of Hopewell traits in Adena mounds or, conversely, Adena traits found in Hopewell mounds. Adena mounds with Hopewell traits were late Adena, and Hopewell mounds with Adena traits were early Hopewell.

Webb produced a table headed "Comparison of Traits of Four Hopewellian Manifestations." It listed 121 traits under the headings of Earthwork, Tomb, House Construction, Cremation, Inhumation, Chipped Stone, Ground Stone, Bone and Antler, Shell, Copper, Mineral, and Textile. The four units compared were Adena, Ohio Hopewell, Copena, and the Trempealeau complex of southwestern Wisconsin. The list was based on what Webb regarded as Adena or Ohio Hopewell traits which seemed to be significant in assessing Hopewell chronology. Of the 121 traits, Adena was credited with 111; Hopewell with 109; Copena with 66; and Trempealeau with 31. While there can be some debate about the value and meaning of such a listing, it was undeniable that Adena and Hopewell shared many cultural characteristics.

Webb sought to arrange the seven major excavated Ohio Hopewell sites in chronological order. Preparing a small selected list of Hopewell traits, he assumed that each trait occurred within a certain time interval, which he represented by a horizontal line, and that the nonuniform distribution of a trait, such as copper earspools, indicated a developmental sequence. It was further assumed that the number of specimens of a particular trait per one hundred burials was a measure of the total number available at that site, and that the larger the number of specimens the later the site.

The Adena People received two major reviews, by Richard G. Morgan (1946) and Jesse D. Jennings (1947), that should be read by any serious student of eastern United States archaeology. Morgan's review is quite critical of method, accuracy, and results, and although it was based on a close study of both Hopewell and Adena, it apparently had no influence upon Webb's second treatise on Adena (1957).

Snow's contribution on the physical anthropology of the recovered and available Adena burials and his comparison of the burials with available skeletal material from Ohio Hopewell sites were valuable additions to the total study. One advantage was that the forty-five male and twenty-eight female skulls from Kentucky sites were certainly some part of an Adena population. The number is inadequate for a confident assessment of all Kentucky Adena populations, but the number of Adena skulls and other skeletal parts from Ohio, Indiana, and West Virginia is even smaller and less adequate, as is the Copena skeletal material from northern Alabama. Snow included what was available and did as much as could be done with it. The Hopewell series, on the other hand, benefited from an earlier study by Hooton (1922) on the Turner burials, from the loan of Hopewell site skeletal material by the Field Museum and by the Ohio State Museum, and from studies by Snow on the crania from four other Hopewell sites.

The Adena physical type was characterized by Snow as round-headed with marked deformation, presumably from the use of a cradleboard in infancy, and also by a circular compression that rounded the skull in a horizontal plane and also elevated it. The face was long, with prominent cheek bones and an unusually wide, bony chin. The Adena were stated to be of medium height, with the males standing 5′6″ and the females 5′2½″.

Compared with Adena physical type, Hopewell was found to be taller and to belong to a northern, longheaded group. There was some evidence of the same cranial deformation on Hopewell skulls. One group of crania from Hopewell sites was quite clearly the same as Snow's Adena type, which Snow interpreted was a result of the fact that Adena culture grew and changed into Hopewell.

A totally inadequate series of seven crania represented the Copena populations of northern Alabama. It was Snow's interpretation that Copena represented a mixed population which was predominantly broadheaded like Adena but intermixed with another strain that showed similarities to the longheaded Ohio Hopewell population. These Adena and Hopewell physical types were all clearly distinct from the early Archaic populations of the Tennessee-Cumberland drainage.

In their conclusion Webb and Snow identified Adena as the first sedentary people in the eastern United States with "developed agricultural husbandry"—the first pottery makers, smokers, mound builders, constructors of earthworks, builders of wooden houses, and the first architects of ceremonial structures. Webb particularly resisted the point of view that Adena was a local, rather early representative of what was then known as the Woodland Pattern. It had been proclaimed by one archaeologist that there was no Woodland culture south of the Mason-Dixon line, and Webb stuck to that interpretation in the rest of his writings. In their "Speculations," Webb and Snow postulated that the source of the Adena populations "lay somewhere in Middle America," and that in the southeast the "process of brachy-cephalization" began with the advent of the ancestors of Adena as they traveled up the Mississippi Valley. The first cultural influences from Mexico into the southeast arrived in late Archaic times with these Adena ancestors, who brought a different cultural heritage and a new economic pattern, finally reaching a homeland in the Ohio Valley. Finding no remains of this cultural complex in the lower Mississippi Valley, Webb and Snow claimed that the Adena culture resulted from a long period of development and growth in the Ohio River Valley.

Early Adena was identified as sites with Adena but no Hopewell characteristics, while late Adena included some Hopewell traits. Webb's Early Adena included the Glidwell and Nowlin mounds of southeastern Indiana, the Redman Mound in Ohio, and the Ricketts, Robbins, C and O Mound 9, and Dover Mound in Kentucky. His late Adena included the type site, the Mt. Vernon Cemetery and the Metzger Mound in Ohio, the Beech Bottom and Great Smith mounds in West Virginia, and the large Wright Mound (Mm 6) in Kentucky.

Another author was represented in the publication on *The Adena People*. I had prepared chapters on the pottery from the Norris Basin of northeastern Tennessee and the Wheeler Basin of northern Alabama which had appeared as appendices in the two reports. I had also worked on pottery from the Pickwick Basin, studied the Fort Ancient and Woodland rock shelter pottery in Kentucky, and written a short paper on Adena pottery. Webb sent me manuscript sections of his Tennessee Valley reports, as he did to a number of others. In April 1943, Webb wrote that he was planning a summary volume on Adena; after some correspondence Webb agreed that I should do a chapter on the pottery. This chapter supported the concept of Adena priority in time over Hopewell, which I had strongly espoused since 1936 (Griffin 1937:274; 1969:468), but maintained that Adena was not the only source of Hopewell pottery. I emphasized that Adena pottery did not move into the Ohio Valley from the south, that although it was related to some southeastern pottery—to Tchefuncte in the Lower Mississippi Valley, to the later Copena complex in northern Alabama, and to early ceramics of eastern Tennessee, Georgia, and northeastern Florida—its closest relationships were to Early Woodland pottery complexes in the northeast and could be "recognized as a significant unit of the widespread Woodland ceramic tradition." I could not then (nor can I now) arrange the Hopewell sites in a satisfactory chronological scheme, and during my correspondence with Webb I strongly criticized his chronology of Hopewell sites. Morgan commented in his review (1946:57) that the proposed chronological sequence of Hopewell sites "is the same as would be obtained by arranging the sites according to the total number of traits present at each site."

During the preparation of *The Adena People,* Webb, Snow, and I carried on an extended correspondence, and I read and commented on much of the manuscript. The three of us met at the Ohio State Museum in Columbus in October 1944, for I hoped that Richard Morgan would collaborate with me on a joint statement on Adena and Hopewell pottery. Beginning in May 1943, I tried to persuade Webb that the several varieties of Adena pottery, from Fayette Thick to Adena Plain, were Early Woodland pottery; that some of the Adena pottery continued into Ohio Hopewell; that Adena and Hopewell were representative of Early and Middle Woodland; and that many of the cultural elements in Adena could be shown to have their origin or prototype in the shell mounds and related early cultures. I tried to persuade Snow that a migration of people from Mexico could not account for Adena culture because there was nothing remotely resembling Adena in Mexico and that there were physical types resembling Adena in Illinois, New York, and the Southeast on an apparently earlier level.

Nevertheless, *The Adena People* remains an important documentation of what was known of Adena mounds and their incorporated materials in the mid-1940s. During the period from 1930 to 1945 a specific kind of history—a history of material culture—developed which at best described the succession of the preserved archaeological assemblages in each culture province. Also, the emphasis was on archaeological data as things in themselves rather than as the values offered by different ways of looking at them.

In 1957 the Ohio Historical Society published a much smaller volume entitled *The Adena People No. 2* with Webb and Raymond S. Baby as co-authors and with chapters by Snow on the physical type and by Robert M. Goslin on "Food of the Adena People." This volume updates the previous study with the addition of forty-eight new mounds to the Adena list, most from Ohio, and by the addition of twenty-four new traits to the Adena trait list. Of the additional sites, the Burkham Stone Mound in Indiana and the Chilton site in Kentucky should not be regarded as Adena; they belong to a late Woodland complex which has been called Newtown (Griffin 1952; Kellar 1960).

A typological study of the artifacts from ten rock shelters in four eastern Kentucky counties persuaded Webb that Adena people had occupied them at some point in time, and it was asserted, but not demonstrated, that the Adena occupation was in the lower level of the refuse. This occupation was regarded as representing temporary winter hunting camps. Such an assertion is not supported by the evidence on the analysis of the faunal and floral remains which were listed as Adena food. The shelters do have occupational debris from Early Woodland times, but it may be doubted that any can properly be called Adena. The assignment of specific foods to a limited period of time or culture group in the shelters cannot be done on the basis of evidence from excavation.

In his chapter on "Adena Portraiture," Snow reiterated his faith in the Mesoamerican origin of the Adena people, but added that there were other early roundheaded populations in the Southeast which had furnished "the roots of the Adena people." Webb and Baby prepared a discussion of the finds of cut-and-worked wolf, puma, and bear jaws as parts of the costumes of medicine men, and acknowledged that this practice was also known in Hopewell. There was also a section on medicine bags and their contents which were placed with burials. This tradition of burying such personal effects is known to have begun in the Archaic and to have continued on into the Mississippi period. There is an extended discussion of engraved and plain Adena stone tablets. Unfortunately, included in this list is a remarkable shell gorget (Figure 45) from the Crab Orchard Springs Mound, Lincoln County, Kentucky. I do not believe the gorget is Adena; rather, it is very similar in style to several gorgets, including one found in Missouri (Wood 1961:39) that is dated no earlier than very late Hopewell.

An extremely important development had occurred between the publication of *The Adena People* and *The Adena People No. 2.* Radiocarbon dating had appeared, and the results were (and still are) a bit difficult to handle for a variety of reasons. Most of the dates on Adena were provided by the University of Chicago laboratory, and many of its dates are now regarded as varying in either direction from the true radiocarbon date without any consistent pattern. In addition to the Adena dates there were Chicago dates on Archaic sites and some Hopewell dates from Ohio. Webb and Baby (1957: 103) accepted "a very respectable antiquity for the major traits of Adena, i.e., from 2450 B.C. to 700 A.D., a span of 3,150 years," and held that the measurements on five Hopewell sites indicated a time range from 600 B.C. to A.D. 1500. Within such a time range, they developed the thesis that Adena-Hopewell provided the inspiration for the art motifs and concepts of the late prehistoric Southeastern Ceremonial Complex.

An interesting change of view in the second volume is that instead of Adena being primarily responsible for the development of Copena culture in Alabama, it is now Ohio Hopewell that extended its influence southward to manifest itself in Copena. A short table was prepared of traits characteristic of Early, Middle, and Late Adena, and the concluding portion of the text hints that there may be some connection between the Late Archaic and Early Adena. Not much emphasis was placed on attempting to separate Early from Late Adena sites or mounds.

Webb's last contribution to the study of the Adena complex was a report with Snow (1959) on the excavation of the Dover Mound in Mason County, Kentucky. The excavation was done in 1950, so that Webb had had time to submit two of the charcoal specimens to the University of Chicago. One of the two dates from the penultimate construction stage was 700 B.C. ± 170 years. Adena Plain pottery was discovered under the mound in the village debris, and this was the only indication of village occupation because, curiously, no village refuse was incorporated in the mound. Data from the mound were used in the preparation of *The Adena People No. 2*, and the Dover report contained very little in the way of comparative data. On the basis of radiocarbon dates, Webb apparently felt that Dover belonged in Early to Middle Adena, even though there were several heavy copper-bar bracelets which should have put Dover into Late Adena according to Webb's earlier argument. Such a placement was also suggested by the presence of mica sheets and crescents, as Webb recognized.

As a result of his excavations of the Cresap Mound in Marshall County, West Virginia, some six and one-half miles south of Moundsville, Don W. Dragoo prepared *Mounds For the Dead: An Analysis of the Adena Culture* for the Annals of the Carnegie Museum in 1963. Cresap Mound had two major periods of construction, the first period having a number of sequential burial depositions and covering layers. Dragoo felt that his careful excavation of the mound provided the previously missing key to the understanding of the cultural sequence within Adena. Dragoo certainly illustrated more material from an Adena mound than had ever been illustrated before, and his comparative section covers more area and cultural groups than those of the previous authors. He presented a comparative trait list for nine Adena mounds in the upper Ohio Valley, but he was not able to identify clearly very Early Adena in that area. Apparently the Grave Creek Mound, never properly excavated, is the best example of the very late period. A list of characteristics of Early-Middle Adena and of Late Adena ("Robbins" complex) is provided, with identifications of several mounds that Dragoo felt belong in each category. Dragoo placed the Nowlin, Robbins, and Dover mounds in Late Adena, whereas Webb felt they were Early. Dragoo also included the Beech Bottom Mound in his earlier group, while Webb had regarded it as Late Adena.

There is a somewhat extended discussion of Adena radiocarbon dates and a listing of them, along with dates from cultural groups which Dragoo used for comparative purposes in the text. He expressed a great deal of dissatisfaction with them, and almost any archaeologist would share that dissatisfaction. Seven of the twenty-four dates Dragoo had available were University of Chicago dates using carbon black, and two were from early runs at the University of Michigan laboratory, which at that time was also using carbon black. This method of counting C_{14} could at times produce good results, but often did not. Dragoo had two dates from the Gulf Oil Company laboratory, one of which was 2506 $\pm$ 175 and the other 3685

± 123 years before 1950. The youngest of these does overlap in its upper range with the lower limits of the oldest of three Michigan dates. For the Cresap Mound, my own guesses based on the radio-carbon dates would be a time-range from about 250 to 100 B.C. The length of time for various burials to be deposited, or the length of time for soil development which Dragoo used for his time estimates, is an even less exact science than radiocarbon dating; therefore it is im-possible to have valid estimates of the difference in age of the depos-its in Cresap without radiocarbon dates.

A number of additional radiocarbon dates have been run since Dragoo's book was issued. One block of five was published (Crane and Griffin, 1972) as the result of Orrin Shane's efforts in obtaining, from the University of Kentucky, collections of additional material from the Kentucky Adena sites. The dates for the big Wright Mound (Mm 6) in Kentucky of A.D. 50 and A.D. 210 would have pleased Dragoo, but the Dover site date of 310 B.C. would probably have frus-trated him. Another reasonable Adena mound radiocarbon date is M-1830 at 2050 ± 140, or 100 B.C., on wood of American red cedar or juniper from Tomb 2 of the Murad Mound in Kanawha County, West Virginia; a second date, M-1829, was 2390 ± 130, or 440 B.C. The excavators, Edward V. McMichael and Oscar L. Mairs (1969), believed that Tomb 1, which produced the older date, had been con-structed somewhat later than Tomb 2. As a final comment on Adena radiocarbon dating it can be said that there are now no sound radio-carbon dates for Adena older than 500 B.C.

Dragoo supports the concept of a gradual growth of Adena from Late Archaic complexes in the eastern United States instead of the theory of a Mexican origin, a position which other archaeologists have supported for many years. On the other hand, he believes that some Adena populations were pushed out of their upper Ohio Valley homes by Hopewell peoples and that they moved to Delaware and Mary-land and eventually into the New York state area. He also believes that the majority of Adena people who moved from the Ohio Valley under Hopewell pressure went to the Tennessee Valley in Alabama and became the Copena Complex. Some of the Adena population he believes were absorbed into the Hopewell society. I have no confi-dence in either movement of people. Dragoo's publication, however, was a significant step in our understanding of Adena.

B. K. Swartz of Ball State University organized a symposium on Adena in March 1970 to help understand problems resulting from excavations near Newcastle, Indiana. The symposium papers were published in 1971 under Swartz's editorship. At this meeting papers were presented on the history of Adena studies by Raymond Baby, and on Adena culture content and settlement by Martha A. Potter of the Ohio State Historical Society. James E. Fitting and David S. Brose presented "The northern periphery of Adena" and discussed various mortuary complexes with some relationships to one another and to Adena. They belong to a time period recognized as Late Archaic and Early Woodland. Ronald A. Thomas of the Delaware Archaeological Board talked on "Adena influence in the Middle Atlantic Coast." His interpretation of the Adena material in the Chesapeake Bay area was that it was the result of a prehistoric trade pattern which had existed before Adena, that it was intensified during the climax of the Adena culture, and that it continued to exist in post-Adena times. Edward V. McMichael drew on his intimate knowledge of West Virginia and the upper Ohio Valley to suggest that many of the mounds in the Charleston area listed by Greenman and Webb should not really be called Adena. McMichael asserted that distinctive regional groups could be recognized near Pittsburgh, in the area of the Grave Creek Mound, around Parkersburg-Marietta, and around the mouth of the Kanawha River. He suggested that comparative analytical study of these geographic groups would be valuable, and also argued that, "considering Adena in its broader aspects, . . . there has been undue cultural imperialism on the part of the Adenaphile" and that many sites included by Greenman and Webb should probably not be regarded as Adena.

Charles H. Faulkner of the University of Tennessee gave a paper entitled "Adena and Copena: a case of mistaken identity." Faulkner concluded that Adena influence and relations were never strong in the Tennessee Valley area and Copena relationships are primarily with Hopewell. The conclusion that Copena relations were with Hopewell and not Adena is also supported by the recent Ph.D. dissertation at the University of North Carolina–Chapel Hill by John A. Walthall of the University of Alabama.

James H. Kellar and B. K. Swartz discussed evidence on Adena in southeastern Indiana. Some of the excavated mounds in this area are clearly identifiable as Adena, but others pose somewhat of a problem. They believe that all of the Adena sites in southeastern Indiana are in the latter part of Adena (Middle to Late in Dragoo's terminology).

There was a short statement on "The Havana tradition" by Howard P. Winters and Nancy Hammerslough of New York University and on the Scioto Hopewell by Orrin C. Shane III of Kent State University. Extensive discussion sessions are reproduced and there are short statements by James Griffin and Charles Callender. Unfortunately, a brief statement by Georg K. Neumann could not be included; he observed that Adena does not have a single distinctive physical type and that the Adena populations were primarily related to north central Late Archaic groups modified by the cultural practice of cranial deformation and other factors.

The group attending the symposium agreed that the term Adena had been used much too loosely and that it was almost entirely a burial and ceremonial complex. It was suggested that careful comparative studies should be done to identify regional characteristics in contrast to broader areal traits. Every effort should be made to identify village and camp sites in order to better comprehend the economic base and total social structure, and changes through time, in local areas. Adena material in the central and upper Ohio Valley was recognized as a series of variants of the latter part of the Early Woodland period, and it was seen that most of the burial practices associated with Late Adena are also found in Ohio Valley Hopewell.

The Adena People figured heavily in those discussions and will be equally important to future research in the prehistory of the Ohio Valley. Archaeologists will be working past Webb's and Snow's interpretation to apply and analyze the data in the book for a long time to come.

James B. Griffin
University of Michigan

REFERENCES

Crane, H. R., and J. B. Griffin
    1972 University of Michigan Radiocarbon Dates XIV. *Radiocarbon* 14, No. 1, pp. 155–94. American Journal of Science, New Haven.
Dragoo, Don
    1964 *Mounds For the Dead: An Analysis of the Adena Culture.* Annals of the Carnegie Museum, Vol. 37. Pittsburgh.
Greenman, Emerson F.
    1932 Excavation of the Coon Mound and an Analysis of the Adena Culture. *Ohio Archaeological and Historical Quarterly* 41, No. 3, pp. 369–523. Columbus.

Griffin, James B.
1952 The Late Prehistoric Cultures of the Ohio Valley *in* Prehistoric Indians of the Ohio Valley. *Ohio State Archaeological and Historical Quarterly* 61, No. 2, pp. 186–95. Columbus.
1937 The Chronological Position and Ethnological Relationships of the Fort Ancient Aspect. *American Antiquity* 2, No. 4, pp. 273–77.
1969 Richard G. Morgan, 1903–1968. *American Antiquity* 34, No. 4, pp. 467–70.

Haag, William G.
1965 William Snyder Webb, 1882–1964. *American Antiquity* 30, No. 4, pp. 470–73.

Hooton, Earnest A.
1922 The Skeletal Remains *in* The Turner Group of Earthworks, Hamilton County, Ohio by Charles C. Willoughby. *Papers of the Peabody Museum of American Archaeology and Ethnology, Harvard University* 8, No. 3. Cambridge.

Jennings, Jesse D.
1947 *The Adena People.* William S. Webb and Charles E. Snow (*University of Kentucky, Reports in Anthropology and Archaeology,* Vol. VI, 365 pp., 7 tables, 28 figures, 10 plates, and numerous unnumbered charts. Lexington, Kentucky, September, 1945). *American Anthropologist* 49, No. 2, pp. 275–79.

Kellar, James H.
1960 The C. L. Lewis Stone Mound and the Stone Mound Problem. *Prehistory Research Series* 3, No. 4, Indiana Historical Society. Indianapolis.

McMichael, Edward V., and Oscar L. Mairs
1969 Excavation of the Murad Mound, Kanawha County, West Virginia. *Report of Archaeological Investigations No. 1, West Virginia Geological and Economic Survey.* Morgantown.

Morgan, Richard G.
1946 *The Adena People.* William S. Webb and Charles E. Snow (*University of Kentucky, Reports in Anthropology and Archaeology,* Vol. VI, 369 pp., 28 figures, 7 tables, 1 map. Lexington, Kentucky, 1945). *American Antiquity* 12, No. 1, pp. 54–58.

Schwartz, Douglas W.
1967 *Conceptions of Kentucky Prehistory. A Case Study in the History of Archaeology.* Lexington, University of Kentucky Press.

Swartz, B. K.
1971 *Adena: The Seeking of an Identity.* Muncie, Ball State University.

Webb, William S., and Raymond S. Baby
1957 *The Adena People No. 2.* Columbus, The Ohio Historical Society.

Wood, W. Raymond
1961 The Pomme de Terre Reservoir in Western Missouri Prehistory. *The Missouri Archaeologist* 12, No. 1, pp. 54–58.

CONTENTS

ILLUSTRATIONS

The
Adena
People

PREFACE

This study of "The Adena People," deals largely with their burial customs and the earth mounds erected over the remains of their dead; and with the physical anthropology of such skeletal material as has been preserved to the present time. On many phases of their mode of life, their social customs and material possessions there is yet only scant information. Even the data on physical anthropology of necessity are derived from studies of a seemingly selected group of individuals. Even the basis of such selection is not known, but only surmised. It is, therefore, recognized that the picture of these people and their culture, which this study is intended to portray, must, in the nature of the case, be incomplete. Although no effort has been spared to make the picture as complete as possible much yet remains to be determined by excavations and studies of the future.

These investigations have been made possible by the cooperation of many agencies and by the aid of many individuals, to whom the authors are greatly indebted. It is a pleasure to make acknowledgement of such cooperative aid, and personal assistance.

The Work Projects Administration, through Mr. George H. Goodman, State Administrator for Kentucky supplied the labor, for the field work of excavation, and for processing the material in the museum over a period of many months, from 1937 to 1942. Without this vital aid this study would have been impossible.

Much of the success attained in procuring the basic information for the reports on site excavations may be credited to the efficient service of Messrs. John L. Cotter, Ralph D. Brown, and John B. Henson, who in succession served as State Archaelogical Supervisors during the period of the field work 1937 to 1942.

Among the field party supervisors, whose work on individual sites contributed greatly to the total body of information, should be mentioned Messrs. John B. Elliott, Claude Johnston, J. C. Greenacre, and John Buckner.

In the laboratory Mr. Ivar Skarland and Mr. H. T. E. Hertzberg directed the processing of the skeletal material 1938–1941 and prepared the reports thereon.

Dr. Henry A. Carey directed the archaeological research at the laboratory and has described many Adena textiles. Mr. Wm. G. Haag made studies of the pottery recovered from the site excavations.

The Ohio State Museum at Columbus through its Director, Mr. Henry L. Shetrone, and the Curator of Archaeology, Mr. Richard G. Morgan sent the large Hopewell skeletal collection to this laboratory for processing and study. Additional cooperation in supplying the authors with photographs and burial descriptions has generously been given.

The Chicago Natural History Museum through Acting Director, Mr. Orr Goodson, and Curator of Exhibits, Mr. George I. Quimby, Jr., kindly loaned the W. K. Moorehead collection of Hopewell skulls to this Museum for study.

The Academy of Natural Sciences of Philadelphia, through its Director, Mr. Charles Cadwalader, and Mr. John P. Carter, extended permission to study the skulls in the Morton Collection at Philadelphia. They provided photographs of crania from the valuable CRANIA AMERICANA; and furnished descriptions of the burial proveniences.

The Peabody Museum, Harvard University, through the courtesy of Professor Earnest Hooton and Mr. Fred Orchard, supplied photographs of the Turner skulls described by Hooton; and loaned the "trophy" skull from the Mariott Mound No. 1 for study.

The Alabama Museum of National History through its Acting Director, Professor Stewart J. Lloyd, made possible the illustrations herein of the Copena skulls. Dr. Alvin V. Beatty, of the Geological Survey supplied the photographs of these skulls.

The Museum of the American Indian, Heye Foundation through its curator, Mr. E. K. Burnett, furnished the photograph and drawing of the Meigs County, Ohio, Adena engraved stone tablet.

Dr. James B. Griffin, Associate Curator, Museum of Anthropology, University of Michigan, has made a study of Adena pottery, and his chapter on "The Ceramic Affiliations of the Ohio Valley Adena Culture" is a valuable addition to this report.

Mr. Georg K. Neumann, Indiana University, kindly offered suggestions and data on the Illinois Hopewell material.

Dr. T. Dale Stewart, Curator of Physical Anthropology, U. S. National Museum, generously supplied comparative data and photographs of Hopewell cranial material in the National Museum.

Mr. Henry B. Collins, Jr., Bureau of American Ethnology, very kindly assisted in obtaining information relative to the Louisiana Hopewell material now at the National Museum.

Dr. J. Otis Brew, Lecturer and Assistant Curator of Southwestern American Archaeology, Division of Anthropology, Harvard University and Mr. Frank M. Seltzer, Head Curator, Department of Anthropology, U. S. National Museum, each read large portions of the preliminary manuscript. Their criticisms and suggestions have been most helpful and stimulating. They are in no way responsible for any errors of fact or judgement which may be included herein.

Dr. Wilton M. Krogman, Associate Professor of Anatomy and Physical Anthropology of the University of Chicago, has made a critical study of typical samples of the Adena and Hopewell cremated skeletal material, sent to him by this museum. His valuable conclusions, quoted herein, have led to a better understanding of the process of cremation by these Hopewellian groups.

Mr. James L. Poole, Lexington, rendered helpful services in the preparation of the Hopewell skeletal material at the Museum Laboratory and in the photography of specimens.

Mrs. Charles E. Snow has rendered valuable service in the preparation of the manuscript and in reading and correcting copy.

THE ADENA PEOPLE

Introduction

It is now more than a hundred years since the first large earth mound, which today is classified as belonging to the Adena Complex (Grave Creek Mound*, Moundsville, Marshall County, West Virginia), was partially excavated. Forty-three years have elapsed since the great mound on the estate of Governor Worthington‡ in Ross County, Ohio, which gave the name of "Adena" to this culture complex, was excavated and reported by Mills**. From these beginnings, excavation and research in prehistory have continued to show the great importance of this prehistoric cultural manifestation in southwestern Ohio and its very considerable extension into and effect upon the prehistory of adjacent regions. Thirteen years have passed since Greenman† published "An Analysis of the Adena Culture." This very complete and extensive study of a large mass of data, the accumulation of previous decades of archaeological excavation by many different investigators in seven states, enabled him to list 70 mounds as belonging to Adena, and to present and describe 59 cultural traits found in common in two or more of these mounds. All serious students of the prehistory of the Ohio River Valley are thoroughly familiar with the scientific methodology underlying this analysis by Greenman. Only those who have undertaken a similar task can appreciate the difficulties which beset the investigator in such a situation. Naturally, Greenman desired to make his analysis thorough and his summary as complete as possible; yet of the 70 mounds believed to show Adena traits, only 16 had been completely excavated. Of the remainder, the degree of completeness of many was not known. In a few cases reports or field notes of the excavator

---

* Tomlinson, A. B., 1838, pp. 196-203.
** Mills, W. C., 1902, pp. 452-479.
† Greenman, E. F., 1932, pp. 369-523.
‡ Thomas Worthington, born July 16, 1773, was Governor of Ohio 1814-18. His estate in Ross County, Ohio, about one mile northwest of Chillicothe, and on the west side of Scioto River, he had named Adena. This name he had adopted from a Greek adverb meaning sufficient, or literally "nothing lacking." Evidently the intention was to convey the idea that this beautiful estate was near perfection or as its name might be freely translated "paradise." On this estate was the great earth mound, which when excavated became the type site of the cultural complex now known as Adena.

were lacking. Besides these difficulties of incompleteness, part of which is due to the individual field techniques used by different investigators, there is inherent in such a problem the difficulty of unifying by interpretation the various forms of records written by many different observers, each using a different vocabulary to describe his finds, and each with a different scientific background which of necessity subjectively colors his classification and interpretation of the facts which he observes and describes. In spite of these inherent difficulties, Greenman produced a very complete series of tabulations of data on Adena culture and brought together a very considerable body of information which previously was widely scattered in the literature. As a result of his patient industry and good scholarship, "An Analysis of the Adena Culture" presented a most complete summary of the data available at that time (1932).

OHIO HOPEWELL

Within the Ohio River Valley, and covering about the same period of time, roughly the past one hundred years, information relative to the prehistoric cultural manifestation known as Ohio Hopewell has also been increasing. This cultural manifestation, one of the most important in the Eastern United States, has come to be regarded as unique among prehistoric manifestations because of evidence of its high artistic development, its great material wealth as shown by the number and variety of its artifacts, and its possession and use of materials from far distant regions. Naturally as other prehistoric cultural manifestations were discovered they were compared to Hopewell of Ohio. Some of these were found to show a degree of similarity to this outstanding cultural expression. To indicate this similarity in cultural traits the broader term of "Hopewellian" came to be used to include Ohio Hopewell and those other cultural manifestations having many and important likenesses to it. In time it was found that Adena also had many traits in common with Ohio Hopewell, and its trait complex might be considered as falling within this broader classification of Hopewellian. Thus, in attempting to describe fully the

Adena cultural complex it is necessary to discuss the relation of Adena to Ohio Hopewell and to other Hopewellian manifestations. Such comparisons constitute a considerable portion of the present problem, and will be discussed in later chapters.

Excavations of the past two decades have revealed many previously unknown manifestations, some far removed from the Ohio Hopewell area, which, because they show similarity to Ohio Hopewell, have demonstrated that at least the influence of this great prehistoric people was widespread in the eastern and central portions of North America. The discussion of this widespread Hopewellian manifestation which will be presented later will give opportunity to introduce a comparative trait list of some of these more important cultural complexes. Before undertaking this larger problem it is necessary to define Adena more exactly, in view of recent new evidence.

New Information on Adena

During the past decade, since Greenman's Analysis was published, the science of archaeology has experienced a period of great activity and development. Much field work has been accomplished, and many more mounds have been investigated, some so large that the cost of excavation probably would have prevented their study had not Federal funds for relief labor been available. Further, during this period field techniques have been improved and extended. There has thus been brought to light a very considerable body of data bearing on Adena culture which necessitates a relisting of Adena cultural traits. Many traits previously unknown have been discovered, and significant relations of old and well-known traits have been made apparent. With this broadening of the base of understanding of what may be considered as Adena manifestations, sites which were previously not included may now with reason be added to this group. Clear and positive evidence, discovered in recent investigations, also suggests that in the case of some sites long since investigated, a re-interpretation of factual data reported from them may be warranted by the circumstances.

From the recent excavations in Kentucky there have been recovered many skeletons sufficiently well preserved to permit measurement and study after cleaning and careful restoration. Notwithstanding the considerable practice of cremation by the Adena people, the extended burials in log tombs have produced sufficient skeletal material to allow the physical anthropologist to draw some very definite conclusions, some of which may be regarded as traits, quite as diagnostic of Adena, as any material culture traits.

Because of these developments it is proposed to offer herein a new Adena trait list, which includes the 59 traits listed by Greenman as well as the many new traits which have been discovered as a result of recent excavations. In retaining the original 59 traits, each shown by its original number in the new listing, it was found desirable in some cases to change the description of the trait in the light of more recent information. The retention of the original number of each trait will enable the critical student to see the new trait list as an extension of the older one and not a thing apart and wholly unrelated to the original concept of Adena. Of the 59 traits listed by Greenman, 56 of them have been found in recent excavations in Kentucky, and there is no reason to discard the other three, although they seem to be rare even in Ohio. It is because of the very careful and fundamental work done by Greenman that it has been possible to accept his trait list in its entirety and use it as a foundation for the new trait list.

On the basis of this new trait list, it is proposed to add to the previously known list of Adena sites, all other sites recently explored which show these traits, and finally it is proposed to submit a map of the Ohio River Valley and adjacent territory (see Map 1) showing the location of all known Adena sites as determined by this new trait list. In attempting this task the purpose is not to restudy the 70 mounds listed by Greenman, but to supplement this list by adding to it those mounds recently excavated, as well as those excavated earlier, where it may be shown that, in accordance with the new trait list, these early explored sites meet the minimum requirement for acceptance.

The Adena Trait List

In the preparation of this new trait list no attempt has been made to follow the "zoological species" methodology used by Greenman. It is well known that sites of any one of the Hopewellian groups (Adena, Hopewell, Copena) are likely to have a very low percentage correlation of traits with the total complex. As information increases, this becomes more and more obvious. With continued excavation, the trait list is broadened, and the percentage of the whole complex possessed by any individual site becomes less. It is recognized that all traits are not of equal importance, and some may have little or no diagnostic value. It is obvious that all traits are more or less subjective, depending for their generality on the manner of their expression, as well as on the basic facts of observation which are sought to be recorded. Even the frequency of occurrence of a trait is not always a measure of its diagnostic value. In view of these facts, no pre-arranged order of traits has been selected. They are not arranged alphabetically or in order of frequency of occurrence. It has been determined that traits shall be listed under group headings, as for example Mound Traits, House Traits, Burial Traits, etc., to enable functionally related traits to appear in association. Thus the order of their listing, while quite arbitrary and artificial, is nevertheless not wholly irrational.

In the list of traits which follows (see page 16), the first column shows the number designating this trait in the new list. In the second column is shown the old number of this trait in Greenman's list, if the trait occurred in his Table A, in which case it had a number. If the trait was mentioned by Greenman in some other of his tables, its table designation "B" or "C" is then indicated in the second column. Thus Greenman's traits are still identified by his designation even though in a few cases the wording of the trait description has been slightly changed. The third column contains a very brief expression of the trait which will generally need much amplification in the chapter entitled "Description of Traits" which immediately follows the trait list. In the fourth column there is indicated the total occurrence of the trait in Greenman's analysis and in the fifth column the number of mounds in which the trait occurred in Greenman's original list of 70 Adena mounds.

The sixth column shows the number of the new sites in Kentucky and the frequency of occurrence of the trait in each. The same method of recording the data in this column is used as in Greenman's original list. This is done wholly in the interest of simplicity and to permit the critical student to integrate the data furnished herein with that of the original tabulation without the necessity of wasting effort in translation procedure. For the purpose of this listing these 20 new Kentucky sites, 17 of which have been recently completely excavated, have been assigned numbers 71 to 90, inclusive, as shown by the following list:

LIST OF ADENA SITES IN KENTUCKY FROM WHICH NEW EVIDENCE HAS RECENTLY BECOME AVAILABLE

Name of Site	Kentucky Survey Designation	Number Designation in New Trait List	Reference in Departmental Reports		
			Volume	Bulletin	Page
Ricketts Mound	Mm 3	71	III	3	71
			III	6	211
Wright Mound	Mm 6	72	V	1	5
Wright Mound	Mm 7	73	V	1	102
Mt. Horeb Site	Fa 1	74	V	2	139
			V	7	640
Drake Mound	Fa 11	75	V	2	170
Stone Mound	Bh 15	76	V	3	223
C & O Mound	Jo 2	77	V	4	298
C & O Mound	Jo 9	78	V	4	315
Robbins Mound	Be 3	79	V	5	379
Robbins Mound	Be 14	80	V	5	379
Crigler Mound	Be 20	81	V	6	508
Crigler Mound	Be 27	82	V	6	506
Hartman Mound	Be 32	83	V	6	535
Mt. Sterling Mound	Mm 1	84	V	1	13
			V	2	205
Gaitskill Mound	Mm 5	85	II		299–303
Stamper Rock Shelter	Wo 10	86	I	4	266
Riley Mound	Be 15	87	V	7	585
Landing Mound	Be 17	88	V	7	597
Tarlton Mound	Fa 15	89	V	7	677
Grimes Village	Fa 14	90	V	7	654

As the result of this new trait list and the broader concept of Adena presented by it, it is inevitable that many mounds in Greenman's list of 70 will be found through additional study to possess many of the new traits heretofore either unnoticed or regarded as unimportant, or found infrequently. As an example, bone combs were found in one mound only (Original Adena) which did not constitute a trait. Recent discoveries now make possible the recognition of ''bone combs'' as an Adena trait, since they have been found in other mounds.

Further, on the basis of this new trait list many mounds explored by early investigators may now be shown to belong to Adena. Such a list has been prepared, the mounds being numbered from 91 to 173 and designated SUPPLEMENTAL ADENA MOUNDS. See page 115.

It is not possible to make a complete listing of all traits from these additional mounds explored before Greenman's list was published. Only traits have been listed, which in the opinion of the authors are sufficient to justify the classification of the site as Adena, since the purpose was only to justify the use of the site in plotting the ''distribution of Adena'', in order to show its geographical spread, and concentration. It is believed to be quite impracticable to study these ''early excavated sites'' in their entirety, as a basis for setting up an Adena trait list. However, where such early sites have offered unmistakable confirmation of some of these recently recognized Adena traits, that fact has been noted in column seven, by inserting the appropriate mound number.

It is also impossible to list completely all of the traits from Adena mounds explored by others within the last ten years, since the reports on many have not been published and the data is only partially available.

However, while *complete listing* of all traits is *not* possible, in column seven of the new trait list there has been recorded the occurrence of a trait in any mound whenever it is known. This is indicated by the mound number in the usual way. Finally in the list of sites, mounds have been numbered as follows: Numbers 1 to 70, inclusive, refer to Greenman's list; Numbers 71 to 90, inclusive, to Kentucky sites recently excavated, as shown on page 13; Numbers 91 to 169, inclusive, refer to sites excavated or otherwise known prior to the publication (1932) of Greenman's list, and not included by him, or to sites excavated since 1932.

It is obvious, for reasons given above, that column seven for the trait list cannot be anywhere nearly complete. No matter how much might be added, it becomes incomplete with the passage of time. Even with this inherent deficiency it does permit the recording of valuable information which aids in defining Adena and which shows how wide is the geographical distribution of some traits which may be quite infrequent in any one locality.

Later, in the chapter on ''Widespread Hopewellian Manifestations'', an attempt will be made to compare Adena traits with those of Ohio Hopewell, Copena, and Trempeleau, and to demonstrate both cultural and chronological relationships.

ADENA TRAIT LIST

1 New Trait Number	2 Greenman's Trait Number	3 Traits	4 Occurrences by Greenman	5 Mounds by Greenman	6 Kentucky Site Numbers with Number of Occurrences in it.	7 Site Number of Non-Kentucky Sites Having the Trait
		Earthwork Traits				
1		Large earthworks associated with other Adena manifestations			74–X 75–X	
3		"Sacred circles" associated with large earthworks			74–2	
4		"Sacred circles" have embankments exterior to the ditch			74–2	
5		"Sacred circles" usually have entrance or gateway			74–2	
6		"Sacred circles" once enclosed a circular structure of vertical posts			74–1	
		"Sacred circles" usually occur in groups of two to eight			74–X	
		Mound Traits				
7	1	Mounds conical		57	71–X 72–X 73–X 75–X 76–X 77–X 78–X 79–X 80–X 81–X 83–X 87–X 88–X 89–X 79–X	114, 125, 126
8	45	Mound one of a group		4		
9	41	Mound in or near "sacred circles"		2	74–1 89–1	

No.	Trait	n	Associated traits (significance codes)	Refs.
10	Mound in or near large earthworks	41 / 3	72-X, 72-X, 79-X, 73-X, 73-X, 73-X, 81-X, 76-X, 74-X, 76-X, 83-X, 79-X, 75-X, 77-X, 87-X, 81-X, 89-X, 78-X, 88-X	114
11	Mounds built on their own villages			111, 115, 116, 77; 13, 56, 59
12	Mound on site of burned house			
13	Mound shows stratigraphy	16 / 10	72-X, 88-X, 72-X, 71-X, 79-X, 72-2, 72-X, 87-X; 73-X, 72-X, 81-X, 79-X, 72-2, 72-X, 77-X; 75-X, 73-X, 72-1, 81-X, 73-2, 77-X; 78-X, 77-X, 75-X, 88-X, 78-2, 78-X; 81-X, 78-X, 76-X, 81-1, 79-X; 83-X, 79-X, 78-X; 83-X	
14	Primary mound contains midden			
15	Secondary and later sections of mound built of sterile clays			
16	Earth quarries formed near mound			
17	Village midden in situ under mound			
18	Mound shows individual earth loads	8 / 8	72-X, 72-X, 71-6, 76-1; 77-X, 75-X, 72-1, 78-7; 78-X, 77-X, 73-2, 79-1, 79-3, 73-X, 79-X, 88-X, 79-X; 79-X, 78-X, 74-1, 81-1; 81-X, 79-X, 75-1	44, 61
19	Impressions of grass, twigs, leaves			
20	Fired areas at mound base	20		61
21	Fired areas on mound surface			
22	Primary purpose of mound to cover burials			
23	Mound built by increments as burials were added	7	71-X; 72-3; 76-1; 83-1	38
24	Constructional use of stone	21		

Tomb Traits

No.	Trait	n	Associated traits (significance codes)	Refs.
25	Horizontal log tombs built on bark covered clay floor	55 / 35	71-7, 79-37, 71-6, 71-1, 81-1, 72-5; 72-13, 81-2, 72-5, 72-3; 76-1; 77-1, 76-1, 77-1; 78-3, 81-1, 79-17	
26	Single log rectangle about body	2	76-1; 79-20, 78-3	
27	Multiple parallel logs about body			
28	Tomb walls shored up with horizontal logs		79-2	61
29	Tomb walls of vertical posts in rectangular pattern			6, 43, 52, 55, 59

ADENA TRAIT LIST—Continued

New Trait Number	Greenman's Trait Number	Traits	Occurrences by Greenman	Mounds by Greenman	Kentucky Site Numbers with Number of Occurrences in it.	Site Number of Non-Kentucky Sites Having the Trait
30		Vertical tomb-posts in corners of rectangular horizontal patterns				20
31		Horizontal log burial platform in tomb			78-2	
32		Log tomb burial on house floor			73-1, 79-6, 80-1	61
33		Log tomb has log supported earth roof			72-4, 76-1, 77-1, 78-2, 81-1	20, 38
34		Vertical post-molds at grave	2	2	81-4, 81-1	
35		Log head and foot rests	28	25	72-7	20
36	56	Log tomb passageway at east			72-4, 81-1	61
37	5	Pit tomb dug below earth surface	5	5	72-1, 75-1, 77-1, 83-1, 83-1, 88-1	20, 38
38	24	Earth or stone embankment about subfloor tomb			72-1, 75-1, 77-1, 83-1	
39		Subfloor tomb closed by log roof			75-1, 77-1, 83-1, 88-1	38, 61
40		Mound erected over subfloor tomb			72-1, 75-1, 77-1	38, 61
41	C	Fire-hardened clay dome or "vault"	8	3	77-1, 78-1	58, 61, 64
		House Traits				57
42		Post-mold pattern circular, diameter 97 feet or more			72-3, 74-1, 76-1, 77-6, 78-4	
43		Post-mold pattern circular, diameter 60 feet or less			72-3, 73-1, 76-1, 79-1, 81-1, 87-2	6, 55

No.	Trait	References
44	Single post set in individual hole	72-X, 73-X, 74-X, 76-X, 77-X, 57
45	Posts set in pairs	78-X, 81-X, 87-X, 76-X, 87-X, 77-X
46	Posts of a pair in line with pattern	72-X, 73-X, 74-X, 76-X, 87-X, 77-X, 91
47	Two posts set in same hole	78-X, 79-X, 81-X, 77-X
48	Pairs regularly spaced in circle	78-X, 73-X, 74-X, 77-X, 78-X
49	Posts incline outward from center of circle	79-X, 79-X, 81-X, 87-X, 77-X, 78-X
50	Multiple occupancy of house sites	72-X, 73-X, 76-X, 87-X
51	Interior concentric circle of single postmolds	72-X, 79-X, 81-X, 87-X
52	Floor area discolored by heat	73-X, 73-X, 76-X, 81-X, 81-1
53	Ash pile on center of house floor	76-1, 81-X, 78-7, 87-2
54	Fire basins in village, circular	77-25, 77-X, 78-9, 83-1
55	Fire basins held burned, broken stones in ashes	77-9, 79-X, 78-8, 87-1
56	Clay fire basins, raised clay rims, "Altars" (3)	77-3, 78-3, 78-3
57	Fire basin, flat sandstones set on edge about basin rim	77-4, 78-3
58	Fire basin had potsherds in ashes	77-7, 78-3, 76-X, 78-1, 56
59	House burned intentionally	73-?, 76-X, 79-X, 77
60	Post-mold pattern rectilinear	72-1, 87-1, 81-X, 78-1, 87-1
Cremation Traits		
61	Cremation partial, remains in situ, house burned over log tomb (3)	76-1, 73-1, 41, 42
62	C Cremation total, in clay basins (3, 2)	71-3, 83-1, 83-1, 113
63	13 Cremation total, left in situ (30, 14)	78-9
64	Cremation partial, extended body in bark lined pit	83-1
65	Cremation in rectangular log-tomb, logs burned	78-5

ADENA TRAIT LIST—Continued

New Trait Number	Greenman's Trait Number	Traits	Occurrences by Greenman	Mounds by Greenman	Kentucky Site Numbers with Number of Occurrences in it.	Site Number of Non-Kentucky Sites Having the Trait
66		Cremated remains redeposited separately in mounds			81–1 74–1	44, 91, 110, 118
67		Cremated remains redeposited in village			86–1	
68		Cremated remains redeposited with extended inhumation in log tomb			71–1 81–2	
69		Cremated remains redeposited separately in log tomb			79–1	
70		Cremated remains deposited with extended burial in subsurface pit			75–4	91, 110
71		Cremated remains spread or scattered on floor of town-house			81–3 79–11 81–1	
72		Communal deposit of cremated remains			78–1 79–1	
73		Artifacts burned with body			71–3 83–X 75–2 73–6 89–X 81–2 74–X 78–5 79–2	44
74		Unburned artifacts placed with redeposited cremations			74–1 75–2 86–X 89–X	
75		Artifacts intentionally mutilated when deposited with cremation			74–1 75–2	56
76		Cremated remains associated with red ochre			89–X 75–3 89–X	

Inhumation Traits

No.	Ref.	Inhumation Traits								Refs
77		Body extended in flesh, on back, no tomb			72-1, 81-1, 72-1	75-3, 83-2, 79-39	76-1, 87-2, 80-1	77-2, 88-10, 81-1	79-19	
78		Body extended on back in earth-walled tombs								
79	2	Body extended, singly in log tombs	55	35	71-3, 79-40, 71-3	72-14, 81-2, 79-3	76-1	77-3	78-2	
80		Two extended bodies in same log tomb			76-1		81-2	76-1		
81		Three extended bodies in same log tomb				79-5				
82	7	Important central graves	25	24	72-5, 83-1, 71-9, 81-3, 71-24, 79-15, 71-2, 81-1	77-1, 87-1, 72-14, 83-1, 72-8, 81-2, 72-3	78-3	79-1	81-1	38
83	11	Use of bark in graves	54	18			75-2	76-1	79-47	59
84		Use of puddled clay in graves					75-1	76-1	78-2	59
85	17	Red ochre on skeleton	13	10			75-1	78-1	79-5	12, 43
86	38	Red ochre, lumps or granular in mound		6						
87	49	Red ochre on artifacts	25	2	71-1, 72-1	89-X, 79-3				1, 10, 53
88		Red ochre applied to skull or long bones								
89	58	Graphite in graves		2	79-2, 71-1	81-1, 81-1	88-X			
90		Graphite applied to skull or long bones								52
91	C	Separate skull in grave with burial—"trophy"?	1	1	79-1	72-1	81-1	88-3		
92		Burial of isolated skulls			72-1, 72-1					108
93		Decapitation, head buried between femora				78-1				123
94	59	Skeletons flexed	2	2	71-1, 88-X					25
95		Extended skeletons arranged in circle								57, 129
96	C	Skeletons bundled	2	1	83-2					155

ADENA TRAIT LIST—Continued

New Trait Number	Greenman's Trait Number	Traits	Occurrences by Greenman	Mounds by Greenman	Kentucky Site Numbers with Number of Occurrences in it.	Site Number of Non-Kentucky Sites Having the Trait
			4	5	6	7
		Flint Traits				
97		Blanks, flint				
98		Celts, flint				
99		Cores, flint				
100		Gravers, flint				
101	8	Leaf-shaped blades, knives	1,369	18	72-45 71-1 88-1 71-1 74-8 71-2 77-15 90-9 79-X 73-11 77-2 74-10 72-2 78-6 72-19 78-8 76-1 78-1 90-3 76-1 77-31 83-1 77-1 86-1	
102		Leaf-shaped blades deposited in cache			86-X 89-1 74-60 81-3 76-1 89-53	1, 12, 29, 54, 66
103		Stemmed projectile points deposited in cache			78-1	6, 7, 54
104	9	Projectile points, stem with parallel sides	112	18	71-2 78-50 90-180 74-X 72-167 87-4 73-23 88-1 74-563 76-6 77-54 81-2	
105		Stemmed points, and scrapers ground smooth on stem edge			87-X 88-X 90-X	
106	36	Projectile points side notched	40	8	71-4 78-1 72-10 78-3 72-3 81-9 73-2 90-27 73-1 83-6 74-49 74-70 90-27 76-1 77-26	
107	48	Drills and reamers	3	3	77-20	

13

No.	Code	Trait	n	n					
108 109	50	Scrapers, flint, hafted / Scrapers, thumbnail	18	2	72-2 72-5 83-3	74-17 73-5 90-24 74-2	77-8 74-11	83-1 77-10	90-12 78-5
110	25	Scrapers, side, flake	17	4	72-47 90-5		76-3	77-10	78-7
		Ground Stone Traits							
111	3	Gorget, bar, expanded center	20	14	71-2 78-9 72-1	72-3 79-2 73-1	74-3	76-1	77-2
112	3	Gorget, reel-shaped	5	5	83-1 74-1 83-5	73-1	75-1	77-2	78-2
113 114	3 / B	Gorget, concave side, convex ends / Gorget, truncated pyramid and semi-keeled	9 / 1	7 / 1	72-2	76-1			
115	C	Gorget, flat, various form, elliptical, triangular, diamond shape	3	3	72-2	72-3 83-6 72-3	74-4 89-1 77-1	76-1	77-2
116		Gorget, conically perforated from one side only							
117 118	10	Pipes, tubular, constricted mouth / Pipes, tubular, slate, long flared mouth	54	18	71-2 78-9 71-1 79-1	72-1	77-1	78-1	85-X
119 120 121	C / 55 / 22	Pipes, elbow, biconical / Pipes, platform / Pitted stones, cup stones	1 / 2 / 8	1 / 2 / 6	71-2 81-1 72-22 87-1	73-2 90-1	76-1	77-1	78-6
122 123	30 / 34	Stone balls / Celts, granite, and igneous rock	6 / 38	3 / 15	71-1 78-3 88-2 78-1	72-25 79-5 89-1	73-3 81-2 90-11	74-58 83-3	76-2 87-8
124 125 126	37 / C	Celts, hematite / Hoes, limestone, sandstone, slabs / Hammerstones	10 / 2	7 / 2	72-18 72-28 87-2	73-1 74-6 90-8 74-5 74-12	76-1 78-5	77-3 81-1	78-1 83-1
127	53	Abraiding stones	4	2	72-7	74-5 74-12	76-1 90-15	81-4	
128 129 130	/ 40	Grooved semi-cylinders and balls / Stone discs / Hemispheres, lime, sandstone	7	5	72-2 73-1 77-3	78-1			90-2

ADENA TRAIT LIST—Continued

New Trait Number	Greenman's Trait Number	Traits	Occurrences by Greenman	Mounds by Greenman	Kentucky Site Numbers with Number of Occurrences in it.	Site Number of Non-Kentucky Sites Having the Trait
131	C	Hemispheres, barite, basalt	1	1	72-4, 74-3, 90-1	
132	43	Hemispheres, hematite	5	4	78-1, 74-3, 89-1, 90-24	
133	54	Boat shaped barite bars	2	2	72-4, 74-23	
134	C	Pestles	1	1	90-3	
135		Steatite vessel fragments			77-8	
136	33	Galena, barite fragments, worked	4	2	76-3, 77-1, 74-10, 90-90	
137	44	Concretions or fossils	4	4	71-1	
138	52	Stones with incised characters	5	2		
139	59	Geodes, cuplike	2	2		
140		Obsidian flakes				
141		Saws, sandstone, lime, granite			72-8	
		Tablet Traits				
142	15	Tablets, rectangular	15	11	73-3, 81-1, 72-1, 74-1, 90-1, 85-2, 77-3, 78-16, 79-1	26, 55, 25, 129, 130
143	C	Tablets, rectanguloid, engraved				25, 26, 129
144		Engraved in relief, one side			72-1	25, 26, 129
145		One side of tablet grooved			73-1	130
146		Tablet engraved on both sides				55, 130
147		Zoomorphic figure duplicated on same plane			85-1, 85-2	25, 26, 129

No.	Ref.	Trait	N	Occurrences	References
148		Engraving bilaterally symmetric about a median line		85–1	25, 26, 55, 129
149		Head and beak of raptorial bird		72–1, 85–1	25, 130, M. C.
150		Joints in zoomorphic form represented by dots or circles		72–1	25, 26, 130
151		Claws of bird		85–1	25, 129, 130, M. C.
152		Five digits in foot forms		85–1	25, 26, 130, M. C.
153		Representation of the serpent motif		85–1	26
154		Human facial mask of death motif		85–1	M. C.?
155		Hand-eye design		85–1	25, 26, 129, M. C.
156		Row of notches at base of tablet		85–1	
		Bone and Antler Traits			
157	2	Awls, cannon bone or scapula of elk	61	71–4, 80–3	53, 1
158	1 / 18	Awls, scapula, deer	12	71–1, 72–1, 86–3, 77–1	1
159	7	Awls, bone or antler	16	78–8, 73–1	
160	4 / 26	Beads, bone	53	71–4	
161	1 / C	Bone combs	2	71–12, 72–2, 73–1	
162	4 / 27	Flaking tool antler or bone	15	79–2, 72–9, 73–5, 76–6, 77–14	38
163	9 / 19	Teeth, animal	15	71–2, 72–3, 79–1	
164	3 / 28	Claws, animal	17	77–1	
165	2 / 32	Projectile points, antler	4	71–2, 73–3	
166	3 / 46	Spatula, metapodal bone of elk	4	72–3, 73–2, 78–4	
167		Spatula flat bone section			
168	2 / C	Animal jaws worked	2	72–1, 77–4	
169		Cut antler sections, drifts		72–4	
170	1 / C	Gorget, human parietal	1	77–1, 72–1, 77–1	
171	6 / C	Handles, bone or antler	8	71–5, 71–4, 77–1, 79–1, 79–1, 88–1	12, 143
172	39	Spoons, carapace of terrapin		71–4	
		Shell Traits			
173	C	Spoons, bivalve shell		71–8, 72–4, 77–1	

ADENA TRAIT LIST—Continued

New Trait Number	Greenman's Trait Number	Traits	Occurrences by Greenman	Mounds by Greenman	Kentucky Site Numbers with Number of Occurrences in it.	Site Number of Non-Kentucky Sites Having the Trait
174	C	Hoes, bivalve shell		4		
175	12	Beads, disk	3,498	15	71-299, 72-1505, 75-X, 79-96	
176	23	Beads, marginella	1,049	5	81-X, 72-152, 76-X, 76-X	
177	31	Pearl beads	242	2	71-135, 71-2	
178	C	Beads, large columella, tubular	7	3	71-X, 83-44	
		Copper Traits				
179	4	Bracelet	133	26	71-3, 72-26, 77-17, 78-10	
180	29	Rings, finger, spiral	7	3	71-5, 72-1, 77-1, 79-1	
181	35	Beads, rolled sheet	825	11	71-7, 75-X, 77-X	
182	35	Beads, drilled nuggets			75-X, 85-145	
183	C	Pins, long pointed rods	1	1	72-1, 81-1	
184	C	Crescent, head ornament?			72-1	99
185	42	Pendants, long strips	8	4	79-11	38
186	B	Gorgets, rectangular			87-1, 84-1	
187	B	Gorgets, reel-shaped	1	1	75-2	40, 56
188	B	Celts			74-2	
		Mica Traits				
189	14	Fragments of designs	200	13	77-2, 78-6, 81-6, 85-X	
190	C	Crescent, head ornament?	1	1	72-2, 79-2, 81-1	

Pottery Traits

No.	Trait	C1	C2	C3	C4	C5	C6
191	Adena Plain	72-3472, 76-202, 79-484, 86-267	73-215, 77-278, 81-121	74-81, 78-376, 87-159			145-13, 148-17, 149-1
192	Limestone tempered check stamp	72-X	74-1				
193	Sand tempered plain	72-X					
194	Sand tempered check stamp	72-X	76-1				
195	Montgomery Incised	72-5		77-3	78-9		
196	Grit tempered 5-line diamond						48-1
197	Johnson Plain	77-2457, 77-102, 77-28	78-2567, 78-98, 78-1				
198	Levissa Cord Marked						
199	Paintsville Simple Stamped						
200	Fayette Thick	73-26	74-156	83-16			146-X, 147-X, 7-X, 34-X, 43-X, 143-X, 145-60, 149-272
201	Woodland Plain, Adena variety	74-14	79-9	83-1			43-X, 145-13, 149-6
202	Woodland Cord Marked	72-X	74-10				
203	Grit tempered check stamp	78-1, 77-1	72-X	73-X	75-X	77-X	
204	Grit tempered fabric marked	77-X, 78-X	79-X	80-X	81-X	82-X	
205	Pottery vessels not used as mortuary offerings	83-X	87-X	88-X			

Textile Traits

No.	Trait	C1	C2	C3	C4	C5	C6
206	Plain plaiting	76-X					1-X
207	Twilled plaiting, rectangular	76-X					
208	Twilled plaiting, oblique	76-X					
209	Multiple braid plaiting	75-X					
210	Plain twining	72-X	76-X				
211	Twilled twining	72-X	76-X				
212	Diamond twilled twining	72-X	76-X	83-X			
213	Chevron plain twining	76-X					12-X

ADENA TRAIT LIST—Continued

1 New Trait Number	2 Greenman's Trait Number	3 Traits	4 Occurrences by Greenman	5 Mounds by Greenman	6 Kentucky Site Numbers with Number of Occurrences in it.	7 Site Number of Non-Kentucky Sites Having the Trait
214		Lattice (bird cage) twining			75-X	
215		Rope, three ply			76-X	
		Physical Characteristics				
216		Physical type. Adena people basically a medium sized brachycephal			71-32 81-3 72-17 83-1 76-4 87-1 77-2 88-7 79-29	12, 28, 43, 55, 59, 143
217		Head deformation. Occipital vertical flattening			Same	
218		Head deformation. Bifrontal planes on each side of forehead			Same	

DESCRIPTION OF INDIVIDUAL TRAITS BY NUMBER, IN ORDER AS INDICATED IN THE ADENA TRAIT LIST

EARTHWORK TRAITS

(1) Large earthworks associated with other Adena manifestations.

Recent investigations seem to show that long extended Adena occupancy of any locality resulted in several forms of earth construction capable of survival to the present time. These remains called earthworks, "sacred circles", mounds, and village sites are often found associated in a group, in various combinations. These groups occur throughout the Upper Ohio River Basin, in West Virginia, Ohio, Indiana, and Kentucky. Any Adena site may have one of more of these forms of prehistoric remains. Some sites have all of them.

A typical group, but by no means one of the largest, is the Mt. Horeb Site,* Fayette County, Kentucky, made up of Site Fa 1, Units A, B, C, and D, and Sites Fa 14 and Fa 15. Here a large earthwork which encloses a small Adena village, has another Adena village in its general vicinity, and in the immediate neighborhood there are two Adena burial mounds, and two "sacred circles", one of which has been proven by excavation to have been built by Adena.** Such groups of related structures pointing to an extensive Adena community usually are found in the vicinity of a fairly large stream; often located on its high bank or on hill crests overlooking the valley.

The **earthwork;** the largest constructions in the group consists of a ditch paralleling one of more embankments, which in various forms usually encloses an area of 25 acres or more. The ditch is usually formed by excavating the earth and throwing it either inward or outward from the enclosed area. Sometimes the earth is thrown both ways. These large earthworks have been called "enclosures", defensive earthworks, or "forts".

Unit B. Site Fa 1, is typical of this form of structure. Its location in relation to other members of its group is shown in Figure 21, page 642, Vol. V. It was surveyed by Rafinesque and illustrated by Squier and Davis,*** who classified it as a defense earthwork.

The fact that such a large earthwork encloses an Adena village; is constructed in somewhat the same manner as a "sacred circle" in the immediate vicinity, which has been proven to be of Adena origin; and the further fact that Adena burial mounds have been found near by; seem to justify the belief of a common origin for all these manifestations. This belief seems to find confirmation in the repeated

* Webb, Wm. S., 1943, p. 139.
** Webb, Wm. S., 1941, p. 155.
*** Squier, E. G., and Davis, E. H., 1848, Plate XIV, No. 3.

close association of these several forms of earth remains on sites having burial mound known to belong to Adena.

Of the ancient works near Charleston, West Virginia, Thomas* says,

> "Along the Kanawha river from three to eight miles below Charleston are the most extensive and interesting ancient works to be found in the State of West Virginia. They consist of fifty mounds varying in diameter from 35 to 200 feet; some eight or ten enclosures containing from less than one acre to fully 30 acres; circular clay lined pits from six to eight feet broad and as many feet in depth and box-shaped stone cists. All are found in the upper river terraces beyond the reach of the highest floods."

In Plate XXVII, and in figures 294-297, he presents a plot of this group of earthworks from which it may be seen that some of these earthworks are large enclosures of many acres, and others which are smaller and circular, are the so-called "sacred circles". Some of these mounds lie inside the smaller circular earthworks. From the various reports of excavation of these mounds Greenman has accepted thirteen (his numbers 57 to 69 inclusive) of these mounds as of Adena origin.

From the reports of explorations of Thomas in this region, the authors feel justified, in the light of the present Adena trait list, even on the very meager evidence available, in classifying an additional seventeen of these Kanawha River Mounds as of Adena origin.

The intent of this Trait No. (1), is to declare, what has now been demonstrated, that large earthworks occur in association with minor enclosures, some of which have been found by excavation to be of Adena origin. These earthworks and enclosures are not known to be associated with any other prehistoric peoples in the regions mentioned, i.e. in Kentucky and West Virginia.

The fact that minor enclosures, the "sacred enclosures" of Squier and Davis, or sacred circles, so-called, are found in great numbers in Ohio, may suggest that some of these earthworks in Ohio had their origin in Adena.

Since the great "geometric earthworks" of the Scioto River Valley, commonly attributed to Hopewell of Ohio, also had many "sacred circles" enclosed within their area, or attached directly to them, or lying on the outside of these geometric earthworks but in their immediate vicinity, one must be profoundly impressed by this coincidence which could hardly be attributed to accident or independent invention, but which would be easily understood if these great cultural groups could be shown to be related in some way to each other.

---

* Thomas, Cyrus, 1894, p. 414.

(2) "Sacred Circles", associated with large earthworks.

The term "sacred enclosure"* as used by Squier and Davis to describe these minor earthworks, was adopted by them in the belief that such works could not have been defensive in character since the embankment formed is exterior to the ditch, which seemed to them to be contrary to good military engineering. Usually these sacred enclosures are circular in form, though they may be square, rectangular, elliptical, crescentic, panduriform, or hexagonal. Since the vast majority of them are circular; and since it is the circular form of these minor earthworks, or "sacred enclosures" which has been shown to be of Adena origin, the term "sacred circles" has been adopted, not because their purpose is certainly known, but because Squire and Davis,* under the term "sacred enclosure', have so well described their construction and occurrence.

Of these minor earthworks they say:

"Occasionally we find them isolated, but more frequently in groups. The greater number of the circles are of small size, with nearly uniform diameter of two hundred and fifty or three hundred feet, and invariably have the ditch interior to the wall. These have always a single gateway, opening oftenest to the east, though by no means observing a fixed rule in that respect.. It frequently happens that they have one or more small mounds of the class denominated sacrificial within the walls."

They usually occur in the vicinity of large earthworks, and sometimes are attached to them as if intended as an integral part of the larger construction. This is well illustrated in the many great sites in the vicinity of Chillicothe, Ohio.**

It has recently been demonstrated that "sacred enclosures", or sacre circles, are of Adena origin.***

(3) Sacred Circles have embankments exterior to the ditch.

This characteristic of these minor earthworks was simply obtained by excavating the ditch and depositing all earth removed on the exterior side. These circles vary in diameter from 50 feet to 500 feet. In a recent study of 76 circular enclosures, the average diameter was found to be 212 feet. The other geometric forms of these minor enclosures are of comparable area. This method of excavation left the central area of the circle unmodified, but gave it the appearance of a mound since it was surrounded by a ditch.

(4) Sacred Circles usually have entrance or gateway.

In many cases the central area in a "sacred circle" was not completely enclosed by the ditch, but a section some 30 feet or more wide was left unexcavataed. These sections were called by Squier and

* Squier, E. G., and Davis, E. H., 1848, pp. 47, 48.
** Squier, E. G., and Davis, E. H., 1848, Plate II.
*** Webb, Wm. S., 1941 p. 167.

Davis "gateways" on the assumption that they served as entrances. The best illustration, so far available, of the gateway of a "sacred circle" is that presented by Lilly,* of the Great Circle, Mound Park, Anderson, Indiana.

(5) Sacred Circles once enclosed a circular structure of vertical posts.

This fact has been demonstrated at Site Fa 1, Kentucky.** The structure was evidenced by a circular post-mold pattern some 95 feet in diameter which contained an estimated 68 pairs of posts. Of these, 62 pairs were found complete and undisturbed, but only remnants of the other 6 pairs were found. Since circular patterns of paired post-molds have now been found on many Adena sites, and have never been reported in any other cultural connection, one is constrained to believe that these structures surrounded by "sacred circles" are of Adena origin. The importance of this discovery should prove to be great, for it offers a direct and simple means of testing for the origin of the many great groups of earth works in Ohio, such as are centered in the region about Chillicothe.

These "sacred circles" may have been, as suggested by Morgan, the meeting place of a phratry or other social subdivision of the tribe, and the enclosed "stockade-like" circular structure may have been built to obtain privacy, and prevent "outsiders" from observing secret ceremonials. Whatever their purpose, there seems to be no suggestion that they had any military value or purpose.

(6) Sacred Circles usually occur in groups of two to eight.

This seems to be a fact easily observed by inspecting topographic surveys of the great mound groups of the Ohio Valley. The reason for multiplicity of such "circles" cannot certainly be known until their use is better understood. However, the suggestion of Morgan*** seems to offer a satisfactory explanation, and it is not at variance with any information at present available. If these "sacred circles" were indeed the private meeting places of a phratry in any tribe, it is easy to understand why there would be two, or four, or possibly more at a single site. It sometimes happens that the embankment of these earth circles is not very high, and the corresponding ditch not very deep. Where cultivation has taken place, they could easily be destroyed. It is certain that many of them have been destroyed and today cannot be seen. In the few cases where such circles occur singly and seemingly removed from all other evidence of occupancy, one is led to suspect that it appears alone only because it is the sole survivor of a former group now largely erased by erosion, cultivation, or recent "improvements" in the locality. Many such groups of

* Lilly, Eli, 1937, Inside cover.
** Webb, Wm. S., 1941, p. 153.
*** Morgan, Lewis H., 1881, p. 216.

earthworks are known to have been partially obliterated, if not almost completely destroyed, in historic times.

Speaking of the Junction Group, Ross Co., Ohio, Squier and Davis* say:

"Similar groups are frequent, indeed, small circles resembling those here represented, constitute in the Scioto Valley, by far the most numerous class of remains. They seldom occur singly, but generally in connection with several others of the same description and are accompanied by one or more mounds; sometimes they are connected with long parallel lines of embankments."

The present authors believe that **every "sacred circle" is of Adena origin,** and that many of them still possess internal evidence of that origin. Careful excavation of the central enclosed area should reveal a **circular pattern of paired post-molds.**

MOUND TRAITS

(7) **Mounds Conical.** G(1).

Most Adena mounds have an approximately circular base and the apex is nearly symmetrically located relative to the base. The present form of many such mounds would suggest that they were once nearly right circular cones, which have suffered by erosion, cultivation, and some of them by specific disturbance within the historic period. While this trait may not be diagnostic of Adena, since non-Adena mounds are also often nearly conical, yet it is a trait of high frequency in Adena, and does serve to distinguish this type of mound from the zoomorphic effigy form of mound of the north-central states and the truncated pyramidal mounds of the Southeast.

(8) **Mounds one of a group.** G(45).

This trait is stated by Greenman as "In a group of three mounds". While this is often true, there seems to be no particular significance to a group of three. From the nature of mound construction and the causes which seem to have led to the starting of the new mounds, it may be inferred that the number of mounds in any immediate locality was somewhat a measure of the length of time the site was occupied, and the importance of the site as a center of population. Many Adena mounds were never more than a few feet high, having been built to cover a burned house on the floor of which a log tomb burial had been made, or to cover cremated remains which had been deposited on the house floor. Sometimes low mounds were built to cover subfloor pit tombs. Unless such a low mound was later chosen as the site of additional log tomb burials, it would remain small and might be easily so reduced in time by erosion, or by cultivation in recent years as now to escape recognition as of human origin. This

---

* Squier, E. G. and Davis, E. H., 1848, p. 65.

is especially true if there were other large mounds in the vicinity to divert attention. It thus happens that where a large Adena mound is found, it is usually accompanied by other smaller mounds in the vicinity. These smaller mounds are sometimes quite inconspicuous and may be found only after a careful search by trained observers.

(9) Mound in or near "sacred circles." G(41).

Five mounds in Greenman's list, No. 20 (Salt Creek Mound, Hocking County, Ohio), No. 52 (Fudge Mound, Randolph County, Indiana), and Nos. 58, 68, 69 (Kanawaha Valley near Charleston, West Virginia), were in or associated with "enclosures". Since it is known today that many "enclosures" are of Adena origin, it is not surprising that mounds inside, as well as many outside, but in the vicinity of such minor earthworks, should have been found to be of Adena origin also. Of the five mounds reported by Greenman, three were inside or near "sacred circles". Two of these, Nos. 68 and 69, were within true circles while Mound No. 20 was inside a small enclosure which was described as a "square with rounded corners". The circular mound base covered almost the entire enclosed area. The other two mounds, Nos. 52 and 58, were within earthworks of much larger size.

Fowke* reports Adena artifacts from a mound inside a "sacred circle" as follows:

"A mile north of Wakefield in Pike County, (Ohio) on the Barnes farm, are the enclosures figured by Squier and Davis as the works in Seal Township. Near the southeast corner of the square enclosure is a mound about three feet high and sixty feet in diameter surrounded by a ditch and an embankment. About eight feet northwest of the center and sixteen inches above the original surface were two or three fragments of human skull and between three and four feet south of them, portions of human femora; these probably were the remains of a body that had laid extended with head to the north.

"Eleven feet south of the center were several pieces of mica, some of them fragments of trimmed and perforatd pieces, others, rough flakes split off from a larger piece; on them lay nine flint blocks or cores. . . . these were partially covered with a large sheet of mica; one of the blocks was chipped into a rough hatchet form. A fcot east of these were two gorgets; one was close grained slates well made with a single perforation; the other of micaceous sandstone with two perforations."

(10) Mound in or near large earthworks. G(41).

Since it is now known that large earthworks, "sacred circles," and burial mounds are all part of the same building complex of Adena, it follows that Adna mounds may be expected to occur in the vicinity of such earthworks. Not every Adena mound, however has such associations. Clearly, some mounds were built quite apart

---

* Fowke, Gerard, 1895, p. 515.

from large centers of occupancy, but other mounds were also erected adjacent to large earthworks and sometimes even enclosed by them. Two such mounds in Greenman's list of 70, i.e., Nos. 52 and 58, were reported inside "enclosures" which were of considerable size, and which could not well be described as "sacred circles", although three other mounds reported by him were enclosed by "sacred circles".

(11) Mound built on their own villages.

This is a nearly universal trait of Adena. The fact was not recognized by the early explorers of mounds in the Mississippi Valley, and the apparent absence of Adena villages has often been the subject of comment and speculation. The fact is that if a large mound was erected on a small village it might cover a considerable portion of the area occupied by the small village, see traits 14 and 17. This is a fortunate circumstance for today our most exact knowledge of Adena villages comes almost exclusively from such fragmentary portions of village as have been preserved from erosion and destruction by being covered by a mound.*

It now appears that Adena villages which were outside earthworks, were never areas of congested population. Rather, the evidence seems to suggest that the pattern of occupancy of an area was to build a few houses, two to five, which constituted a habitation group, at a distance of perhaps 1000 feet from the next nearest group. A village or a community might have consisted of scores of such habitation groups somewhat widely scattered over several square miles of area.

Except for the fact that Adena dwelling houses and "townhouses" were often burned, and mounds erected exactly on their sites, it is very doubtful if evidence of such structures and the villages would have been preserved to the present time.

(12) Mound on the site of burned house.

It is now known that Adena Folk practiced house burning after burial of the dead on the house floor.** Sometimes the house was burned over a deposit of cremated remains,*** on the house floor. When the house was burned in connection with a burial, a mound was erected over all. Thus many Adena mounds were almost exactly over the site of a burned house.

The presence of the house, its size and form, are often shown by post-mold patterns deep in the subsoil below the house floor. Sometimes the hard burned clay floor is found. Rarely are portions of the house to be seen except their remains as a layer of charcoal and ashes covering rather exactly the area of the post-mold

---

* Webb, Wm. S., 1940, p. 48, and 1942, p. 307.
** Webb, Wm. S., 1941, p. 233.
*** Webb, Wm. S. and Elliott, John B., 1942, p. 431.

pattern. Since it was customary to cover burials on the house floor by a small earth mound built inside the house before it was burned, the charcoal remains of the burned house often appear as a thin convex layer of ashes and charcoal extending over the house floor and **over** the surface of the small mound erected at its center.

As an evidence of house burning over a primary mound built on its floor while the house was still standing, the thin charcoal layer resulting from a burned house has been reported by early excavators many times. In describing their excavation of a mound near Chillicothe, which was later classified as of Adena origin (Greenman's No. 2), Squier and Davis* say:

> "The charcoal layer is a frequent though by no means invariable feature in mounds of this class, and would seem to indicate that sacrifices were made for the dead, or funeral rites of some description, in which fire performed a part, celebrated."
>
> * * * * * * *
>
> "The fire in every case was kept burning for a very little time, as is shown from the lack of ashes, and by the slight trace of its action left on the adjacent earth."

Of a mound near Waverly, Ohio, Fowke** says:

> "The feet of the skeleton lay on hard-burned undisturbed earth, from which the ashes had been carefully removed . . . The head of the second skeleton was two feet farther east than that of the first, and rested on a fire-bed; near its skull were found fragments of bones of a very young child. The fire-beds at the head and feet of these two were each about four feet across, another north of them was six feet across, and the earth beneath it was regular in shape. On these bodies and ash beds, over a space of some fourteen feet in diameter, earth had been deposited to the thickness of a foot at the center, running to an edge all around; above this was a thin layer of charcoal with its margin resting on the original surface; and over this the mound had been built."

Evidence of house burning over a primary mound on its floor is furnished by Moorehead*** when in speaking of a mound on the Scioto River, Chillicothe, he says:

> "The height was seven and a half feet, the diameter at the base, fifty-five feet. . . .
>
> * * * * * * *
>
> "The only variation from the yellow clay of which the mound was built was a stratum, about three inches in thickness, of clay burned to a bright red. It had nearly the same curvature as the mound's surface, the edge resting upon the general level at about ten feet from the center on every side."

This was obviously a primary mound, the surface of which had been burned when the house was destroyed. If its surface, as he says,

---

*Squier, E. G. and Davis, E. H., 1843, p. 163.
** Fowke, Gerard, 1902, p. 370.
*** Moorehead, Warren K., 1892, p. 146.

followed the surface of the larger mound erected over it, it would have been 20 feet in diameter and about three feet high in the center. It is to be regretted that he did not seek for a post-mold pattern. Usually if one follows these hard burned clay strata to the house floor, the wall post-mold pattern is to be found in the subsoil at the edge of the clay floor, which seems to suggest that oftimes the primary mound erected inside the house on the house floor while the house was still standing was conical, and covered the entire floor area. A mound three miles southwest of Wilmington, Ohio (Greenman's No. 25), was found by Moorehead* to have been built on the site of a house which had been burned. Of it he says:

> "The structure is thirty feet in diameter and two and a half feet in altitude. . . . .
> "The mound is presumed to be a house site, as posts extend into the structure to a depth of three feet and form a square twelve feet on each side. The posts were burned and charred so that little remained of them."

This mound accepted by Greenman as an Adena mound yielded a grooved sandstone tablet. The rectilinear pattern of wall post is rare —but not unknown in Adena** (see trait 60).

(13) **Mound shows stratigraphy.** G(16).

This is a very frequently observed situation in Adena mounds. Greenman states the trait as "Primary stratigraphy". After the erection of a primary mound to cover a log tomb, or a burned house, the mound was often left to weather and accumulated a humus zone on its surface. In many cases later log tombs were intruded into this primary mound, on its sides, or within its central apex. Always these new tombs were covered with new earth brought in from the vicinity. Usually this increment not only covered the new burial, but was extended to cover the entire primary mound. Thus the mound grew in height and in area. The very considerable size of some Adena mounds is due to the fact that secondary, tertiary, and even quaternary sections have been erected over relatively very modest primary mounds. This trait has been frequenty recognized by early excavators and is well illustrated by the Adena† mound of Ohio, G(1); by the Great Smith†† mound, G(59) of West Virginia; and by Wright††† mound (Mm 6) of Kentucky.

Probably the best possible demonstration of this trait in any mound would be obtained by a complete vertical slice through it, thus revealing a profile. Since the early excavators never used such technique, it is interesting to note from their observations how strati-

---

* Moorehead, Warren K., 1892, p. 107.
** Webb, Wm. S., 1940, p. 51.
** Webb, Wm. S., 1943, p. 588.
† Mills, William C., 1907, Figures 1 and 19.
†† Thomas, Cyrus, 1894, p. 425, Figure 298.
††† Webb, Wm. S., 1940, p. 12.

graphy revealed itself. From present evidence it seems that many times a cremation was deposited, or a log tomb erected, on a house floor. A primary mound was erected to cover the burial, all inside the house. Finally the house was burned and a secondary mound was erected over all. This left in such cases, a core, in form approximating a right circular cone, in the center of the mound at it base. The earth used in building the primary mound often contained much village midden which being loam, did not pack tightly. It was often covered by the secondary mound made of sterile clays—from the subsoil, tough when moist and hard when dry. If a mound was investigated by tunneling there would be a very slight chance to see any evidence of the burned house, or of the post-mold pattern in the subsoil, but still its stratigraphy would be revealed in part.

Note the report of Thomas* on Mound 23 of the Kanawah Valley Group near Charleston, West Virginia, (Greenman's No. 61) in which he says in part:

> "The tunnel carried in at the base from the south side was 10 feet wide and 8 feet high. For a distance of 20 feet it passed through the hard gray material of which the body of the mound was composed. Here it entered suddenly into a mass of soft earth of various colors that had been brought from the hill-sides and bottoms near by. A short distance from this point the casts and remains of the timbers of the large central vault began to appear, but before reaching the interior the tunnel passed over a small refuse heap evidently belonging to an age preceding the date of the building of the mound."

In this language Thomas says there was a primary mound of surface earth, a core, inside a 20 foot thick secondary mound. Since this stratigraphy now has been found many times, covering house floors it is easy to guess that there was a house pattern under this mound although none was reported.

In fact, it appears in the report that a subfloor pit had been used for burial before the erection of the central log vault, and the primary mound over it.

(14) Primary mound contains midden.

The base of many Adena mounds is a burned house in the village. The earth forming the primary mound was scraped up from the surface in the vicinity and thus contains much midden material. In fact, today the apparent dearth of Adena villages is in part accounted for by the fact that the primary mound was erected on the village and thus covered a part of the occupied area. The adjacent area was literally scraped over, and all earth and debris on it in the humus zone was used to construct the primary mound. It is quite apparent in the excavation of some Adena mounds as illustrated by

---

* Thomas, Cyrus, 1894, p. 428.

mound (Mm 6)* that this scraping of the surface about the mound area actually left the mound base as much as one foot above the level of the surrounding area. Thus most of the midden debris of Adena villages which can be found today has either been covered over by the primary mound or incorporated in it during its construction.

(15) Later mound sections built of sterile clays.

The erection of the primary mound from the earth of the humus zone left only the subsoil clays exposed in the immediate vicinity. Later sections of the mounds were built of these subsoil clays, and are hence usually quite sterile of cultural debris. Adena villages seemingly were never very large. Where large mounds were constructed, the later sections were often built from earth carried several hundred feet. This earth was usually sterile because, even though it was taken from the surface, its source was outside of the deposit of village debris.

(16) Earth quarries formed near the mound.

The digging of the hard tough clays with which to build a large mound was, perhaps, as much of a problem as its transportation several hundred feet to its place on the mound. Obviously the clay was not equally easier to dig in all places, so where digging was easiest, there cavities were formed. These are usually broad shallow depressions in the earth's surface, in the vicinity of the mound. Their surfaces today, still a few feet below the level of the general terrain, show practically no humus zones compared to the surrounding region. The building of a large mound must have been a task of many months, probably running into years. Such earth quarries surely would catch and, for a time, hold rainfall. This would have the effect of softening the hard clay subsoil and perhaps make it easier to dig. Recent excavation of mounds in Kentucky show that the individual loads of earth, when dumped, did not spread, i.e., they were generally not dry crumbly earth, but definitely chunks of moist plastic clay. Earth quarries, because of their ability to catch water, and thus soften the clay, and render its detachment and transportation somewhat easier, may have been intentionally formed by the builders of Adena mounds. Whether their existence is intentional or fortuitous may never be demonstrable, but in many cases their presence is obvious. Where mounds today must be removed and the site left level after excavation, earth quarries are a potential asset to the investigator since they offer a place for easy disposal of the mound earth. The "normal loading" so often reported by explorers of Adena mounds, is believed to have been made possible by having available near by a supply of **moist** clay.

---

* Webb, Wm. S., 1940, p. 12.

(17) Village midden in situ under mound.

The importance of this fact for Adena has been only recently recognized. The lack of evidence of the existence of Adena villages has long been known, and the fact has been the basis of much speculation. This absence of Adena villages has been attributed to many causes, among them, great age of Adena, long periods of erosion, inability or carelessness of investigators in searching for such evidence, etc. Recent excavation has shown that mounds erected on a village site inevitably cover a part of the original village. Much of the remaining portion outside of the mound base is destroyed or removed in the building of the mound. After a burial mound is erected over a group of houses in a village, occupation probably did not continue on that exact spot but was, perhaps, removed to a new site distant a thousand feet or more, thus no new debris would accumulate in quantity about the mound base. The excavation of mounds (Jo 2-Jo 9) have suggested another reason for the paucity of Adena villages. This suggestion is that the Adena people rarely, if ever, lived in a large compact village, but in scattered house groups, a few houses, perhaps four or five closely associated, the groups being separated several hundred feet from their next neighbor. Under such circumstances, even with long continued occupancy, the midden deposit would never be deep anywhere. When at the burial of an important person a mound was built over a house floor on which the burial lay, the mound covered and contained in its primary structure most all of that village debris. In a house group where no mound was constructed, its identity as a village would be easily lost since the debris was so thin. Whatever the reason, today Adena villages usually exist only under mounds, although traces of at least one have been found inside an earthwork believed to be of Adena origin.

Many early excavators have found these thin strata of Adena village middens under mounds, but did not recognize them for what they were, and so made only casual reference to them in reports. As an illustration Moorehead* reports on the Quick Mound near Loudonville, Ashland County, Ohio in part as follows:

"We sunk a trench eight and one half feet wide and nine feet deep and continued the same around the mound, widening it at the bottom. * * * * *

"It was erected upon a burnt floor or base. Above this was a dark streak one half inch wide; then a layer of ashes and pottery fragments and burnt bones one half an inch thick. A hard burnt 'pan' or floor one inch thick and cement-like in character was above this. It seems to have extended over a space 12 x 15 feet. * * * * *

"Animal bones, chiefly deer, were in the ashes below the hard floor. Some fifty of these were found and about 400 pottery fragments." .

* Moorehead, W. K., 1897, pp. 178-179.

Although Moorehead did not seem to recognize it, here was a village midden, animal bones, potsherds, under a house floor, erected on the village debris. He found the skeleton buried on this house floor, over which the mound had been erected, but he did not find or recognize any evidence of a house, at least none was reported.

(18) Mound shows individual earth loads.

This is frequently observed in Adena mounds. Sections of the mound built of clays of different colors, show each load as it was deposited. Often the clays from different areas about the mound, or from different depths in the subsoil showed a wide range of color variations, red, brown, yellow, blue, and light grey. When the clay was moist, each load remained compact and was pressed down into a lenticular mass weighing about 30 pounds, more or less. This seems to be the average load carried up in the buiding of the Adena mounds. When the deposit of new earth was on a horizontal surface, the lens of the clay was horizontal; if the surface on which it was deposited was sloping, the lens took that slope. Observation of the tilting of these individual loads is often a good index of the order of events in making the fill in different portions of the mound. When individual loads are found above an Adena tomb, the roof of which has collapsed, observations on the dipping, shearing, and faulting of individual loads is the best possible means of determining the original tomb depth, and the original position of the tomb roof. Such observations on the amount of shearing of individual loads is often confirmed by finding the original tomb roof position, indicated by the molds of the roof poles on the tomb edge. In excavations of Adena sites a careful reading of profiles showing "loading" is absolutely essential to avoid serious destruction of features before they are fully exposed.

Of mound 23 in the Kanawaha Valley group near Charleston, West Virginia (Greenman's No. 61) Thomas* says:

"There was a marked dissimilarity between the northern and southern sides of this mound, the former being a compact mass of variously colored soils from different points in the vicinity, in alternate horizontal layers. The separate loads of those carrying it in were plainly defined and the different sizes of these small masses indicate that many persons, some much stronger than others, were simultaneously engaged in the work."

(19) Impression of grass, twigs, leaves, etc. G(20).

An inspection of a number of these impressions found during excavations seem to indicate that most of them are of coarse grasses, such as usually grow in swamp land near a river bank. In several instances where this has been observed in mounds, small present

---

* Thomas, Cyrus, 1894, p. 430.

day swamps were not far distant, and coarse grass was still to be found in the vicinity. This may mean nothing more than that builders of the mound found it convenient to transport a load of earth on to the mound by uprooting a large tuft of swamp grass and depositing it, grass, roots, and dirt all together on the mound. There are, however, instances of small limbs and twigs which have been impressed into clay surfaces, the sides of pits or the sloping sides of mounds or tombs. Some of these twig impressions seem to suggest that when the clay surface was moist and soft, and possibly slick, the twigs with leaves were laid down to permit walking over the surface, while the construction was going on. Such twigs and leaves would become imbedded in the clay, and later when they were covered might leave impressions. Such impressions are usually found on surfaces from which the over-burden of earth breaks away readily, which suggests that the twigs were merely used by the builders to maintain a footing on a slippery clay surface in the process of mound construction.

(20) **Fired area at mound base.**

Since mounds were often erected over burned houses, the central floor of which usually had been a fireplace, it is not surprising that burned house floors at the base of mounds are very noticeable features. Many early explorers reported such burned area covered with ashes and charcoal at the mound base, and some concluded that such findings indicated a **ceremonial** preparation of the mound base by fire, and the intentional deposit of an ash layer. Such explanations are founded on nothing more substantial than imagination and speculation by the authors, and seem calculated to excuse by the magic word "ceremonial" what would otherwise have been an irrational and pointless procedure of the builder of the mound.

This trait seems to be a natural consequence of building mounds on old village sites, and oftimes over a specific house floor, on the center of which there had been a hot fire, perhaps for some considerable time, used in the ordinary processes of domestic economy.

(21) **Fired areas on mound surfaces.**

While not very common, this trait has occurred with sufficient frequency to justify its listing. No reason has so far been demonstrated for burned areas as sometimes appear on the side of the mounds. Such surfaces were not left long in the open, but seem to have been covered with earth during mound construction. Such burned areas may be merely the result of fires used for the comfort of workers in cold weather, or for the purpose of giving light at night. They seem not to have been long continued at any one point, and usually no bone or stone debris is to be found in direct association with them, which seems to exclude such fires as designed for cooking.

(22) Primary purpose of mound to cover burials.

This trait is obvious to all investigators of Adena mounds. Every Adena mound either covers a log tomb where extended burials were made, a cremation, or a subfloor tomb containing one or more burials. No other use for an Adena mound has ever been discovered. Certainly they were not domicilliary. No Adena dwelling house has ever been discovered **on a mound.** The Adena mound surely served the ceremonies associated with death—not life. Some earth mounds in the Adena area have been excavated by earlier explorers who found a few Adena artifacts in them, but no burials. Such mounds have been reported as "unproductive", the investigator sometimes stating that the purpose of the erection of the mound was not discovered. Such reports usually show within themselves that the techniques of excavation used **could not** have revealed evidence of a house structure had it been present, or a deposit of cremated remains on a house floor even if it had existed.

(23) Mound built by increments as burials were added.

This is not the equivalent of trait 13—"Mound shows stratigraphy." Mounds are often built over a long period of time by additions of small tombs each of which is covered with new earth brought upon the mound. The mound thus grows slowly in size—but may never show an internal humus line, and may have no major sections superposed, thus indicating no evidence of natural stratigraphy. This increment burial trait is well illustrated by the Robbins mound*, Be 3, in Kentucky. In such cases where burials are intruded into mounds, the additions may be so small that they do not overlap, and hence such additions furnish no clue to relative chronology.

(24) Constructional use of stone. G(21).

Occasional use of flat stones about graves, or as minor additions to log tombs has been noted in Adena mounds. Several areas have been found on interior surfaces of mounds, which were floored with flat slabs of limestone or sandstone. There seems to be no great significance in this trait except to show that stone was used occasionally where it was available. Its use, seemingly, was not a primary objective. Surely in large mounds, containing elaborate log tombs, there was occasion for much "travel" of up and down the mound surface in connection with mound and tomb construction and in connection with whatever ceremonies may have been associated with the burial of important personages. The mound surface was usually steep, as shown by "loading", and, being of clay, was slick when wet, making passage over its surface difficult. (This fact is well demonstrated in the experience of recent excavators working on mounds

---

* Webb, Wm. S. and Elliott, J. B., 1942, p. 377.

in winter weather.)   Such usuage of stone as is shown sparingly in Adena mounds may be wholly due to attempts at construction of temporary paving as an aid to necessary travel up and down the steep sides of a mound at times when footing was difficult.

The Wright Mound Mm 6 (Site No. 72 in trait tabulation) had, of its three areas floored with stone, one in which the individual stones were each laid horizontally,. but in a row extending up the slope of the tertiary mound.   All had been covered when the quaternary section of the mound was added.   This construction was less extensive but probably similar in purpose to that in the Seip* Mound No. 2 of Ohio, regarded as of Hopewell origin.

TOMB TRAITS

(25)   Horizontal log tombs built on bark covered clay floor.   G(2).

Under trait (2) log tombs, Greenman indicated that half of his list of 70 mounds held 55 log tombs.   He does not attempt a detailed trait analysis of tombs.   Recent excavations have revealed a mass of detailed information relative to tomb construction.   While variations exist among individual tombs in any site, yet even these variations are repeated in other sites, so exactly as to indicate procedures which were well understood by people widely separated geographically, and which were carefully followed out in detail.   That is, there are recognized "traits" within the log tomb burial procedures.   A frequently observed log tomb trait is that they were constructed of **horizontal logs laid on a bark covered clay floor.**   The logs resting on plastic clay and covered with mound fill, leave remarkably clear impressions after their decay.   It is also remarkable how little residue is left of large logs a foot or more in diameter.   The impression of the bark is so perfect that it is easy to discern the kind of tree from which the log was cut.   The bark imprint of hackberry, walnut, ash, and elm are easily detected in log tomb molds.   Only rarely does the mold show a smooth surface indicating that the bark was removed before the log was placed.   In most mound clays, the log passes into a very small amount of loose black residue on the very bottom of the mold, but a whitish stain is often left over the remainder of the log mold, probably the result of the growth of mildews or other minute fungi.   Details of construction of log tombs with horizontal molds are listed in the following traits.

(26)   Single log rectangle about body.

The simplest form of log tomb is constructed of four logs, usually laid on a layer of bark, to form a rectangle with approximate interior dimensions of width 3 feet and length 7 feet.   The extended body is laid in this rectangle.   It may or may not be covered with

* Mills, Wm. C., 1917, p. 12.

bark or puddled clay or both, and the tomb is closed by poles laid across the short dimensions. This wooden roof supports the earth piled over it and leaves the body in a cavity the depth of which depends on the diameter of the side logs. When these logs decay they leave their impressions as a depressed rectangle about the skeleton. Sometimes these simple single log rectangles are square and may contain two bodies. The rectangular form may contain, along with a single extended skeleton, the deposited cremated remains of another body. Rarely, do they contain only a deposit of cremated remains.

Sometimes the single log rectangle has a second tier of logs laid just above the first making the cavity inside the tomb two logs deep. This gave greater clearance between the body in the tomb and the log roof which enclosed it. This condition left only a single horizontal log mold rectangle about the body, but the extra height of the tomb wall produced by the second tier of logs is disclosed by observations on the depth the tomb roof fell when it collapsed, as shown by the shearing and faulting of earth loads above it.

(27) **Multiple parallel logs about the body.**

This is an elaboration of the simple log rectangle. Additional logs are laid parallel to the single log rectangle on both sides and ends. Tombs with three or more parallel logs on a side are not uncommon, and tombs have been found which had six logs on a side. Such tombs may thus spread over an area of 25 to 30 feet square. The purpose of the extra logs, other than to form a platform about the remains is quite conjectural. Often they do not serve any obviously useful purpose. However, in some cases it appears that where two parallel logs were used to surround the body on all sides, a third log laid on top of the two parallel logs, and covering the crevice between them, may have been used. Such a third log would have elevated the roof poles of the tomb roof, and given greater "clearance" between the tomb roof and the extended body, which sometimes, after the scattering of red ochre or graphite over it, was covered with bark, or puddled clay, or both, or left open in the tomb. The only "proof" **of a third log,** since it could leave no mold in the clay, is the distance that the tomb roof fell, as shown by the "sheared" loading. If this distance exceeded the diameter of the largest log producing molds in the clay, one may rationalize a third log on top of the two in a pair. Excessive tomb roof collapse is usually associated with elaborate tomb construction where there are two or more log molds parallel to each other surrounding the body.

(28) **Tomb walls shored up with horizontal logs.**

Sometimes the log tomb was constructed at the bottom of a pit four to six feet deep. Sometimes the tomb was intruded into the sloping side of a mound. These left vertical or nearly vertical earth walls to prevent the collapse of which, logs were laid up in log pen fashion, crossed at the ends. The cracks between the logs were closed with bark. This produced horizontal log impressions one above another, and even though the roof had collapsed, the height of the shoring indicated the depth of the tomb.

This is also observed in tombs constructed by first building an earth wall about the tomb area. Shoring with horizontal logs was sometimes necessary to prevent spreading of loose earth into the tomb area. The first of these conditions is well illustrated in Burial 13, Mm. 6—see page 37 and the second by Tomb 5, Be 27, see page 511, Fig. 3 C, Volume V.

(29) **Tomb walls of vertical posts in rectangular pattern.**

Rarely the walls of a pit tomb were shored up by vertical posts, as shown by the Coon Mound* (43) and the Great Smith Mound** (59). In the Coon Mound these vertical posts were from 5 to 8 inches in diameter and from center to center were from 6 inches to 23 inches apart, enclosing a rectangle 12.6 x 15 feet. The ends of these posts were set in a trench dug to receive them. The walls of the tomb being lined with bark, the spaces between the vertical posts were thus closed.

The tomb in the Great Smith Mound was 12 x 13 feet and it had a height of 6 feet at the "eaves" and about 10 feet at the "comb" of the roof. Walls were made of vertical logs set close together. Says Thomas:**

> "The sides were plastered with a mixture of clay and ashes and possibly lined with bark; the roof was covered with bark and poles."

So far this trait has not been found in Kentucky but it has been reported four times from three other states, twice from Ohio (Greenman's Mounds Nos. 6† and 43), once from Indiana (Mound No. 52) Fudge Mound†† and once from West Virginia (Mound No. 59), Great Smith Mound.

In the Fudge Mound not only did the body lay inside a rectangular pattern of vertical post-molds, in the pit, but there was about the mouth of the pit a rectangular pattern of one inch stake holes, and enclosing that pattern, a larger rectangular pattern of three inch stake holes. While horizontal log tombs are rectangular in form, it is somewhat astonishing to note rectangular structures of vertical posts used for burial in mounds, since for dwellings made with vertical posts, the pattern in Adena is characteristically circular, only a few rectangular structures having been so far found in village sites. This trait may rep-

---

* Greenman, E. F., 1932, Fig. 22.
** Thomas, Cyrus, 1894, p. 426.
† Moorehead, Warren, K., 1899. p. 132.
†† Setzler, Frank M., 1931, p. 30.

resent a "survival" in Adena or a new concept borrowed from an outside source. If so, the source from which it was derived is not apparent since all other well known forms of rectangular structures of vertical posts are later than Adena.

(30) Vertical tomb-posts in corners of rectangular horizontal pattern.

This trait has not been found in Kentucky but it appears to be an important trait although rare. It is a combination of vertical and horizontal logs in tomb construction.

This trait was first reported by Thomas from the Davis Mound, Hocking County, Ohio, (now Greenman's No. 20). This tomb was in the center of the mound which in turn was in the center of a "sacred enclosure", in form a square with rounded corners. Of this tomb Thomas* says:

"The logs of which it was built were completely decayed, but the molds and impressions were still very distinct so that they could be easily traced. This was about 10 feet square and the logs were of considerable size, most of them nearly or quite a foot in diameter. At each corner had been placed a stout upright post, and the bottom judging by the slight remains found there had been wholly or partially covered by poles.'"

This tomb trait has not only been found in Adena, but is reported from Hopewell as well.

Shetrone** describes Burial 10 in Mound 25 at Hopewell Site as follows:

"Burials 9 and 10 the first discovered in the interior mound were uncremated adults with only minor artifacts accompanying them. The grave of Number 10, however, was an interesting example of the timbered structures characteristic of Hopewell burials. It measured 7½ feet long by 3½ feet wide and was composed of exceptionally large timbers some of which were above 6 inches in diameter. At each corner there had been set a post for support of the structure, while exteriorly there had been driven stakes to hold the three tiers of logs in place. At the point shown on the floor plan there was found an extensive log-mold the timber of which had been burned."

(31) Horizontal log burial platform in tomb.

The base of most log tombs was a layer of bark, usually a single layer of strips laid parallel to each other. Exceptional cases have been noted where two layers were used, the second layer of strips being placed at right angles to the first. In rare instances, as a substitute for this bark layer, a layer of horizontal poles or logs was used (see Tomb 29, p. 403, Vol. V). The purpose of this extra expenditure of logs is not clear, though it may have been connected with the desire to leave the tomb open and accessible from the outside for a

---

* Thomas, Cyrus, 1894, p. 448.
** Shetrone, H. C., 1926, p. 67.

season. This last is more fully discussed in connection with Trait No. 88.

(32) Log tomb burial on house floor.

The custom of burial of deceased persons in, under, or on the floor of their houses was widespread among certain Indian groups in the southern states in early historic times (see p. 241, Vol. V). The trait there was usually associated with burning of the house over the grave. This combination of traits, as revealed by recent excavations, seems to have been present in Adena. A review of the reports of early excavators (see p. 244, Vol. V) seems to indicate that this trait of burial upon the floor of dwelling houses was fairly common in Adena, although not always recognized as such by these early writers.

The fact of burial on a house floor is easy to demonstrate, but its purpose is not so clear. However, there is evidence of a circumstantial sort which seems to indicate that it may have been desirable in some cases to leave an Adena tomb open, i.e., uncovered, and the body, perhaps, exposed for a season after burial. This evidence is partially discussed in Trait 88. If the body was to be left exposed for a season (see Trait 34), it is easy to see that any house, or better, the deceased's own house, would be a convenient and natural place to choose for such a purpose, particularly if the house was soon to be destroyed by fire in any event (see Trait 88).

(33) Log tombs have log supported earth roofs.

This is a general trait in Adena log tombs. It is believed to be much more universal than can always be demonstrated by excavation. The cross log supports for the earth roof, over log tombs, were never much stronger than necessary, to permit the tomb to be covered. The structural engineering of these roofs was none too good. As a result, early decay, and excessive weight of earth caused the roofs to collapse into the tomb. The fallen logs soon decayed completely, and as centuries passed, evidence of the roof as such gradually disappeared. The collapse usually destroyed any possibility of molds being formed by the roof logs, as did occur in the case of the logs of the tomb walls. Evidence for believing in tomb roofs comes therefore, mostly from observations on the tilting and faulting of earth lenses above the tomb floors.* So common is this trait that in most Adena mounds, well trained excavators, by observing in a profile the tilting of individual loads, can predict the exact position of a tomb floor before the excavation reaches it; in like manner, once the floor is established, the tilting and shearing of earth lenses above the floor definitely locates the first position of the log supported tomb roof.

---

* Webb, Wm. S. and Elliott, John B., 1942, p. 385.

(34) **Vertical post-molds at grave.**

In a number of well-preserved Adena log tombs, vertical post molds* of small individual posts have been found associated with the burial. These have been found at the head and foot of graves, or on all four sides, somewhat irregularly placed. Their purpose is not certainly known, but they suggest that they may have served to support a light canopy, or some kind of a temporary structure erected at the grave. They are much too light to have been part of any heavy roof support. Here again is the suggestion that possibly for a season these tombs remained open, and the body was protected by some kind of open structure with a light temporary roof.

It is also quite possible that such vertical posts may have served as trophy posts upon which was hung the trophies, clothing, and other property of the deceased which might have been displayed at the grave.

In any event evidence points in many cases to the destruction by fire of these posts, and presumptively all that was attached to them, at the grave, before the grave was covered.

Another suggestion relative to the possible reason for these post holes is given by Thomas. Of the cemetery mound at Mount Vernon, Ohio, (Greenman's No. 38) Thomas** says:

"In the central portion of the mound, resting on the original surface of the ground was an irregular quadrilateral stone inclosure. This was built up loosely of rough surface sandstones, all with the weathered side up. . . . .
"Within the space enclosed by the wall and extending partly under it on the east side, was the circular pit, 12 feet in diameter and 2.5 feet deep. The sides were slightly sloped, giving it a basin-like shape. . . . .
"The skeleton which was badly decayed lay at full length with the head at the west margin of the pit, and the feet toward the center, around it a quantity of decayed vegetable matter possibly the remains of bark wrapping. On the under jaw was a crescent-shaped piece of copper. . . . .
"Just outside the eastern wall were four small pits or holes in the natural soil each about a foot in depth and 9 inches in diameter. Two of these were filled with a dark brown "sticky substance" in which were a number of split animal bones. A careful study of this exceedingly interesting mound leads to the conclusion that it was a work of considerable time, the various steps in its construction being about as follows:
"First, the small holes were dug possibly to hold posts on which a scaffold was built to support the corpse, the split bones being cast into them after the posts were removed for burning when the final burial took place. Next when the time came for this, the central pit was dug, and the skeleton, the flesh being removed, was deposited in it, then the layer of ashes sprinkled over the bottom (and over the skeleton) and the pit filled up. . . .
"After this a wooden covering was probably placed over the pit and the stone wall built around it. There can scarcely be a

---

* Webb, Wm. S., 1940, pp. 36, 43, 46.
** Thomas, Cyrus, 1894, p. 445.

U. K.—4

doubt, judging by the fact that the weathered sides of all the stones were uppermost, that a considerable time had elapsed before the mound was built, possibly a number of years."

It is interesting to note that this trait "vertical post-molds about graves" has been noted on Hopewell sites also. Of the burials in Seip Mound No. 2, Mills* says:

"Near the large graves a cluster of small post-molds, varying in number from 5 to 7 would be found. These posts were usually placed about one foot apart, but not in any particular form. Frequently the floor around the posts would be covered with great quantities of charred cloth, ornaments, and implements, and occasionally the floor would be covered with mica. . . . . The mica was usually placed so as to cover the floor completely, and only the natural mica crystals, split in many pieces were used. It seems very probable that the cluster of posts near the graves were the sacred shrines for the dead, and here the clothing and very frequently some of the interesting ornaments, such as cut and polished human jaws, large effigy eagle claws, bear teeth set with pearls, pendants of ocean shells, and shell and bone beads in great numbers, and in a few instances copper ornaments were found with the charred woven fabrics, so promiscuously placed on the floor surrounding the posts. At one of the shrines a quantity of charred rope about 4 feet in length and a number of effigy eagle claws made of bone were found. The rope was 3-ply and made of coarse bast fibers perhaps that of Bass-wood."

It is well known that in some Hopewell log tombs stake holes by the side of the log molds seem to indicate supports for a second log rectangle resting on the first or lower one. Such stake holes are not to be regarded as the equivalent of the post-molds as indicated by this trait No. 34.

(35) Log head and foot rests.

So far this trait has been noted in only one Adena mound, but it occurred definitely in four instances at that site. Inside the inner rectangle of logs constituting the log tomb, short logs about two feet long were laid transversely, one under the head, the other under the feet. This had the effect of raising slightly the head and feet. With the decay of the log rests, the head and feet of the skeleton appear over the log molds. That the head rest was used as a sort of pillow, is shown in one case (see page 47, Vol. V) by the use of a small bundle of cane stalks laid under the head of the body on this log head rest. These are reminiscent of the clay head and foot rests found in Copena graves in Guntersville Basins on the Tennessee River in Alabama.** It will be remembered that Copena shows many Hopewellian traits.

Of the burial at the base of the mound near Chillicothe—(Greenman's No. 3), Squier and Davis*** say:

---

* Mills, Wm. C., 1917, p. 20.
** An Archaeological Survey of Guntersville Basin (M. S. not yet published).
*** Squire and Davis, 1848, p. 164.

"It was deposited with its head toward the south; and unlike the one above described, had been simply enveloped in bark, instead of having been enclosed in a chamber of timbers. "Just at the head and also at the foot of the skeleton had been placed a small stick of timber, probably to retain the covering of bark in its place."

This is believed to have been an instance of such head and foot supports.

(36) **Log tomb passageway at east.** G(56).

This trait is supported by two mounds Nos. 19 and 43 of Greenman's list. Its significance is uncertain but, as pointed out by Greenman, the log tomb in Mound 19 was enclosed within a gravel wall which had a gateway to the east. It is known today that the "Sacred Enclosures" as described by Squier and Davis are of Adena origin. The larger portion of these are circles most of which have gateways. There is indicated a decided preference for the eastward direction for these gateways (see p. 161, Vol. V). Of 101 enclosures listed from five states, 76 are circular. Of these 76, there were 26 open due east, and within the quadrant East to North inclusive, there were 48 with gateways so oriented. In Site Be 20, see page 519, Vol. V, a circular structure probably used for communal purposes, had a "passageway at the east", if the townhouse entrance may be so regarded. In some elaborate tombs, passageways may have been placed to provide access to the tomb's interior, for a definite period immediately after the burial.

(37) **Pit tomb dug below earth surface.** G(5).

The statement of this trait is an attempt to distinguish the actual excavations of a pit below surface level in a village, for the purpose of constructing a tomb, from the method employed to accomplishing the same form of construction by building up earth walls several feet high in the form of a rectangular basin and constructing a tomb inside the rectangle. While both were covered with logs and a mound erected over the tomb yet the process was quite different. Sub floor tombs are quite common in Adena. Greenman states this trait as "Subfloor graves."

(38) **Earth or stone embankment around subfloor tomb.** G(24).

When subfloor tombs were excavated the earth thrown out in excavation was left to form a ridge or ring about the tomb mouth. This earth was never used to fill the pit. Sometimes flat limestone or sandstone slabs were carried to the site and laid on the surface of the earth ridge about the pit mouth. They did not have their origin in the excavated pit. In some of the Adena mounds in Ohio described by Greenman the stone consisted of large gravel excavated from the pit, and used to form a circular embankment about the excavation.

(39) Subfloor tomb closed by log roof.

Since the earth dug from subfloor tomb pits was never used to fill it, the cavity had to either be filled or closed by a roof before a mound could be built on the spot. Because of the considerable size of some subfloor pits the covering logs had to be of considerable size to cover the long span. The logs which were laid from side to side, due to decay and weight of earth above them finally collapsed, leaving impressions of their ends in the wall about the pit mouth. This trait has also been noted in Copena, in Pickwick Basin of Alabama.*

(40) Mound erected over subfloor tomb.

Mounds were erected over subfloor tombs to cover the excavation and the earth embankment about the tomb mouth. These mounds are not very large in size but tend rather to be of medium size or smaller. Often there are no burials in such mounds other than those made in the pit.

(41) Fire hardened clay dome, "Vaults". G(c).

These clay domes were called by Thomas "beehive vaults". They were made of clay and ashes and were very hard. They contained bone fragments. Greenman shows 8 of these vaults as occurring in 3 mounds, as follows, 57-1, 61-6, and 64-X. A review of the original report by Thomas will show that mound 61 did yield 6 of these clay vaults on the first excavation, and upon its completion 5 more were found, or a total of 11. There have been found, therefore, counting the two recently found in Kentucky, one of which is shown on page 300, Vol. V, 15 vaults from 5 mounds. Their purpose remains as yet undiscovered but they appear to be associated with log tombs, and may have been used to contain or cover the cremated remains of an individual—hence the ashes and bone fragments in association as reported.

HOUSE TRAITS

(42) Post-mold patterns circular, diameter 97 feet or more.

The fact that Adena house patterns are circular is now well established by the findings of 23 such patterns on 9 sites in Kentucky. Records of earlier investigators give abundant evidence that such patterns have been previously found elsewhere, but they were not recognized as house patterns. These patterns occur in the hard clay

---

* Webb, Wm. S. and De Jarnette, David L., 1942, Plate 25-2.

subsoil in the old villages, under mounds, and are clearly discernable and unmistakable. The diameters are easily measured. The structures seem to fall into two classes: those having circles 97 feet or more in diameter, a total of four, and those having diameters of 60 feet or less, a total of nineteen. So far **none has been found with diameters between these dimensions.** It is suspected that the significance of this division, if it continues to be verified by future excavations, will be found in the fact that the smaller size circles were houses, each of whch had a single roof over it, and the larger circles indicate structures no one of which had a single roof over the entire structure because of its excessive diameter. Scattered post-molds in the interior of some of these large circles suggest that "rooms" built against the inside walls of the circle may have had roofs. This would have left a central area without any roof. This area in the center of large circles often shows fire action on the structure floor.

(43) **Post-mold pattern circular, diameter 60 feet or less.**

The convenient size dwelling house for Adena seems to have been about 37 feet in diameter, although this dimension varies from 21 to 59.5 feet in houses on different sites. The median diameter is 37 feet and the average is 37 feet. Sixty feet seems to have been about the limit in size which would permit the construction of a roof over all, if indeed they were so large. No roof has ever been found, but its existence is predicated upon the discovery of interior post-molds arranged in a regular pattern which might indicate roof supports.

(44) **Each post set in individual hole.**

All Adena structures whether with circular patterns (usual), or with rectangular patterns (very rare) appear to have had each post set in a hole rather than in a trench. Holes were excavated larger than the post, by using sharp flat sticks. These sticks were thrust down into the tough clay hardpan, and used to chisel out chunks of clay which were probably removed by the hand. Longitudinal sections of such post molds invariably show the long striated tool impressions in the clay walls. Often the holes were dug three feet deep. —a laborious undertaking even today with modern steel tools. Rarely it has been found that two posts were set in the same hole, the hole being made proportionally larger than for a single post. In no case has any suggestion of a trench been found in any Adena site as an aid in setting posts in the hardpan. See Trait 47 for the manner of filling postholes.

(45) **Posts set in pairs.**

This is a characteristic Adena trait which seems diagnostic. Every circular post-mold pattern, as well as the few rectangular patterns found on Adena sites, show by their molds the pairing of posts. To date this trait has not been reported so far as known from other areas outside the Adena area, or in other cultural association although circular patterns of post-molds are not uncommon in the Southeastern United States. It appears that some early excavators* of mounds in Ohio had actually observed this pairing of post molds on Adena sites, but attached no significance to it. Because so many Adena traits are observable in Ohio Hopewell, it was natural to anticipate that evidence of this trait might also have been found. It is just possible that it has been previously noted in Hopewell. Of the mound floor of the Edwin Harness Mound, Mills** says:

> "I am inclined to believe that such a roof existed, although no definite proof of such a roof, other than the uprights to support it were found in the mound. The posts forming the outer row varied in size from six to ten inches. However, **a very great number of the upright supports consisted of a combination of smaller posts placed together,** and this was evidenced by the post molds showing a number of small posts placed together. In a number of instances these posts had been split, and in several cases posts seven inches in diameter were split and used for support."

It is suspected that Mills was here describing a system of paired posts, made by splitting a post in halves, and setting the halves apart, thus making "a combination of small posts". It would have been very desirable to have studied a base chart of this post-mold pattern from the Harness Mound if such had ever been made. It is a matter of regret that no such chart is now available at the Ohio State Museum. There is thus the strong suggestion, not yet proven, that Hopewell used "paired post" in house construction. For further discussion of paired post molds see Vol. V, page 365.

(46)   Posts of a pair in line with the patterns.

This trait is also unique in Adena. It seems to stem from some construction requirement in the building of walls in Adena houses. One might suppose that if walls were to be laid up of logs or small poles they would have found it convenient to place the line of the pair of posts at right angles to the line of the wall and by binding together the post of a pair at the top, produce a very good wall support. It is quite apparent they did not desire this effect, and deliberately chose the parallel position, doubtless with good reason. This would seem to suggest that the technique of wall construction was universally understood among them and thus it followed a definite pattern, to produce a satisfactory and doubtless characteristic result.

---

* Thruston, Gates P., 1897, p. 73, and Fowke, Gerard, 1902, p. 362.
** Mills, Wm. C., 1907, p. 29.

(47) **Two posts set in same large hole.**

This trait so far has only rarely been discovered in Adena houses, and has been found only once in Kentucky. It appears, however, to have been found (but not recognized) in at least one other early excavated site in Ohio, see Mound 91* which has been classified as Adena by these authors partly on a basis of possessing this trait. Due to the laborious process of digging a post hole in tough clay, this trait may represent an economy cf labor. For a single post 6 inches in diameter it would require a hole perhaps 14 inches in diameter. It migh be just as easy, perhaps, easier, because of "elbow room" to dig a hole 24 inches in diameter, to hold two posts. If such holes were rightly spaced, and the two posts set on opposite sides of the same hole, the seeming necessity of pairing could be accomplished by bringing posts in adjacent holes near enough to each other to form the pair, and thus there would be a great saving of labor since, if two posts were put in each hole, only half as many holes would be required. For illustrations of this trait, see page 432, Vol. V.

When single posts are set in a hole, the hole is filled with earth rammed in on one side only, the post being generally set against one side. Often broken artifacts and cultural debris are found in the post-hole fill. Where two posts are placed in the same hole, it appears that the posthole may not have been completely filled at once, since they are sometimes found filled with ashes, burned stone, broken bone and the same cultural debris that is usually found cn the house floor. If the posthole remained open after placing of the post, long enough to accumulate this debris as the result of occupancy of the structure, which seems to be thus suggested, it may mean that the construction of the wall (woven of cane, twigs, and small limbs) was such as to support the post in positions without having the hole filled with earth. To have had the post free to move in the hole during wall construction conceivably, may have been an advantage.

(48) **Pairs regularly spaced in the circle.**

The spacing of pairs is generally remarkable for its regularity when one compares one house with another, although there may be some variation in the spacing in a particular house pattern. It has occurred that in single houses this variation is greater than exists between different houses on the same or different sites. The usual spacing between posts of a pair is 1.5 feet center to center, and between pairs from 3.5 to 5 feet from center to center of a pair.

(49) **Post inclines outward from center.**

This universal trait in Adena houses of small size evidently served a useful purpose. If the house had a roof, the eaves would

---
* Moorehead, Warren K., 1892, p. 69.

overhang the walls by a greater margin if the walls leaned outward. This would make for better drainage, and drier walls. Whatever the reason for outward inclination of the posts, it was accomplished in two ways. Holes were dug with the inclination desired, and the post set in each was pressed against one side of the hole in line with the wall, and the hole was filled, which gave each post the same outward slant. Sometimes the posthole was dug with vertical walls, and the post set in it so that the base of the post was against the inside of the hole at the bottom, and against the outer side edge of the hole at the top. The slant of a post of given size was thus determined by the diameter of the posthole, as well as by the diameter of the post.

(50) Multiple occupancy of house sites.

Where portions of the old village have been preserved by being covered by a mound, the clay subsoil reveals circular post-mold patterns crossing each other so that three or four may be interlocked.* Obviously these houses were not all simultaneous. So in an area where post-mold patterns appear as a cluster of house sites, perhaps, there never was more than a single house on the spot, at any one time. No case has been found where a new Adena house had been constructed exactly over an older one, by renewing posts or making repairs, as has been found frequently among the remains of structures of other prehistoric peoples.** New houses on a particular area usually had different diameters from the old, and were slightly displaced. The interlocking of circular post-mold patterns of Adena house sites can harly be regarded as valid stratigraphy, since such manifestations do not generally lead to a determination of the relative chronology of the structures. If several houses successively used the same surface of the clay hardpan for the house floor, each house would show its series of post-molds arranged in a circle, and while the patterns would intersect, the holes in general would not touch each other, leaving no clue as to which was dug first. Had these house patterns been trenches, the resulting indication of chronology would be much more satisfactory. When as a matter of accident holes from two different patterns did touch, it has seemed impossible so far to demonstrate chronology.

(51) Interior concentric circle of single molds.

In houses of the small type, i.e., less than 60 feet in diameter, there is usually observed a series of single post molds, four or six which are placed in a regular pattern on a circle concentric with the main pattern. These interior post molds suggest roof supports.

---

* Webb, Wm. S., 1942, p. 308, and 1940, p. 51.
** Webb, Wm. S., 1938, p. 163.

Earlier excavators* have reported single post molds in circles under under the center of mounds under circumstances which seem to indicate that at times more than six posts may have formed this inner group.

(52) Floor areas discolored by heat.

The central portions of all Adena house patterns whether there is a deposit of ashes or not, show discoloration of the clay floor by heat. Usually there is evidence of hot fires, perhaps, long continued, as indicated by deep ash beds and by deep discoloration of clay floors. Ash beds on house floors show they are in situ and undisturbed.

(53) Ash piles on center of house floor.

These ash piles often show accumulation of charcoal in the outer ring where the heat was less intense and pure white ashes in the central area where combustion was complete as would be expected. That is, these ash heaps are in situ and undisturbed. They often show such cultural debris as would indicate they were used for cooking as well as heating. Occasionally human bones have been found in quantity in such ash heaps, which is taken to mean that human cremation might have taken place in such surroundings. However, it is very difficult, if not impossible in such cases, to distinguish between a cremation in situ and a deposit of cremated remains. In at least one case (see Mound Be 3, page 427, Vol. V), the accumulation of human bone fragments was so great as to suggest a deposit of cremated remains on the house floor. Lest such an accumulation of burned human bones in a central fire basin might suggest to some, possible evidence of cannibalism, it should be pointed out that if this interpretation be accepted, one should also expect to find accumulation of animal bones about such fire basins for the same reason; since large numbers of animals were certainly used for food. Such accumulations of animal bones are not found on Adena house floors.

(54) Fire basin in village, circular.

Such fire basins are circular or nearly so, and are from 3 feet to 5 feet in diameter. The simplest form is a concave basin in the clay subsoil, without any special construction details. They are usually full of ashes, and show the effect of heat by discoloration of the clay.

(55) Fire basins held burned, broken stone in ashes.

These blocks of sandstone or river pebbles show the action of fire. Many are cracked as if by sudden cooling which suggests their possible use in hot-rock cooking. Some stone fragments in fire basins may be the result of attempts to line the basin with flat stone.

---

* Moorehead, Warren K., 1899, p. 133.

(56)   Clay fire basins, raised clay rims. "Altars?" G(47).

These basins are concave basins in the old village floor which have been plastered with puddled clay and a rim several inches high raised about the edge. The effect of the fire is to harden these basins to brick-like texture. They are usually circular in form, and in size may be as much as 8 to 10 feet in diameter. Greenman has pointed out the confusion which has existed in the uses of the term "Altar" by some early writers. It is apparent that these clay basins with raised clay rims have been found by early excavators and called by some "Altars." It is possible that some of these larger fire basins were used for cremation, see Trait 62.

(57)   Fire basins, flat sandstones set on edge about basin rim.

This is a trait of no great frequency. Flat stones set up on edge make an effective rim to a clay basin. The clay surface of these basins may have flat stones laid in them, see page 589, Vol. V.

(58)   Fire basins had potsherds in ashes.

This trait seems to indicate that these basins were used for cooking and other household processes, and when utility vessels were broken, the sherds were left in the fire.

(59)   House burned intentionally.

Evidence that houses were burned is quite objective. That they were burned intentionally is much more difficult to prove. Evidence for this belief rests on the fact that small mounds were erected inside standing houses to cover log tomb burials, or cremations placed on the house floor. The destruction of the houses by fire after the building of these small mounds inside them would seem to be the result of intention. This order of events is often repeated in Adena mounds, and the evidence for its occurrence is quite convincing. It is believed that early excavators often found this condition but did not fully recognize the significance of the evidence. In describing the excavation of a mound at Monongahela, Pa., (Greenman's No. 56), Thomas says:

"On the eastern side of this level, near the break of the ravine, and close to a never-failing spring, stands the largest mound above the one at McKee's rocks, measuring 9 feet in height by 60 feet in diameter. Beginning on the eastern side, a 6-foot trench was run in for 35 feet. At 17 feet from the point of beginning was found a thin layer of charcoal and burn dirt, which at this point was between 3 and 4 feet from the original surface. This, which seems to have resulted from burning weeds and trash that had sprung up when the building was temporarily arrested at this stage, continued for 12 feet with an upward slope nearly corresponding with that of the top of the mound, showing that the latter had been built from the center upward and outward, and not by a succession of horizontal layers. This is further shown by the arrangement of the different sorts of dirt used in its construction, which show a central core or nucleus, with the successive deposits extending over it from side to side. Underlying the bottom of the mound was a tough gray clay, varying in thickness. On this the mound had been built up."

This Mound No. 56 shows clearly that the burials were made on a house floor, a mound was erected over them inside a house, the house was burned, firing the surface of the small mound and leaving ashes and charcoal over it. And finally a larger mound was erected over all. Of course, Thomas* did not find evidence of post-mold pattern, he did not look for it and had little chance to see it in the single radial trench which he dug. It seems highly probable that such a post-mold pattern could have been found had he sought for it, as was done in Site Bh 15, in Kentucky. See p. 229, Vol. V.

(60) Post-mold patterns, rectilinear.

This is a relatively rare trait in Adena. Only three sites in Kentucky have, so far, shown paired post molds in straight lines, and only two of these have rectangular house patterns.** In one of these house patterns one side of the rectangle has no post molds, and in the other pattern one side cf the rectangle had only three post molds, one at each end and one in the center of the side, see Vol. V, P. 588, Fig. 2.

This suggests that in rectangular houses, one side was left open, or if closed, it was by some other means than a permanent wall like the other three sides of the house. It may have been closed by hanging woven mats, of by curtains of skins. These would have required no posts set in the hard pan on this open side of the house.

Moorehead*** reports a mound 3 miles southwest of Wilmington (Greenman's Mound No. 25) as covering a house site where the posts (vertical) formed a square twelve feet on each side.

CREMATION TRAITS

(61) Cremation partial, remains in situ, house burned over log tomb. G(13).

Until recently cremation has been considered to play a very minor role in Adena. In fact, many of the early explorers regarded cremation as an evidence of non-Adena affiliation. However, Greenman presents evidence of it, 30 occurrences in 14 mounds of the 70 mounds listed as Adena. In his description of this trait, he included partial along with total cremation. Today there is evidence to indicate that these types of cremation properly may be separated on a basis of partial cremation as accidental, and total cremation as defi-

---

* Thomas, Cyrus, 1894, p. 495.
** Webb, Wm. S., 1943, p. 588.
*** Moorehead, Warren K., 1892, p. 107.

nitely intentional. Partial cremation seems to have been produced sometimes in a log and bark tomb burial made on the floor of a house, over which a small mound of earth was erected within the standing house. If the mound was not large, and the logs and bark not too well covered, then, when the house was later burned, it sometimes happened (accidentally) that fire found its way into the log-bark burial and these smoldering logs under the small earth mound and under the ruins of the burned house, produced a partial cremation of the body in situ. The part of the body burned, and degree of completeness of cremation of any part of the body, are matters of chance, depending on how well the internal fire could acquire sufficient oxygen for complete combustion. This "crucible" action chars the wood and bone not fully burned, smokes and discolors fabrics about the body, and produces a typical partial cremation. An excellent illustration of this occurrence was found at site Bh 15*—the Morgan Stone Mound.

In a mound within the city limits of Chillicothe, excavated by Squier and Davis,** they found excellent evidence of a partial cremation in a log tomb on the floor of a house, over which a primary mound had been erected on the house floor. When the house was burned it not only left a layer of charcoal over the surface of the primary but fired the log tomb to produce a partial cremation. Of this mound they say:

"It was situated within the corporate limits of the city of Chillicothe, and was originally about 25 feet high, though now reduced to about twenty. The customary shaft was sunk from its apex. At six feet below the surface a layer of charcoal corresponding in all respects with that described in connection with the first example of mounds of this class was found. . . . Upon the original level of the earth was found a deposit or layer of charcoal and ashes six or eight feet square and from six inches to a foot in thickness. In this layer were discovered fragments of human bone, a stone hand-axe; several thin pieces of copper which had been worked into shape, and also a number of stones of the harder and less common kinds, fragments of sienite, gneiss, etc. . . .
"The fire in this case had been a strong one, as is evidenced from the fact that the skeleton had here been almost entirely consumed. That is, it had also been heaped over while burning, which was shown by the charcoal which was coarse and clear, and by the baking of the earth immediately above it. In some instances, in which burial by incremation has been practiced, the entire skeleton is traceable. In such cases it has been observed that the charcoal occurs beneath as well as above the skeleton, demonstrating that the body had been placed upon a pyre of some sort before burning. . . . .
"This mound is nearer to enclosures than any other of the class yet examined."

This mound now regarded as belonging to Adena has been designated No. 92 in the new list of Adena sites.

---

* Webb, Wm. S., 1941, p. 231.
** Squier, E. G. and Davis, E. H., 1848, p. 165.

The report of Andrews* on the excavation of the Silas H. Wright Mound, Green Township, Hocking Co., Ohio (Greenman's Mound No. 42) presents evidence of house burning over a primary mound which covered an extended burial in a log tomb. The tomb caught fire and the logs were partially charred but the body in the tomb was not burned. This tomb had been built on the floor of a house on which had been made a deposit of cremated remains, while Andrews found no house, he wondered how the clay above the tomb could have been so heavily burned. He says in part:

"In the center of the mound, perhaps, 5 or 6 inches above the original level, with a layer of brown loam between, we found a large and mixed collection of bones, all burnt and in very small fragments. They rested above some ashes, a very thin layer, but were themselves embedded in a dark brown dirt. These bones were spread over a surface of perhaps 5 feet long and 2 feet wide. They evidently had been burned before burial in the mound. In the clay and dirt, perhaps 3 inches above the layer of burnt bones, we found a part of the bones of a body which had been evidently buried without cremation. No trace of fire could be detected either upon these bones or upon the brown earth connected with them. Above the stratum of brown earth which was from 4 to 6 inches thick, we found a thin layer of earth black with charcoal perhaps 2 inches thick. Above this layer was another of a brown loam, slightly reddish as if it had felt the fire somewhat. Above this reddish brown loam was a horizon of charred wood, although the wood was gone in places which in others it was 6 inches thick. There were indications of pretty large timbers or logs forming a structure something like a cobhouse of children or a rail corn crib of the western farmers. These timbers were in places only charred, and the charred ends were preserved. The direction in which the charcoal wood lay was for the most part from north to south. The unburned body also lay in the same direction. Over the charred wood horizon was red burnt earth and clay. The amount of this burnt clay was very great. Directly over the buried body it was nearly 3 feet thick and elsewhere it was from one to two feet in thickness. Some of it is hard almost like brick and of a bright brick red. Much of it, although equally burnt, was not compacted, but was soft and flowing like kiln-dried sand or like Indian meal. . . . . "How such a large mass of clay could be burnt by a fire on top, I cannot understand, and it is more difficult to suppose that the comparatively small fire on the line of the charred wood under the clay could have oxydized the iron in such a large mass of clay. In the burning on the level of b, (charred wood) the fire must, in part, have been a smothered one, producing as it did, charred wood."

In considering partial cremation, its accidental aspect needs to be kept in mind. It is quite possible that when the log tomb was made on the floor of the house and a small earth mound erected over it, there was no intention, and possibly no expectation that the body would be burned. Early explorers have reported conditions found in

* Andrews, E. B., 1877, p. 67.

mounds which seem to prove that the burning of the house did not always result in firing the logs of the log tomb. In such case, there would be **no cremation,** even though the mound inside of the house showed the action of fire over its surface. In describing such a condition where a burial, because it was well covered with clay, was not burned when the house was fired, although its log tomb was charred, Andrews* says:

> "No fragments of charcoal were **found in the heavy mass** of red burned earth, extending over the center of the mound. How such a large mass of clay could be burnt by a fire on top, I cannot understand."

Today we understand such a situation. The clay of the small mound on the house floor was burned when a house over it was destroyed by fire. Andrews did not find evidence of the house—he did not look for the post-mold pattern. He excavated only the center of the mound by a single trench. For other illustrations of this partial cremation—house-burning burial complex, see reports of Andrews** and Putnam*** and comments thereon, pages 246-247, Vol. V.

When partial cremation does occur because of its accidental nature, very different results would be produced in different burials. This accounts for the varied forms of description of this condition, as observed by the early explorers.

(62) **Cremation total, in clay basins.** G(C).

It appears that when a total cremation was desired, which was quite a general practice in Adena, a concave basin was scraped out in the Adena village, usually in the clay hardpan. This basin, either circular or elliptical, about 8 feet in longest dimensions, may or may not, have had a clay rim. Here the body was burned in a hot fire—a fire so hot as to disintegrate chunks of sandstone, break and burn flint, bone, and antler artifacts. It is apparent that some attention was given to this procedure by the attendants, since all large bones are thoroughly calcined and broken into small pieces.

Similar cremations may have occurred, however, in the clay fire basins on a house floor. In some cases, the procedure seems to have been to gather up the cremated remains, ashes, charcoal, burned artifacts, stone fragments, etc., for redeposit elsewhere. Greenman reports three crematory basins from two mounds. Evidence of cremation has been frequently found by early excavators in mounds certainly belonging to Adena. However, since cremation was not regarded generally as an Adena trait, such mounds formerly were

---

* Andrews, E. B., 1877, pp. 68-70.
** Ibid., pp. 59-60.
*** Putnam, F. W., 1887, pp. 551-553.

excluded from Adena classification, even though they did not possess a single other trait which was not a known Adena trait.

(63) Cremations, total, left in situ.

Sometimes after a cremation was completed, it was left in situ in the village, being covered over in various ways. Sometimes they were covered over with village midden. Sometimes they were covered over with a layer of puddled clay, and then with surface earth from the village. Sometimes a platform of logs was laid over the spot and all covered with earth. When the logs decayed, they left their imprints in the clay above the cremation in situ (see Fig. 10-3, p. 321, Vol. V). More frequently a log rectangular tomb was erected about the cremated remains, and all was then covered with village surface earth (see p. 327, Vol. V). This particular tomb contained a **multiple cremation** and was made of two parallel logs on all four sides, as shown by their imprints in the clay platform on which they lay. This cremation in situ is in many respects similar to Burial 86 in the Seip Mound* No. 1, which was a deposit of the cremated remains of three individuals placed separately inside a log rectangle.

(64) Cremation, partial, in bark lined pit.

Since the Adena people knew so well how to produce a total cremation when desired, it is difficult to understand the production of a partial cremation except as an accident, or as a consequence of other processes which did not have cremation as a major objective. Partial cremation sometimes occurs in pits, where a body, laid on bark, wrapped in textiles, and covered with bark at the bottom of a pit, is set on fire and covered before complete combustion can consume the skeleton. For an illustration, see Burial No. 7, Hartman Mound, Site Be 32, Vol. V. Circumstances seem to suggest that such burial pits may have been kept open for a reason after the placement of the body—perhaps to allow a period for it to "lie in state." Small vertical post-holes about some graves seem to suggest that a sun shade or light canopy or temporary roof may have been built over the pit tomb. Possibly these posts were merely standards upon which trophies, the clothing or other property of the deceased were hung at the time of burial. Whatever their purpose, before the pit was filled, the canopy or other material may have been burned. Such an anrangement would account for the partial burning of the bark, textiles, and the body in a pit tomb. Whatever the reason for such partial cremation, and whatever means were used for its accomplishment, it is certain that the smoked, charred, and stained fabric, bark, and bones in pit tombs indicate the presence of fire in the pit, but demonstrate no really serious attempt actually to consume a human body.

---

* Shetrone, H. C., and Greenman, E. F., 1931, p. 399.

Whether the partial burning is an accident, incidental to the destruction of a burial canopy, or other material; or is intentional in connection with some ceremonial procedures, matters not; this type of partial cremation differs from other forms, and it is believed it should be listed separately as a trait.

It does show the action of fire about the burial in a pit, and was a wholly ineffective method of producing a cremation if that was the intention.

(65)   Cremation in rectangular log tombs, logs burned.

This is a recently discovered Adena trait, so far found only five times on a single site (Jo 9, see page 339, Vol. V). It is suspected that it has been found by other excavators heretofore, but not distinguished from other forms of cremation. Here the body is uniformly burned, as well as the logs forming the rectangle, and the degree of the destruction by fire tends toward completeness. In general the body seems to have been laid extended on a log-pole platform with side logs as in a log box tomb. The whole is burned, body and logs underneath. The side logs are often found partially preserved as charcoal, which suggests that they were covered with some earth before they were completely burned. It is quite possible that a crematory pyre was prepared of combustible material under the log-pole platform on which the body was placed. It may be the log rectangle about the body was partially covered with earth to represent a log tomb. When fire was applied the central and uncovered portion where the body lay was perhaps the hottest part and this resulted in practically complete cremation of the body. The body and crematory pyre were undisturbed except by the fire and all were covered over without being disarranged. This type of cremation is different from cremations in situ in basins, for there the remains must have been stirred in the fire to cause all bones to be completely calcined. It also differs from a partial cremation in a log tomb on a house floor, for here the cremation is as complete for one part of the body as another, there is no house floor and no post-mold pattern. The burning is evidently intentional. A partial cremation on the house floor as explained, has the appearance of being accidental.

It may be noted that in all log tombs used for extended inhumations, the molds indicate that nearly perfect logs, straight and of uniform diamater, without side limbs were used. In log tomb cremation, the logs of the rectangle have been known to be crooked, not worked off bluntly at the end, and to contain limb forks. Clearly these logs were not seemily as carefully selected as those for regular log tombs, perhaps because they were soon to be burned. (See p. 320, Vol. V.)

(66) **Cremations, remains redeposited separately in mound.**

Redeposited cremated remains are often found in Adena sites. Usually the pile of burned human bones with burned stone artifacts, and quite frequently, with fragments of the clay lining of the crematory basin, is found as a cache by itself, in a mound under such circumstances as to prove it to be a redeposit. That is, at the place where found there is an entire absence of the evidence of fire, yet the contents of the cache, of human bones, artifacts, etc., show they have been heavily burned. One cannot, of course, know all of the circumstances of time and place from observation of such a deposit, but it would appear quite reasonable to suppose that at death of an individual the body was cremated in a basin in the village or, perhaps, on the floor of his own house, doubtless with proper ceremonies, and when completely cremated, the residue and all that remained with it—burned stone, artifacts, burned clay, etc., may have been gathered into some form of suitable container and retained to such a time as might be convenient to deposit it in a mound in the process of erection, or, as explained in Trait 68, in a log tomb of a friend or relative which happened to be open. Lacking such an opportunity it could be deposited in a hole in the ground of the old village (see Trait 67), or if the cremation took place in the open, the cremation in situ could be covered and so left (see Trait 63). While such related details are highly subjective, such rationalizations rest upon the observed facts that there have been found all of these varied "end products" of the human body on Adena sites.

Such a redeposit is reported by Moorehead* from the excavation of his mound No. 6, Brown Co., Ohio, near St. Martins, in which he says:

"Our first find was made at a point about eighteen feet distant from the center. Here we came upon a large pile of burned earth and charcoal intermingled with fragmentary remains of human bones which had been burned until they were almost destroyed, but as there was about a bushel of small pieces it was obvious that several bodies had been cremated. They had not, however, been burned on the spot, for not only did the surrounding earth show no evidence of the intense heat that would have been required to reduce them to the condition in which they were found, but the mass itself showed the curvature of the mound's surface, the end nearest the center being about two feet higher than the first struck.

"Several similar but smaller masses were found on the original surface at various distances from the center."

This mound is now classed as an Adena Mound No. 110 in the new list of Adena Sites.

---

* Moorehead, Warren K., 1892, p. 70.

U. K.—5

(67)   Cremations redeposited separately in village.

This indicates the deposit of burned human bone with or without artifacts in a village site without any association with a mound, a tomb, or any other special feature. Occasionally the excavator comes upon such deposits in quite unexpected places. There seems to be no explanation for such placement except the desire to dispose of the cremated remains. Such remains indicate by their surroundings that they are redeposits and are not cremations in situ since evidence of fire in the surrounding soil is absent. Some of the cremations at Site Jo 9 may have been redeposits, but because of the considerable evidence of fire everywhere in the old village, one could not be sure. An excellent example of this type of redeposit was found in the ash bank in the Stamper Rock Shelter.* It was accompanied by a large cache of artifacts all of which are typical Adena products.

(68)   Cremated remains deposited with extended inhumation in log tomb.

The finding of such deposits accompanying extended burials in log tombs raises the question of their purpose and method of accomplishment. This might seem to be merely a means of disposal of the cremated remains. However, in the elaborate log tomb 16 x 25 feet in the Crigler Mound (Be 20, Ky.), the extended burial was accompanied by two piles of cremated remains carefully deposited each in a separate corner of the tomb fartherest removed from the center of the house. One of these deposits contained the remains of at least two individuals. Such placement of two cremated remains on the raised clay platform, one at each end of the tomb, but in subordinate positions and accompanying this extended burial in a very elaborate tomb, would seem to indicate more than mere disposal of these remains. One could hardly doubt that these cremations were prepared for this purpose, whether before or after the death of the person occupying the central position, of course, cannot be known, and were carefully placed in the positions as found. Since the tomb was quite large enough to have accommodated many extended burials if they had cared to so use it, the cremations suggest that it was desired that these burials accompany the central one—yet perhaps they were not entitled to log tomb burial but only to cremation which was much more generally used.

It is of course possible that such cremations represent members of the same family or household, who having died previously, were cremated and their remains retained until they could be placed in the grave of this more important personage.

(69)   Cremated remains redeposited separately in log tombs.

This is a rare trait as so far reported for Adena. It is important since it is complimentary to trait No. 63, where a total cremation left

---

* Funkhouser, W. D. and Webb, Wm. S., 1930, Fig. 29, p. 274.

in situ, is surrounded by a log rectangle before being covered over in the old village. Here a cremation is redeposited on a bark floor surrounded by a log rectangle of the usual size for an extended burial. The cremated remains were covered by a layer of puddled clay, which in turn was covered with another layer of bark. In case of Burial No. 84 in Tomb 51, Site Be 3*, additional logs were laid about the burial to raise the wall height so that a roof of poles could be laid crosswise and thus seal the burial in a closed chamber. This trait as well as trait 63 shows an important connection between cremation and inhumation in log tombs. They seem to represent an attempt to use in part **both** types of burial, in one the cremation remaining in situ, and in the other the cremation being redeposited. It is hoped that the careful recording of data in future excavations of such burials, may lead to the discovery of some significance in this combination of burial practices.

(70) Cremated remains deposited with extended burials in subsurface pits.

This trait has recently been found to occur at one site,** in Kentucky. That is, the cremated remains of at least four individuals were separately deposited on the bottom of a large subsurface pit. These deposits were placed near the pit walls, the central area being occupied by three extended burials. All burials were placed at the same time.

The significance of such deposits is not apparent. It may be only a convenient means of disposal of the cremated remains of the individuals which were awaiting burial. It, however, may mean cremations accomplished at the time of placement of the extended burials, with the purpose of having such burial accompaniment.

(71) Cremated remains spread or scattered on the floor of a townhouse.

In the two cases in which this trait has been observed recently, one house floor had a heap of ashes of human remains, in which at least parts of eleven skeletons could be identified.

On the other house floor the cremated remains of a least three individuals, and probably twice that number, had been widely scattered over an area of about 25 x 40 feet. A part of this area was a raised clay platform, which, after the scattering of the burned human bones over it, was covered with a layer of bark and thus formed the base of an exceptionally large Adena tomb.

* Webb, Wm. S. and Elliott, John B., 1942, p. 400.
** Webb, Wm. S., 1941, p. 174.

(72) Communal deposit of cremated remains.

Only very recently has the trait of depositing together the cremated remains of more than one body been positively demonstrated for Adena, although previously suspected from the quantity of bone fragments found in several deposits. Not until the large deposit on the house floor of the Robbins Mound, Be 3, Ky., was proven to contain at least eleven individuals, was a critical study made of other deposits. Several of these have now been proven to be deposits of more than one individual. This is a highly technical task for an experienced physical anthropologist. Usually the bone fragments are so small and so badly burned that recognition of the identity of any single piece of bone requires the service of a skilled technician. The proof of multiple deposit consists in finding some bone of a skeleton occurring repeatedly in the mass of debris. The auditory meatus portion of the temporal bone has been found to be very useful for this purpose since it is easily identified and seems to escape complete destruction as frequently as other identifiable bone portions. It is also easy to distinguish the right from the left bone, which adds validity to the determination by elimination of the chance of duplication. There can now be no doubt that Adena practiced communal deposits of cremated remains. Whether or not they practiced multiple cremation is not as yet determined. It is suspected, but so far proof has not been established beyond question.

(73) Artifacts burned with the body.

Few artifacts other than copper could survive the fires of cremation and remain intact. There have been found with cremated bones, flint projectile points, broken by heat. Sandstone tablets are very frequently found broken by heat in crematory deposits. Spatula antler flaking tools, and bone combs have been found broken and burned with cremations in situ. Copper bracelets and copper reels have gone through the fires of cremations with no apparent serious injury. This trait does not deny, however that unburned artifacts are found deposited with cremated remains.

(74) Unburned artifacts placed with redeposited cremations.

Artifacts other than those of personal adornment of body or clothing are very seldom found in Adena burial association. Beads of shell or copper, mica head dresses, copper bracelets, finger rings or reel-shaped breast-plates are all objects of personal adornment and would naturally be attached to the body or the clothing. Artifacts of utility, tubular pipes, projectile points, expanded bar gorgets (regarded possibly as atlatl weights), bone combs (regarded as carding devices—not hair combs), antler handles, and carapace spoons, are very rarely found in the burial offerings in Adena. It is, therefore, the more surprising to find cremations accompanied by artifacts of utility which have themselves not been burned. However, very large flint points, shale pendants, copper daggers encased in textiles, have all been found accompanying deposits of cremated remains in mounds. One of the best illustrations of this practice in Adena has been found in a rock shelter in Eastern Kentucky. Adena peoples evidently roamed the counties of Eastern Kentucky and lived under the rock shelters. Perhaps, these were but transient hunters or travelers, but in an ash bed under the Dillard Stamper Shelter No. 1 in Wolfe County,* there was found a deposited cremation accompanied by Adena type stemmed projectile points, a cache of leaf-shaped flint blades, a flint celt, two antler handles, three awls made from the scapula of deer, and several antler spatula flaking tools. All of these artifacts are of utility, and all typical of Adena. None of them showed any effect of fire. While such deposits of unburned artifacts with Adena cremations are rare, it is, in view of the facts, noteworthy that this trait should occur at all.

(75) Artifacts intentionally mutilated when deposited with cremations.

This, like all other traits dealing with artifacts associated with burials, is rare in Adena. However, it definitely does occur. In the Drake Mound** (see pp. 181-183, Vol. V), a stone reel was broken into two pieces and deposited with the cremation. At the same site a copper reel was battered with the cutting edge of a blunt tool—perhaps a hafted celt. It was gashed seven or eight times—heavily dented and marred, but not cut through, and then folded and hammered. In the Tarlton Mound Site, Fa 15,† a cache of flint blades was deposited with a cremation. Of a total of 28 blades, 21 were broken seemingly by intention. While such instances of intentional mutilation of artifacts in Adena are comparatively rare, it is known to have occurred four times in three sites.

In this connection interest attaches to the gorget from Mound 56, Monongahela, Pa., described by Thomas†† as follows:

"The copper gorget was rectangular in form, 3 x 4¼ inches in size, with incurved sides, and had two holes on the longer axis. It had been doubled over along this axis until the opposite sides were in contact and then hammered down flat.'"

Here, certainly is a copper reel—showing intentional mutilation at the time of burial, and seemingly duplicating the situation in the Drake Mound Fa 11, Kentucky.

Mutilation of artifacts deposited with cremations is also a Hopewell trait. Of Burial 1, Mound No. 8, of the Mound City Group,

---

* Funkhouser, W. D. and Webb, Wm. S., 1930, Fig. 29.
** Webb, Wm. S., 1941, p. 141 and pp. 181-183.
† Webb, Wm. S., 1942, p. 664.
†† Thomas, Cyrus, 1894, p. 495.

Mills* offers the following description of the burial and his concept of the trait:

"The grave, a slight depression upon the floor, contained the cremated bones of one individual with which were 16 copper artifacts consisting of breast plates, ear ornaments and pendants. These specimens were hammered and doubled together with the idea of destroying their intrinsic value, a proceeding customary when objects were placed in open graves, the idea being to preclude the possibility of their being stolen by derelict members of the tribe for personal use. This "killing" ceremony seems to have been widespread and aside from the practical purpose served may have carried with it something of the idea contained in the cremation ritual—the release of the spiritual essence of the object In the instance of incombustible artifacts the breaking or mutilating of the object may have served as did cremation with those which were combustible. That this procedure was anything more than a common sense precaution, however, is not indicated definitely for in the more pretentious burials of the mounds of the group, where the cremated remains immediately were covered by a primary protecting mound, artifacts as a rule were deposited entire. The only definite inference to be drawn is that the broken and mutilated artifacts placed with the dead served equally well the purpose of perfect specimens."

(76) Cremated remains accompanied by red ochre.

The use of red ochre in graves, in various ways, in connection with extended inhumation in the flesh is well known. Whatever its purpose the custom extended to deposits of cremated remains also. Such use of red ochre has so far only been found with cremated remains which were accompanied by outstanding deposits of artifacts, see Vol. V, p. 664. Since artifacts deposited in Adena mounds are known to have been painted and some covered by red ochre, the deposit of red ochre with these cremations may be only an attempt to cover the artifacts which accompany them. Careful future investigation may clarify this point.

INHUMATION TRAITS

(77) Body extended, in flesh on back, no tomb.

The extended inhumation is definitely characteristic of Adena. Often the body is encased in bark and laid in the earth of a mound under construction without any suggestion of log or earth walled tomb. Such burials usually show no evidence of a pit having been dug, and no collapse of any earth roof. One must conclude that such bodies were laid on the surface of the mound without surface disturbance, and covered with earth. There is often to be found traces of bark, but usually no artifact of any kind. It sometimes happens that such skeletons are very well preserved.

---

* Mills, Wm. C., 1922, p. 255.

(78) **Body extended on back in earth-walled tomb.**

The intent here is to describe the simple tomb constructed of earth, no pit having been dug. The usual method seems to have been to prepare a level surface over which a layer of bark was laid down, always with outside of bark downward. On this, earth was piled about the edges to form a wall enclosing a rectangular area about 3.5 feet by 8 feet. The wall may be from one foot to three feet high. This interior pitlike cavity, made by transporting earth from elsewhere, has thus a sloping interior surface. This surface is usually covered with another bark layer, the first layer of bark having been covered by the earth wall except in the central open area. On this second bark layer the body is placed. Small poles are laid from wall to wall transversely to support a bark cover over which earth is placed. These have been called earth-walled tombs. They differ from the simple bark burials only in having made earth-walls, and the bark, poles, earth supported roof. There is no interior log rectangle, and there are no log molds about the body.

(79) **Body extended in log tomb, singly. G(2).**

This is the familiar log-tomb burial of Adena. Under this trait Greenman describes different forms of log tombs. These have been discussed in this analysis under tomb traits. It is sufficient to say that there is a wide variation in form, size and elaborate care in the construction of these tombs, all of which seems to point to the conclusion that those accorded log-tomb burials were exceptional persons entitled for some reason to this evidence of special esteem. Greenman reports the maximum dimension of log tombs to be length 19 feet and width 12 feet. The principal tomb in Creigler Mound, Be 20, Kentucky, was 24 feet long and 17 feet wide at roof level.

(80) **Two extended bodies in same log tomb.**

This has occurred so frequently as to raise the question of a possible reason for this fact. Two individuals could, of course, die at the same time, but if only one died, the burial of the first could hardly wait for a second death. In all such cases, it is clear the burials were simultaneous. The positions of the bodies is, in such cases, varied. In six cases in three mounds the bodies of the pair were placed parallel side-by-side. In one case the body of one was superposed over the other, parallel. In two instances of double burial in the Ricketts Mound, Mm 3, Ky., the two bodies of the pair were placed end-for-end, but one superposed over the other. In the central subfloor grave in the original Adena mound, there were two skeletons parallel but in reverse position, end-for-end. In the subfloor grave of the Landing Mound, two bodies, both males, side-by-side, parallel, were placed in the bottom of the pit, and covered by a pole and bark roof, and a dismembered body, another male, was laid on top of the log-pole tomb roof.

(81) **Three extended burials in same log tomb.**

This has been found six times in two mounds. In one case, one of the bodies was reverse end-for-end relative to the other two. These multiple burials of Adena may be simply a matter of accidental death coupled with a desire to save the trouble of construction of additional tombs. However, if one reads carefully the record of early excavators, it will be noted that such burials have been reported on numerous occasions. Taken in connection with the deposit of cremated remains in log tomb burials, under such circumstances as to indicate intentional planned associations, these multiple burals may point to the intentional, or it may be, the voluntary destruction of some individuals in order to follow in death, an important personage. While such explanation of multiple burial is highly speculative, one form of evidence if it existed might be an aid in reaching a decision; namely, evidence in the accompanying skeleton of physical violence. Such evidence has not been found, although sought for. However, the lack of such evidence does not at all preclude the possibility of human sacrifice upon the death of a notable, by means such as strangulation which was used by the Natchez.* This would leave no trace on the skeleton. The problem of multiple burial in Adena which may include deposit of trophy skulls, or deposit of cremated remains, needs additional careful observation in future excavation of Adena sites.

(82) **Important central graves.** G(7).

The term central grave is here used, as by Greenman, to indicate any form of inhumation in log tomb or subfloor pit, placed at the center of the mound. As pointed out by Greenman, many Adena mounds contain a central tomb, and no other burials. Those mounds which have many burials often have a central one, the most elaborate one, and often the first one made in the mound. This trait was early recognized, and in the conviction that everything of importance was to be found at the center of the mound as stated by Fowke,** the technique of excavation of many early investigators was so developed as to explore the mound center and but little else. This was done by sinking round wells, or vertical shafts, down from the mound apex (which must have been quite inconvenient from the standpoint of the disposal of slack earth), or by tunneling from the side, or by a radial trench cut into the center. Because of the use of these techniques it is not surprising that post-mold patterns and village middens were not found and many cremations and log-tomb burials on house floors were not recognized as such. Because of a recognition of this trait, Adena came to indicate a collection of traits determined by the in-

---

* Bushnell, David I., Jr., 1920, p. 101, and Swanton, John R., 1911, pp. 138-157.
** Fowke, Gerard, 1902, p. 376.

vestigation of important central graves only. That is, Adena came to be little else than a burial complex of important central graves.

(83) **Use of bark in graves.** G(11).

This is almost a universal trait of Adena. Bark was used to wrap about the body when buried singly. Bark covered the floor on which earth walled tombs and log tombs were erected. Bodies lay on bark, and were usually covered with bark. Even cremations were often deposited on bark. Bark of all kinds seems to have been used but elm, hackberry, ash, and walnut were repeatedly used in the Kentucky mounds.

(84) **Use of puddled clay in graves.**

This was a fairly common practice. Clay in the form of plastic layers often covered the bark floor of tombs. Often the body was covered by a thin layer of plastic clay before a top coating of bark was put over it. In log tombs with an interior rectangle of logs, plastic clay was often used to fill the space between the logs and thus completely encase the body. This clay is hard, dry, and nearly impervious to water. Suggestions have been made that it was mixed with ashes. Of course, one cannot disprove such a statement made by early excavators, but in limestone regions in the vicinity of marl deposits the clays are often bluish white in color, and are often found in swampy lowlands. Such clay is always plastic, easy of access, and when dry has white streaks mingled with blue. This does give an impression that the clay had been mixed with wood ashes. It is this clay which is often found in graves, and it is this type of clay which seems to have been used to build the "beehive vaults" of West Virginia and eastern Kentucky.

Thomas* says of the principal central burial in the Great Smith Mound near Charleston, West Virginia (Greenman's No. 59):

> "It lay on the bottom of the vault, stretched horizontally on the back, head east, arms by the sides. East wrist was encircled by six heavy copper bracelets. . . . .
> "A fragment of the bark wrapping preserved by contact with the copper shows that it was black walnut. A piece of dressed skin which had probably formed part of the inner wrapping was also preserved by the copper. From the clay with which this was connected we may possibly infer that the body was wrapped in a dressed skin, this plastered over with a coating of clay (it seems to be clay and ashes mixed), and this surrounded by bark. Upon the breast was a copper gorget."

This copper gorget was a "reel shaped" gorget. With this skeleton was also found a steatite platform pipe.

---

* Thomas, Cyrus, 1894, p. 425.

(85) **Red ochre on skeleton.**   G(17).

This trait was reported by Greenman as occurring 13 times in 10 mounds. It has recently been found to occur 13 times in an additional six mounds. The intent of this trait is to state that red ochre in quantity was poured on or over the body at burial. There can be no doubt of the intentional use of red ochre in graves, but the promlem is much more complicated than a simple recognition of the fact. In many cases the powdered ochre seems to have been placed in a container or in a pile over the hips and lower extremities. If it was deposited on the body at burial, it would probably reach the skeleton after the passage of the flesh and cause a staining of the bones as observed. Under such circumstances it would be expected that the ochre which did not adhere to the bones would be found near by as a stain in the soil. This is sometimes true, but the problem of the deposit of ochre comes from the fact that sometimes bones are found so stained, with no evidence of ochre in the surrounding soil, leading to the suggestion that the ochre was applied at paint, in such cases, directly to the bones. This means the bones previously must have been denuded of the flesh and then have been accessible to persons from outside the tomb, i.e., the tomb would have to be open. Thus it would appear that some of the 13 cases reported by Greenman might well be listed under trait 88. Evidence on this point will be presented later.

Of the single burial on bark at the base of a mound near Chillicothe (Greenman's No. 3), Squier and Davis* say:

"From certain indications it was at first thought the bark in the vicinity of the skeleton had been painted of a red color, as portions adhered to the bones, giving them a reddish tinge. This probably resulted from other than natural causes."

(86) **Red ochre, lumps or granular in mound.**   G(35).

Greenman reports this as occurring in six of his list of 70 mounds. So far it has not been found in Kentucky mounds, except as reported in graves.

(87) **Red ochre on artifacts.**   G(49).

This trait is reported by Greenman as occurring 25 times in two mounds. It has been found twice, once in the Ricketts mound, and once in the Tarlton Mound, Fa 15, in Kentucky. It is not easy to determine what the significance of this trait may be. If, as it appears, there was a deliberate attempt to place ochre on artifacts, it then has some significance. If, on the other hand, ochre is merely found on artifacts in the grave where ochre was placed with the body,

---

*Squier, E. G. and Davis, E. H., 1848, p. 165.

it may, so far as the artifacts are concerned, be only an accident. In Mound 54, Beech Bottom, West Va., red ochre is reported as painted on flint projectile points in fine oblique lines. This is obviously an intentional application of ochre as paint.

(88) **Red ochre applied to skull or long bones.**

As thus stated, this is a new trait. The intent is to emphasize the application of the ochre, in the form of paint, to the skull or long bones, with all that this implies as distinguished from Trait No. 85 which indicated the placing of ochre in the grave. This Trait No. 88 means the flesh must have been removed from the bone, and the grave either was uncovered or accessible from the outside. On this point Moorehead* says of his Mound 40 which became No. 10 in Greenman's list:

"It is evident that the skeleton had been buried after the flesh had been removed from his bones as the lower jaw and bones of the hands were covered with a coating of red ochre of uniform thickness while the surrounding earth, except that immediately in contact with the bones in question showed no trace of the coloring matter."

The condition described by Moorehead is precisely what has been observed elsewhere, but one hardly need assent to his conclusion that the burial took place **after the flesh had been removed.** It is believed that had the flesh been removed before burial it would have been very difficult, if not impossible, barring the retention of ligimentous articulation, for the aboriginees to have placed the bones so nearly in anatomical order as they are found.

Mills,** in speaking of Burial 13 of the Adena Mound, says:

"The skeleton had been wrapped in three distinct layers of bark and was in a fair state of preservation; the skull was badly crushed and several of the arm bones were broken; the tibia and fibula of both legs were painted red; evidently the flesh had been removed from the bones, the paint then placed around them and the whole then covered with a plaster made of mud."

In discussing the painting of human bones, Hrdlicka† has this to say:

"In Ohio painted bones were found by Prof. E. W. Putnam (Turner group of mounds) and by Mr. W. K. Moorehead. The latter writes†† me on the subject as follows:

"Painted bones have been found in a mound at Omega, Ross County, Ohio; in Jackson County mound, Ohio, and in two mounds within the corporate limits of Chillicothe. One of the latter was discovered by Mr. Clarence Loveberry, assistant curator of the above (Ohio Archaelogical and Historical) society. The others were found by myself. Near Green Camp, Marion

---

* Moorehead, W. K., 1892, p. 164.
** Mills, Wm. C., 1907, p. 22.
† Hrdlicka, Ales, 1904, p. 612.
†† Letter dated September 21, 1897.

County, Ohio, in a stone grave 6 feet below the surface, Mr. Loveberry discovered a skeleton entirely painted.

"All of these were coated with red pigment or ochre, including in nearly every case all of the larger bones. There are other instances in which just the hands, or the feet, or, perhaps, the skull were coated. These are usually from mounds, either large or small. Bones on which the pigment was simply heaped were clearly distinguished by the surrounding soil being also stained. "I have never observed instances in which skeletons were coated with yellow or black paints. (We have found yellow and white mineral paints near the hands of skeletons several times.) "We have never found painted bones in stone mounds. They are invariably in earth mounds or stone graves."

In speaking of the possible distinction attaching to the individuals accorded elaborate log-tomb burials, Greenman* says of the Coon Mound central burial:

"The erection of a mound of this size over the remains of a single individual is very suggestive and the presence of red pigment on the tibia of the skeleton is of further significance."

The statement of Romans** on the customs of the Choctaw relative to the use of skull painting is interesting and suggestive. He says:

"As soon as the deceased is departed, a stage is erected and the corpse is laid on it and covered with a bear skin; if he be a man of note, it is decorated, and the poles painted red with vermilion and bear's oil. . . . the head being painted with vermilion (after the flesh has been scraped off) is with the rest of the bones put into a neatly made chest. . . . "

After quoting the above, Greenman says, "a number of other Adena type mounds have contained skeletons, parts of which were **painted with red ochre.**" This is taken to mean that he believed the ochre was **applied** by some means **directly to the bone.**

In Kentucky recent excavations have revealed the presence of red pigment, coating the bones of the lower extremities of some skeletons where the presence of red ochre in the graves was not noticed by the investigators. This condition has occurred at Site Be 3 on Burial 66, and at Site Mm 6, Burials 15 and 16.

On the skull of Burial 8, Mm 6, probably a young adult female, there was found red ochre pigment in two distinct transverse bands on the front of the skull. One of these bands crossed immediately above the orbits while the other was several inches above it on the upper portions of the frontal bones.

Across these two red bands a vertical strip of graphite about an inch wide extends from the top of the frontal bone down the forehead touching the tips of the nasal bone and extends on to the front teeth.

---

* Greenman, E. F., 1932, p. 410.
** Romans, B., 1775, p. 88.

It seems impossible to explain the presence of the graphite on any basis other than direct application to the bone. This graphite strip seems to overlay or cross on top of the red ochre bands. This seems to demand the previous application of red ochre to the skull.

This trait is accepted by the present authors on the present evidence as valid. The question remains how could this painting be accomplished in an extended burial in a log tomb.

It is believed that when burial took place in an Adena log tomb, in most cases a period of many days elapsed after the burial was made, while the body "lay in state" surrounded by its burial paraphernalia, much or little, before the tomb was finally closed and the mound erected over it. Doubtless, during this period burial ceremonies were conducted, some of which may have had the intent of preservation of the body. (In mounds of the Hopewell* group and Seip Mound No. 1** a number of cases are on record where copper nasal supports were introduced, seemingly for this purpose.) Under such condition, the time would come when the flesh fell from the bones of the skull, or could be removed easily and the skull painted. Whether this painting was done because "he was a man of note" as in the case of the Choctaw, or not, need not particularly concern us here, except in passing, it may be well to note that those Adena skeletons which have had their skulls painted, usually occupy central tombs of rather elaborate construction. This point is further discussed in the chapter on comparison of burial traits of Adena and Hopewell.

This assumption that some time elapsed between the burial and the erection of the mound over the tomb seems necessary to account for the facts. It may be well to point out circumstantial evidence which seems to confirm this "open grave period". (1) Slight disturbance of single bones from correct anatomical order have been frequently noted under circumstances which could hardly be explained as the result of a collapsed tomb roof or the work of burrowing animals, as for example, femurs have been found placed in non-anatomical order, as reported by Moorehead.*** (2) The use of short logs in elaborate tombs definitely as head and foot rests by which the extremeties of the skeleton were propped up to slightly elevated position (see pages 35 and 38, Vol. V). (3) The use of a bundle of cane stalks as a pillow (see page 46, Vol. V). (4) Small vertical post molds about the central rectangle in elaborate tombs seem to indicate the necessity for a small temporary structure over the grave, a sort of canopy or light shelter or sunshade. One might consider that such a canopy would not have been erected if the grave was to be filled immediately, since it would seem to serve no useful purpose in such case (see pp. 43 and 46, Vol. V). (5) Possibly the desire to

---

* Shetrone, H. C., 1926, Fig. 24.
** Shetrone, H. C. and Greenman, E. F., 1931, p. 409.
*** Moorehead, W. K., 1892, p. 153.

expose the body after death within its tomb, yet under some kind of cover may have been a factor in causing occasional burials on the floors of dwelling houses.   (6) The exposure of the body in the tomb, whether the tomb was completely open to the elements or only accessible to persons through a restricted passageway would give point to the placement of "trophy" skulls with the deceased.   (7) If tombs which were kept open were to be visited by interested persons for a season, the reason is explained for flooring large horizontal areas with logs about the mouth of elaborate tombs, which happened to be high up on the side of mounds, and the occasional use of flat stones laid on the sloping sides of the mounds about tombs. (8)   At least two mounds in Greenman's list, Nos. 19 and 43, had elaborate tombs which had "passageways at the east".   Here seems to be specific proof that in these two tombs at least for a season, access to the tomb's interior could be had from the outside.

The danger of drawing conclusions from such "circumstantial evidence" is inherent in all such speculations.   However, such evidence offers to intellectual curiosity, a challenge to devise an explanation.   To be worthy of further consideration such explanation must cover a wide range of observations, and be contradicted by none. The "period of an open grave" is rationalized on such a basis.

Skulls, to which red ochre has been intentionally applied after the removal of the flesh, have been found in a Hopewell site under circumstances which make the interpretation of the significance of this trait quite difficult.

In the intrusive pit in Mound 3 of the Turner Group, Willoughby[*] reports as follows:

> "The extended skeletons of a man and a woman lay upon the bottom near its center. . . . .
>
> "About the two skeletons were sixteen crania of men arranged at regular intervals. . . . .
>
> "The sixteen skulls were unaccompanied by other bones. They were probably family relics, connected with or belonging to the man whose skeleton occupied the center of the grave.   Thirteen of them have superficial scratches or cuts on their surface, apparently made with flint knives in the process of removing the flesh.   Some of the skulls had been painted red, and red ochre still adheres to the surface of six.   It is more common on the forehead, facial bones and jaw, but in one skull it occurs about the base as well and in this and one other on the temporal fossa. Five of the skulls have one to four perforations about ⅛ inch in diameter, in the wall of the cranium.   The sixth example has eleven perforations and another apparently started. . . . .
>
> "The position of the holes seems to indicate that at least a part of them were intended for the passage of a suspending cord. Others may have been used for the insertion of feathers or other decorations."

---

[*] Willoughby, Chas. C., 1922, p. 60.

(89) **Graphite in graves.** G(58).

This is reported in two mounds by Greenman and has been found in two mounds in Kentucky.

(90) **Graphite applied to skull and collar bone.**

This trait seems to have occurred under conditions similar to that of trait 88. This trait has been found at two sites in recent excavations in Kentucky. The occurrence of this trait at Mm 6 on Burial 8 is noted in connection with trait 88.

At Site Be 20, Burial 11, the large young adult male skeleton which occupied the central position in the elaborate tomb, had a wide transverse band of graphite across the forehead just above the orbits, and graphite had been applied also to the upper surfaces of the collar bones. This is the same skeleton whose lower extremities were found covered by a large quantity of red ochre both in chunks and powder form.

It was noted that the lower surfaces of bones of the lower extremities, the pelvis and the arm bones were found to be stained with a dull black pigment, where they rested on the floor of the grave. Chemical analysis* of the stained bone tissue and of fortuitious encrustations showed ferric iron. This black stain, in the opinion of the late Dr. R. N. Maxson** may have been brought about by the presence of red ochre during the period of decomposition of the body with the formation of carbon and asphaltic compounds.

Numerous examples of this same black iron compound have been found in the bones of skeletons at Site Be 3, Burials 30, 36, 74, 57, 83; at Site Be 17, Burials 3, 5, 13, and 15; and at Site Mm 6, Burial 8.

(91) **Separate skull in grave with burial, "Trophy"?** G(C).

This trait under the title "Trophy skulls" was noted by Greenman in Table C, since it had occurred in but a single site, the Fudge Mound of Indiana, Greenman's No. 52. There have now been found two other instances of a separate skull buried in an Adena tomb, in association with a complete skeleton, under circumstances which point to it as an intentional inclusion of a skull at the time of burial, and not the head of a recently decapitated body. This suggests that such a clean skull may have been the valued "property" of the deceased individual in whose grave it was placed. This extra skull seems less well preserved than the skull of the skeleton which it accompanied, which suggests that it may have been dry before burial, and in such condition that disintegration might have been more rapid than in the case of a body buried in the flesh. There has been found no evidence in this skull, as in the trophy skulls of Hopewell***, that it may represent an enemy who was conquered, scalped, etc. One of

---

* At the time the semi-micro analyses were made, all reagents were tested before their use to show the absence of iron.
** Maxson, Dr. R. N., Professor of Chemistry, Univ. of Ky.
*** Shetrone, H. C., 1926, Figs. 5, 6.

these skulls, Burial 38, Site Be 3,* shows traces of red ochre over its entire surface. The other instance of a "trophy" skull is Burial 7, Site Mm 6.**

(92) Burial of isolated skulls.

This has been found six times in four sites. The skull is buried or deposited without any evidence of a grave and without any other part of the skeleton in association except in some cases, the axis and atlas, which evidently remained attached. The reason for this decapitation is not clear, since no information is available of the disposition of the remaining portion of the body. No headless bodies without skulls in association have been found in Adena sites. Knowing the prevalence of cremation in Adena, one may speculate on its use as a means of disposal of the extra bodies. Some deposited cremations have been found with no skull portions visible, but obviously such absence proves little or nothing. Also human bone fragments have been found in and about fire basins on village sites, see Trait 53. In the Seip No. 1 and the Harness Mounds, two Ohio Hopewell sites, isolated skulls were deposited on top of a pile of cremated bones.

(93) Decapitation, head buried between femora.

This trait has been found only once in Kentucky. It is such an irrational procedure as to definitely suggest some kind of ceremonial significance. It has been reported as occurring in the Kiefer Mound of Miami County, Ohio. The Kiefer Mound was not classified as belonging to Adena in the original 70 mounds. Today, it should be so regarded in view of the proof that engraved tablets are of Adena origin. In this mound*** three of the twelve skeletons arranged in a circle under the mound were buried with the skull between the femora. The Kiefer Mound, thus, has Adena Trait 95 as well as Trait 93, and also seven tablet traits.

(94) Skeletons flexed. G(59).

This is a rare occurrence in Adena, only two instances being reported by Greenman in two mounds. One burial, that of a child, from the Rickets Mound Mm 3 has been so classified. It may have occurred in the Hartman Mound, Site Be 32, in Kentucky, but due to aboriginal disturbance the evidence is not conclusive. In no case has the exact position of arm and leg bones been reported.

(95) Extended skeletons arranged in a circle. G(C).

This trait occurred in Mound 57 in Greenman's list, but since it was in only one mound, the trait was not regarded by him as an Adena trait. He described this trait as "skeletons in wheel-shaped

---

* Webb, Wm. S. and John B. Elliott, 1942, p. 398.
** Webb, Wm. S., 1940, p. 27.
*** Shetrone, H. C., 1930, p. 93.

formation". In this mound, the Criel Mound,* Kanawha County, West Va., one extended burial was at the center of a group of eleven. The other ten were arranged, extended, five on each side in a semi-circle with feet toward the center about the central burial. The Kiefer Mound** No. 129 and the Wilmington Mound*** No. 126 had this trait also, but were not accepted by Greenman as Adena mounds since so little was known about them. In the Kiefer mound 12 skeletons were extended, "like spokes in a wheel", with heads together near the center, feet outward. Both of these mounds yielded engraved stone tablets. Since the engraved tablets have been found in Kentucky definitely in Adena mounds, there can be no reason now to doubt that the use of these tablets constitutes a very important Adena trait. Thus one may conclude that the Kiefer and Wilmington mounds also should be classed as Adena. The Landing Site Be 17, Kentucky, had about a central pit containing 5 burials, six burials nearly equally spaced extended on the arc of a circle of about 17.5 feet radius. When these three mounds are added to the Adena list, Trait 84 then rests on an occurrence in four mounds, one in West Va., two in Ohio, and one in Kentucky.

(96) **Skeletons bundled.** G(C).

Sometimes the bones of a skeleton are found in a mound, deposited in a pile, not in anatomical order. This suggests that they may have been in a bundle when deposited; hence the term "bundle burials" used to describe this condition. These burials are sometimes called reburials. This implies an exposure of the body in the flesh for a sufficient time after death to permit the passage of the flesh. The bones of the skeleton would then be cleaned and put into some light hamper or container and stored for a time awaiting final disposition. This final disposition in both Adena and Ohio Hopewell was sometimes cremation and deposit of cremated remains in a mound. In some cases the bundle of bones was deposited in a mound without cremation, thus producing a so-called "reburial" or a "bundle burial". This is a rare trait in Adena reported by Greenman as occurring in only one mound (No. 53) in his list. This mound, the McEvers Mound†, Montezuma, Pike County, Illinois, is now considered by some to be more closely related to Illinois Hopewell than to Adena. However, Mills†† reported two "reburials" from the Adena mound and Black‡ has reported four from the Nowlin Mound in Indiana. The Hartman‡‡ mound Be 32, Kentucky has

---

* Thomas, Cyrus, 1894, p. 415.
** Shetrone, H. C., 1930, p. 93.
*** Welch, L. B., and T. M. Richardson, 1879, pp. 40-48.
† Fowke, Gerard, 1905, p. 8.
†† Mills, Wm. C., 1902, p. 460.
‡ Black, Glenn A., 1936, p. 299.
‡‡ Webb, Wm. S., 1943, p. 542.

yielded two. There can be no doubt therefore, that rarely Adena as well as Hopewell of Ohio deposited the bundled bones of skeletons in mounds, sometimes within the graves of other individuals.

FLINT TRAITS

(97) Blanks, flint.

The village sites of Adena show that flint blanks were brought from the quarries, roughed out by percussion, and but little specialized. These blanks are often found broken on the village site, and may have served as crude implements even though unspecialized.

(98) Celts, flint.

Celts of flint were roughed out by percussion, and very carefully made nearly rectangular by secondary pressure fracture. The sides are straight—the pole is nearly square in section and relatively flat. The cutting edge is thin. Generally the whole surface is heavily ground and highly polished. However, the grinding is never sufficient to obliterate the facets formed by chipping. Most are relatively small in size being of the order of 60 mm broad by 150 mm long, although some are much larger.

(99) Cores, flint.

Cores are the central portion of blocks of flint from which long thin flint flakes were thrown off. They show the characteristic conchoidal fracture. They are found infrequently on Adena villages.

(100) Gravers, flint.

These are flint flakes, usually as large as a projectile point, where by secondary and tertiary chipping a long, very fine point has been worked out. Site Fa 1, Ky., has recently yielded, from the village surface, a number of gravers with a very interesting curved point, made by cutting in a deep notch by chipping, and enlarging the bottom of the notch nonsymmetrically. This may be the tool which was used to engrave tablets.

(101) Leaf-shaped blades or knives. G(8).

This artifact is very abundant in Adena. Greenman's Trait No. 8 regards these articraft as projectile points only. The term "knife" has been added in the belief that they often show internal evidence that they were used for cutting, became dull, and were retouchd by secondary chipping. From this it is inferred many were used as knives.

(102) Leaf-shaped blades deposited in cache.

This has occurred with sufficient frequency to indicate some special reason for it. It may be that in some instances when these caches accompanied the dead, these flint knives were regarded as somewhat unfinished, possibly to be completed in the world of spirits, and therefore, represented potential value, since being unspecialized they still could be made into knives, scrapers, projectile points, drills, reamers, or gravers, at pleasure. While such caches are found as burial offerings, they are also found apart from burial association. Caches have been found in villages and in mounds out of association with burials, and in mounds, and under rock shelters in burial association. The contents of a typical cache is illustrated in Figure 27, p. 661, Vol. V. These were finished knives, seemingly some of them had been used, dulled by use, and resharpened by secondary chipping.

(103) Stemmed projectile points deposited in cache.

This is a deposit of well-finished, and usually rather heavy, projectile points. A typical cache is illustrated in Fig. 15, p. 335, Vol. V. Such points may be atlatl darts, and the cache may represent the supply carried by an individual. Such caches have been reported from many other sites.

(104) Projectile points, stem with parallel sides. G(9).

This is the most commonly recognized Adena point. It is usually well and carefully made—from medium to heavy as projejctile points go—being from 3.5 to 5 inches or more in length. The size and weight of these points would seem to suggest the use of the atlatl rather than the bow.

(105) Stemmed points and hafted scrapers ground smooth on stem edges.

A very considerable proportion of all Adena stemmed points, as well as hafted scrapers show definite grinding and smoothing on the edges of the stem. This seems to have been done to prevent the cutting of the lashing which secured the point to the shaft or scraper to the handle.

(106) Projectile points side notched. G(36).

These were early recognized as Adena points. They are fairly common.

(107) Drills and reamers. G(48).

These are numerous on village sites of Adena, and were surely the tools by which gorgets were drilled from one side only with very exactly drilled conical perforations. The cataloguing of this trait by Greenman shows one drill from each of three sites. That is, out of 70 mounds, only three sites reported drills and those only one each. This fact emphasizes how Adena was, until recently, only a "mound burial complex". Excavations in Kentucky have included villages. In one village 20 drills were found under Mound Jo 2. Twenty-nine drills have been recently recovered from the Peter Village, Unit I, Site Fa 1, Kentucky.

(108) Scrapers, flint, hafted.

These have the appearance of projectile points from which the point, including, perhaps, one third of the blade, has been broken off. The broken end is then modified to produce a sharp but blunt scraping edge. While they have the appearance of broken projectile points, it is doubtful if many of them are such. It seems highly probable that these were made as scrapers originally. The hafting is only inferred from the fact that the scraper has a stem—usually with parallel sides, and often with a convex base. The edges of the stem are often smoothed by grinding.

(109) Scrapers, thumbnail, flint. G(50).

This trait Greenman reports from only two mounds. Recent excavations of villages under Adena mounds show it to be very frequent in occurrence. This type of scraper may have been hafted, but the blade or scraping end is much like the hafted type, the proximal end is somewhat pointed, and could have been inserted in a hollow bone or antler handle of Adena type. Such a combination would doubtless have been an efficient combination. So far none has been found in such association. Recent continued searching of the surface of a proven Adena site in Fayette County, Ky., has yielded many flint scrapers of this type, see Fig. 22A, p. 645, Vol. V.

(110) Scrapers, side, flint, flake. (G)5.

Greenman speaks of these as knives—flint flakes. Doubtless many were so used, but many are made from curved flakes showing conchoidal fracture. These would be rather difficult to use as knives, but as scrapers over a convex surface, Adena man probably had no more efficient tool.

GROUND STONE TRAITS

(111) Gorget, bar, expanded center. G(3).

Under trait No. 3, Greenman included all forms of stone gorgets. In this analysis they have been separated into types since some of these forms may not, in fact, have been gorgets at all. The expanded bar gorget is, perhaps, the most frequently found and is, perhaps, diagnostic of Adena. It is flat on one side, convex on the other. It is made of slate, sandstone, or limestone, and may or may not be perforated. When perforated, there are usually two holes about one fourth of the gorget length apart, drilled from the flat side. Gorgets of this type with a single central perforation have been found. There seems to have been little or nothing observed in their actual occurrence in burial associations to justify the term gorget. As has been pointed out (page 444, Vol. V), they are usually found in the region of the hips or lower extremities, are most frequently found lying parallel to the body and flat side up. This seems to suggest that they could have been atlatl weights attached to the back of the flat atlatl bar, flat side against it. When an atlatl was included as a burial offering, it was usually laid in the grave, handle near the hand of the individual, bringing the "gorget" into the position found. In at least one case * there was a well worked antler handle found in the same grave, practically in alignment with the stone weight and by estimation at the proper distance from it to indicate that they may have been parts of the **same atlatl.** This may account in part for the occurrence of bone and antler handles in the Adena complex.

(112) Gorgets, reel-shaped.

These are made of slate and limestone. They seem to be true gorgets, that is, they were suspended about the neck and usually have two perforations. They have been previously discussed at some length, see page 192, Vol.V.

(113) Gorget, concave side, convex ends.

These are of slate or limestone and usually have two perforations. They are not numerous and are very rarely found in numbers more than one to a site. One was reported from the Original Adena Mound and one is illustrated in Fig. 12, page 239, Vol. V.

(114) Gorgets, semi-keeled and truncated, pyramid, rectangular base. G(8).

These gorgets are very similar in general form. They are best described by reference to Ancient Monuments of the Mississippi Valley,** page 237, Fig. 126, Nos. 1 and 2. They usually have two perforations and are made from slate, limestone, sandstone, or hematite. It is believed they may have been used as atlatl weights. Five have been found in a single site in Kentucky (see page 545, Vol. V).

(115) Gorgets, flat, various forms.

These gorgets made of sandstone, limestone, slate, or shale may be elliptical, rectanguloid or triangular or diamond shaped with one or two perforations.

(116) Gorgets conically perforated from one side only.

This trait seems to be diagnostic of Adena. The conical perforation seems to have been accomplished by the use of a flint reamer. Where gorgets of any type have one flat and one convex face, reaming is invariably done from the flat face.

(117) Pipes, tubular, constricted mouth. G(10).

These pipes are about five inches long and about three-fourths of an inch in diameter. They are made of limestone, or sandstone. The form is illustrated in Fig. 34, page 56, Vol. V. These pipes al-

* Funkhouser, W. D. and Webb, Wm. S., 1935, Fig. 18.
** Squier, E. G. and E. H. Davis, 1848, p. 237.

though seemingly diagnostic of Adena, are usually found sparingly on any single site. Of Greenman's seventy mounds, seventeen of these mounds had a total of twenty-two pipes, i.e., fourteen mounds had one each, one mound had two pipes, and two mounds had three pipes each. One of these was the Original Adena Mound. The notable exception to the scarcity of pipes in any one site is the Beech Bottom Mound in West Virginia (Greenman's No. 54). This had a total of thirty-two. These were all found in a portion of the mound called the Central Cone. The excavators, Bache and Satterthwaite*, spoke of them as "tubes" rather than pipes since the flattening at the "mouth" end was not present. On this point the authors say:

> "None of our specimens show this flattening or wedgelike bevelling at the base, with the possible exception of three. . . . This flattening is slight, irregular and rough, and probably results from smoothing damaged tube."

The authors point out that various uses for such tubes have been suggested, as shaman's blowing or sucking tubes**, horns or trumpets***, whistles****, telescopic instruments†, nasal inhaling devices‡.

It is plain that many writers have been disinclined to accept them as smoking devices. Bache and Satterthwaite attempted to answer the question by having the contents of some of these tubes analyzed. The volatile combustible component of these samples ran as high as 60 per cent, as the result of which, the investigator states that,

> "It would be quite natural to conclude that this material could be the incrustation resulting from smoking tobacco or similar substances."

It must be obvious that the finding of thirty-two such tubes together in a single site indicates something quite out of the ordinary. Either these tubes were not made for the same purpose as those with flattening at the "mouth" end, or else these represent the unfinished product in the process of manufacture at this site.

From the some twenty new sites recently investigated in Kentucky four sites have yielded one pipe each and one had three. A total of seven pipes from five sites. Such numbers would seem to be much too small to indicate any general use of such tubes in any very prevalent habit of smoking. These pipes usually found singly in important log-tomb burials may be part of the paraphernalia of medicine men as described by Willoughby‡‡, see Trait 118.

---

* Bache, Charles, and Linton Satterthwaite, Jr., 1930, pp. 133-163.
** Jones, Charles C., 1873, pp. 359-365.
*** McGuire, Joseph D., 1897, p. 383.
**** Moorehead, Warren K., 1917, p. 135.
† Schoolcraft, Henry F., 1845, pp. 369-420.
‡ Read, M. C., 1879-1880, p. 53.
‡‡ Willoughby, Charles C., 1935, p. 97.

(118) **Pipes tubular, long slate, flared mouth.**

These pipes are also characteristic of Adena, but much less numerous than the smaller tubular variety. They are made of slate, and specimens have been found which are thirteen inches long. The type is best illustrated in "Ancient Monuments"*, page 224, Fig. 122, No. 1. This pipe is reported as taken from a mound near Chillicothe, Ohio. A broken specimen shown in Fig. 7-1, page 314, Vol. V, was taken from Mound Jo 2,** Johnson County, Kentucky.

It is difficult to believe that these tubular pipes were ever used as tobacco pipes for smoking. Slate, which takes a high polish, and is not too difficult to work, is poorly adapted to use as a pipe in smoking since the heating of the fire in the body of the pipe would destroy the polish of slate and probably induce early fracture, in such long slender tubes. A cylindrical tube 5.5 inches long, with flared end, made of sheet copper was taken from the George Connett Mound, on Wolf Plains near Athens, Ohio, by Andrews†. From his description of this mound it is clearly an Adena mound, showing partial cremation of a body in a log tomb, laid upon the floor of a house. The log tomb was covered over by a small primary mound on the house floor and the house was then burned. The fire obtained access to the logs of the tomb, producing a partial cremation. This copper tube was found in the center of this charred and partially cremated log-tomb burial. It was more exactly described later by Putnam††. This copper tube could hardly have been a convenient means of smoking. Copper has so low a specific heat and is so good a conductor of heat, that had one attempted to burn tobacco or other material in this tube by smoking, the thin copper tube would have been too hot to hold in the hand, much less to have permitted its being put to the lips of the smoker. Such a copper tube, however, could have served as a shaman's device, as well as if made of stone, bone or wood.

(119) **Pipes, elbow biconical.** G(C).

This type of pipe is made of sandstone. It is not numerous in Adena. One specimen from Kentucky is illustrated in Fig. 10, page 222, Vol. III.

(120) **Pipes, platform.** G(55).

These pipes are rare in Adena sites. One each was found in Mounds 54 and 59, both in West Virginia. These were straight based steatite pipes. A curved-base sandstone monitor pipe was found **under** Mound Be 20, Ky., see Fig. 12, page 528, Vol. V.

---

* Squier, E. G. and E. H. Davis, 1848, p. 224.
** Webb, Wm. S., 1942, p. 314.
† Andrews, E. B., 1877, p. 61.
†† Putnam, F. W., 1882, p. 108.

(121) Pitted stones, cup stones. G(22).

These are numerous in Adena villages. They may have served as anvil stones. One is illustrated in Fig. 36, page 61, Vol. V. The pits are hemispherical depressions about 1.25 inches in diameter. Usually there are many such pits in the face of the stone—sometimes the pits overlap. Pitted stones believed to be of Adena origin found in rock shelters of Eastern Kentucky are illustrated in Fig. 25, p. 269, Vol. I.

(122) Stone balls. G(30).

This is a rare trait so far found only once in Kentucky in Adena mounds.

(123) Celts, granite, and other igneous rock.

Under the term "stone celts", Greenman reports 38 specimens from 15 mounds. Many of these must be granite, although not so stated, from the obvious preference of Adena for igneous rock for making celts, although they did use flint and occasionally hematite. On any Adena village broken granite celts are very common. It is a fact of personal observation that many celt fragments are the rounded pole end. The reason why this end should show such a marked preponderance in the debris, may be that the celt was used for hammering. When the pole end was broken off, usually about a one inch section, a new pole could be made quickly and the use of the same artifact continued. Broken poles of celts, from Site Fa 1, Kentucky, are illustrated in Fig. 22C, page 645, Vol V.

(124) Celts, hematite. G(37).

Highly polished small celts of hematite were used by Adena. They were not nearly as numerous as the flint or granite celts, but were very highly polished, and often quite small.

(125) Hoes, limestone or sandstone slabs. G(C).

Hand hoes seemingly unhafted, were made from slabs of limestone, sandstone, or shale. The slab was roughly pecked into a rectangle about 7 inches broad by, perhaps, 16 inches long. One end was left square and blunt, while the other was chipped to a sharp edge. They all show use and are polished as if used to excavate earth. Broken hoe blades are frequently found in the mound fill (see Fig. 35, page 59, Vol. V). A very good specimen taken from the ash bank in Wilson Cove, Lee County, Kentucky, is illustrated in Fig. 24, page 68, Vol. I, Departmental reports.

(126) Hammerstones, flint concretions and sandstones.

In some villages hammerstones are very numerous. They were made from a block of sandstone, or from a flint concretion. They show abrasion by battering. Occasionally one is found obviously broken in half. It is strange that hammerstones have not been reported by Greenman, who mentions only one occurrence—that of a "grooved" specimen. Hammerstones of Adena were usually not grooved. Perhaps, the failure to report them previously is due to the fact that they occur only in villages, although one would expect some to have been incorporated in mound fill. For illustration see Fig. 35, page 59, Vol. V.

(127) Abraiding stones. G(53).

These are usually flint blocks or concretions, which have one very rough surface which shows use as a grinding and abraiding instrument.

(128) Grooved stones, semicylinders and balls.

Under the term "grooved stones", Greenman describes under his trait No. 15, stone tablets which often have several longitudinal grooves on one face. In this trait No. 128 the term "grooved stones" designated a class of objects illustrated in Fig. 37, page 62, and Fig. 13, page 158, Vol. V. Their purpose is unknown. In other culture complexes they have been called among other things, net sinkers. In Adena they have one flat face and are believed to have served as atlatl weights. Recent surface collections at the Adena Site Fa 1, Ky., made from inside the earth works, have recovered many of these objects made from galena (lead sulphide) associated with barite heavy spar (barium sulphate), see Fig. 22C, page 645, Vol. V.

(129) Stone discs. G(40).

These discs are not numerous. Fragments of a limestone disk have been found which was about 6 inches in diameter (see Fig. 59, page 108, Vol. V).

(130) Hemispheres, Limestone, sandstone.

They are usually considered rubbing or polishing stones, and are illustrated in Fig. 34-L, page 56, Vol. V.

(131) Hemispheres, barite, basalt. G(C).

Similar in form and purpose to those of limestone and sandstone (see Fig. 34, page 56, Vol. V).

(132) Hemispheres, hematite. G(43).

Highly polished—a form of rubbing stone—not very frequent in occurrence.

(133) Boat-shaped, barite, galena, bars.

These stones are about 1.5 inches long and about .5 of an inch broad. They have the boat-stone shape except that the flat face is not excavated. About half of them have the double sloping perforations of boat stones. The other half are unperforated. Barite, (barium sulphate) occurs in outcrop veins in Central Kentucky and usually carries with it a considerable percentage of galena (lead sulphide) and "black jack" (zinc sulphide). These last two mentioned minerals in crystal form are usually seen in small traces in the artifacts made from barite. The Adena village site Fa 1, Kentucky, continues to yield barite fragments, many of which were worked pieces of triangular prisms. It is believed they were atlatl weights (see illustration Fig. 25, page 655, Vol. V).

(134) Pestles. G(52).

These are very rare on Adena sites, only two being reported by Greenman. The absence of lap stones or mortars as accompanying artifacts, seems to suggest they did no grinding of food in great quantities as some other prehistoric peoples seem to have done.

(135) Steatite vessel fragments. G(C).

These are quite rare on Adena sites, but now have been reported from two sites.

(136) Galena, barite fragments, worked.

These were probably made in attempts to make "boatstones", "hemispheres", and beads of this material. They occur in village midden.

(137 Concretions or fossils. G(33).

These are rare, but they show that Adena man recognized the unusual, and potentially useful objects.

(138) Stones with incised characters. G(44).

None have been found in recent excavations. There is nothing which can be added to Greenman's description.

(139) Geodes, cuplike. G(52).

No new occurrence.

(140) Obsidian flakes. G(59).

No new occurrence.

(141 Stone saws.

These are made from sandstone or limestone slabs about 7 mm. thick. They are beveled from both sides along one edge, to produce a sharp straight edge from 25 to 75 mm. in length. This edge is then notched very regularly with 14 to 22 notches per 5 cm. One saw was made from a small granite celt. These serrated edges show abrasion and occasionally a broken tooth, which is taken to mean that they were used as saws. Eight saws were found in one village site under Mound Mm. 6, Montgomery County, Kentucky. See Fig. 34, page 56, Vol. V. It is believed that as other Adena villages come to be investigated, this trait will rest upon additional evidence.

TABLET TRAITS

(142) **Tablets, rectangular.** G(15).

These tablets, made of sandstone, rarely of slate, are about 3 x 4 inches and up to .5 inch in thickness. They have fairly straight edges, and flat sides with slightly rounded corners. They were described by Greenman as "Grooved stones", because many of them have on one face, one or more long grooves as if made by an attempt to sharpen a bone awl against them. They have been called sharpening stones by some because of this supposed use. A few tablets have one or more grooves on both sides. A few are ungrooved. These tablets often occur as burial associations, particularly with cremations, being often burned and broken by the crematory fires. These associations seem to indicate that they were valued by their owners beyond ordinary blocks of sandstone. Fig. 12, page 324, Vol. V, illustrates such a tablet with a cremated burial.

(143) **Engraved tablets, rectanguloid.** G(C).

These tablets are modified and specialized rectangles, which still retain their general form, but whose edges may be convex (Grave Creek), or slightly concave (Cincinnati), or otherwise modified (Berlin). Eight of these tablets are described in detail and the form is shown (see pp. 117-123, Vol. V).

Recently another engraved stone tablet has come to light. This tablet, the property of the Museum of the American Indian, Heye Foundation, was a part of the collection of William M. Fitzhugh, acquired by it in 1936. Through the courtesy of the Heye Foundation there is presented in Figure 1, a photograph of this tablet together with a drawing showing in detail the engraved design. The tablet is about 5.5 cm broad, 9.5 cm long and .6 cm thick. The long edges are slightly concave, one end is nearly straight and the other end slightly convex. It is engraved on only one side, the reverse side being smooth and slightly convex. The record of this tablet states only that it was "found in a mound on Olive Hayman's farm, Saxon, Meigs County, Ohio, by Marion West and William Hogue". It is a matter of regret that we do not know the location more exactly, but from the record, the site very probably was not more than fifty miles southeast of Chillicothe. Whether or not this tablet was in burial association is not known, but the fact that it seems to be unbroken and that it came from a mound might justify the assumption that it was a burial offering. If one compares this tablet with the Wilmington tablet, one is struck by the close resemblance between the two, both in the figure represented, and the technique employed. There is obviously portrayed the head and beak of a raptorial bird, and the talons, in what seems to be a crude attempt at bilateral symmetry. For the purpose of reference, since the mound from which it came is unknown, it will be referred to as the Meigs County Tablet and designated in the trait list as M. C.

Archaeologists will recall the discussion of the authenticity of the Wilmington Tablet, or as it is sometimes called, the Richardson Tablet, because it was taken from the same mound as another tablet, the Welsh Tablet, which for obvious reasons was regarded as a fraud. The Richardson Tablet has long been under grave suspicion, and for some time a reproduction of this tablet has been displayed in the National Museum in a case marked "Frauds". Recently discovered finds of unquestioned authenticity, depicting similar motifs, have tended to diminish the suspicion formerly attached to the Richardson Tablet. This Meigs County Tablet, because it is similar to the Richardson Tablet in general design, may come under the same cloud of suspicion as to its authenticity. In this connection it may be remarked that the footform of the raptorial bird as depicted is very similar to that presented on the Florence* Mound human skull gorget found by Ohio State Museum in 1938. Under such circumstances it is doubly a matter of regret that the record of the provenience of the Meigs County Tablet is not more exact. Another en-

Figure 1. Meigs County Tablet. Courtesy of the Museum of the American Indian, Heye Foundation, Cat. No. 19/2732.

* Webb, Wm. S., 1940, p. 126.

graved tablet was recently reported from Meigs County, Ohio, by Ellis*.

(144) Engraved in relief, one side.

Nine such tablets have so far been found. All are mound finds, most are known to have been found in grave associations. Some are undoubtedly of Adena origin. All are so similar that, lacking evidence to the contrary, reason would ascribe to all of them the same origin, in Adena. Of the eight known engraved tablets, seven are stone, and one is very hard clay.

(145) One side of tablet grooved.

Of the nine known engraved tablets three are grooved and one has a circular depression on the reverse side. This seems to suggest their kinship to the unengraved tablets which are often found grooved on one side in a very similar way. Such tablets are usually worked from fine grained sandstone, and these grooves appear to be the result of their use as whetstones for producing bone awls.

(146) Tablets engraved on both sides.

This trait occurs in two tablets. In one, the Grave Creek tablet, the figures which are geometrical, are different. While in the Berlin tablet, the same figure is duplicated rather exactly in bilateral symmetry, relative to the two faces.

(147) Zoomorphic figure, duplicated on same plane.

This trait is shown by four tablets. It has been suggested that this duplication is an attempt of the primitive artist to represent both sides of the object. The figures represented are highly conventionalized.

(148) Engraving bilaterally symmetric about a median line.

This trait occurs in five of the eight tablets. This symmetry is not absolutely perfect, but apparently the artist strove for it. In a former comparison of the well known Adena tablets this author** called attention to many similarities of these tablets with the copper eagle breastplates of Ohio Hopewell. These breastplates possess bilateral symmetry, and some of them are symmetric about two independent axes.

Recently Quimby† called attention to birch bark cut-out patterns used by certain Northern Algonkian groups as reported by Speck††, to obtain symmetry of design in decoration on birch-bark containers. Quimby suggests that Hopewell of Ohio could have used birch bark or other thin material capable of being folded, to produce the symmetry of design found in Hopewell artifacts of mica and

---

* Ellis, H. Holmes, 1944, p. 449.
** Webb, Wm. S., 1940, p. 124.
† Quimby, Geo. I., Jr., 1943, p. 630.
†† Speck, Frank G., 1937, p. 68.

copper. While absolute proof of the use of birch bark cut-out designs by Hopewell probably cannot be proven, Quimby infers such use because of the very considerable similarity observable between Algonkian and Hopewell design. By the same token it might now be suggested that Adena may have obtained symmetry of design as shown on certain engraved tablets by the use of folded cut-out patterns of birch bark or other like material. Thus symmetry in design and similarity in motif may point not only to a close connection between Adena and Hopewell but also to a connection between Hopewell and Northern Algonkian groups.

(149) Head and beak of raptorial bird.

Three of these engraved tablets show this highly conventionalized bird head. It seems very significant that this figure should be so very similar to that represented on Hopewell copper gorgets from the Mound City group, (see page 125, Vol. V). The same figure is reported by Morgan engraved on a circular gorget cut from a human skull found in the Florence Mound (see page 126, Vol. V). Moorehead* reports this same figure engraved on bone from Hopewell Mound 25. Also Shetrone** reports, from Burial 11, Mound 25, a copper head dress representing this form, of which he says:

> "At the top of the skull lay an elaborate head dress, with large oval copper wings on either side. This birdlike head dress has been assembled on a saucer-shaped wooden base, parts of which were fairly well preserved. Along the margins of the wings lay in place small designs cut from mica which evidently had been fastened to them for ornamentation. The remains of a bonnet-like appendage of woven fabric indicated the original form of the complete head dress and to this fabric had been sewed large pearl beads, bear's claws, bird feathers, and the head of a small raptorial, presumably a hawk."

(150) Joints in zoomorphic form represented by dots or circles.

This trait is shown in four of the tablets.

(151) Claws of bird represented.

This trait is shown in four tablets and is also well represented on the gorget made from a human skull reported from the Florence Mound. A conventionalized design of claw carved on a human femur was reported by Moorehead*** from Burial 281, Mound 25 of the Hopewell Group. From the same mound, Burial 47, Shetrone reported two specimens in cut mica representing the claws of a bird.

(152) Five digits in foot forms.

Four tablets show this similarity. This trait was pointed out by Willoughby**** in his comparison of the highly conventionalized designs of Hopewell copper gorgets.

---

* Moorehead, Warren K., 1922, p. 162.
** Shetrone, H. C., 1926, p. 290.
*** Moorehead, Warren K., 1922, Plate LXXXII.
**** Putnam, F. W. and Willoughby, C. C., 1896, pp. 302-323, Vol. XLIV.

(153) **Representation of the serpent motif.**

This interpretation which was suggested by Willoughby* may be seen in two tablets, the Cincinnati tablet discussed by him and the Gaitskill stone tablet which is much less conventionalized. The serpent seems to have had some symbolic significance in Adena as well as in Hopewell. One of the best illustrations of this motif in Ohio Hopewell is the mica image from the Turner** Mound. It should be kept in mind that this image was that of a "horned" or "plumed" serpent with rattles. This concept in Hopewell may well have come to Hopewell from Adena.

Griffin*** has recently called attention to the report of Putnam****, on the excavation in 1887, of a village site and a mound south of and in the immediate vicinity of the Great Serpent Mound in Ross County, Ohio. Griffin recently inspected potsherds, and other artifacts, now in the Peabody Museum of Harvard University, taken by Putnam from his mound. He concludes that the pottery taken from the mound and from the lower level of the village site is Adena pottery, and that the artifacts and form of burials can be associated with the Adena-Hopewell complex.

An inspection of the artifact illustrations presented in Putnam's report show that most of them are identical with Adena forms, and particularly one illustration on p. 888, described by Putnam as an "ornament cut from crystal of galena, found in grave". This object is clearly a boat-shaped weight, flat on one side with double conical drillings. It seems to be identical in form with artifacts reported from Adena mounds***** in Kentucky regarded as atlatl weights.

(154) **Human facial mask (death motif?).**

This is rare in Adena, and best shown in the engraved stone tablet from the Gaitskill Mound†. The trait is also to be found in Hopewell of Ohio as shown by Moorehead‡. This trait may also be illustrated in Hopewell by the sculptured head found with Burial No. 36 of the Seip Mound No. 1 and recently described by Morgan††.

(155) **Hand-eye design.**

So far this trait is quite rare in Adena, but it has been found. The engraved clay tablet taken from the base of the Gaitskill Mound‡‡ demonstrates that Adena did use this symbol although it is found infrequently.

---

* Putnam, F. W. and Willoughby, C. C., 1896, pp. 302-323.
** Willoughby, Charles C., 1922, p. 69.
*** Griffin, James B., 1943, p. 56.
**** Putnam, Frederick W., 1890, p. 871.
***** Webb, Wm. S., 1943, pp. 649 and 655.
† Webb, Wm. S., 1940, p. 122.
‡ Moorehead, Warren K., 1922, Fig. 21.
†† Morgan, Richard G., 1941, p. 384.
‡‡ Webb, Wm. S., 1940, p. 123, Fig. 67.

(156) Rows of notches at base of tablet.

This seems to be merely an embellishment having no known significance, yet five of the tablets show this similarity.

BONE AND ANTLER TRAITS

(157) Awls, cannon bone or scapula of elk (Wapiti).

From the original Adena Mound eleven awls made from elk scapula were taken. Mound 53 yielded 50 awls made from the cannon bone of elk. These last were perhaps similar to the awls used at Seip Mound No. 1, to peg down the fabric canopy. If Mound 53 is finally to be regarded as an Illinois Hopewell site then elk cannon bone awls may be a Hopewell trait, while elk scapula awls are properly ascribed to Adena.

(158) Awls, scapula of deer.

From the original Adena mound some 12 awls of this type were obtained. They have not been specifically reported from other early excavations, but again some of the undesignated bone awls may be of this type. They have been found in two Kentucky sites.

(159) Awls, bone or antler. G(18).

Doubtless Adena people made great use of bone as awls, since it is shown that they carved animal jaws, made circular gorgets out of human skulls, and produced very efficient bone combs. However, awls seem to have been placed with the dead very infrequently, and like any other bone artifact, its life is limited in any village midden. The total awls of bone or antler reported by Greenman is only 80 specimens from 9 mounds. Two of these mounds, Nos. 1 and 53, each had a special type of awl and between them had a total of 73 leaving only 16 awls in the seven other mounds. Many of these were bone splinters, but it has been shown in recent excavations that the ulna of deer and black bear were often used to make awls. Certain types of bone awls are so distinctive that their use has been separately designed as special traits Nos. 157 and 158. Trait 159 includes ulna awls and all other forms not included in these special traits.

(160) Beads, bone. G(26).

Only four mounds in Greenman's list of 70 mounds show this trait. It has been found only once in Kentucky. In Mound No. 9, with a cremated burial were found bone cylindrical beads much burned when the body was cremated. Only eight remained in such condition that they could be identified.

(161) Combs, bone. G(C).

This trait was not listed by Greenman in table "A" since it occurred in only one mound, the original Adena Mound. It has now been found in three other mounds in Kentucky. These combs are well made, deeply carved from sections of very heavy animal bone.

To obtain greater breadth, two bone sections were very exactly fitted together edge to edge and parallel. They seem to have been bound together in this position (see page 224, Vol. III, these reports). The purpose of these bone combs is not certain. The study of certain textiles may indicate that bear's wool was spun into thread. It has been suggested that these combs may have been carding tools used in the preparation of textiles. Combs have been found partially burned in the fires of cremations. This may indicate they were used as hair ornaments, or objects of personal adornment.

(162) **Flaking tools, antler or bone.** G(27).

Many of these have been found in recent excavations. Those of antler have been usually reduced to a heavy spatulate form, both ends bluntly rounded. These have been found burned, broken and mingled with cremated human remains.

(163) **Teeth, animal.** G(19).

The incisors of rodents may have been used as graving tools. Bear canines may represent the remains of a bearjaw gorget. Teeth of animals have been found recently in three sites.

(164) **Claws, animal.** G(28).

Three sites yielded 17 occurrences in Greenman's list. No new occurrences have been found.

(165) **Projectile points, Antler.** G(32).

This is definitely an Adena trait—but not one of great frequency of occurrence, probably because such specimens were very poorly preserved in village midden.

(166) **Spatula, metapodal bone of elk. (Wapiti).** G(46).

This is definitely an Adena trait, but rare. Two sites in Kentucky have yielded five specimens. See illustration, page 224, Fig. 12-A, Vol. III, these reports.

(167) **Spatula, flat bone sections.**

Nine specimens have been found in three sites. Large bones were split longitudinally and one section worked down to a flat, blunt blade.

(168) **Animal jaws, worked.** G(C).

Definitely an Adena trait but of rare occurrence. See illustration page 66, Fig. 42-C, Vol. V.

(169) **Cut Antler sections.**

This trait is fairly frequent in Adena villages. Sections of antler some three inches long seem to have been used as drifts. The rounded ends show battering as if they were interposed in percussion between the hammer and the object struck.

(170) **Gorget, from human skull.** G(B).

One was found in the Westenhaver Mound, Greenman's No. 12. Site No. 2 has produced one, and an engraved gorget from a human skull has recently been found in the Florence Mound, Ohio. Through courtesy of Ohio State Museum this gorget is illustrated in Figure 69, page 126, Vol. V. Moorehead* also reports from a mound in Ross County, Ohio, (Greenman's No. 11) the finding of a human calvarium worked into the form of a cup.

(171) **Handles, bone or Antler.** G(39).

Four sites have recently yielded specimens. There is reason to suspect that some antler handles may have served on atlatls. (See discussion of Trait No. 111). For illustrations see Fig. 31-F, p. 441, and Fig. 7-2-F, p. 314, Vol. V.

(172) **Spoons, carapace of terrapin.**

Three Kentucky sites have produced six specimens. (See illustration, page 224, Fig. 12-D, Vol. III). These carapace spoons have also been found in many rock shelters of eastern Kentucky. See Fig. 24, p. 268, and Fig. 45, p. 291, Vol. I. When so found they are in association with other artifacts regarded as of Adena origin.

SHELL TRAITS

(173) **Shell Spoons.** G(C).

These are cut from a bivalve shell. They are some three inches long and about 1.5 inches wide. The general form is subrectangular, with corners much rounded. The spoon retains the natural curvature of the shell, and often shows much wear (see Fig. 42-F, page 66, Volume V). They are not numerous but have been found in three sites in Kentucky. (See illustration, page 224, Fig. 12, K-N, Vol. V.)

(174) **Hoes, shell.** G(C).

These have been reported from four of the list of 70 Adena mounds. No new occurrences have been noted. They are made from a bivalve shell by cutting a large hole through it for insertion of a handle and were probably used in scraping up the earth with which the mound was constructed. (See Fig. 9, page 12, Adena Report**.)

(175) **Beads, shell, circular disk.** G(6-12).

This is the type of shell bead most frequently found in Adena burials. Greenman expressed the belief that they were made from marine conch shells, probably Busycon perversum. They are in size from .25 of an inch to an inch in diameter.

(176) **Beads, Marginella.** G(23).

Five mounds of the list of 70 showed this trait. Three mounds in Kentucky have produced this type of bead.

---

* Moorehead, W. K., 1892, p. 179.
** Mills, Wm. C., 1907, p. 12.

(177) **Pearl beads.** G(31).

Pearl beads in Adena are always rare. Only two mounds of the original list of 70 possessed them. Pearls have been found in only one site in Kentucky in very small numbers. They were undrilled, but were in burial association.

(178) **Cylindrical shell beads.** G(B).

These have been mentioned by Greenman as found in Mounds 35 and 39 of his list. These are evidently made from the columellas of very large marine gastropods. They vary in length from half an inch to an inch or more and may be half an inch in diameter. The description of bead types by the early explorer was not exact, and in many cases the type found cannot certainly be known. Enough have been found to demonstrate that Adena used marine shell forms for bead manufacture, and that the columella of large gastropoda were cut and worked down into cylindrical beads. If they were not so completely worked down, a portion of the spiral whorl of the columella still showed on the beads. One site in Kentucky produced 44 beads from columella, 21 of which still showed the large spiral groove of the columella, and 23 were worked down to cylinders. Some of the large beads of the original Adena mound appear to have been made in this way.

COPPER TRAITS

(179) **Bracelets, copper.** G(4).

This is a very distinctive Adena trait, of high frequency of occurrence. Seven mounds in Kentucky have yielded 72 copper bracelets. The bracelet, usually a nearly circular rod bent into an elliptical form with its free ends nearly touching, is made of a single nugget of native copper. This nugget usually was hammered into a thin sheet which is folded once across the center, and starting with this folded straight edge, the folded sheet is rolled up into as tight a cylindrical roll as is possible by hand rolling. This cylinder is then bent to form a bracelet of sufficient size to permit putting the hand through it. They are usually found on a fore arm of the skeleton, often several together, and frequently a skeleton will have copper bracelets on both fore arms. Many textile specimens are found preserved because of the proximity of copper bracelets.

(180) **Rings, copper.** G(29).

Copper finger rings are made after the technique of bracelets, the rolled cylinder being made of very thin sheets. The cylinder is then bent about a finger forming one, two, or even three spiral loops about the finger.

(181) **Beads, rolled sheet of copper.** G(35).

Sheet copper was rolled into hollow cylinders, and cut into cylindrical beads of lengths varying from .25 inch to 1.5 inches. They are usually strung on strings about the neck. Frequently the string is preserved by the copper salts.

(182) **Beads, drilled copper nuggets.**

These are nearly spherical beads of a few millimeters diameter, drilled with a small hole. Such beads were sometimes strung and the string wrapped about the forearms. At least that is the position in which they are found on the skeleton. A string of such beads thus served as a bracelet.

(183) **Pins, long, copper.**

These pins are about 3 inches in length; they are cylindrical, about an eighth of an inch in diameter, one end being pointed. They are so far quite rare in Adena.

(184) **Crescents, copper.** G(C).

Greenman reports a copper crescent from Mound 38 of his list. Another has been reported from Kentucky (see page 69, Vol. V). This one seems to have been beaten quite thin and cut into a crescent form quite similar to the sheet mica crescent, and seems to suggest possible imitation of a feather plume, one end being possibly attached to the head and the other left free. However, they may have been suspended as gorgets, or breast ornaments. Of the specimens from Mound 38, Thomas* says:

> "On the under jaw was a crescent-shaped piece of copper
> . . . . and about the head the remains of some textile fabric."

(185) **Pendants, copper strips.**

These copper strips about three inches long and about half an inch wide, are perforated at one end for suspension. Such pendants have been found at the waist of a skeleton, suggesting suspension from a belt about the waist. (See Fig. 31, page 440, Vol. V).

(186) **Gorgets, copper.** G(42).

This trait as described by Greenman occurred nine times in five mounds of his list. These gorgets are mostly thin sheets of copper of near rectangular shape. Five of them from Mound 18 were found about the wrist of a skeleton, which suggests that while they may have been pendants they were not gorgets in the true sense. Recently the Riley Site Be 15, Kentucky, has yielded one copper gorget, taken from under the chin of the skeleton.

(187) **Reel shaped copper gorgets.** G(B).

Only one such gorget was reported by Greenman from his list of 70 mounds. It was found on the breast of a skeleton in Mound 59, the Great Smith Mound of West Virginia. Greenman describes it as an "H" shaped gorget. Now that three copper reels have been found

---

* Thomas, Cyrus, 1894, p. 445.

in Kentucky, and Adena has been shown to have this trait which seems to have had further development in Hopewell of Ohio, and Copena in Alabama, (see page 192, Vol. V), the importance of this trait is apparent.

A copper reel was reported by Thomas* from the Crall Mound at Monongahela, Pa., (Greenman's No. 56). He describes this artifact in the following way:

"The copper gorget was rectangular in form, 3 x 4¼ inches in size, with incurved sides, and had two holes on the longer axis. It had been doubled over along this axis until the opposite sides were in contact and then hammered down flat."

This surely represents an Adena reel which had been intentionally mutilated before deposit as a burial offering. The evidence shows that a mound had been built on the floor of a standing house and the house burned—all over a central pit which contained burials.

(188) **Celts, Copper.** G(B).

Copper celts are rare in Adena. Greenman reports a single copper celt from the Ulrich Mound (G 32). The Fisher Mound, Unit C, Fa 1, Kentucky has yielded two copper celts. Copper celts were scarce in Adena seemingly because the supply of copper was generally restricted, and quite insufficient to permit manufacture of artifacts of utility. In the few sites where copper celts are found, in Adena, it would seem to indicate that such sites are quite late in the history of Adena. In early Adena celts were made entirely of stone. It would seem that when copper became available, the copper celt largely replaced the stone celt.

MICA TRAITS

(189) **Mica, fragments of designs.** G(14).

It is most unfortunate that sheet mica crumbles so easily that designs cut from it so often lose their form and appear as merely a mass of cut fragments. This has been reported from 13 mounds of Greenman's list of 70, which produced some 200 fragments. Some 15 fragments have been found in four mounds in Kentucky. The trait would suggest that Adena had begun to cut and use designs from sheet mica, but they were not very well preserved when placed with the dead, where they must in some cases be subjected to the fires of cremation, or possibly to disturbance incident to the falling of the roof of a log tomb.

(190) **Crescent.** G(C).

Only a single mica crescent was reported from the original list of 70 mounds. This specimen came from Mound No. 1—the original Adena mound. Five specimens have now been found from three

---

* Thomas, Cyrus, 1894, p. 495

other mounds in Kentucky. As is the original specimen, these sheets of mica are cut in crescentic shape, and sections were overlapped to obtain greater length. These sections were sewed together, probably by a textile thread, the sections being perforated for that purpose. The sections are usually found in disorder about the head of the skeletons, but by observing the perforations and by bringing holes in apposition, it has been possible to restore these crescents, see Fig. 45, page 70, Vol. V. They are similar in general form and size to the copper crescents. They may have been used as plumes like "feathers" in a headdress, where one end of the crescent is attached to a head band and the other end is free. However, they may have been suspended about the neck as gorgets.

POTTERY TRAITS

(191) **Adena Plain.**
For a description of this type, see page 75, Vol. V; also Griffin, 1942.

(192) **Limestone tempered check stamp.**
Mentioned on page 81, Vol. V.

(193) **Sand tempered plain.**
Mentioned on pages 81 and 669, Vol. V.

(194) **Sand tempered check stamp.**
Mentioned on page 81, Vol. V.

(195) **Montgomery Incised.**
See Figure 2. For a description of this type see page 264, Vol. V; other references are pages 80-81, 345-48, Vol. V.

(196) **Grit tempered 5-line diamond.**
Found only at Mound Camp, Site No. 48.

(197) **Johnson Plain.**
For a description of this type, see pages 341-42, Vol. V.

(198) **Levissa Cord Marked.**
For a description of this type, see pages 343, Vol. V.

(199) **Paintsville Simple Stamped.**
For a description of this type, see page 344, Vol. V.

(200) **Fayette Thick.**
For a description of this type, see pages 667-69, Vol. V.

(201) **Woodland Plain, Adena variety.**
For a discussion of this trait see page 223 of this report.

(202) **Woodland Cord Marked.**
For a discussion of this ware see page 222 of this report.

(203) **Grit tempered check stamp.**
Briefly mentioned on page 346, Vol. V.

(204) **Grit tempered fabric marked.**
Briefly mentioned on page 346, Vol. V.

(205) **Pottery vessels not used as mortuary offerings.**
This is a negative trait and as such may be criticized. However, in view of the abundance of pottery which is evident on Adena villages, and the very considerable amount incorporated in mounds erected on village sites, which was the usual procedure, it is little short of remarkable that the absence of pottery in burial associations should be so universal. This is in strong contrast with the customs of other peoples of the southeastern United States. On this basis the trait seems valid. In the very few recorded instances where nearly whole vessels have been found in mounds in questionable association with burials, it appears that in every case the vessels may have been part of the house furniture, and the burial was made on the house floor. The vessels seem to have been left in the vicinity of the burial and to have been broken by the falling house when it was burned as in the case of Morgan Stone Mound, see page 232, Vol. V.

The only instance known of a pottery vessel reported as found in the vicinity of a burial, is that of "a broken earthen jar" found by Mills* in the Adena mound, "near the head of a skeleton". This jar was not photographed, and no further description was ever published. At present its location is unknown. It is barely possible that this find represents only a large sherd found near a burial, and like other sherds, would indicate only a chance inclusion in the mound, since village midden was often scraped up and used in mound construction. If so, such accidental association would be in accordance with the results of the investigation of other Adena sites.

TEXTILE TRAITS

(206) **Plain plaiting, basket or checker weave.**
Weft movement over-one and under-one warp strand. Weft, two-ply, clockwise twisted. Warp, two-ply, clockwise twisted. (See pages 269 and 280, Vol. V.)

(207) **Twilled plaiting, rectangular mesh.**
Weft movement over-two and under-one warp strand. Weft, two-ply, clockwise twisted. Warp, two-ply, clockwise twisted. (See pages 270 and 280, Vol. V.)

(208) **Twilled plaiting, oblique mesh.**
Over-two, under-one, technique; warp and weft elements at oblique angle (about 55°) with each other instead of at right angle. (See page 275, Vol. V.)

---

* Mills, Wm. D., 1902, p. 458.

Fig. 2. Restored vessel. Montgomery Incised. Maximum dimension of restoration—height 37 cm, diameter at shoulder 24.5 cm. See Trait 195.

(209) Multiple-ply braid plaiting.

Twilled movement over-two, under-two, each successive element advanced by one stitch, elements make angles of about 60°, width 72 cords counted in straight line from edge to edge. (See page 187, Vol. V.)

(210) Plain twining.

Weft strands twisted on each other to enclose single warp strand. (See pages 269, 270, 280, Vol. V.) Also, plain twining with widely spaced wefts and a very loosely twisted or **braided,** three-ply, counter-clockwise twisted warp.

(211) Twilled twining.

Weft strands twisted on each other to enclose two warp strands, each successive weft element advanced by one stitch. Proximity of warps prevent their zig-zag movement. (See pages 270, 271, and 280 Vol. V.) Weft, two-ply, clockwise twisted. Warp, two-ply, clockwise twisted.

(212) Diamond twilled twining.

Alternate pairs of weft strands alternate in splitting pairs of warp strands.

1. With moderately coarse warp and weft elements evenly spaced. (See pages 273, 274, 275, 280, Vol. V.)
2. With very fine warp and weft elements evenly spaced. (See pages 276, 280, Vol. V.)
3. Relatively widely spaced, pliable, warps. (See pages 273 and 280, Vol. V.)
4. In general, both weft and warp are two-ply, clockwise twisted, but single-ply warp also. (See pages 273, and 280, Vol. V.)

(213) Chevron twining.

Plain twining, save that alternate pairs of weft strands are twisted about each other, in opposite directions. Weft, two-ply, clockwise twisted. Warp two-ply clockwise twisted. (See pages 271, 280, Vol. V.)

(214) Lattice (bird cage) twining.

It has three elements instead of the usual two. Two passive, one active. (See page 188, Vol. V.)

(215) Ropes.

Three-ply, wound around fabric to prevent loosening of fabrics from body. (See page 272, Vol. V.)

PHYSICAL CHARACTERISTICS

(216) Physical type.

The Adena burial skeletons indicate a group with an average calculated stature of 5 feet 6 inches for males; 5 feet 2½ inches for females; broad shoulders, long forearms and lower legs, and occipitally flattened round heads. Approximately 89% (31 of 35) of the adult males, 92% (22 of 24) of the adult females are brachycephalic. Only one male and one female skull has a cranial index below 75.

This physical type is very different from the earlier, slighter, undeformed dolichocephalic riparian Shell Heap people. It is equally significant that the later Hopewell people of Ohio with their characteristic, long, narrow skulls with roof-shaped sloping sides, their long angular faces and larger body size. (See section on **Adena Skeletons** (page 251).

(217) **Head deformation.**

Occipital. Approximately 92% of all Adena skulls of both sexes (89% all males, 95% all females) are flattened at the back to a medium or pronounced degree, the deformation plane nearly vertical in the erect head. (See Plates 6, 7, and 8.)

(218) **Head deformation.**

Bifrontal. Nearly one-third (32%) of all Adena skulls of both sexes (37% males, 27% females) all ages have flattened areas on each side of the forehead alone and to the outside of the frontal bases. This combination of deformation, bifrontal-occipital, is probably caused by, possibly unintentionally, the use of the cradleboard in infant care.

It is remarkable that the same type of deformation is found characteristic of 26% of the Ohio Hopewell skulls, notwithstanding the effect of this trait, they appear quite distinctive. (See section on deformation, page 257).

List of Adena Mounds

In order to simplify the tabulation of data relative to the Adena Mounds in Greenman's List and the Supplemental List, it has been found convenient to designate by number the publication in which each site is reported; and to indicate in the list the volume and page in that publication where the report on that site may be found. There follows a list of publications with the numbers designating each. Thus, for example, in the tabulation data on Adena mounds, in the columns designated "Original Report" or "Other Reference" the notation 5,XXI–210 would indicate that the report of the site was to be found on page 210 of Volume XXI of the Ohio Archaeological and Historical Society Quarterly.

LIST OF PUBLICATIONS AND THE NUMBERED DESIGNATION OF EACH AS USED IN THE LISTS OF ADENA MOUNDS

1. Ancient Monuments of the Mississippi Valley, Squier and Davis
2. Archaeological History of Ohio, Fowke
3. Primitive Man in Ohio, Moorehead
4. Certain Mounds and Village Sites, Mills
5. Ohio Archaeological and Historical Society Quarterly
6. Unpublished Notes, W. C. Mills, Ohio State Museum
7. The Mound Builders, MacLean
8. Forty-fourth Annual report of the Bureau of American Ethnology, Fowke
9. Twelfth Annual Report of the Bureau of American Ethnology, Thomas
10. The Monterama Mounds, Missouri Historical Society Collections, Volume II, Number 5.
11. Report of Field Work, Moorehead, Ohio Archaeological and Historical Society Quarterly
12. Recent Mound Explorations in Ohio, Academy of Science of Philadelphia, Fowke and Moorehead.
13. Journal of the Cincinnati Society of Natural History
14. Mounds in Pike County, Ohio, American Archaeologist, Columbus
15. Ohio State Journal, March 27, 1930
16. Unpublished Data, M. A. Hontine, with Ohio State Museum
17. American Pioneer
18. Cincinnati Enquirer, October 9, 1927
19. Records of the Past, Volume VI, Chara K. Baylis
20. The Lee Mound, H. R. McPherson
21. The Ambos Mound, W. K. Moorehead, Third Annual Report of the Ohio State Academy of Science
22. Unpublished Data, Ohio State Museum
23. The American Journal of Science and Arts, Volume XLII, O. C. Marsh
24. Western Reserve Historical Society Transactions, Volume III, Archaeology of Ohio, M. C. Read
25. Smithsonian Institution Report, 1866, I. Dille
26. Fifth Annual Report of the Bureau of American Ethnology, Thomas
27. History of Perry County, C. L. Martzoff, Columbus, Ohio
28. Annual Report, Peabody Museum, Volume II, E. B. Andrews
29. Annual Report, Peabody Museum, Volume III, F. W. Putnam
30. Indiana History Bulletin VII, F. M. Setzler
31. Smithsonian Institution Report, 1882, G. W. Homsher

32. Bulletin Number 8, Bureau of American Ethnology, Thomas

33. Smithsonian Institution Report, 1879, F. Jackman

34. Proceedings of the Indiana Academy of Science, 1910, F. W. Gottlieb

35. Indiana History Bulletin IX, F. M. Setzler

36. Mound Builders, H. C. Shetrone

37. Records of the Past, Volume IV, David I. Bushnell

38. Museum Journal, Volume XXI, University of Pennsylvania, Charles Bache and Linton Satterthwaite, Jr.

39. Blueprint, Kiefer Mound, J. A. Raynor, Ohio State Museum

40. Proceedings of the Academy of Natural Science of Philadelphia, 1895, Fowke

41. The American Antiquarian and Oriental Journal, Chicago

42. Indiana History Bulletin, Volume XIII, Number 7

43. Century Magazine, Volume XXXIX

44. Unpublished data, American Museum of Natural History, New York City

45. Republican Gazette, Lima, Ohio, June 27, 1893

ADENA MOUNDS AS LISTED BY GREENMAN (1932)

Mound Number	Diameter in Feet	Height in Feet	Burials	Location	Mound Name or Number by Observer	Reported by	Original Report	Other References
				OHIO				
1	141	26	33	1.5 Mi. N. W Chillicothe, Ross County	Adena	Mills	5, X–452	4, I–5 10, I–131
2	90	22	1	6 Mi. S. Chillicothe, Ross County		Squier & Davis	1, –162	2, –359 7, –52
3	80	15	1	1 Mi. N. Chillicothe, Ross County		Squier & Davis	1, –164	2, –354
4	40	5	1+	3.5 Mi. N. Chillicothe, Ross County		Squier & Davis	1, –156	2, –353
5	225	35	1	Chillicothe, Ross County		Moorehead	11, VII–126	
6	200	25	1	Chillicothe, Ross County		Moorehead	11, VII–132	
7	50	8	15	On East Side of Scioto River 3 Mi. East, Chillicothe, Ross County	Md. No. 36	Moorehead	3, –148	
8	70	6	2	3 Mi. East Chillicothe, Ross County	Md. No. 39	Moorehead	3, –155	2, –348
9		13	5	Near Slate Mills, 4 Mi. W. Chillicothe, Ross County	Md. No. 45	Moorehead	3, –158	
10	65	20	1	N.W. Edge of City, Chillicothe, Ross County	Md. No. 40	Moorehead	3, –162	2, –354 1, –171
11			9+	N.W. Edge of City, Chillicothe, Ross County	Md. No. 43	Moorehead	3, –168	2, –355 1, –171
12	90	16	15	W. Bank of Scioto River, 6 Mi. S.W. Circleville, Pickaway County	Westenhaver	Mills	5(26)–227	4, (II)–245
13	200	34	1	On Deer Creek, 2 Mi. S.W. Yellow Bud, Ross County	Metzger	Moorehead	12, –314	
14	60	11	6	Concord Tn., 3.5 Mi. S.W. Frankfort, Ross County	Md. No. 17	Moorehead	3, –131	

ADENA MOUNDS AS LISTED BY GREENMAN (1932)—Continued

Mound Number	Diameter in Feet	Height in Feet	Burials	Location	Mound Name or Number by Observer	Reported by	Original Report	Other References
15	115	33	3	Deerfield Tn., Ross County	Deercreek	Dun	13, VII-194	
16	88	18	8	Paxton Tn., Ross County	Overly	Mills	6,	2, -362
17	80	13	5	PeePee Tn., N. Edge of Town, Waverly, Pike County	Pike No. 1	Fowke	14, I-62	8, -509
18	75	10	11	Mouth of Beaver Creek, Newton Tn., 3 Mi. S. Piketon, Pike County	Van Meter	Fowke	12, 308	2, -376
19	130	18	3	3.5 Mi. S. Piketon, Pike County	Md. No. 12	Fowke	2, -377	
20	115	23	1	Salt Creek Tn. across County line near Adelphi, Hocking County	Salt Creek	Thomas	9, -446	2, -339
21	21	3.6	2	Lick Tn., Jackson County	Wernke	Mills	5, XXI-210	4, II-96
22	50	6	1+	Jefferson Tn., Jackson County		Richards	15, -1	
23	50	9	1+	New Market Tn., Highland County		Houline	16,	
24	110	23	1	7 Mi. of Wilmington, Clinton Co.	Md. No. 82	Moorehead	3, 110	
25	30	25		3 Mi. S.W. Wilmington, Clinton County	Md. No. 77	Moorehead	3, -107	2, 380
26	75	27	2	Cincinnati Md., Hamilton County	Cincinnati		17, -195	2, -383 7, -105 1, -274
27	200	45	6+	Anderson Tn., Hamilton County		Brilmayer	18, -4	
28	50	6	8+	Ross Tn., Butler County		MacLean	7, -192	

ADENA MOUNDS AS LISTED BY GREENMAN (1932)—Continued

Mound Number	Diameter in Feet	Height in Feet	Burials	Location	Mound Name or Number by Observer	Reported by	Original Report	Other References
29	40			Jackson Tn., 2.5 Mi. W. Farmersville, Montgomery County	Ulrich 1	T. B. Mills	5(28)-162	4III-153
30	40		1	Jackson Tn., 2.5 Mi. W. Farmersville, Montgomery County	Ulrich 2	T. B. Mills	5(28)-162	4III-153
31	40		2	N.W. Porton German Tn., Montgomery County	Ulrich 3	T. B. Mills	5(28)-162	4III-153
32	45×83	15	8	Jackson Tn., 1.3 Mi. S.W., Farmersville, Montgomery County	Fortney	T. B. Mills	5(28)-162	4III-153
33	45×65	4	3	Monroe Tn., Preble County	Lee	McPherson	20	
34	75	45	12	Jefferson Tn., Preble County	Ambos	Moorehead	21, -7	
35	90	8	27	Near Greenlawn Bridge, Columbus, Franklin County			22	
36				Columbus, Franklin County			22	
37				Near Alum Creek, Columbus, Franklin County				
38	80	11	1	In Cemetery at Mt. Vernon, Knox County		Thomas	9, -444	2, -329
39	80	10	14	2.5 Mi. S.W., Newark, Licking County	Taylor	Marsh	23, -1	24, -90 2, -333
40			1	Licking Tn., Licking County		Dille	25, -360	7, -53 11, V-173
41	120	27	1	Hopewell Tn., Perry County		Moorehead	11, VII-138	26, -46
42	80	10	1	Green Tn., Hocking County		Andrews	28, -68	27, -45 2, -339
43	132–158	30	1	The Plains Athens Tn., Athens County	Coon	Greenman	5, (XLI)-366	28, -57

ADENA MOUNDS AS LISTED BY GREENMAN (1932)—Continued

Mound Number	Diameter in Feet	Height in Feet	Burials	Location	Mound Name or Number by Observer	Reported by	Original Report	Other References
44	85	18	2	Athens Tn., Dover, Athens County	Woodruff	Andrews	28, –71	2, –336 29, –105
45	40	6		Athens Tn., Athens County	Connett	Andrews	28, –62	9, –678 26, –47 1, –64
46	40	6		Athens Tn., Athens County	Md. No. 4	Andrews	28, 59	2, –336 2, –338
47	90	12	3	On Cat's Creek, Adams Tn., 1 Mi. above Lowell, Washington County		Moorehead	3, –26	
INDIANA								
48	83	12	3	Brookeville Tn., Franklin County	Mound Camp	Setzler	30, –467	
49	60	15	27	Franklin County	Glidwell	Homsher	31, –721	
50	40	7	1	Rush County	Kinsley	Jackman	33, –376	32, –50
51	150	7	3	Hanover Tn., Morristown, Shelby County		Gottlieb	34, –159	
52	100	8	1	Randolph County	Fudge	Setzler	35, –27	1, –93(2) 36, –248
ILLINOIS								
53	136	28	2	Montezuma, Pike County	McEvens	Bushnell	37, –202	9, –21 10,
WEST VIRGINIA								
54	72	13	1	Beech Bottom, Wellsburg, Brooke County		Bache and Satterthwaite	38, –133	
55	286	69	3	Moundsville, Marshall County	Grave Creek	Tomlinson	17, –196	2, –324 7, –91

ADENA MOUNDS AS LISTED BY GREENMAN (1932)—Continued

Mound Number	Diameter in Feet	Height in Feet	Burials	Location	Mound Name or Number by Observer	Reported by	Original Report	Other References
				PENNSYLVANIA				
56	60	9	8	Monongahela	Crall	Thomas	9, –495	
				WEST VIRGINIA				
57	173	33	14	Kanawha Valley, 3–8 Mi. below Charleston	Md. 1, Criel	Thomas	9, –415	26, –53
58	35	4	1	Charleston	Md. 11	Thomas	9, –418	26, –55
59	175	35	8	Charleston	Great Smith	Thomas	9, –425	26, –51 2, –328
60	100	15	2	Charleston	Md. 21	Thomas	9, –428	26, –56
61	100	25	7	Charleston	Md. 22	Thomas	9, –428	2, –329
62	95	8	1	Charleston	Md. 23	Thomas	9, –431	
63	84	6	2	Charleston	Md. 25	Thomas	9, –431	
64	95	21	4	Charleston	Md. 27	Thomas	9, –431	
65	100	25	1	Charleston	Md. 30	Thomas	9, –432	
66	50	6	7	Charleston	Md. 31	Thomas	9, –413	
67	20	7	1	Charleston	Len's Creek	Thomas	26, –55	9, –411
68	20	3		200 ft. from Md. 66 Charleston		Thomas	9, –413	
69	50	5	4	Charleston	Elk River	Thomas	26, –55	9, –412
				TENNESSEE				
70	28	5	9	Loudon	Md. 3 Bat Creek	Thomas	9, –392	

LIST OF SUPPLEMENTAL ADENA MOUNDS

Mound Number	Diameter in Feet	Height in Feet	Burials	Location	Report Reference	Author	Author's Mound Designation	Finds as Reported by Excavator. Which Now Seem to Point to Adena Origin. Parenthesis ( ) Indicates Present Interpretation
				OHIO				
91	45	7	14	Paint Creek, 2 M. S.W., Chillicothe, Ross County	1(62) 2(349)	Squier and Davis	Mound "E"	"Function Group", Associated "Sacred Circle", charcoal layer, extended burial. (Burial in fire basin on house floor. House was burned before mound erected.)
92	25			In the City, Chillicothe, Ross County	1(165)	Squier and Davis		On base of mound, layer of charcoal and ashes, partially cremated skeleton; charcoal **under** and **over** skeleton; **clay above** skeleton was burned; granite celt, thin strips of worked copper. (Here was a log tomb on house floor, covered by small mound. Tomb logs fired when house was burned.)
93	50	7	2	In edge of City, Chillicothe, Ross County	1(171) 3(165)	Moorehead	Mound 41	Log tomb, burial encased in bark. One of a group of four mounds. Greenman lists his Nos. 10 and 11 as Moorehead's Nos. 40, 43.

LIST OF SUPPLEMENTAL ADENA MOUNDS—Continued

Mound Number	Diameter in Feet	Height in Feet	Burials	Location	Report Reference	Author	Author's Mound Designation	Finds as Reported by Excavator, Which Now Seem to Point to Adena Origin. Parenthesis ( ) Indicates Present Interpretation
94		13		In edge of City, Chillicothe, Ross County	3(168)	Moorehead	Mound 42	One of four mounds, cremation deposited on house floor, covered by primary mound seven feet high. (House burned and mound erected over all.)
95	90	3	2	Waverly, Pike County	2(368)	Fowke	Mound 2	Two bodies on center of house floor, covered by primary mound. (House burned and mound built over all.)
96	100	10	1	Waverly, Pike County	2(370)	Fowke	Mound 3	Extended burial covered with bark, on ash bed in center of house floor, post-molds charcoal covered floor. (Burned house.)
97	80	35	3	Waverly, Pike County	2(371)	Fowke	Mound 4	Bodies extended, fire bed on floor at mound center. (Burial on house floor.)
98	65	16	6	Waverly, Pike County	2(372)	Fowke	Mound 5	Bodies extended, log and bark layer, copper beads with cremation on center of floor. Primary mound 8 feet high. (Cremated burial deposited on house floor.)

LIST OF SUPPLEMENTAL ADENA MOUNDS—Continued

Mound Number	Diameter in Feet	Height in Feet	Burials	Location	Report Reference	Author	Author's Mound Designation	Finds as Reported by Excavator, Which Now Seem to Point to Adena Origin. Parenthesis ( ) Indicates Present Interpretation
99			3	Waverly, Pike County	2(373)	Fowke	Mound 6	One extended burial, two deposited cremations; two copper rods, two gorgets, one shale, one banded slate.
100			2	Waverly, Pike County	2(373)	Fowke	Mound 7	Extended burial, in subfloor pit, under mound center; bear canines and molars ground, i.e. bear jaw gorget. (i.e. cut animal jaws.)
101			2	Piketon, Pike County	2(374)	Fowke	Mound 8	Deposit of cremated remains on house floor; two flint knives, two pipes, all burned; house burned. (Hence, charcoal layer over all. Mound erected on house site.)
102	80	3		On Scioto River near Jasper, Pike County	2(375)	Fowke	Mound 9	(Mound built over a burned house which had a few rocks on roof to hold on bark slabs. Probable cremation on house floor.)
103	80	3	2	Jasper, Pike County	2(375)	Fowke	Mound 10	Bones on layer of wood and ashes, covered by wood and bark, and by stones before mound was erected over them.

LIST OF SUPPLEMENTAL ADENA MOUNDS—Continued

Mound Number	Diameter in Feet	Height in Feet	Burials	Location	Report Reference	Author	Author's Mound Designation	Finds as Reported by Excavator. Which Now Seem to Point to Adena Origin. Parenthesis ( ) Indicates Present Interpretation
104	75	9	2	On line between Scioto and Pike Counties, Pike County	2(379) 40(512)	Fowke	Mound 13	Bodies extended on house floor; house burned and mound erected over all; mound showed stratigraphy, mica crescents.
105	25	2	1	Stonelick Township, Clermont County	3(60)	Moorehead	Mound 1	Extended burial, conical mound, granite celt, bone awl, layer of charcoal under stone pavement.
106	18	1.8		Lick Township, Jackson, Jackson County	4, II, (96) 5, XXI, (210)	Mills	Mound 3 Werneke	Small mound over deposited cremated remains with Adena artifacts on a house floor: 2nd Werneke is Greenman's Mound 21; Mills says they are Hopewell.
107	57	5	3	On Clarksville Pike, 2 M. NW, Wilmington, Clinton, County	3(109)	Moorehead	Mound 81	Skulls on charcoal layer, banded slate gorget; diorite celt, cremation partial.
108	50	8	5	Just North of Village, Marathon, Clermont County	3(63)	Moorehead	Mound 2	Layer of bark over clay burned area (house floor) under clay, postholes, suggest burned house; one cremation, burial of separate skull.

LIST OF SUPPLEMENTAL ADENA MOUNDS—Continued

Mound Number	Diameter in Feet	Height in Feet	Burials	Location	Report Reference	Author	Author's Mound Designation	Finds as Reported by Excavator. Which Now Seem to Point to Adena Origin. Parenthesis ( ) Indicates Present Interpretation
109	30	4	2	Wayne Township, Clermont County	3(67)	Moorehead	Mound 5	Conical mound inside sacred circle, extended burial covered by sheet mica.
110	70	7	3	1.5 M. North of Village, St. Martins, Brown County	3(68) 2(381)	Moorehead	Mound 6	Conical mound, communal deposit of cremated remains circular post-mold pattern under mound center; 25 feet in diameter. Holes 20 inches in diameter (ie. each had two posts in hole. Holes three feet apart. Burned clay layer was house floor. Extended body buried in house fire basin.)
111	55	7.5	3	E. side Scioto, 3 M. from Chillicothe, Ross County	3(146)	Moorehead	Mound 35	Extended burials, deposited cremations, copper and shell beads. (The primary mound which covered burials on house floor had its surface burned when house was burned. Primary mound 20 feet in diameter.)
112	50 X 95	13	2	On second terrace, Chillicothe, Ross County	3(151)	Moorehead	Mound 37	Mound 36 is Greenman's Mound 7. (Earth quarry near by, stratum of ashes seems to be house floor, extended burial, child on house floor.)

LIST OF SUPPLEMENTAL ADENA MOUNDS—Continued

Mound Number	Diameter in Feet	Height in Feet	Burials	Location	Report Reference	Author	Author's Mound Designation	Finds as Reported by Excavator, Which Now Seem to Point to Adena Origin. Parenthesis ( ) Indicates Present Interpretation
113	32	2.5	6	Cryder Farm, near Adelphi, Ross County	9(471)	Thomas		Five skeletons partially cremated in subfloor pit. One deposited cremation. Mound in center of circular ditch. Stone gorget, stone tube.
114	60	3	1	Seal Tn. 1 M. North, Wakefield, Pike County	40(515) 1(66)	Fowke		Mound associated with "sacred circle", body extended, mica fragments trimmed and perforated (crescents). Sandstone, slate gorgets.
115	36	5		Perry Tn., Vera Cruz, Brown County	10,XX, (551) 2(380)	Putnam	Schmitz Mound	(Appears to be erected over a burned house on floor of which was either a cremation or an Adena log tomb, burned.)
116	60	5		Perry Tn., Vera Cruz, Brown County	10,XX, (553) 2(381)	Putnam	McCafferty Mound	(Built over a burned house. postmolds, ash bed.)
117	60	6		Edwards farm, 2 M. from Reading, Hamilton County	10,XVI, (175) 2(384)	Putnam	Gould Mound	Conical mound inside "sacred circle". Mound surface covered with burned clay. (Primary mound erected on house floor before house was burned.)

LIST OF SUPPLEMENTAL ADENA MOUNDS—Continued

Mound Number	Diameter in Feet	Height in Feet	Burials	Location	Report Reference	Author	Author's Mound Designation	Finds as Reported by Excavator, Which Now Seem to Point to Adena Origin. Parenthesis ( ) Indicates Present Interpretation
118	114	30		Wolf Plain, Athens Tn., Athens County	28, II, (55)	Andrews	Beard Mound	Conical, partially excavated, showed loading and grass impression. Loads dipped toward center. (i.e. collapsed roof over subfloor pit.) Associated with many "sacred circles" on Wolf Plain.
119			2	Wolf Plain, Athens County	28, II, (62)	Andrews	Woodruff Connett No. 3	Skeleton extended, c o p p e r beads, ashes and burnt clay at base. Mound No. 4 of this group is Greenman's No. 45.
120	80	9	1	Wolf Plain, Athens, Athens County	28, II, (63)	Andrews	Zenner Meadow Mound No. 13	Associated with "sacred circle". Mound covered, deposited cremation with ashes, not in situ.
121	60	15		Wolf Plain, Athens, Athens County	28, II, (64)	Andrews	Zenner Large Mound	Group of three mounds with four "sacred circles". Ashes in quantity at floor level. Under mound center. Excavation discontinued after "cave in" due to earlier excavation which yielded pipes.

LIST OF SUPPLEMENTAL ADENA MOUNDS—Continued

Mound Number	Diameter in Feet	Height in Feet	Burials	Location	Report Reference	Author	Author's Mound Designation	Finds as Reported by Excavator, Which Now Seem to Point to Adena Origin. Parenthesis ( ) Indicates Present Interpretation
122		18		Wolf Plain Dover Tn., Athens, Athens County	28, II, (65)	Andrews	Mound 10 School House Mound	Top cut off to make site for school. Leather garment—three strings, copperbeads attached. Mound in group with "sacred circles".
123	40	8		East of Wolf Plain, Athens, Athens County	28, II, (67)	Andrews	Mound 28 Judge Jewett Mound	Charcoal and burned earth in mound. Cremated human bones at base in center.
124	52	7	1	Butler Tn., 10 M. E., Mt. Vernon, Knox County	9(441)	Thomas	Staats	Circular low stone wall at edge of mound. Conical heap of gravel at center of mound base, with lower human jaw. Covered by layer of ashes. All covered by clay layer.
125	45	4		Mt. Vernon, Knox County	9(443)	Thomas	Hammond	Base of mound covered with charcoal and ashes. Central core of surface soil covered by clay layer. Deposit of burned human bones and ashes. Greenman's Mound 38 at Mt. Vernon.
126	35	4	1	Howard Tn., 7 M. N.E, Mt. Vernon, Knox County	9(446)	Thomas	Shipley	Subfloor pit with extended burial.

LIST OF SUPPLEMENTAL ADENA MOUNDS—Continued

Mound Number	Diameter in Feet	Height in Feet	Burials	Location	Report Reference	Author	Author's Mound Designation	Finds as Reported by Excavator, Which Now Seem to Point to Adena Origin. Parenthesis ( ) Indicates Present Interpretation
127	135	12	15	Baum Works on Paint Creek, De Hart's Mills, Ross County	9(484)	Thomas	Pyramidal Mound	Erected over a burned house, circular post pattern, deposited cremations, extended burials in cedar log tombs.
128				About 1 M. E. of Hopewell Site, Union Tn., Ross County	22	Shetrone 1921	Anderson Mound	Tubular pipe, three stemmed flint points, two leaf-shaped flint blades, expanded bar gorget. Carapace of terrapin spoon.
129	12		17	At Piqua, Miami County	36(93)	Rayner	Kiefer	Twelve skeletons arranged in circle, head to center, about a circular fireplace 8 feet in diameter. Three of these skeletons had head detached and placed between femora. Five additional skeletons found. One copper celt, one unperforated slate gorget, ten circular sandstone discs, one with red ochre on it. One-half of engraved tablet. (Kiefer tablet.)
130				Lick Tn., Berlin, Jackson County	41, I, (73)	Sylvester		No burials. Engraved tablet (Berlin) which showed red ochre on it. With it another sandstone tablet grooved on both sides. Also a piece of graphite.

LIST OF SUPPLEMENTAL ADENA MOUNDS—Continued

Mound Number	Diameter in Feet	Height in Feet	Burials	Location	Report Reference	Author	Author's Mound Designation	Finds as Reported by Excavator, Which Now Seem to Point to Adena Origin. Parenthesis ( ) Indicates Present Interpretation
131			14	In Peepee Tn., 1.5 M. N. of Waverly in Pike County, between two forks of Crooked Creek	5, VII, (159)	Clarence Loveberry 1887	Hayes Burial Knob	Three galena boatstones with two holes each, two granite bar gorgets, body nearly cylindrical but flat on one side, with expanded ends, bone beads, three stone chisels.
132		7		New Market Tn., Highland County, Hillsboro quadrant	22	M. A. Honline 1896	Honline	Slate pendant, slate celt flared bit, ovate flint blade, fragments of mica crescent, tablet grooved on both sides.
133	50		2	S. of Omega Station in Tn. 6 N., R. 21 W., S.W. Qt., Sec. 4, Jackson Tn., Pike County, on second terrace	5, V, (219)	Moorehead 1896	J. W. Barger	Two copper beads, copper bracelet. One skeleton was "painted". Base of mound burned to brick color and hardness.
134				Near Loudonville in Sec. 27, Tn. 19 N., R. 15 W., Ashland County	5, V, (178)	Moorehead	Quick Mound II	Skeleton on house floor, potsherds in midden under floor.
135				North of Waverly; in Ross County, in S.E. Qt, Sec. 3, Tn. 6 N., R. 21 W.	5, V, (219)	Moorehead	J. C. Corwin Mound I	Moorehead reported a "cremated skeleton". Ohio State Museum has burned flint blades, notched with pointed base called "turkey tail", galena boatstone and drilled gorget.

LIST OF SUPPLEMENTAL ADENA MOUNDS—Continued

Mound Number	Diameter in Feet	Height in Feet	Burials	Location	Report Reference	Author	Author's Mound Designation	Finds as Reported by Excavator. Which Now Seem to Point to Adena Origin. Parenthesis ( ) Indicates Present Interpretation
136			1	About ¼ M. E. of Walhonding Tn. 6 N., R. 9 W., Coshocton County	5, V, (191)	Moorehead 1896	Workman	Sixty-eight blades in cache associated with traces of bone.
137			11	In S.E. Qt., Sec. 30, Tn. 10 N., R. 21 W., Madison Tn., Pickaway County	5, VII, (124)	Clarence Loveberry and Moorehead	Bauer	Eleven burials; some showed wood in grave. Fine-grained sandstone gorget.
138				Paxton Tn., close to (N.E. of) Seip Site, S.E. of Dills	22	Mills 1911	Overly	Six flint stemmed points, slate pendant, expanded bar gorget, shell beads.
139				Sec. 10, Tn. 6 N., R. 18 W., Jackson County in west bend of Fourmile Creek	5, VII, (163)	Clarence Loveberry	Burn's	Slate gorget with two perforations.
140				4 M. N. of Miamisburg in Jefferson Tn., Montgomery County	22	Ohio State Museum	Swope	Expanded bar gorget, slate handle of form of Adena, carved antler handle.
141				N.W. Qt. of S.W. Qt. Sec. 17, Tn. 5 N., R. 18 W., Jefferson Tn., 4 M. W. of Oak Hill, Jackson County	22	Steven H. Richards 1930	Davis	Copper bracelet, pitted hammer stone, four notched points, flint drill, seven mica fragments, worked, with perforations.

LIST OF SUPPLEMENTAL ADENA MOUNDS—Continued

Mound Number	Diameter in Feet	Height in Feet	Burials	Location	Report Reference	Author	Author's Mound Designation	Finds as Reported by Excavator. Which Now Seem to Point to Adena Origin. Parenthesis ( ) Indicates Present Interpretation
142				Jackson Tn. on W. side of Scioto River, N.E. of Fox, Pickaway County	22	Greenman	Wolford	Multiple cremation, three or more individuals. Village site in field near by, produced grit tempered potsherds, tubular pipe and five stemmed Adena points.
143	60	4.5	4	Jackson Tn., ¾ M. N.W. of Fox, Pickaway County	22	R. G. Morgan	Florence	Extended burials on bark, bark covered, Adena artifacts.
144	100	6	1	South Union Tn., Ross County	22	R. G. Morgan	Dunlap	Central log tomb and Adena artifacts.
145				Mound and village site, S. of, and in the immediate vicinity of Great Serpent Mound, Ross County	43(871)	F. W. Putnam	Serpent Mound, Village Site	Adena pottery and galena boat stones.
146				6 M. S. of Newark, Licking County	44	G. A. Dorsey 1895	Schwartz	Mound and village, Adena artifacts reported by Dr. J. B. Griffin.
147				6 M. S.E. of Newark, Licking County	44	G. A. Dorsey 1895	Orr	Mound and village, Adena artifacts reported by Dr. J. B. Griffin.

LIST OF SUPPLEMENTAL ADENA MOUNDS—Continued

Mound Number	Diameter in Feet	Height in Feet	Burials	Location	Report Reference	Author	Author's Mound Designation	Finds as Reported by Excavator, Which Now Seem to Point to Adena Origin. Parenthesis ( ) Indicates Present Interpretation
				INDIANA				
148	60 × 198	15	11	Sec. 16, Tn. 6 N., R. 1 W., Dearborn County	42(207)	Glenn A. Black	Nowlin	Log tombs, Adena artifacts.
149	80	6.5	8	In Whitewater Tn., 2.25 M. W. of the Ohio State line on the S. side of Syers Run, Franklin County		Frank M. Setzler	Whitehead	Quartz tempered pottery, fragments of slate gorgets expanded center, stone celts, log molds.
				WEST VIRGINIA				
150	30	3	1	3 M. below Charleston, Kanawha County	9(415)	Thomas	Mound 2	Mound inside "sacred circle". Human bones on hard baked floor.
151	25	3	2	3 M. below Charleston, Kanawha County	9(415)	Thomas	Mound 3	Base of mound "well baked by fire". Burial extended on mound base on ashes, coals, fire-boards. Mound near gateway of "sacred circle".
152	112	9		4.5 M. below Charleston, Kanawha County	9(418)	Thomas	Mound 8	Inside square enclosure of 20 acres. Human bones on center at base.

LIST OF SUPPLEMENTAL ADENA MOUNDS—Continued

Mound Number	Diameter in Feet	Height in Feet	Burials	Location	Report Reference	Author	Author's Mound Designation	Finds as Reported by Excavator. Which Now Seem to Point to Adena Origin. Parenthesis ( ) Indicates Present Interpretation
153	65	5		5 M. below Charleston, Kanawha County	9(423)	Thomas	Mound 15	Near enclosure, fire basin on floor contained ashes and charred bone.
154	30	2.5	1	5 M. below Charleston, Kanawha County	9(423)	Thomas	Mound 16	Near Mound 15. Banded slate gorget with burial.
155	20	1.5	1	5 M. below Charleston, Kanawha County	9(423)	Thomas	Mound 17	Burial at center of mound at base, near Mounds 15 and 16.
156	65	4.5		5.5 M. below Charleston, Kanawha County	9(424)	Thomas	Mound 18	Firebasin at center, bed of charcoal, ashes, skeleton, broken flint.
157	100	4	1	5.5 M. below Charleston, Kanawha County	9(431)	Thomas	Mound 24	Near Greenman's Mound No. 61, Thomas' No. 23. Burned bones on bed of charcoal and ashes on natural surface at center.
158	35	4	1	5.5 M. below Charleston, Kanawha County	9(431)	Thomas	Mound 26	Mass of charcoal, ashes, black earth and charred base.
159	40	4		5.5 M. below Charleston, Kanawha County	9(431)	Thomas	Mound 29	Charcoal and ashes near Mound 27 (Greenman's 63) and Mound 30 (Greenman's 64).

LIST OF SUPPLEMENTAL ADENA MOUNDS—Continued

Mound Number	Diameter in Feet	Height in Feet	Burials	Location	Report Reference	Author	Author's Mound Designation	Finds as Reported by Excavator. Which Now Seem to Point to Adena Origin. Parenthesis ( ) Indicates Present Interpretation
160	50	4	2	6 M. from Charleston, Kanawha County	9(432)	Thomas	Mound 32	Skeleton on mound base hematite celt and flint projectile point.
161	54	5	3	6 M. from Charleston, Kanawha County	9(433)	Thomas	Mound 34	Fire bed on mound floor, 3 charred human skeletons, artifacts burned.
162	34	3		6 M. from Charleston, Kanawha County	9(433)	Thomas	Mound 36	Skeleton on subfloor pit.
163	60	7		6 M. from Charleston, Kanawha County	9(433)	Thomas	Mound 37	Fire bed under mound at base. Charred human bones.
164	30	5	1	4 M. up Elk River, Charleston, Kanawha County	9(412)	Thomas		Skeleton at mound base extended, copper beads.
165	30	3		6 M. up Elk River, Charleston, Kanawha County	9(412)	Thomas		Group of small conical mounds. Layer of charcoal, ashes, bone fragments.
166	50	4	2	6 M. up Elk River, Charleston, Kanawha County	9(412)	Thomas		Two skeletons on charcoal, ashes on natural surface under mound.

LIST OF SUPPLEMENTAL ADENA MOUNDS—Continued

Mound Number	Diameter in Feet	Height in Feet	Burials	Location	Report Reference	Author	Author's Mound Designation	Finds as Reported by Excavator. Which Now Seem to Point to Adena Origin. Parenthesis ( ) Indicates Present Interpretation
167	60	7	2	South Side, below Kanawha River, Winfield, Putnam County	9(434)	Thomas		Earth baked by heavy fires. Left charcoal, ashes, calcined bone. At bottom, two decayed skeletons. Stone and hematite celts.
168	50	5		2 M. below Buffalo, Putnam County	9(435)	Thomas		Human bones beneath a layer of charcoal and ashes.
169	30	5		S. side of River, Putnam County Line, Mason County	9(435)	Thomas		Group of 5 mounds, fragments of pottery "composed of pounded stone and clay".
170	300	20	6	S. side Kanawha River, 5 M. above mouth, Mason County	9(436)	Thomas		Natural surface had been leveled up by clay. Then a bark floor was laid down and covered with a layer of ashes. Log vault 12 feet square contained six adult skeletons and some children, extended in ashes. Cast of log 6 to 14 inches in diameter. Vault covered by heavy cross timbers upon which a layer of heavy sand-stone rocks was laid.

LIST OF SUPPLEMENTAL ADENA MOUNDS—Continued

Mound Number	Diameter in Feet	Height Burials in Feet	Location	Report Reference	Author	Author's Mound Designation	Finds as Reported by Excavator. Which Now Seem to Point to Adena Origin. Parenthesis ( ) Indicates Present Interpretation
171	60	20	1 M. W., Barbourville, Cabell County	9(439)	Thomas	Mound 7	One of group of 10 mounds. Mound contained a small interior mound, a "core" 4 feet high, 20 feet in diameter. Under core were prostrate skeletons under a layer of charcoal, ashes.
			KENTUCKY				
172			½ M. E. of Taggart (Tygarts) Creek, Greenup County	45	Charles Wertz and M. Palmer	James King	Mound one of seven. Copper bracelets, beads, log tomb, mica, bone beads.
173			On Kentucky side of Ohio River near mouth of Scioto River, at South Portsmouth, Greenup County		University of Kentucky	Old Fort Earthworks	Adena artifacts. Report not yet published.

THE ARENA OF ADENA OCCUPATION

in the

OHIO RIVER BASIN

There is presented in Map 1, the location of 66 sites in the Ohio River Basin, classified by Greenman (1932) as Adena Sites. These sites are distributed by states as follows:

Ohio 45
West Virginia 15
Indiana 5
Pennsylvania 1

Two sites in Greenman's list of 70 mounds, Nos. 53 and 70 are not shown. Mound No. 53 is the McEvers Mound, Montezuma, Pike County, Illinois, by some now regarded as probably belonging to Illinois Hopewell, and Mound 70 is the Bat Creek Mound in London County, Tennessee, which because of the evidence available may be considered to fall within the historic period. Its connection with Adena is also doubtful. These two sites lying so far beyond the drainage area of the upper Ohio River, have, for the purpose of this study, been omitted. It now appears that Mound No. 4 of Greenman's list is identical with Mound No. 5 of the Hopewell Group and should thus be excluded from Adena classification. This error made by Greenman was a very natural one in view of the map shown by Squier and Davis* in Plate XIX. Their report on this mound showed a cremated burial with ten copper bracelets and sheet mica which, in the absence of any other information, might well have justified its classification as Adena. This seeming error illustrates what is sought to be emphasized in this study, that is, the very great similarity between Adena and Hopewell burial sites frequently found.

Further, it now appears that the Deer Creek Mound listed by Greenman as No. 15 is identical with his No. 13 the Metzger Mound. Again this very natural error, namely the failure to recognize these two descriptions as referring to the same mound, came about from the inadequacy of the reports concerning them. Mound No. 15, the Deer Creek Mound, was only partially explored

---

* Squier, E. G. and Davis, E. H., 1848, Plate XIX.

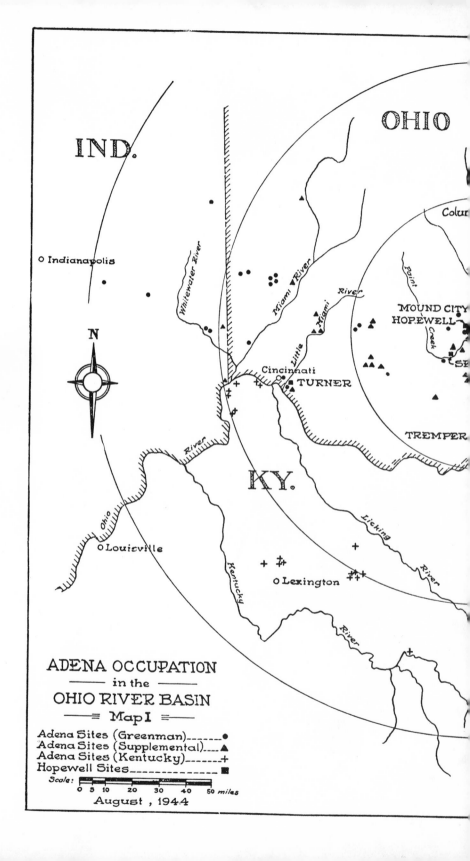

ADENA OCCUPATION
— in the —
OHIO RIVER BASIN
☰ Map I ☰

Adena Sites (Greenman)_____●
Adena Sites (Supplemental)___▲
Adena Sites (Kentucky)_____+
Hopewell Sites_____■

Scale:

| 0 | 5 | 10 | 20 | 30 | 40 | 50 | miles |

August, 1944

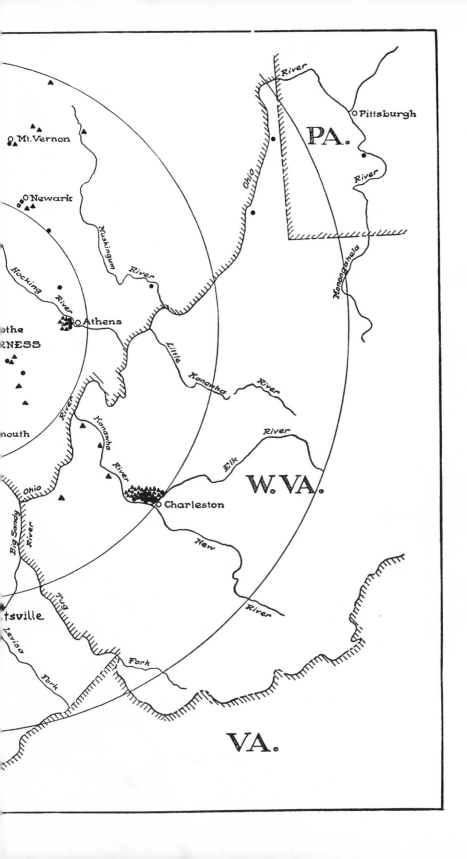

by Walter A. Dun† about 1884, and was reported in the Journal of the Cincinnati Society of Natural History. This same mound, under the designation "The Metzger Mound", Greenman's No. 13, was again explored by Moorehead‡ in August, 1894, ten years later. Although he noted evidence of a previous investigation, Moorehead did not mention the report by Dun published in 1884, of which he may have been aware. Since no connection between these two excavations was indicated, Greenman naturally assumed the Metzger Mound and the Deerfield Mound were separate sites. Such an error is easily understandable, and again illustrates what has been previously mentioned, namely, the very great difficulty in getting exact and complete information from the reports of early excavators which are scattered in inaccessible places. Thus, the 70 mounds listed by Greenman have been, for the purpose of this study, reduced to a total of 66 by the deletion of Numbers 4, 15, 53, and 70 for the reasons indicated.

A further comment on Greenman's listing may be of service to future students of Adena. In Greenman's "Analysis of Adena Culture" he lists under the designation of "Other Mounds" the Wilmington Mound excavated by Welch and Richardson about 1879, from which they removed the well known "Wilmington Engraved Tablet". By this listing of the Wilmington Mound under the caption "Other Mounds" one may infer that this mound was not classified by Greenman as an Adena Mound and hence not included by him in his list of 70 Adena sites. The facts seem to be that this mound, first explored in 1879 and again in 1890 by W. E. Myer of Cathage, Tenneseee, acting for W. K. Moorehead, was reported by Moorehead* as his Number 77. This mound is listed by Greenman as No. 25. Thus Greenman's Mound No. 25, correctly classified as Adena, seems to be the source of the Wilmington tablet, excavated about 1879.

To the 66 Adena Sites in the states of Ohio, West Virginia, Indiana, and Pennsylvania, shown on Map 1 by dots, there have been added 20 sites in Kentucky, numbered 71 to 90, inclusive, which have been recently excavated and classified as Adena. These are indicated by crosses. Thus the distribution of these 86 sites in five states, which have been previously classified as of Adena

† Dun, Walter A., 1884, pp. 194-203.
‡ Moorehead, Warren K., 1894, pp. 314-321.
* Moorehead, Warren K., 1892, p. 107.

origin, may be taken to indicate the known area of Adena occupation in the Ohio River Basin.

There is presented also in Map 1 the location of the six great Hopewell sites of Mound City, Hopewell, Seip, Harness, Turner, and Tremper. The first four of these are located in the general vicinity of Chillicothe, in which area there are to be found many geometrical earthworks, commonly regarded as of Hopewell origin. The sites of Tremper and Turner are about 50 and 75 air line miles, respectively, from Chillicothe. These sites thus designate the known Hopewell area of occupation in Southwestern Ohio.

With the city of Chillicothe as a center, three circles have been drawn with radii of 50, 100, and 150 miles, respectively. Of these 86 Adena Sites located on this map, only 19 sites lie outside of the circle of 100 miles radius, about the great Hopewell center. Of these 19 sites only one is more than 150 air line miles distance from Chillicothe. It will be noted that the distribution of these Adena sites within this area is fairly uniform, when one considers that only sites which have been proven by excavation to be Adena are indicated on the map. Any non-uniformity in distribution of these sites may thus, in part, be regarded as the result of the selection by invest'gators of sites for excavation. Certain it is that in Kentucky there are many mounds known to exist in the vacant areas shown in Map 1, which have offered some evidence of Adena origin, but which cannot be so classified without excavation. An inspection of Map 1 must impress the reader with the compactness of the Ohio Hopewell and the Adena areas, and with the fact that the smaller Ohio Hopewell area is almost exactly centered in the larger Adena area. If there be no fundamental connection between Ohio Hopewell and Adena, it is more than remarkable that the congestion of Hopewell earthworks along the Scioto River and its tributaries should occur so near the center of the area occupied by Adena.

It may be pertinent to remark that the Trempealeau† area in Wisconsin, the manifestation of which has been designated Basic Hopewell, thus suggesting that Ohio Hopewell may have been derived from it, is about 520 air line miles to the northwest of Chillicothe. The Marksville Site in south-central Louisiana, which

---

† McKern, W. C., 1931, p. 238.

has also been suggested* as a possible habitat of the early ancestors
of Ohio Hopewell, is about 760 air line miles to the southwest of
Chillicothe.

When Greenman, in 1932, selected his list of mounds as constituting the Adena manifestation, he was guided in his selection
by the 59 traits which he had shown to be characteristic of Adena.
With the present revised Adena trait list which includes more than
200 traits, as a basis, it is possible now with reason, to include other
sites in the Adena list, which Greenman did not feel justified in
accepting at the time his analysis was made. The broadening of
the trait list, the acceptance of cremation as an important Adena
trait, the recognition of house burning by Adena, and the proof
that the builders of Adena Mounds also built earthworks, and circular enclosures, permits one to justify the acceptance of many
sites, previously investigated, for which some of these new traits
have been previously reported. Many mounds investigated by early
excavators in the Ohio Valley were only partially excavated. From
some of these mounds only very meagre information is available,
yet there are many cases where the evidence points strongly to
Adena origin. There are also some mounds which have been excavated since 1932 which show abundant evidence of Adena origin.
Thus, some 83 additional mounds have been listed under the title
"Supplemental Adena Mounds", distributed as follows:

In Ohio	mounds numbered	91	to	147 inclu.,	total 57
In Indiana	mounds numbered	148	and	149	total 2
In West Virginia	mounds numbered	150	to	171 inclu.,	total 22
In Kentucky	mounds numbered	172	and	174	total 2

Total............ 83

On Map 1 these "Supplemental Mounds" are also shown.
They are indicated by small solid triangles. The addition of these
83 mounds, shown by triangles, to the 86 plotted as dots and
crosses on Map 1, does not change the position of the center of
distribution of Adena sites, or alter whatever significance it may
have in relation to the Ohio Hopewell area. It must be understood
that the admission of some of these sites to the Adena list is on very
meagre evidence and some students may not agree with this classification in all cases. It is possible that future excavations or
additional evidence may make a reclassification of some of these

* Ford, J. A. and Willey, Gordon R., 1941, p. 340.

sites desirable. The deletion of any such doubtful sites, however, from the Adena list would not weaken the argument or invalidate in any degree the significance of distribution of the remainder.

Whatever connection Hopewell of Ohio may have had with Adena, the fact remains that the six great excavated Ohio Hopewell sites, closely associated, in a compact area, lie about the center of a much greater area occupied by Adena, as shown by some 169 excavated sites each presenting, in view of the extended trait list, more or less positive evidence of Adena origin.

THE RELATION OF ADENA TO OTHER HOPEWELLIAN MANIFESTATIONS

The development of the list of cultural traits for Adena serves, within limits, to define this cultural complex. The detailed descriptions of these traits present as complete a picture of the habits, customs, and material possessions of these people as it seems possible to obtain at this time. However, such a definition of the Adena complex does not relate these people in time or space to the other peoples of their region or define the limits of their occupancy. The map showing their known spatial distribution which can report only sites already investigated, shows only an approximation of their habitat. The total area once occupied by the Adena people was doubtless much greater than that reported. It must be left to future investigation to determine how extensive was their domain.

The relation of Adena to other prehistoric peoples, particularly to Hopewell of Ohio, has long been a problem of major importance. It is believed that the solution of this problem might well have been much farther advanced, long ere this, had Adena been discovered first and thoroughly studied before Hopewell with its great wealth of material culture and its abundant evidence of high artistic development had so impressed the imagination, the language and the technique of all early investigators. However, as the result of accident or ill fate, Hopewell was discovered first. Its great material wealth and extensive use of cremations produced a profound effect on the imagination of the observers and on archaeological investigation. A new vocabulary including such terms as "altars", "sacrificial mounds", "sacred circles", "temples", "ceremonial" artifacts, etc., came into vogue. Archaeological field techniques were even so modified as to restrict them to the *excavation of Hopewell mounds only*. Other types of sites were regarded as "unproductive". Village sites were neglected; post-mold patterns were discovered but not investigated. Pits were dug into the center of mounds, or tunnels at base level were run into the center of a mound from one side, and if the mound failed to yield Hopewell artifacts in abundance it was often abandoned without any real attempt having been made to discover the reasons for its construction. Many ''non-Hopewell'' mounds in the Ohio River Valley have been thus partially destroyed in the past century by otherwise able scientists—always with the same explanation—namely, such mounds were ''unproductive''. Small wonder then that the advancement of understanding and the solution of this problem has been so slow. The science of archaeology owes much to Dr. William C. Mills of Ohio, who early advocated a complete and thorough investigation of every site attempted because of his conviction that only by such complete investigation could truth be obtained.

With the recent investigations in Kentucky there has come an understanding of the great importance of cremation in Adena. Other evidence which has been slow in accumulating, now points to a very close relationship between Adena and Hopewell. This evidence seems to force the conclusion that Hopewell material culture in Ohio is an outgrowth or local development of the Adena cultural manifestation with the later stages of which it was probably contemporary.

This is not a new idea. This concept in various form has often been expressed by other writers as a possibility, but the proof heretofore was usually considered as inconclusive. As has been suggested, Mills laid the basis for a satisfactory solution of this problem when he insisted on complete and thorough investigation of every site attempted. It is interesting to note his belief in a vital connection between Adena and Hopewell. Mills[*] excavated the Adena mound in 1901 and the Westenhaver[**] mound in 1915. Between those dates he had completed the Harness[***] mound in 1907 after it had been subjected to four previous partial explorations (Squier and Davis, 1846; Putnam, 1885; Moorehead, 1896; Mills, 1903) and he had also excavated the Seip[†] Mound No. 2 in 1909. Of course, he was familiar with the excavations for the Peabody Museum of the Turner[††] sites from 1882 to 1908, of Moorehead's[‡] work in the Hopewell group in 1891-92 and of the work of Squier and Davis[‡‡] in 1846 when they discovered the famous

---

[*] Mills, Wm. C., 1902, p. 5.
[**] Mills, Wm. C., 1917, p. 245.
[***] Mills, Wm. C., 1907, p. 5.
[†] Mills, Wm. C., 1909, p. 5.
[††] Willoughby, Charles C., 1922.
[‡] Moorehead, Warren K., 1922.
[‡‡] Squier, E. G., and Davis, E. H., 1848.

cache in Mound 8 of the Mound City Group. Mills was thus well able to understand the problem of a possible relationship of Adena and Hopewell. It is interesting to note that he classed the Adena mound and the Westenhaver mound (now known to be Adena) as Hopewell. In his conclusions on the Westenhaver excavation Mills* says:

"The examination of the Westenhaver mound shows that it belongs to the early Hopewell culture, and in many ways resembles the Adena mound, located near Chillicothe. These mounds represent an interesting and distinct stage in the development of the Hopewell culture, to which they undoubtedly belong, as evidenced by the possession and use of copper, the skillful carving of stone, and other characteristics of the highest of the several cultures of the Ohio aborigines. However, the use of copper, artistic stone carving and other marks of the typical Hopewell peoples are not so frequent as in the mounds representing the highest development of that culture, while on the other hand, evidences and influences attributable to the lower cultures are more abundant. While the use of the sacred fire ceremony appears to have held a prominent place with these intermediary peoples, as well as with their more advanced prototypes, they appear not to have reached the plane where cremation of the dead was practiced.

"With evidences of cultural advancement through any considerable period of time so obviously lacking, as regards the aboriginal inhabitants of the Ohio valley, it is perhaps gratifying to note that here, at least, in tracing the history of the Hopewell culture, we have at last something very definite. The evolution from a lower to a higher plane is exemplified in the Adena and Westenhaver stages, with such mounds as the Seip and Harness intermediate, and the Hopewell and Tremper mounds representing the highest development.

"Future explorations doubtless will more clearly demonstrate this cultural development and furnish examples of still other stages in the process."**

Here Mills followed the previous concept of all early investigators—namely that cremation was an evidence of *high* cultural development. He thus assigns Tremper mound to the highest cultural level attained by Hopewell. Recent investigation seems to present evidence pointing in exactly the opposite direction. That is, cremation was used by Adena—and thus probably by Hopewell,

* Mills, Wm. C., 1917, p. 284.
** Mills, William C., 1917, p. 284.

for disposal of the remains of the "common people", "the masses", and extended burial in the flesh seems to have been reserved for the selected few. High development of culture would therefore be measured by the skill and artistic achievement manifested in the artifacts found with inhumations, rather than by the practice of cremations. On such a basis Tremper can not be assigned to the top of the cultural ladder—but must be put at the foot of the ladder, the lowest cultural level of Ohio Hopewell, for reasons to be presented later.

It is plain that since Mills found no cremation in the Westenhaver mound and only two cremations in the Adena mound he concluded that these manifestations of "early Hopewell" "appear not to have reached the plane where cremation of the dead was practiced". If without considering cremations, he concluded that the Adena-Westenhaver manifestation was so much like Hopewell that he classified it as an early stage of Hopewell, he certainly would have found no reason to change his opinion, had he known, as is proven today, that Adena not only practiced cremation, but frequently used communal deposit of cremated remains as a form of disposal of the dead.

In discussing Adena in "Culture Problems in Ohio Archaeology", Shetrone* sees difficulty in establishing any close relationship of Adena with Hopewell because of "many fundamental differences between the traits of the two groups." He says in part:

"While the affinities of the Adena type of mounds are apparently strongly with the Hopewell culture, and their classification as such, in a marginal sense, doubtless is justifiable in a broad scheme of handling, there are many fundamental differences between the traits of the two groups. Aside from the use of copper and other material from distant sources, very few traits of the Adena type will be found to correspond in any degree to those of the Hopewell type. In the dearth of culture horizons, stratigraphic and other evolutionary evidences in the Ohio area, it would be gratifying to find that the Adena type of mounds represents an earlier phase of the Hopewell culture; but if this should prove to be the case, we must suppose a very considerable period of time necessary for the Adena people so completely to change their distinctive traits, and to evolve into the typical Hopewell culture variety. Evidences of long-continued habitation in the area, necessary

---

* Shetrone, H. C., 1920, p. 144.

to such a change, naturally would be expected to manifest themselves as examination of the tumuli proceeds. Aside from their apparent affinity with the Hopewell, the Adena mounds do not suggest relationship to any outside archaeological area or historic tribes.''*

This last sentence contains a profound truth which may not be neglected. The seeming necessity for a ''considerable period'' for Adena to develop into Hopewell will be discussed herein later.

The conclusions of Shetrone are quite logical if they are based on what he considered to be some seventeen ''distinctive Adena traits'' among which he listed the following:

(a) Mounds unaccompanied by earthworks.
(b) Absence of indications of prestructures of upright timbers.
(c) Sites of mounds unlevel and showing no evidence of previous use.
(d) Erection of mounds often begun by piling logs and brush upon sites or bases.
(e) Non-cremations of the dead.

It is to be noted that four of these are ''negative'' traits and as such are unsatisfactory expressions, and all five are in direct disagreement with recently acquired data. Under trait (a) above, it may be noted that Greenman listed six of his 70 mounds as having trait 41, ''mounds in an enclosure''. Further ''sacred circles'' have been proven to be of Adena origin,** and they are often associated with extensive earthworks. It is now known from recent excavations in Kentucky that the great earthwork on the Kentucky side of the Ohio River opposite Portsmouth, Ohio, is of Adena origin.*** Evidence for believing that many earthworks and so-called ''Sacred Enclosures'' with which they are associated are of Adena origin is presented in the new trait list.

As opposed to trait (b), several dozen circular post-mold patterns of paired posts have been found under Adena mounds which shows not only that there *were* ''*prestructures*'' of a *very definite pattern*, but also that in most sites the floors were (c) *very level*. Since Adena practiced house burning over the dead and the erection of mounds on such sites, logs and brush charcoal

---

* Shetrone, H. C., 1920, pp. 160 and 161.
** Webb, Wm. S., 1941, p. 167.
*** Report on this excavation has not yet appeared in print.

at a mound base (d) are now considered to represent the residue of a burned house, which was not swept away before the mound construction began. Cremation of the dead (e) is now demonstrated for Adena, and it is known to have been the chief means of disposal of the dead on some sites, even communal deposit of cremated remains being not unknown. Evidence of these traits is presented in the section "Description of Individual Traits".

In view of these very recently determined Adena traits, one feels justified in emphasizing the importance of the statement of Shetrone that "the *affinities* of the *Adena type of mounds* are apparently with the *Hopewell culture*"; and also the statement that "Aside from their apparent affinity with the Hopewell, the Adena mounds do not suggest relationship to any outside archaeological area or historic tribes", but at the same time depreciating the importance of the difference between the traits of the two groups. This difference, which now is small, seems to be decreasing with increasing knowledge as the result of continued exploration. Such differences as are still apparent seems now to be largely those of quantity, not of kind. These recent explorations in Kentucky were directed when opportunity offered toward Adena mounds, rather than to other types of sites because of the prophetic and stimulating statement of Shetrone* made in 1930 in "Mound Builders" when in speaking of Adena he said, "Far too little is known of the Adena type of mounds, and further exploration promises to enhance the importance of the culture". This is exactly what has happened. With increased information the importance of Adena has greatly increased.

Greenman** seems to have been the first to attempt to systematically arrange the evidence in support of an intimate relationship between Adena and Hopewell. While he did not commit himself positively to a chronological relationship only, he did discuss the evidence to be adduced pointing to an Adena—Hopewell chronological sequence. In his comparison of Adena and Hopewell he says,

> "But there is at least one element of Adena culture which is strongly suggestive of a developmental process with its end point in the Hopewell, namely, the relative size of

---

* Shetrone, H. C., 1930, p. 169.
** Greenman, E. F., 1932, p. 487.

the log tomb considered in connection with the proportions between cremation and inhumation. The average size of the log tomb in the Adena group is much greater than in Hopewell, and only nine per cent of Adena burials are cremated whereas in the Hopewell 77 per cent are cremated.''

Greenman sees possible further confirmation of the Adena-Hopewell sequence in the possible development of copper breastplates of Hopewell, from Adena stone gorgets; in the increase of the use of copper for ornamentation only in Adena to its wider use for ornamentation and utility in Hopewell. He suggests that the evidence of engraved tablets and even the development of pipes and other artifacts might support such a developmental sequence. Perhaps his most illuminating statement on this point is contained in his summary, when he wrote*,

"Finally, to a large extent, it is a different numerical predominance of the same or similar traits which constitutes the difference between Adena and Hopewell.''

This statement finds overwhelming justification in the evidence from recent excavations.

It is very interesting to note how Black**. after his excavation of the Nowlin Mound in Indiana, and long critical study of the Adena-Hopewell problem, reaches the same conclusions as Mills and Greenman but from entirely different data. In discussing the prehistory of Green County, Indiana, Black says:

"The traits exhibited by the mounds in Green County are most nearly paralleled by those of the Hopewell and Adena cultures. The two cultures have long been known to have many traits in common and it has been suspected that the Adena peoples formed some ethnic division or group of the Hopewell people. Greenman's splendid analysis of the Adena culture, covering as it does the states of Illinois, Indiana, Ohio, Pennsylvania, and West Virginia, leaves the material cultural pattern of these people very clearly defined. It also brings out, more than ever, the affinities of the two cultures. This similarity is more noticeable in the states of Illinois, Iowa, Wisconsin, and Indiana, where many of the traits, supposedly distinctive of the Adena culture, are found to be just as common in Hopewell mounds.''

---

* Greenman, E. F., 1932, p. 493.
**Black, Glenn A., 1933, pp. 318 and 327.

And as a further conclusion Black* says:

"It seems to the writer that outside of Ohio, where both the Hopewell and Adena Mounds are highly specialized, there are few, if any, definite distinguishing characteristics between the two cultures."

It should be remembered that this is the well considered opinion of a critical student who has had abundant opportunity to study these cultural manifestations both in the field and in the laboratory. It is plain that he has not allowed his judgment to be overwhelmed by the great material wealth of the Hopewell of Ohio, and has thus been able to see it otherwise as culturally very similar to Adena. This last quotation relative to the lack of distinguishing characteristics, outside of the Ohio area, is profoundly true. Its validity rests on a solid foundation, to be discussed later, after additional evidence from physical anthropology has been introduced.

---

* Black, Glenn A., 1933, pp. 318 and 327.

ELEMENTAL HOPEWELL

More than ten years ago (1931) McKern* showed that in Wisconsin there were to be found mounds yielding Hopewell-like artifacts and having burial customs which as he says "show striking similarities and as striking differences", with the Ohio Hopewell complex of traits. As a result of his studies based on the excavation of some fourteen mounds and campsites and other mounds not excavated, in Trempealeau County, Wisconsin, he concluded that this area showed a Hopewellian manifestation, somewhat less highly developed than Ohio Hopewell, which he designated as a "Wisconsin variant of the Hopewell Culture". This manifestation later came to be called "Elemental Hopewell" or, as suggested by him "Basic Hopewell", on the assumption that *there was a basic culture complex widely* spread (how widely no one fully knew) which was represented in the Wisconsin area by the Trempealeau County finds, and out of which presumptively Ohio Hopewell may have developed. Naturally this new "variant" of Hopewell would in time come to be compared also with Adena. This came about when Black** reported in 1936 on his excavations of the Nowlin Mound in Dearborn County, Indiana. In 1935 at Indianapolis the Committee on State Archaeological Surveys of the National Research Council had met to discuss a tentative classification of the Archaeological manifestations of Central North America in terms of the McKern taxonomic system. Black made his comparison of Adena (of which the Nowlin Mound was an example) with Hopewell, with the then new taxonomic system in mind when he said,

> "It has long been recognized by those familiar with the problems of this area that Adena and Hopewell have much in common. The analogies are especially marked between the foci composing the Adena aspect and those foci which make up the Elemental aspect of the Hopewellian phase. This writer feels that these analogies are so marked as to prevent, at times, the drawing of a definite line of distinction between the two, and that Adena warrants a place in the classification more closely affiliated with Hopewellian than is intimated by the set up tentatively established."

* McKern, W. C., 1931, p. 237.
** Black, Glenn A., 1936, p. 301.

While perhaps no one could seriously object to Black's concept of the problem and his expression of the facts as indicating a close relationship of Adena with Elemental Hopewell, the purpose of this paper is to show that there is now an even closer and more fundamental relationship of Adena (as now modified) with Ohio Hopewell than can be demonstrated for Elemental Hopewell of Wisconsin. Or stated bluntly, the thesis is that IF THERE BE AN ELEMENTAL OR BASIC HOPEWELLIAN MANIFESTATION ANYWHERE OUT OF WHICH OHIO HOPEWELL MIGHT HAVE GROWN, THEN AT LEAST ONE COMPONENT OF THAT BASIC MANIFESTATION IS ADENA.

Obviously this thesis contemplates in the term Adena, the original concept of the complex described by Greenman, as enlarged, modified, and defined by the trait list included herein. Until Adena had been thus modified and extended it is not surprising that McKern* saw little significance in such a comparison with Elemental Hopewell when he wrote,

> "A detailed comparison of the Trempealeau culture with the Ohio Adena culture, suggested by the extended burials in bark lined pits occurring in the mounds classified as Adena, shows little in common between the two, as opposed to a preponderance of insurmountable dissimilarities.

> "In summary, the Trempealeau Culture is typically Hopewellian in its artifacts, Hopewellian with certain marked omissions in its burial practices and decidedly unlike Hopewell in its structural mound features."

In this connection it may be remarked in passing that those *omissions in burial practices,* cremation and allied traits, *are precisely those* in which Hopewell is *similar* to Adena, and those structural mound features in which Trempealeau differs from Ohio Hopewell are *precisely those* in which Trempealeau is like Adena, (i. e., subfloor pits, earth embankments about pit mouth, bark-lined floors, pole and bark roof over pit, mound built over pit without filling pit with earth removed from it.)

This is not to deny a very close (and obvious) connection between Trempealeau and Ohio Hopewell, but to suggest that the material culture of Trempealeau may be a manifestation of late Hopewell rather than ancestral to Ohio Hopewell.

---

* McKern, W. C., 1931, p. 238.

In the comparison of any two archaeological manifestations obviously all traits of whatever kind should be considered insofar as they yield information on such fundamental problems as cultural unity, chronology, or distribution. However, one must admit that in such an evaluation, all traits are not of equal value. An investigator who seeks to be absolutely objective oftimes deceives himself by subjectively attaching to one trait or group of traits a greater importance than he does to others. Where one does subjectively color his thinking by such weighting in his relative evaluation of traits, in all honesty he should admit his bias and he should expect therefore the validity of his conclusions to stand or fall on the validity of such evaluations. In dealing with this broad problem of Hopewellian manifestations these authors have been forced to the conclusion that such relative weighting of traits is not only subjectively difficult to avoid, but is scientifically valid, and in many cases absolutely necessary to reach correct understanding of some archaeological problems. As an illustration, if two sites show the same detailed burial customs, but one has copper and the other does not, these authors would be inclined to attach greater importance to burial customs than to the possession of copper, because of the belief that burial customs are more deeply rooted in the customs of the people, are of long development, and change more slowly than traits derived from the possession of copper, which might conceivably be brought about by a sudden discovery of a convenient source of material, or by a contact with a distant people through a trade route, made more or less suddenly available to one group but not to the other. Much can doubtless be said in opposition to the concept of weighting of traits as a basis for drawing conclusions but this much can certainly be said in its favor: there is no known way of expressing an archaeological trait which will guarantee its statistical equality with another. The belief is expressed that some of our misconceptions of the Hopewellian problem arise from a too positive regard for the statistical equivalence of all traits.

Believing in the relatively great importance of burial traits as compared to artifact traits generally there is reproduced the "Table of comparative burial traits" used by McKern[*] to compare "Ohio Hopewell Culture" with Trempealeau Culture. The word-

[*] McKern, W. C., 1931, p. 237.

ing of the trait descriptions is, of course, not changed from the original; however, with certain slight modification it might be more illuminating. To this table another column has been added for Adena and following it, additional burial traits of Ohio Hopewell have been added. They are separated from the McKern list of traits by the double line. This table is certainly not complete, but it has not been further extended since the intent is to indicate that by comparing burial traits only, there is shown for Adena a closer relationship to Ohio Hopewell than it is possible to show for the "Trempealeau Culture", which has been designated Elemental or Basic Hopewell.

TABLE OF COMPARATIVE BURIAL TRAITS

Burial Peculiarities	Ohio Hopewell Culture	Trempealeau Culture	Adena Trait Complex
Burial Traits Listed by McKern			
Log molds associated with burials	×		×
Bark associated with burials	×	×	×
Rectilinear area for burials	×	×	×
Rectilinear subfloor pits for burials	×	×	×
Humus cleaned floors for burials	×	×	×
Bark covered burial floors	×	×	×
Extended-in-the-flesh burials	×	×	×
Flexed-in-the-flesh burials	× (rare)		× (rare)
Disarticulated bone burials	×	×	× (rare)
Cremation	×		×
Crematory or altar basins	×		×
Burial of fine artifacts with the dead	×	×	×
Compound flesh burials	×	×	×
Additional Burial Traits			
Redeposit of cremated remains	×		×
Communal deposit of cremated remains	×		×
Cremated remains, deposited in grave with extended burial	×		×
Use of puddled clay in graves associate..	×		×
Destruction (intentional) of fine artifacts	×		×
Burial of artifacts with cremated remains	×		×
Human skulls as trophies	×		×

Obviously in this very important group of traits centering about burial customs, Adena shows a much closer relation with Ohio Hopewell than does Trempealeau. However, the absolute value of the percentage correlations may mean little or nothing since the trait list must be considered to be incomplete and by slightly changing the statement of the traits, a different numerical result could be obtained. The purpose of such a comparison is to demonstrate that if the *burial customs* of Ohio Hopewell did evolve from some basic or lower level of culture, it would have been easier to have attained its high degree of specialization by starting with Adena than by starting with Elemental Hopewell of Wisconsin, since the changes necessary would have been much less.

WIDESPREAD HOPEWELLIAN MANIFESTATIONS

One evidence of the widespread influence of Ohio Hopewell in the south has been noted in Copena of Alabama. In 1934* as the result of excavation in the Wheeler Basin on the Tennessee River in Northern Alabama some seven mound sites were found to yield a complex of traits in which the use of copper and galena in the graves became conspicuous. It was possible from these seven sites to present a list of 36 traits with which each of these sites had a measurable correlation. This complex of traits was designated as Copena because of the COP(per-gal)ENA which so regularly occurred in most of the graves. Within this list of traits many were obviously similar to Ohio Hopewell. Of these 36 traits it was found that 32 of them had been observed in one or more of seven Hopewell sites. Those selected for comparison were the Hopewell, Turner, and Mound City Groups, the Tremper, Harness, and Hazlett Mounds, and the Seip Mounds 1 and 2. At that time an attempt was made to justify the consideration of Copena as a cultural complex, fairly homogeneous within the Valley of the Tennessee River in Northern Alabama and clearly separable from all other trait complexes in that region. Because Copena was related in some way to Ohio Hopewell, if only in a very subordinate position, the following statement was made:**

"By thus conceiving the Hopewell complex of traits as the result of a high development of an able people, who, over a long period of time, drew to themselves the best cultural and material wealth from a large area, and like any metropolis of modern times radiated a powerful influence on customs and techniques to all less-favored areas, one comes to understand that it is hardly to be expected that any other area in the United States is likely to be found showing a cultural complex comparable in wealth and variety with the Hopewell of Ohio. For this reason, the absence in the copper-galena complex of many important Hopewell traits is to be expected, and this fact as an aid in defining the copper-galena complex is not so significant. But the fact that some 32 of the 36 traits of the Alabama complex are found on Hopewell sites, and not in any other well-developed complex, by contrast, is very important."

---

* Webb, William S., 1939, p. 189.
** Webb, William S., 1939, p. 197.

Later in the excavation of Pickwick Basin* in Northern Alabama in 1936-38, five additional mounds and two village sites were found and assigned to Copena. These new sites enabled the former trait list to be revised and extended to include 45 mound traits and 45 village traits, of which 18 traits were held in common. That is, a total of 72 traits were recognized as belonging to Copena. Many of these traits, for example, copper reels, disarticulated skulls, extended burials, graves covered with logs and bark, red ochre in graves, and the intentional destruction of artifacts placed with the dead, occur in both Ohio Hopewell and Adena, while other traits like copper breastplates and copper ear spools, while relatively abundant in Hopewell, are found only very rarely in Adena. It is not the purpose of this paper to review the Copena complex here, but merely to call attention to this Hopewellian complex widely spread along the Tennessee River in Northern Alabama, and to point out that, as has been reported,** the copper reels found with Copena, Adena, and Hopewell seem to offer a suggestion of chronological relationship of these three related and yet separable trait complexes.

It may, in this connection, be added that the excavation of Guntersville Basin*** on the Tennessee River in Northern Alabama in 1938 still further increased the trait list of Copena by adding among other traits, the communal deposit of cremated remains, and the use of puddled-clay head and foot rests. The Copena complex of traits thus rests on a secure basis as a manifestation fairly homogeneous in itself, much like Adena, perhaps equally like Hopewell, yet showing very little to suggest the very high artistic development and elaborate cremation practices so characteristic of Ohio Hopewell.

It now appears well established that Hopewellian manifestations are to be found far beyond the limits of the Ohio Hopewell area. They are known to occur in Louisiana****, Arkansas, Mississippi†, Florida††, New York†††, Illinois‡, Missouri, Kansas‡‡, Mich-

---

* Webb, William S., and David L. DeJarnette, 1942, p. 301.
** Webb, William S., 1941, p. 192.
*** Manuscript yet unpublished.
**** Fowke, Gerard, 1928, p. 405; Setzler, F. M., 1933; and Ford, J. A., and Willey, Gordon, 1940.
† Moore, C. B., 1908.
†† Greenman, E. F., 1938, p. 327.
††† Ritchie, William A., 1938, p. 94.
‡ Cole, Fay-Cooper, and Deuel, Thorne, 1936, p. 18.
‡‡ Wedel, Waldo R., 1938, p. 99.

igan*, Minnesota**, Wisconsin†, and Tennessee††. As information increases, evidence of the further spread of this highly developed cultural complex will undoubtedly be found. The interpretation of these finds and the determination of their relative chronology are still largely unsolved problems. Whether the Hopewellian manifestation in these areas were culturally ancestral to, or descendants and beneficiaries of Ohio Hopewell, are still problems of the future, the solution of which will be advanced more rapidly and certainly by additional field exploration rather than by additional speculation. However, there are straws which show the direction of the wind. In attempting the solution of this baffling problem by establishing a relative chronology, it is considered wise to give considerable weight to physical anthropological data, to burial traits, and to mound, tomb, and house construction traits rather than to artifact traits chiefly.

Returning to the primary problem of this study, namely, the relation of Adena to Ohio Hopewell, it would be highly desirable to be able to compare complete trait lists of Ohio Hopewell, Trempealeau, and Copena, with Adena. This at present is very difficult to do. Hopewell, Trempealeau, and Copena are yet largely described as burial complexes. Relatively little is known of their dwelling houses or villages, their artifacts of utility, or the manner of life of the people. Certain it is that no trait list comparable in detail with that of Adena has yet been made available, although the list for Hopewell, in the report of Seip Mound No. 1 goes far in that direction. A completely satisfactory comparison is, therefore, impossible at this time. However, a comparison of partial trait lists, even though incomplete, still provides the best means of understanding relationships.

Such a trait list, can have only a limited significance by itself, but when traits begin to show a chronological relationship (see chapter on chronology) the comparative trait list begins to have much more significance. However, its most fruitful interpretation becomes available only after the physical anthropology of the peoples possessing these traits has been determined.

In the following trait list no attempt has been made to pre-

* Coffinberry, W. L., 1875, p. 293.
** Bennett, John, 1944, p. 336.
† McKern, W. C., 1931.
†† Putnam, F. W., 1882, p. 106.

sent a complete list of traits for Hopewell, Copena, and Trempealeau. Such information is at present not available. The list does present important traits in Adena which have also been found in these other Hopewellian manifestations. The few non-Adena traits which are presented have been included because they seem to be significant as indicators of Hopewell Chronology.

The relation of the Hopewellian Manifestations is discussed in the chapter on "Conclusions."

COMPARISON OF TRAITS OF FOUR HOPEWELLIAN MANIFESTATIONS

Adena Trait No.	Trait List — Occurrence Symbols — Trace *, Moderate †, Frequent ‡, Predominant **	Adena	Hopewell	Copena	Trempealeau
	Earthwork Traits				
1	Large earthworks associated with mounds	‡	**		
2	Circular enclosures associated with earthworks	‡	‡		
4	Circular enclosures have "gateways"	**	**		
6	Circular enclosures occur in groups of two to eight	**	**		
	Site in vicinity of large stream	**	**	**	**
7	Mounds conical	**	**	**	**
8	Mounds occur in groups	**	**	**	**
9	Mounds in or near circular enclosures	†	†		
10	Mounds within large earthworks	†	**		
11	Mounds built on their own village	**	**	**	*
12	Mound covers house floor	**	**		
	Evidence of house burning on mound base	‡	†		
13	Mounds show stratigraphy	‡	‡	*	
14	Primary mounds contain midden	**	†	†	*
15	Secondary sections made of sterile earth	**	‡	‡	‡
16	Earth quarries formed near mound	‡	†		
17	Village midden in situ under mound	**	†	†	
18	Mounds show individual earth loads	**	‡	†	‡
20	Fired areas at mound base	‡	‡	†	
22	Primary purpose to cover burials	**	**	**	**
24	Constructional use of stone	*	‡		
40	Mounds erected over subfloor pit	†	†	†	‡
42	Mounds cover post-mold patterns	**	‡		
58	Fire basins on house floor held pot sherds	†	†		
	Tomb Traits				
26	Rectangular tombs, of single horizontal logs	‡	‡		
27	Multiple horizontal log rectangle about body	‡	†		
25	Tomb floor covered with bark	**	‡	‡	†
30	Vertical tomb post in corners of horizontal log pattern	†	†		

COMPARISON OF TRAITS OF FOUR HOPEWELLIAN
MANIFESTATIONS—Continued

Adena Trait No.	Trait List — Occurrence Symbols Trace *, Moderate †, Frequent ‡, Predominant **	Adena	Hopewell	Copena	Trempealeau
33	Tomb has log supported earth roof	**	**	†	
34	Small vertical post molds at grave	‡	‡	†	
32	Log tomb burial on house floor	‡	‡	†	
37	Subfloor pits used for burial	‡	†	‡	**
38	Earth or stone embankment about pit mouth	‡	‡	†	**
39	Subfloor pit tomb closed by log roof	**		‡	‡
35	Head and foot rests, logs or clay	†		‡	
	House Construction Traits				
	Post-mold pattern encloses circular area	**	‡		
44	Single post set in individual hole	**	**		
	Post-mold pattern in spiral to form entrance	*	*		
	Cremation Traits				
62	Cremation in clay basins	‡	‡		
66	Cremated remains redeposited separately	‡	‡	‡	
70	Cremated remains redeposited with extended bu.	‡	‡		
72	Communal deposit of cremated remains	‡	‡	*	
73	Artifacts burned at cremation	†	‡	*	
74	Unburned artifacts deposited with cremated remains	‡	‡	‡	
75	Artifacts intentionally multilated when deposited	‡	‡	‡	
76	Cremated remains associated with red ochre	‡	†	†	
	Inhumation Traits				
78	Bodies extended in the flesh	‡	‡	‡	†
81	Multiple extended burials in same grave	‡	‡	*	‡
82	Important central graves, bodies extended	‡	‡	*	‡
83	Use of bark in graves	**	‡	‡	‡
84	Use of puddled clay in graves	‡	‡	‡	
85	Red ochre deposited on extended burials	†	‡	**	
91	Separate skulls in grave—trophy	*	†		
92	Burial of isolated heads	†	†	†	
94	Skeleton flexed	*	*	*	
96	Bundle burial, disarticulated bones	*	*	*	‡
	Burial of fine artifacts with extended burials	‡	**	‡	†
	Evidence of smothered fires in subfloor burial pits	†	*	†	
	Chipped Stone Traits				
98	Celts, chipped flint	†		*	
101	Leaf-shaped blades flint	**	‡	*	†
104	Stemmed projectile points flint	**	‡	‡	‡
106	Side notched projectile points flint	†	†		

COMPARISON OF TRAITS OF FOUR HOPEWELLIAN MANIFESTATIONS—Continued

Adena Trait No.	Trait List / Occurrence Symbols / Trace *, Moderate †, Frequent ‡, Predominant **	Adena	Hopewell	Copena	Trempealeau
107	Drills—reamers, flint	‡		*	
	Obsidian chips, and blades		**		†
125	Hoes, chipped stone slab, rectangular	‡		**	
	Ground Stone Traits				
111	Gorget, bar, expanded center	‡	‡		
112	Gorget, reel-shaped	‡	†	*	
117	Pipes, tubular, constricted mouth	‡			
119	Pipes, elbow, biconical	†		†	
	Pipes, biconical, large zoomorphic		†	†	
120	Pipes, platform, monitor	*	**	†	†
	Pipes, platform, zoomorphic		‡		
123	Celts, small rectanguloid	‡	†		
	Celts, circular section, large pointed pole		†	**	
130	Hemispheres, rubbing stones, cones	†	†		
133	Boat-shaped stones	‡	†		
	Tablets, rectangular	‡		*	
136	Galena-barite, artifacts and fragments	**	†	**	†
149	Head, beak, claw of bird incised on stone, bone, copper	‡	‡		
	Stone artifacts intentionally broken before deposit	†	**	‡	
	Hand eye design in clay or hand cut in mica or copper	*	†		
	Human facial mask or death motif	*	*		
	Bone and Antler Traits				
157	Awls, cannon bone, deer or elk	‡	‡	*	
158	Awls, scapula deer or elk	‡			
161	Combs, bone	†	†		
163	Teeth, small mannals, worked	‡	‡	†	
	Teeth, canine bear, cut, drilled, worked		‡		†
165	Projectile points, antler tip	‡		*	
168	Animal jaws, cut worked	†	†		†
170	Gorgets, human skull (parietal)	†	†		
172	Spoons or ornaments from carapace of terrapin	‡	†		
171	Handles, bone or antler	‡	†		
	Shell Traits				
175	Disk, beads	‡	†	‡	
177	Pearls, and pearls drilled	*	**	†	
178	Beads, tubular, large columella	‡	†		
	Containers, large marine shell, cut		**	**	

COMPARISON OF TRAITS OF FOUR HOPEWELLIAN
MANIFESTATIONS—Continued

Adena Trait No.	Trait List Occurrence Symbols Trace *, Moderate †, Frequent ‡, Predominant **	Adena	Hopewell	Copena	Trempealeau
	Copper Traits				
179	Bracelets	**	†	†	
180	Finger rings, spiral	‡			
181	Beads, cylindrical, rolled sheet	‡	‡	†	**
182	Beads, drilled, nuggets	†		†	
183	Pins, awls drills hairpins	*	‡	*	
184	Crescents, breast ornaments	*	‡		
186	Gorget or breast plates	*	**	‡	
187	Gorget, reel-shaped	‡	†	‡	
188	Celts	*	**	‡	‡
	Earspools	*	**	‡	†
	Conjoined tubes		†		*
	Beads, buttons, copper covered		‡		†
	Reels, copper intentionally mutilated	*	*	*	
	Mineral Traits				
189	Mica, art forms and designs	*	‡	*	
190	Mica, crescents	†	**		
	Silver covered buttons, ear ornaments, tubes		‡		†
	Meteoric iron, button covered, and fragments		†		
	Textile Traits				
206	Plain plaiting, basket or checker weave	‡	†	*	
207	Twilled plaiting, rectangular mesh	†	†		
209	Multiple-ply braid plaiting	*	*		
210	Plain twining close woven	†	†	†	
210	Plain twining open woven	†	†	†	
211	Twilled twining	*	**		
212	Diamond twilled, twining, relatively widely spaced pliable warps	†	†		
212	Diamond twilled twining, both weft and warp are two-ply, clockwise twisted	*	*		

EVIDENCE OF
GRADUAL DEVELOPMENT OF TRAITS IN HOPEWELL

Returning now to the statement of Shetrone* relative to the problem of the development of Hopewell material culture out of Adena, he states in "Culture problems in Ohio",

> "It would be gratifying to find that the Adena type of mounds represents an earlier phase of the Hopewell culture, but if this should prove to be the case, we must suppose a very considerable period of time necessary for the Adena people so completely to change their distinctive traits, and to evolve into the typical Hopewell Culture variety."

Today, it may be said, in view of recent discoveries, that this necessity for a considerable period of time for Adena to change their traits, seems largely to have vanished. This assumption has become less necessary because it is possible today to find in Adena the *beginnings* of *many* of the customs which in Hopewell blossomed into important and highly specialized traits. Since Adena already had them, these traits did not begin in Hopewell, and it was, thus, *not* "necessary for the Adena people so completely to change their distinctive traits", etc. This is well illustrated in the practice of cremation, the increased use of copper and mica, and in the development of artistic carving of stone and bone.

When Greenman discussed the possible evolution of Adena into Hopewell, he also presented evidence which he considered opposed this concept of more or less gradual transition. He** says:

> "Against this evidence is (1) the scarcity of definite stages in a developmental series, and (2) the great length of the intervals which separate the few that exist. In the Hopewell new forms are presented suddenly and fully developed, like (3) the earspool, (4) the clay platform underlying the log tombs, (5) the gravel-covered primary mound, (6) elaborate mica designs, (7) the use of obsidian, (8) the great variety of effigy and geometrical forms in copper, (9) the effigy platform tobacco pipes, (10) and the geometrical inclosure."

---

* Shetrone, H. C., 1920, pp. 160-161.
** Greenman, E. F., 1932, p. 491.

The numbers in parenthesis are no part of this quotation. They have been introduced here merely to facilitate reference in this discussion to these "objections". The rebuttal arguments are offered in this same order and similarly numbered.

(1) It is asserted that there is no scarcity of definite stages of this developmental series. The entire purpose of this paper is to present such stages in order. A systematic presentation of the evidence will be attempted later in this paper.

(2) As pointed out above, the discovery of many of the highly developed Hopewell traits, in an incipient form in Adena makes unnecessary the assumption of *long time intervals* between successive stages. It is believed that neither the earspool, nor any other Hopewell artifact ever "was presented suddenly and fully developed". Traits which illustrate this gradual development may well be chosen from those mentioned above by Greenman. In what follows the development of these selected traits is discussed following the same order.

While the earspool is regarded as a very "diagnostic" trait in Hopewell, after all it was except in very late Hopewell, actually relatively scarce in the total population. In the total summation of copper earspools from the six most important Hopewell sites (i.e., Hopewell Group, Turner Group, Mound City Group, Tremper Mound, Harness Mound, and Seip Group) there were only 378 earspools. Since these are usually found in pairs this represents only about 189 individuals, or about 19 per cent of the more than 974 estimated burials from these six important groups of Hopewell sites that had copper earspools. The point is, the vast majority of these Hopewell people, more than 80 per cent of the individuals, probably *did not* have copper earspools.

What is much more important, the distribution of copper earspools among Hopewell sites is *very nonuniform*, indicating a definite developmental trend. For example, in the Hopewell Group 85 burials produced 131 earspools or at the rate of 161 spools per 100 burials. In the Tremper Mound for an estimated 378 burials there were only eight earspools or about two spools per 100 burials. Tremper Mound (see chapter on chronology) is now regarded as the earliest of the six great Hopewell sites, one of the first to begin and the earliest abandoned, while the Hopewell site was one of the last sites to be discontinued. Further, of the eight copper earspools actually found at Tremper some were of a cruder form (one side being flat instead of concave). Here is evidence that the copper earspool did not appear suddenly but developed not only from a crude form at Tremper to a finished form at Hopewell, but in its use from two per 100 burials to 166 per 100 burials. Further, in Tremper where the copper spools were few and still crude in form there were to be found stone rings believed to be ear ornaments. With only two copper ear-spools per 100 burials at Tremper and an even less rate per 100 burials for stone-ring ear ornaments at Tremper, it is not unreasonable to suppose that some ornaments could have been made of wood or other perishable material, and with their decay the record of their existence lost. The copper earspool in Hopewell could well have developed as a substitute for stone rings or for some other perishable material, used in the same form, the substitution being made possible only after and because copper had become relatively abundant in Hopewell. At least one copper earspool has been found in a late Adena mound, namely the Metzger Mound, Greenman's No. 13. Incidentally, this mound shows in the profile diagram that a small primary mound was covered by a layer of ashes and charcoal, which definitely suggests a small primary mound built on the floor of a house to cover an ordinary Adena log tomb burial, after which the house was burned and a secondary mound erected over all. The investigator found the burned clay floor under the mound, but the pit and trench which he dug did not permit the finding of a house wall pattern. From this mass of evidence the site was clearly to be classed as Adena but because of the earspool, a Hopewell artifact, this mound is believed to be late Adena, probably contemporary with very early Hopewell, from which the earspool was obtained; and since copper earspools were then scarce, even in Hopewell, only one was found in this late Adena mound.

The suggestion that Adena had some kind of ear ornaments is not without foundation. The magnificent tubular pipe taken from the original Adena mound presents one of the very few human effigies which have been found in an Adena site. The delineation of this human figure certainly shows some form of elaborate circular or ring like ear ornament precisely like the stone rings found at Tremper. Since it must be considered that this figure very probably protrays actual conditions rather than the pure imagination of the maker, and since such ring ear ornaments have not been found in Adena, one might conclude that if they existed, they were made of wood or other perishable material. It may be pertinent to point out that in this figure, it appears that a large perforated plug had been thrust through the softer portion of the lower ear which was stretched into a loop to hold this plug of relatively large size. It may be significant that in Hopewell, by the use of copper ''cymbals'', the same enlarged, circular effect with depressed center, could be obtained but with only a relatively slight perforation of the lobe of the ear. This suggests that Adena, if it had no copper ear ornaments, possibly had their counterpart in some other material.

Terra-cotta figurines taken from the Turner[*] site show the human form, with ear plugs of considerable size and length thrust through the lobe of the ear. These clearly did not represent copper ''double cymbal'' ear ornaments (see a, Plate 21). All of this points to a long period of development of the copper earspool in Hopewell, and not to a sudden appearance. It seems to suggest that circular ear ornaments in early Adena were made of wood or other perishable material. In late Adena copper had begun to appear as at Metzger Mound. In early Hopewell (Tremper) stone rings were used, possibly as substitutes for some perishable forms, since only a few individuals had stone earrings. Also in early Ohio Hopewell (as at Tremper Mound), copper earspools of crude form began to be made in a form similar to that presented by the Adena pipe image. In late Hopewell, as at the Hopewell site, copper earspools became so common that some 78 per cent of the burials had such spools. But apparently the antique form of wooden plug, or other perishable material type, did not disappear entirely from Ohio Hopewell, if one regards the Turner site images as portraying customs in dress with factual accuracy. It is, of course, conceivable that these pottery figurines may not indicate an actual survival of these large cylindrical ear plugs, but they may have been a portrayal of their own antique but discarded customs, which early in Hopewell history they had adopted from Adena. In any case the argument is the same; they present evidence of a long developmental series.

---

[*] Willoughby, Charles C., 1922, Plate 21.

(4)   The clay platform underlying the log tomb of Hopewell is *not presented suddenly and fully developed.* It is found in Adena in all stages. The clay platform in its simplest form was, it is believed, a simple house floor on which burials were made. Usually, the floors were covered with bark. Later, when a body was to be put in a single log tomb, after burial the log tomb rectangle was often filled with puddled clay up to the level of the top of the crib logs. This seems to have led to sealing the body in puddled clay by first placing on the bark floor of a rectangular log tomb, a layer of puddled clay. The body was then placed on this clay layer and covered by another layer of puddled clay. It was thus easy to seal in the body completely. Thus the bottom clay layer constituted an elevated "clay platform". Sometimes when it was used in Adena, instead of adding the second puddled clay layer to cover the body, the body was covered with bark only, and the tomb sealed instead, by its log roof. The body thus lay on a raised clay platform, within a closed log tomb. In Mound Jo 2, Kentucky, this raised clay platform was obtained at the bottom of a sub-floor pit, for the burial of two bodies, by digging out the hard clay subsoil to the depth of approximately a foot, about the rectangular surface upon which these bodies were laid. It seems certain that the "burial platform", therefore, does not *"appear suddenly and as fully developed",* in Hopewell, but it seems to have come about from burials on the house floors in Adena, coupled with a desire to "seal the body in clay". Having developed the custom of using two layers of clay to "seal in" the body, the trait was later modified to use only one layer in cases where a log tomb had a log roof which completely closed the tomb. In this way, clay platforms developed in Adena. It should be noted *as very important* that in Hopewell sites, as for example Seip Mound No. 1, where Hopewell cremations were deposited on "clay platforms"—*in every case,* the clay platform was surrounded by a log rectangle and covered by a wooden roof precisely like a regulation Adena tomb. Of the Seip Mound, Shetrone and Greenman* say:

> "No platforms were without log-molds. The greater number showed evidence of but one horizontal log on each of its sides, but because of the ultimate collapse of log cribs around the

---

* Shetrone, H. C., and Greenman, E. F., 1931, p. 481.

platform it was often difficult to determine the original number of logs.''

In view of the known extensive use of puddled clay in Adena log tombs, and the continued use of log rectagles about clay burial platforms in Hopewell, the evidence presents a striking similarity in burial customs amounting almost to identity, and leaves no place for any "sudden appearance of clay platforms".

(5) The gravel covering of primary mounds, by Hopewell is hardly to be regarded as a unique trait. True, it does occur in Ohio Hopewell, but since the excavation of the Coon Mound by Greenman*, we have his very exact description of the intentional placement of the gravel dug from the bottom of the central pit tomb of an Adena mound. Here it was used as an elevated circular ridge to cover the clay thrown out from the central pit. It was not cast out in haphazard fashion, but as he says:

". . .was thrown out and carefully spread over the base into a symmetrically rounded wall whose crest was from 12 to 15 feet from the edge of the tomb. . . . The surface of the gravel circle was as smooth as the coarse material of which it was made would permit.''

If we may consider that the earth ring found about the subfloor pit of the Coon Mound really constituted the "primary structure", then here Adena did intentionally use gravel to cover the primary earth construction. The appearance of this trait in any event must depend on the location of the site and on the geology of the terrain. In Kentucky, mostly outside of the area of glaciation, there are no glacial gravel beds, and river gravel beds are not common. Adena here did not use gravel. There was none to be had. No case is known of the failure of Adena to use stone or gravel if it was easily obtainable at the site. In the small mound, Be 32—where stone was available—they did use it as a ring about the pit mouth.

(6) Elaborate mica designs were not "presented suddenly and fully developed" by Hopewell. The extensive use of mica and its cutting into pictorial and symbolic forms did reach a high state of perfection in late Hopewell. The high development of mica cutting seems in Hopewell to follow a similar development in cutting of beaten copper sheets. However, mica cutting had its

---

* Greenman, E. F., 1932, p. 387.

beginning in Adena, where, like copper, it was far less plentiful than in Hopewell. Thirteen of Greenman's 70 mounds had complete or fragments of cut mica designs. Adena has produced in Kentucky five occurrences of mica crescents, apparently portions of head or breast ornaments, and many mica fragments which appear to be disintegrated cut mica artifacts placed with the dead. One such was found in the original Adena Mound. In this same mound, a very good portrayal of a raccoon was found cut from shell, which shows that the cutting of zoomorphic forms had already begun, using such material as was available to them, and the art having begun, awaited only an adequate supply of suitable material such as mica or sheet copper to demonstrate the high native ability of the prehistoric artisan. This supply of suitable material such as mica or sheet copper became available when by trade and travel to far distant regions, new sources of material were discovered. Such discoveries may have come suddenly, and thus greatly accelerated such arts in middle to late Hopewell, but the point is, this art had its origin in Adena and had progressed as far as the material available would allow.

(7) The use of obsidian may have the appearance of "sudden presentation". This, however, does not in any way oppose the concept of long development. The working of obsidian, by pressure, and percussion fracture used precisely the same techniques as are used in working flint. Both Adena and Hopewell had developed this art to high levels. The forms used by them are not greatly different. When, again, by trade or travel, Hopewell was fortunate in procuring an abundant supply of obsidian from some remote area, probably the present Yellowstone Park region, nothing further was necessary for Hopewell to produce its exquisite specimens in obsidian, its technique of manufacture having already been thoroughly mastered by a process of long development, which may well have had Adena in its line of transmission. Adena had no obsidian because it had come and gone before obsidian was made available to its area.

(8) The explanation of the variety of effigy and geometric forms in copper in Hopewell is essentially the same as for mica. This very high artistic development in copper *did not present itself suddenly*. Copper breastplates, copper reels, and copper crescents are found sparingly in Adena. The lack of copper, that

is, its unavailability, may be considered the primary reason why effigy and geometric forms in copper did not appear in Adena in quantity. The scarcity of copper and the high regard in which it is held in Adena may be illustrated in the copper gorget from Burial 1, Site Be 15, which was made from several very thin pieces of copper, each so small that they were placed in position to overlap and were perforated along the margins while overlapping. This permitted them to be sewed together, or otherwise attached, thus forming a single piece large enough to make a small gorget, 2.3x6.3 inches. This is a great contrast to the condition at Seip Mound No. 1 where there were 46 copper breastplates, some of which had maximum dimensions of breadth about 6 inches and length about 11 inches; and where one out of many copper celts weighed 28 pounds.

Attention has been called to the carving of stone tablets in Adena. Some of these characters represented in stone by Adena are precisely the same symbolic and conventionalized figures cut in copper and carved in bone by Hopewell. This can mean only that the same ceremonial significance and conventionalized symbolizations which developed in stone in Adena extended on into Hopewell, and were, in copper retained by Hopewell in the very highest and latest expressions of its art. The absence of these forms in copper in Adena is to be attributed to the absence of an abundant supply of copper. These high expressions of art in copper in Hopewell did not therefore *present themselves suddenly and fully developed.* On the contrary, they appeared in Hopewell in great quantity only after an abundant supply of copper had come to Hopewell, and when they were produced, many of the best artistic forms showed internal evidence of having been derived by development directly from Adena. This is illustrated by the comparison of the carved stone tablets of Adena with the incised copper breastplates of Hopewell. In particular, the head of the raptorial bird presented on the Wright*, Berlin, and Wilmington tablets and on the bone gorget from the Florence Mound must certainly be regarded as portraying basically the same concept as the incised Hopewell copper ''eagle'' plates from the Mound City Group.

(9) Again the effigy platform tobacco pipe did not present

* Webb, William S., 1940, p. 115.

itself suddenly in Hopewell. The effigy platform pipe was by no means the only Hopewell pipe. From the six great sites compared by Shetrone and Greenman, which show a total of 278 effigy platform pipes, there are indicated 147 plain platform pipes which are believed to be the older form. Some of these plain pipes have straight bases, that is, they are not curved as are many of the effigy pipes. Straight-based platform pipes of steatite have been found in Adena. Straight-based platform pipes of very simple form were much more numerous among early Algonquian tribes occupying the region south of the Great Lakes and eastward to New England. The straight-based platform pipe, according to Willoughby*, is one of a group of artifacts designated as "Old Algonquian". Under this term he attempted to express its antiquity and indicate its wide spread distribution in the northeastern United States from New York to Maine. Certainly its distribution extends far beyond the Ohio Hopewell area, and evidence (see Map 2) points to its greater antiquity. There is no reason to believe, therefore, that this form of pipe "suddenly appeared" in Hopewell. It is highly probable that Ohio Hopewell's first pipes were of this simple early Algonquian type. From this simple form Hopewell may have developed the straight-based monitor pipe, then the curved-based monitor pipe, and finally, the curved-based effigy pipe of late Hopewell, the highest development. Certainly there is no reason to believe that effigy platform pipes were either "suddenly presented", or came to Hopewell fully developed.

A very late Adena site, Be 20 in Kentucky, has just yielded a single curved-based monitor pipe, another evidence that late Adena may have been contemporary with early Hopewell.

(10) In the matter of earth enclosures, Greenman shows that six of his seventy mounds were in earth enclosures. It has recently been demonstrated that sacred enclosures are of Adena origin. (See Vol. V, No. 2, p. 152). This means that the development of Adena is closely related to the construction of earthworks where so many of these sacred circles are to be found. The great earthworks on the Kentucky side of the Ohio River at South Portsmouth are now known, as the result of explorations, yet unre-

---

* Willoughby, Charles C., 1935, p. 89.

ported, to have been built by Adena*. Hopewell, therefore, did not present suddenly these great earthworks, but they had their beginnings in Adena communities and it is believed many were erected *before* Ohio Hopewell had reached its highest development. On the basis of excavations in Kentucky these authors venture to predict that many of the earthworks of Ohio, often regarded as the product of Ohio Hopewell, will be some day demonstrated to be of Adena origin. In particular, it may certainly be expected that careful excavation of so-called "sacred circles", will yield circular post mold patterns, where posts are set in pairs. This will obviously require that excavations be conducted using such technique as will make it possible to reveal such evidence where it still exists. Further, some of the mounds enclosed by such earthworks, or otherwise associated with them, should reveal small primary mounds covering burials on dwelling house floors. The evidence that the house had been burned before a secondary mound was erected over all in general would remain as an ash and charcoal layer over the primary mound. This, if sought for, will be found in the future even more frequently than it has been reported in the past when found and not understood.

Thus, it may be asserted with confidence that recent evidence seems to make the concept of "sudden presentation" of fully developed traits in Hopewell, particularly the traits mentioned by Greenman, quite untenable.

Finally it should be said that even if in Ohio Hopewell "new forms were presented suddenly and fully developed," that fact would hardly be sufficient to establish the argument of Greenman against gradual transition of Adena into Hopewell. So active a group as Ohio Hopewell, showing evidence of extensive contact with distant regions might well have been expected to suddenly produce, or pick up something new. Even so, the fact remains that in the majority of the important Hopewellian traits one is now able to see evidence of gradual transition of Adena into Hopewell.

---

* The report of these excavations has not yet been published.

COMPARISON OF BURIAL TRAITS
ADENA AND HOPEWELL

As has been previously explained, the authors are inclined to attach much greater importance to burial traits of a people than to their artifact traits, when seeking possible relationship between two archaeological manifestations. This conclusion is derived from the conviction that burial traits which may at first arise from the sheer necessity for the disposal of the dead are developed under the guidance of the social and religious concepts of a people and after long continued usage come to have the authority of law. Certainly death is one of the major crises in the life of the individual and must produce a definite social effect upon the community. The magnitude of this effect would be in proportion to the influence and importance of the deceased in the community. Naturally the community reaction to the loss of one of its members would be a formal expression of group solidarity, the manner of such expression being determined by many influences, among which are historic precedent and tradition, social customs, economic condition, and religious beliefs. Burial practices which gave rise to observed archaeological burial traits were accomplished by means of ceremonies and procedures undoubtedly requiring general public approval, as well as the specific approval of constituted authority. Burial practices and the resultant traits which point to them may thus be conceived as the social act of the body politic, in contrast to, for example, the manufacture of a particular type of artifact which may be considered the act of an individual, in which society generally had no interest, and on which it exerted little or no control.

If this concept of the inherent nature of burial traits is valid, one might expect burial traits to be much less subject to change than material traits in any group. Being more constant in time, burial traits would be more likely to persist in new locations to which they might be transported than any artifact traits. On this basis, the social inertia inherent in burial customs would make them quite stable in new situations and cause them to persist under new circumstances, with a minimum of change. This is not to say that developmental changes in burial customs are impossible, but quite to the contrary, burial customs are capable of change, but they should be expected to change much more slowly than traits relating to material wealth. If this be true, similar burial traits should be of prime importance in establishing close connection between peoples, if such connection exists, and conversely dissimilarity in burial customs would seem to indicate a fundamental difference in peoples, even if material traits were similar.

Heretofore, many of the comparisons between Adena and Hopewell have centered about artifacts. The great material wealth and high artistic techniques of Hopewell were contrasted with the relative poverty and lack of development of Adena, to prove a lack of connection between the two. The supposed (and asserted) non-cremation of the dead by Adena was contrasted with, in some cases, the total cremation in Hopewell, again with the effect of demonstrating a lack of connection between the two cultural complexes. Cremation in Hopewell, being associated with high material and artistic development, thus came to be regarded as an evidence of, and a synonym for, high cultural development and communal deposit of cremated remains was even accepted as an evidence of the highest development within Hopewell. This had the effect of inverting the relative chronology within the Hopewell complex, and of heightening the contrast and emphasizing the difference in development when compared with Adena, since Adena by Shetrone's* definition had no cremation.

In undertaking the comparison of burial customs of Adena with those of Hopewell as proposed, it is necessary to review certain very basic Adena traits associated with their burial customs, and to understand these traits in relation to each other. It has been established that Adena had quite a varied practice connected with the disposal of the dead. These may, however, be integrated under two general heads: (1) Inhumation, (2) Cremation.

INHUMATION**

Bodies were buried extended in the flesh, in log tombs. The body was laid upon bark or puddled clay, and covered by one or

---

* Shetrone, H. C., 1920, pp. 160-161.
** Traits mentioned herein are described in detail on pages 70 to 82.

both materials, the tomb being closed by a roof of bark, poles, or logs, before all was covered over with earth. There seems to be a wide range in variation within this trait, extending from the simple burial of an extended body wrapped in bark, through burials in subfloor pits with log roofs, to the elaborately constructed log vaults, sometimes associated with stone, found in the center of large Adena mounds. Such burials often occupy the central position in a mound. In many cases they are the only burials in the mounds, and when other burials do occur, it is apparent that these central burials were the first made, and that the mound was erected primarily to cover them. Usually such burials and their tombs are the most elaborate. These burials usually are accompanied by important artifacts, relatively numerous and of the highest quality. Such tombs are often larger than need be for a single burial. Such burials are often accompanied by other burials certainly made at the same time—but so placed as to suggest they were in a secondary position, and placed in specific relation to the important central burial.

This burial procedure has impressed many excavators of Adena mounds with the idea that the individual thus buried was not a usual person, but one of distinction. This is illustrated by Greenman's* statement relative to the important burial in the Coon Mound when he says:

> "While extreme caution is necessary in making deductions regarding social status from the manner in which the dead are buried, it seems worthwhile in the present instance to suggest that the individual entombed in the Coon Mound was a person of considerable importance. The erection of a mound of this size over the remains of a single individual is very suggestive and the presence of red pigment on the tibia of the skeleton is of further significance."

Finally, such burials obviously represent a very small minority of the total population at any site. Certainly the total number of individuals given log tomb burials, could not in general, in any reasonable time have built the mounds, earthworks, and log tombs occupied by them, or associated with them. This seems to force the conclusion that the individuals buried in Adena log tombs represented a selected minority of the total population—

---

* Greenman, E. F., 1932, p. 408.

apparently an honored group, on the basis of the evidence. Why they were thus buried, or how selected, need not concern us here, for there remains the much more important question—what means was used for the disposal of the rest of the population? This is the real question, the answer to which is basic to an understanding of Adena. It will be discussed later.

Coupled with this trait of inhumation in log tombs, of what seems to be a certain selected few, is definitely the practice of house burning in Adena. Log tombs were constructed centrally on the floor of a dwelling house, and after the body was placed in the log rectangle and covered with bark and clay in various combinations, and the log tomb was closed by a roof of bark, poles, or logs, a small primary earth mound on the house floor was raised over the log tomb, and finally the house was burned down. The fact that sometimes partial cremation resulted need not here concern us, for it is believed to be accidental in such cases and thus no indication of any intention. This house burning was followed by the erection of a secondary mound to cover the site of the burned house. After the large secondary mound was completed, pits for other log tombs might be dug into it or cremated remains might be deposited on its surface. All such new burials would be covered with new earth brought upon the mound in considerable quantity often producing tertiary, quaternary, etc., sections of the mound. These later added sections may or may not be symmetrically placed relative to the primary mound.

Sometimes, in lieu of the log tomb burial as the initial phase of an Adena mound, a subfloor pit was dug. Here bark and puddled clay again were used to form a burial area, and always there is to be found evidence of fire or ashes in the pit. Often deposits of cremated human remains are placed in subordinate positions in such graves. The pit was usually closed at the original surface by logs, poles, and bark before a mound was erected over all. It should be observed that all Adena mounds cover either log tomb burials, and/or cremations, or subfloor pits which contain inhumations, and/or redeposited cremations. No Adena mound has ever been properly excavated which did not show either one or another of these traits. It may or may not have later additions, but always it has this initial stage. Inasmuch as original log tomb burials were sometimes made on the floor of a house, and often cremated remains were deposited on a house floor, and in all such cases a small earth mound was built on the house floor to cover the burials in these various forms, the house when it was burned fell on a small earth mound already erected on its floor. This small mound, with burned surface, formed a core over which the larger mound was later erected. This sequence of events in Adena must be kept clearly in mind when making comparison with Hopewell burial customs.

CREMATION*

Turning now to the other general method of disposal of the dead by Adena (cremation), here we again notice a rather varied procedure. Cremations in clay basins in the village were quite common. It is quite possible that some of these cremations were made within a standing house, the cremated remains being gathered up and redeposited elsewhere, thus seemingly making it unnecessary to burn the house. If the remains were cremated and left in the fire basin in the house, the house was burned and a mound erected over all, but first a small mound within the house on the house floor was built to cover the cremation. However, cremations did seemingly occur in the open air in the village, and were often left in situ, but sometimes were surrounded by a log rectangle placed about the remains after the crematory fires were burned out. Such burials were covered in various ways by using puddled clay layers, bark, poles, logs, and finally earth. There are usually no artifacts in such graves. Such burials of cremated remains are left in the village, unmarked, and their location often lost, as they have been found disturbed by later aboriginal house construction on the site.

Since most Adena villages were perhaps never very large nor their middens very deep, because of the seemingly widely dispersed occupancy of Adena in any area, such cremation evidence would not remain indefinitely and it would not be preserved unless such villages had been covered by a mound and thus preserved. Even the habit of the Adena people of literally ''scraping up'' the village midden in order to build mounds may account for the destruction of such evidence in many small villages. It is frequently observed that fragmentary burned human bones are

---

* Traits mentioned herein are described in detail on pages 59 to 70.

found scattered in the fill of Adena primary mounds. Where portions of villages still remain intact under mounds, cremations left in the midden, without artifacts, unmarked in position, except by the log rectangles about them, which are shown today only by the log molds, are usually quite numerous. So much so that one is constrained to believe that cremation was a usual and common practice in Adena, and the nearly universal means used in the disposal of the dead of the whole population.

That the individuals thus cremated were not "selected individuals" is suggested by the lack of artifacts for the majority of such burials, their redeposit is unmarked in the village, except by the log rectangle, and a general lack of any special preparation for such graves is noticeable. Frequently cremated remains were gathered up and redeposited in various ways—in mounds while they were being built; in log tombs of other persons, but in subordinate positions; sometimes scattered widely on the floor of a townhouse, or deposited together (multiple deposits) in the center of a house floor. Always the house in such cases was later destroyed by fire. The whole intent seems to be to dispose of the cremated remains in the easiest way possible, many being left in situ in the village. Thus the suggestion seems inescapable that cremation was not reserved for the favored few as was log tomb inhumation, but was used as a burial method for the great majority, the multitude, the persons who required less care, whose graves were usually unmarked and contained few, if any, accompanying artifacts, and who, for the lack of a better term, might be called the common people, the masses.

These authors believe that the great majority of the Adena people were cremated soon after death and the charred bones placed in unmarked graves under the thin village middens on the scattered and widespread occupation sites where they had lived. These village middens, small and thin, have long since disappeared due to soil erosion, cultivation, and the action of time, unless covered by a mound. Skeletal remains from which the physical anthropologist may today draw conclusions are thus in Adena limited to the group selected, by what process we do not know, for inhumation in log tombs.

If the above conclusions on inhumation and cremation in Adena be substantially correct, one may assume that Adena man considered burial in a log tomb accompanied by artifacts, and the erection of a mound, as evidence of a higher estate, perhaps more honorable than cremation. Where custom dictated cremation in any particular case, it would be easy to suppose that the desire by the friends of the deceased to approximate the highest estate of burial possible for them to obtain for the remains of a friend, may have been the motive leading to (a) deposit of cremated remains in the log tombs of others, or (b) the redeposit of cremated remains in earth mounds while they were being built, or (c) the deposit of cremated remains on a house floor, where because the house would be burned and a mound erected over all, there would be a measure of similarity to log-tomb burials. Lacking any of these opportunities which obviously would not always be available, it would be quite natural to build a miniature log tomb about the cremated remains in situ in the village. Thus one may be led to understand that much of the variation which is observable in the disposal of the cremated remains in Adena may be only the manifestation of a desire to give the cremated burial as much of the appearance of, advantage in, or prestige of, a log-tomb burial as it was possible to obtain. While such subjective rationalizations may be wholly in error, the evidence remains that Adena, after cremating many individuals, left many of them in wholly unmarked graves, but in some cases attempted to associate the cremated remains with various aspects of log-tomb burial. Rationalizations as to the basis for this action are quite apart from the facts that such varied dispositions were made of the cremated remains of Adena, as shown by recent archaeological excavations. It is precisely this series of practices and procedures in the disposition of cremated remains in Adena which makes the comparison with the practice of cremation in Hopewell so very significant.

In undertaking to make a detailed comparison of Adena with Hopewell burial customs, one is confronted with the problem of determining what actually is typical of Hopewell. There is, as a matter of fact, quite a variation in burial procedures among the six great Hopewell sites. Two of the six great Hopewell sites, Mound City and Tremper, are reported as using cremation only; while in other sites, as Seip No. 1, elaborate log tomb burials are an important feature. It may be that this variation is even greater among Hopewell sites, than that between some Hopewell sites and Adena. In order to avoid, at first, the discussion of this internal variation among Hopewell sites, it may be more satisfactory to choose a particular Hopewell site for comparison with Adena, by which means likenesses and differences may be dealt with, more specifically. Following this procedure, the great Hopewell Group has been chosen for comparison, primarily because its great wealth of material culture has caused it to be commonly regarded as one of the highest, if not the very highest, manifestation of material wealth and artistic development of the Hopewell people. In attempting to evaluate the evidence furnished by this prehistoric site, one is impressed with the relative poverty of exact information on burial customs now available, despite the magnificent body of artifacts which this site has yielded to many investigators.

The first investigation by Squier and Davis, which completely demolished some of the smaller mounds, gave no information of any value in the comparison of burial traits. Their work, however, here and elsewhere, did give rise to the terms "Sacrificial Mounds", or "Altar Mounds", as distinguished from "Mounds of Sepulture". Under the term "Altar Mounds" they classified some of the mounds of the Hopewell Group, and thus fastened upon Hopewell, and the minds of many early investigators, whatever concepts were connoted by the terms "Altar" and "Sacrificial". It is interesting to note in passing that Greenman classified one of their "Sacrificial Mounds" as an Adena Mound (Greenman No. 4). Since the manner of excavation of Squier and Davis* as well as their form of description of their finds was determined by their concept of the trait of the builders of the mounds, it is well enough to recall their statement relative to this mound (Greenman's No. 4). They say in part:

> " . . . . the basin, in this instance, measuring seven feet in diameter by eight inches in depth. This basin was then carefully paved with small round stones . . . . Upon the altar thus constructed was found a burnt deposit . . . . The deposit consisted of a thin layer of carbonaceous matter, intermingled with which were some burned human bones, but so much calcined as to render recognition extremely difficult. Ten well wrought copper bracelets were found, placed in two heaps, five

---

* Squier, E. G., and Davis, E. H., 1848, p. 157.

in each, and encircling some calcined bones—probably those of the arms upon which they were originally worn . . . .

"Assuming, what must be very obvious from its form and other circumstances, that this was an altar and not a tomb, we are almost irresistably led to the conclusion, that human sacrifices were practiced by the race of the mounds. This conclusion is sustained by other facts, which have already been presented, ..."

When Moorehead excavated this great site and completely removed some more of these mounds, and partially excavated many others, he seems to have accepted the ideas of Squier and Davis for he reported finding "altars", and spoke of offerings associated with them. Although Moorehead collected a magnificent body of artifacts from this site and excavated more than 150 burials, his published report does not indicate the relative number of cremations and inhumations. While he describes artifacts found in some detail, he seems to have made no attempt to study burial customs generally, and thus offers no aid in a comparison of burial traits. As a result of these previous explorations and other forms of destruction such as the building of highways and railroads; when the Ohio Museum Survey came to excavate this site in 1925, there remained undisturbed only five of the original 29 mounds, and portions of nine others which were able to furnish some information. It is to this survey and the report of Shetrone that one must turn as the sole source of information on burial customs of the Hopewell Group.

From the remnants of the mounds of this once great site Shetrone reports 85 burials as follows:

Inhumations, extended in the flesh........................ 51
Cremations 32
Deposit of bundle of bones.. 2

Of the 51 extended burials, 21 bodies were stated to have been extended in 18 log tombs, since there was one double and one triple burial within log rectangles. It is quite possible that more than the stated 21 bodies were so buried for it appears that timbered structures were characteristic of Hopewell. Mound No. 25, a very large mound, was found to cover several smaller interior mounds. In one of these, Burials 9 and 10 are described by Shetrone* as follows:

"Burials 9 and 10, the first discovered in the interior mounds were uncremated adults, with only minor artifacts accompanying them. The grave of Number 10, however, was an interesting example of the timbered structures characteristic of Hopewell burials. It measured 7.5 feet long by 3.5 feet wide and was composed of exceptionally large timbers, some of which were above 6 inches in diameter. At each corner there had been set a post, for support of the structure, while exteriorly there had been driven stakes to hold the three tiers of logs in place. At the point shown on the floor plan there was found an extensive log-mold, the timbers of which had been burned."

Here then is evidence of log tombs in Hopewell much like the log tomb of Adena, and Shetrone points out that they were "characteristic" of Hopewell. It is interesting to note that the tomb walls were built three logs high, the logs held in place by stakes. This is an illustration of economy as compared to Adena, where to obtain the same effect Adena often laid down three logs, placed two logs in the second tier and one on top. That these tombs had log roofs much the same as Adena is plain. Of Burial 34, Mound 25, Shetrone** says:

"With this typical uncremated burial were found some of the more interesting of the many specimens secured from Mound 25. A feature of the burial was the size of the log structure enclosing it and of the individual logs employed. The dome-like aperture above the grave, resulting from the decay and falling down of the log structure, was strikingly large and bold, reaching almost to the top of the mound which at this point was ten feet in height. In the illustration it will be noted that the gravel strata of the primary mound have broken off and dropped down with the loose earth filling the cavity."

Along with this evidence of log tomb burial, and the collapse of log roofs, it will be noted that such burials contain "some of the most interesting of the many specimens", etc. Here again is the suggestion that extended burials in elaborate log tombs were those of unusual or selected persons.

---

* Shetrone, H. C., 1926, p. 67.
** Shetrone, H. C., 1926, p. 87.

The details of the log tomb construction seem to be exactly like Adena and to have about the same range of variation.

Of Burial 25, Mound 25, Shetrone* says:

"In this typical burial the bark bed and covering of bark were strongly marked, the covering having been laid transversely across the body."

Even in this small detail in placing the bark transversely, the procedure here follows Adena custom. Note that this is said to be a typical burial.

The use of raised platforms inside a rectangle of logs and the occasional use of stone as in Adena is also observable in Hopewell.

Of Burial 11 Shetrone** says:

"Burial Number 11 comprised the skeleton of a middle-aged individual 5 feet 8 inches in height. The raised earthen platform on which it lay was enclosed by a pretentious log structure, two logs deep, which measured 10 feet long by 6 feet wide. The logs were held in place by small posts at the corners and by stakes and large stones at the ends and side exteriorly. While most burials of the mound had coverings of bark on which the body was laid, in this burial the platform had a covering of fine gravel to a depth of one inch."

It thus appears that so far as the burial trait is related to extended burials, the procedures of Hopewell are precisely the procedures of Adena. This similarity in custom extends even to such minor details as the manner of placing the bark layers in graves.

As stated above, of the 85 burials reported by the Ohio Museum Survey as found by them in the Hopewell Mounds, 32 of them were cremations. All 32 appeared to be the deposit of cremated remains. Of this number 10 were said to have been enclosed by small log rectangles, a trait recently observed in Adena villages.

Of Burial 39, Mound 25, Shetrone*** says:

"Burial Number 39 was a cremated one, occupying a raised platform 3 feet 4 inches by 2 feet 3 inches in size, with log enclosure. This burial, as is true of many other cremated burials of mounds, was exactly similar in its preparation to graves containing uncremated skeletons, with the exception that its dimensions are less."

---

* Shetrone, H. C., 1926, p. 83.
** Shetrone, H. C., 1926, p. 68.
*** Shetrone, H. C., 1926, p. 90.

Here in Hopewell is the same trait as in Adena, which seems to be the result of a desire to give a deposited cremation something of the appearance of a log tomb burial.

In Adena cremated burials, the bone fragments are usually so small that it is difficult to recognize individual bones. Behind the concept of cremation is the assumption that at death a body was burned in a hot fire, and usually in a clay basin. By stirring the fire, bones were reduced to small pieces. Here at the Hopewell site, there is noted what appears to be a different result.

Of Burial No. 7, Mound 4, Shetrone* says:

"Burial Number 7 was a typical cremated burial and was placed beneath the shoulders and back of Burial 4. There was the usual amount of coarsely charred bones, deposited without preparation and . . . . four copper earspools . . . ."

Here it is to be noted is a cremation in the grave of an extended burial. This is like similar burials in Adena, but the remains here are *coarsely charred*. This suggests that they were not burned as completely as might have been possible. Further, four copper earspools suggest the possibility that two individuals provided the burned bones, that is, here is the suggestion of multiple deposit of mixed bones, a trait already noted in Adena.

Further of Burial 1, Mound 20, Shetrone** says:

"Burial Number 1 occupied approximately the center of the mound, and consisted of the usual amount of coarsely cremated skeletal remains resting upon an elevated earthen surface about three inches higher than the surrounding floor."

Here again is the emphasis on *coarsely* cremated bones. This seeming difference in bone residue raises the question of the method by which the cremation was accomplished.

In a footnote in connection with Mound 2 Shetrone*** says:

"The characteristic basins found in mounds of. the Hopewell culture have been designated as altars by several writers. Since with one or two exceptions the surveys of the Society have not found them to contain offerings, the most plausible explanation seems to be that they served as places of cremation."

* Shetrone, H. C., 1926, p. 34.
** Shetrone, H. C., 1926, p. 52.
*** Shetrone, H. C., 1926, p. 22.

It will be noted here that Shetrone states an opinion—not an observed fact. He speaks of an explanation of the presence of these clay basins on the hard floor of these mounds. Obviously, having in mind the "sacrificial" concepts of Squier and Davis, and the "altars" of Moorehead, he might have expected to find in these basins the evidence of "sacrifice", the evidence of their use as "altars". What was revealed at this great Hopewell site was that in most cases the *basins were empty*. In one case, Mound 26, there was a deposit of artifacts in a basin, but they were not burned. Two deposits in Mound 17 which might under the concepts of Squier and Davis have seemed to justify their term "altar", were described by Shetrone[*] as follows:

> "The mound was composed of clayey loam of the surrounding surface .... There were no burials of human remains. Instead, the mound seems to have been erected over the site of two distinct and important sacrificial or ceremonial offerings of artifacts.

> "Ceremonial Offering Number 1, south of its center, occupied an oval space 5 feet by 7 feet, along side and partly filling a rectangular basin of typical form, measuring 22 by 26 inches. Perhaps a cubic yard of the peculiar yellowish-green clay so often associated with burials and deposits of the Hopewell type had been placed upon the oval space mentioned, and upon and intermixed with this were the following objects ...."

(Here follows a long list of artifacts.)

> "Many of the finer specimens among the above were undamaged while others had been intentionally broken ....

> "There was evidence of considerable burning in connection with this cache, and a good deal of charcoal and charred wood were in the deposit. However, it appears that the burning had not taken place where the objects were deposited, and the fact that in several instances portions of ceremonially broken specimens were not included in the cache, leads to the presumption that the ceremonial fire had been kindled elsewhere, and that the offering afterwards was scooped up and carried to the place of deposit."

In this language Shetrone makes it clear that the so-called crematory basin was a "place of deposit" for this large collection of mutilated and unmutilated artifacts, and *not* an *altar* upon

---

[*] Shetrone, H. C., 1926, p. 44.

which they were burned. Had this basin been excavated by Squier and Davis, or by Moorehead, it probably would have been described by them as a "sacrifice on an altar."

Shetrone* continues:

"Deposit Number 2 was located well toward the northern margin of the mound and marked *the first instance,* insofar as the present Survey is concerned, *where a deposit or offering of great importance* was placed directly within a basin. The basin in this instance was of typical form and measured 18 inches by 22 inches at the rim. It was carefully constructed and was burned red to a considerable depth beneath its base. The deposit of specimen filled and extended outward from the basin covering a circular space 4½ feet across. The objects were intermingled with earth, clay, and charcoal, apparently intentionally."

* * * * * * *

"As in Deposit Number 1, specimen in the second cache were ceremonially broken up, but to a lesser degree. Something near one-half the total number were undamaged or slightly broken, while most of the others, broken in two or more parts, were readily restored. While several fragments of human skull were identified with this cache, it, like Deposit Number 1, appears not to have been accompanied by cremation of human remains."

Here again Shetrone makes it plain that this was a "deposit" of artifacts in a basin, not a burning of artifacts in situ. Note also fragments of skull were not burned.

When Mills re-examined Mound No. 8 of the Mound City Group, he reached a similar conclusion relative to the great central basin from which Squier and Davis had in their previous investigation taken the remarkable find of effigy pipes and other artifacts.

Squier and Davis** gave the impression that this great cache of pipes, copper, and other artifacts was a "sacrifice" burned within an "altar". They assumed that this great mass of material had been burned in place by hot fires. Of it they say:

"The pipes were much broken up—some of them calcined by heat, which had been sufficiently strong to melt copper, masses of which were found fused together in the center of the basin."

---

* Shetrone, H. C., 1926, pp. 47-49.
** Squier, E. G., and Davis, E. H., 1848, p. 152.

When Mills* re-examined this "altar" he concluded that the deposit had not been burned in this basin. Of it he says:

"However, a glance at the basin, once more exposed to view, was sufficient to show that the supposedly intense sacrificial or crematorial fires of Squier and Davis never had occurred therein. As so often noted in the crematory basins of other mounds of the group, this one had undergone extensive repairs. Continued use of these basins as crematories, with alternate heat and moisture, resulted in all instances in damage in the way of checking and cracking. In this particular basin, this cracking had been very pronounced, the separation being as much as one inch in width. These cracks, as well as portions of the floor which had been altogether broken away, were neatly repaired by filling with puddled clay, bluish-drab in color. The fresh clay used in these repairs was entirely unburned, and showed no contact whatever with fire. In view of this fact, it becomes clear that cremation or burning of the deposit found in this basin had occurred elsewhere."

Thus Mills reached the same conclusion from Mound No. 8 at Mound City that Shetrone did from these great deposits at Hopewell.

It is plain from the above lengthy presentation that these basins were not altars in the general accepted meaning of the term, that is, places where "sacrifices were burned".

What then was the purpose of these well-made clay basins? When Shetrone reached the conclusion that these basins were not altars, it was then that he wrote, "the most plausible explanation seems to be that they served as places of cremation", as quoted above.

One should understand that this opinion was the considered judgment of a man who had abundant opportunity to see the material in the field, and who was wholeheartedly seeking the truth only. As such, this opinion should carry great weight. It is, therefore, with some hesitancy that the present authors would undertake to offer a different interpretation. It is done only because it seems necessary properly to evaluate all evidence related to Hopewell burial customs.

The opinion expressed by Shetrone that these basins were crematory basins seems not to be supported by any evidence from

* Mills, W. C., 1922, p. 261.

the Hopewell Group of mounds. The basins were *all* empty when found except as previously noted. They were so clean of any evidence of cremated remains that it was often a matter of special note.

The term cremation is here taken to mean the burning of a body in the flesh, presumptively after death. The present objection to the term "crematory basin" arises from the fact that:

(1) There is not a particle of evidence to show that human bodies were burned in such basins at the Hopewell Group of Mounds;

(2) Of those basins listed by Shetrone, the sizes of the basins and the number of mounds in which each was found are as follows:

Mound No.	Basin size in inches	Form
1	None given	Rectangular
2	44 x 35	
3	Small	
4	None given	
7	None given	
8	2 ft. in diameter	Circular
11	3.5 ft. in diameter	Circular
17	20 x 28	Rectangular
	22 x 26	Rectangular
	18 x 22	Rectangular
	Mutilated	Rectangular
18	15 x 16	Rectangular
20	17 x 22	Rectangular
24	22 x 28	Rectangular
25	48 x 37	Rectangular
26	20 x 26	Rectangular
	22 x 28	Rectangular
28	27 x 23	Rectangular

Shetrone thus reports on the size of 13 basins. One described as small and another as mutilated have no reported dimensions. Of the 13 basins two were circular and eleven rectangular. It will be noted that all are small, much too small to permit the burning of an extended human body. Even the largest of these basins is too small to permit the building of a fire large enough, and hence hot enough, to consume a human body.

(3) The cremated remains found at Hopewell site were often deposited on earthen platforms surrounded by log rectangles. These platforms for the deposit of such remains were on the average larger than the so-called crematory basins. It might be

reasonably expected that basins used for cremation would be at least as large as the platforms used to retain the much reduced residue of the crematory process.

For these reasons these authors prefer to believe that these basins were ''fire basins'' placed on a house floor, probably near its center, but where the house was large, and more than one basin was built, they may have been nonsymmetrically placed. These fire basins were hard burned, discolored by heat, and often cracked as the result of long use as fire places for heating and possibly for cooking. Near some of these basins large potsherds, major portions of broken vessels, were occasionally noted. This suggests domestic use of such basins since it is now known that pottery vessels were not intentionally used in burial association in either Hopewell or Adena.

If this long discussion has lowered the exalted status of these clay basins from *sacrificial altars* to *crematory basins,* and finally to *simple fire places* used in the domestic life of the household, what is the effect of this change in status on the understanding of the burial customs at Hopewell Group of mounds?

The authors are led to believe that, excluding Mound 25, to be discussed later, the mounds of the Hopewell Group, 28 small mounds inside the enclosure and 9 outside, were built to cover dwelling houses on the floors of which were one or more fire basins used generally in the processes of domestic economy. It is believed that each of these houses so marked by fire basins on the house floor was the habitat of a single family group or social unit. It is believed that these houses were by no means all of the houses that at one time or another may have been erected at this great site. However, they do represent the houses, on the floors of which, for reasons suggested later, it was decided to place an extended burial. This would be done only in the case of the death of a person entitled to a log tomb burial, possibly an elaborate burial. The process of making such burials seems to be identical in both Hopewell and Adena. They were prepared by erecting on the house floor a rectangular pen of logs of the proper depth and area. The inside floor of the log structure was covered with puddled clay, thus producing a raised clay platform which was usually covered with bark. On this floor the body was extended with artifacts. The body was then covered with puddled clay or bark, either or both, and the log tomb roofed over with poles and bark. Over this a small mound would be built on the house floor. As has been suggested, such a log tomb burial would hardly be provided for any one except a prominent person, perhaps the owner of the house, or the head of the family or social group. Since the dwelling house was soon to be burned after such a log tomb burial was made on its floor and covered by a small mound, one must account for the other burials in association. On this point Shetrone* says of Mound 25:

> "To account for the multiple burials *apparently repre-senting family groups found* in this *and other mounds* of the culture it becomes a logical supposition that some form of temporary burial and reburial obtained with the Hopewell peoples, as with certain historic tribes."

This supposition of Shetrone seems to be fully justified by the evidence and today can even be put in more exact terms. Using the assumption of Shetrone one may suppose that when an elaborate burial of some important person was to be made in a log tomb on a dwelling house floor, and the house was thus soon to be destroyed by fire, all other less important members of the family or household group, who had previously died, and whose skeletal remains had been kept for such an occasion, would be cremated and deposited on the house floor of the house which was in life their home. These cremations of bones, not bodies, might perhaps have been performed outside of the house in the village nearby, but they could have been done on the very small fire places found on these house floors. While these fire places were not nearly large enough to permit the destruction of a human body, they might have served for the burning of a dismembered human skeleton. That they did so serve for the cremation of bones but not of bodies is definitely suggested by the constant reiteration of Shetrone as he describes the deposits of cremated remains as being "coarsely cremated." This means that those bodies whose skeletons were thus cremated were prepared for this final disposition long before cremation. In order to obtain the skeletons of their dead for a temporary period of preservation, many historic tribes exposed the bodies of the deceased

---

* Shetrone, H. C., 1926, p. 179.

on scaffolds for a period of a month or more, after which time
the remains were taken down, the bones completely denuded of
the flesh and put into a hamper for preservation.

Such procedures incident to the death of a Choctaw were
described by Romans* and quoted by Bushnell** as follows:

> "As soon as the deceased is departed, a stage is erected
> . . . . and the corpse is laid on it and covered with a bear
> skin; if he be a man of note, it is decorated, and the poles
> painted red with vermillion and bear's oil; . . . . The stage
> is fenced round with poles, it remains thus a certain time but
> not a fixed space, this is sometimes extended to three or four
> months, but seldom more than half that time . . . . the day
> being come, the friends and relations assemble near the
> stage, a fire is made, and the respectable operator, after the
> body is taken down, with his nails tears the remaining flesh
> off the bones, and throws it with the intrails into the fire,
> where it is consumed; then he scrapes the bones and burns
> the scrapings likewise; the head being painted red with ver-
> million is with the rest of the bones put into a neatly made
> chest (which for a Chief is also made red) and deposited in
> the loft of a hut built for that purpose, and called bone
> house."

Thomas*** refers to the burning of the posts which had
supported a scaffold, at the time of removal of the body. The
custom of destruction by fire of property on the occasion of the
death of an important person was known in many historic tribes.
If the Hopewell people had a custom of scaffold exposure similar
in any degree to that of the Choctaw, it may be supposed that the
clothing, robes and other textiles investing the body on the scaffold
may well have been burned at the same time the flesh was removed
from the skeleton and burned. Such a practice could probably
never be demonstrated for the Hopewell people, but if they did
have such a custom, all that would be required to account for the
burned textiles, mingled with pearl and shell beads and other
artifacts frequently found in such deposits, would be to assume
that the residues remaining from the destruction of the scaffold
and the burning of the vestments of the deceased were gathered
up and retained along wtih the disarticulated bones of the skeleton
to such time as the bones might be cremated, and all might be

---

* Romans, Bernard, 1775, p. 89.
** Bushnell, David I., Jr., 1920, p. 95.
*** Thomas, Cyrus, 1894, p. 446.

deposited on their own house floor. To such honored remains they may well have added some new, unused, and unburned artifacts when making the final deposit. Since the original material may have required storage for a considerable time, this fact may have led to the destruction or mutilation of artifacts of value included in these cremated remains, according to the suggestion of Shetrone.

This assumption that the clothing and the burial wrappings of the exposed burial were burned at the time the body was denuded of the flesh and the flesh burned, leaving the skeleton to be disposed of by cremation later, implies a very complicated procedure, a "double cremation" as it were. One may well ask why could not this be accomplished in one operation? The reasons for this assumption are as follows:

(1) Hopewell did have some (not many) bundle burials.

(2) On the floor of many mounds (Mound City) Shetrone* reports "deposits" of burned and broken artifacts, accompanied by burned textiles and other carbonaceous material. Most of these artifacts like beads, and animal teeth, are the types attached to clothing. Such deposits are *not* mingled with burned human bone.

(3) In general, deposits of individual cremated human remains show no mingling with the material of the "artifact deposits" as would be the case if a body with clothing and artifacts had been burned together.

(4) In communal deposit of cremated human remains and in the communal deposit of artifacts, there is a strict separation, of artifacts and cremated human remains.

(5) The use of many "trophy" skulls by Hopewell indicates that some bodies were, in part at least, denuded of the flesh. These trophy skulls, discussed more fully later, show polishing, grinding, cutting, drilling, scraping, and gouging of the surfaces; evidence that much labor was expended upon them in their preparation. It is hard to believe all this would have been done if the skull was to be immediately buried or cremated. This evidence seems to point to a period of preservation or storage as cleaned bone. The trophy skulls are generally of the same physical type as the skeletons which they accompany in the burial, which makes unnecessary the assumption that they were necessarily of enemy origin.

---

* Shetrone. H. C., 1926, p. 107.

The occasion for the final deposit of such remains would presumptively be the death of the head of the family. On such an occasion we may assume the important personage would be laid in a log tomb on the floor of his house with his most valued relics about him, including headdress, and other artifacts, perhaps trophy skulls if he had them, and perhaps accompanied by his wife who may have been sacrificed in order to accompany him in death. The log tomb would be closed by a roof and about it on the house floor there would be deposited the cremated skeletal remains of all who had long been dead, but whose remains had been retained for this occasion. Such deposits would be made in small rectangles in imitation of the more important log tomb burials. Finally there would be brought in the accumulated residue of the burned artifacts, clothing, and perhaps burial wrappings used by these individuals, when their bodies were exposed on scaffolds, these would be deposited on the house floor in any convenient place, sometimes using the fire basin as a receptacle, but often being placed in a pile by themselves.

After a primary mound had been erected over the entire house floor, the house would be burned down and then the mound may or may not have been increased in height and diameter, to form a mound of the type remaining to the present time.

Because of a desire to obtain a maximum of information on the process of cremation by Hopewell and by Adena, and because it was hoped that the residues of cremated burials might still show internal evidence of what it was that was cremated, *i. e.*, whether a body in the flesh or dry bones from which the flesh might long have been separated; it was determined to seek technical advice on the subject. Dr. Wilton M. Krogman, Associate Professor of Anatomy and Physical Anthropology of the University of Chicago, was known to have had an interest in somewhat similar problems in connection with his work as consultant to the Federal Bureau of Investigation[*].

Accordingly typical samples of cremated burials from the Seip Mound No. 1 and from Mound 25 of the Hopewell Group, in Ohio, and from the Coon Mound in Ohio and the Stone Mound (Bh 15, Adena) in Kentucky were submitted to him for study.

---

[*] Krogman, Wilton M., 1939.

Dr. Krogman after a careful investigation of a considerable mass of material was able to separate out significant specimens which contain evidence on the point at issue. These samples are presented in Figure 3 with some of the comments of Dr. Krogman. Basically, it appears that when bones in a dry condition are

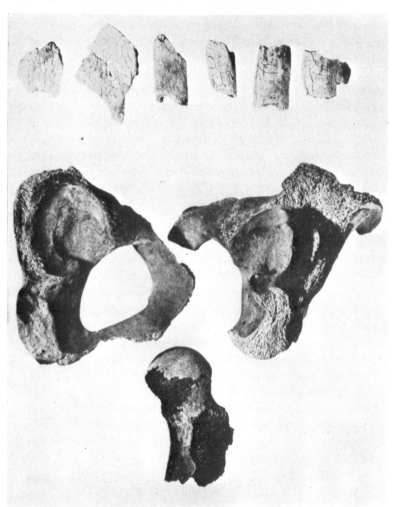

Fig. 3. In top row, fragments of skull and long bones show "checking" both inside and outside, indicating the burning of dry bones. In lower portion of illustration fragments of large bones show by incomplete combustion and the retention of remains of endosteum that the body was burned "in the flesh".

incinerated, besides being calcined, they show cracking or "checking" as he says "like the patina of age in an oil painting". However, if a body should be burned in the flesh, besides possibly showing an incomplete incineration of bone, it is often possible to see under a low power magnification the remains of incompletely consumed endosteum. Dr. Krogman states that it is particularly difficult to distinguish between the burning of a body in the flesh and the burning of green bones, that is, bones from which the flesh has but recently been removed. As difficult as the problem inherently is, Dr. Krogman was able to draw conclusions which in the light of other archaeological evidence seems to be very satisfactory. His statement follows:

> Upon the basis of the archaeological material examined by me I feel warranted in the following observations:
> (1) The people of the Hopewell culture practiced cremation mainly on defleshed and dried bones, though not to the exclusion of fleshed cremation; (2) The people of the Adena Culture practiced cremation mainly on fleshed bodies, though not to the exclusion of de-fleshed dried bones.
> In other words, both cultures practiced both types of cremation, the Hopewell concentrating on the one form, the Adena on the other.

It is, of course, obvious that many of the detailed burial customs herein suggested cannot be demonstrated for Hopewell. It is doubtful if it will ever be possible to discover many of the major procedures of this complex and highly developed prehistoric social organization. However, the suppositions made enable one to account for the following definite facts and observations relative to Hopewell burial customs:

(1) Burial by what seemed to Shetrone to be family groups.

(2) Inhumation in log tombs of important persons; the cremation of others.

(3) Small size of the fire basins at Hopewell site.

(4) The partially burnt textiles, clothing mingled with pearl and bone beads, and other artifacts burned elsewhere and deposited on the house floor.

(5) The communal deposit of such burned remains, since if all the remains of one family were to be kept till finally de-

posited, and all were to be placed on the same house floor, there was no need to keep them separately.

(6) The bundle burials of bones by Hopewell, since they had, in keeping, skeletons denuded of the flesh, which were sometimes though rarely deposited on the house floor without being cremated, (see bundle burials, Mound 4).

(7) Communal cremation and communal deposit of cremated remains, since in the retention of disarticulated bones of skeletons of the same family, destined to be deposited at the same time and in the same house, there would be no purpose in keeping them separated if it was more convenient to store them together, or if bones of different individuals became unintentionally mixed. In fact, if such bones were to be cremated, multiple cremation of many individuals together would be easy to understand.

(8) The Auxiliary Mounds as reported by Shetrone fit into the pattern of occupancy.

Relative to these Auxiliary Mounds outside the great enclosure, their presence only demonstrates that they were some of the house sites of lesser importance which by virtue of deposits of cremated remains on their floors or other connection with cremation happen to have had mounds built over them. On the floors of these mounds there were found burned areas, with animal and bird bones, potsherds, scraps of mica and other artifacts, including bear canines, and sandstone gorgets.

Encircling the floor of these mounds in some cases were ridges of coarse gravel 6 inches high and spreading outward 3 to 5 feet wide.

Of Mound Number 33, Shetrone[*] says:

"While several post molds were found interiorly, they could not be definitely located around the margins. Nevertheless, the evidence appears to indicate that the mound covered a lodge or house-site, where domestic activities prevailed."

Locations of the others of the supplemental mounds may be noted on the map. Their examination was on a lesser scale, a repetition of that of Mound 33 including Mounds 30 and 31, on the lower terrace. In every instance potsherds, flake knives, mica fragments, and flint flakes were found and in each, usually at the center, was the burned space suggesting a fire place.

---

[*] Shetrone, H. C., 1926, p. 111.

It may be objected by some that if all of these small mounds both inside and outside the great enclosure were house sites, why were there not more evidences of post mold patterns? It should be stated that the failure to find post mold patterns does not prove that they were never there. Such patterns are difficult to find under all circumstances. They may have been obscured by the gravel banks or ridges encircling the floor areas, and it is possible that they may in part have been destroyed about the edges of the mound in mound construction. While it would have been a matter of great satisfaction to all students of Hopewell to have had post mold patterns observed, certain it is that the failure to find them does not demonstrate their absence. It is quite possible that the excavations may not have extended sufficiently far from the mound center to have encountered the post molds had they been there, and the techniques then in use were probably inadequate to reveal their presence.

Further, if it be admitted that each of these small to medium size mounds, both inside and outside the enclosure, represents a house site, in which family burials were made, the problem raised by Shetrone* is largely answered. He raises the question in a final paragraph in discussing this problem when he says:

"Within the large enclosure at the points indicated on the Map are small areas containing evidence of occupation, such as fragments of bone, flint flakes, occasional flake knives, potsherds, and bits of mica. Dark soil and burned stone indicate limited occupancy of the site, and nothing commensurate with the importance of the group, and the problem as to where its builders and occupants lived remains a puzzling one."

The present authors believe that these small areas showing evidence of occupancy were house sites, which for some very natural reason never became the burial place of a prominent person, and hence were not selected as sites for mound construction. It is conceivable that a family may have occupied a house until it became so decrepit that a new house was needed. They might thus select a new site a short distance away, within or without the enclosure, build a new house, and after removal to it leave the old house to fall into decay or be otherwise destroyed. In such case the small evidence of occupancy by a single family

---

* Shetrone, H. C., 1926, p. 112.

would leave, at this time, very meagre surface indication of a former house site. Mounds were erected over house sites *only* when the house had been used as a burial place of the head of the family or other important personage. At such time, after a log tomb burial had been made on the house floor; and after the cremated remains of other members of the household had been deposited on the house floor; the house was burned and a mound erected over all.

To these authors the answer to Shetrone's puzzling problem is plain enough. Every one of the 38 mounds (excepting for the moment, Mound 25) was a house site where much activity connected with ordinary village life was carried on. Such house sites only become synonymous with death as the result of the final use to which they were put in the final days before the house was destroyed by fire. The problem of Shetrone "remains a puzzling one" only because he was convinced that the mounds did not cover dwelling houses. He seems to have been led to this conclusion because he considered the fire basins on the house floor as having been constructed primarily for cremation purposes, hence they were "crematory basins". Thus, the house, if there was one, was primarily a charnel house, and not a dwelling house.

The "puzzling problem" arose because he thus refused to accept the only evidence of habitation sites this great earthworks is able to offer.

MOUND 25

Consider now Mound 25, which was reserved for special study because it was by far the largest of the group; was located very near the center of the great earthwork, and was itself surrounded by a smaller enclosure. Certainly any explanation of the life or the people of the Hopewell Group must include the evidence furnished by this great structure.

In the summation of the "evidence accruing from examination" of the mound, Shetrone* says in part:

> "The oval area corresponding to the floor of the mound as a whole—some 470 feet long by approximately 130 feet maximum width—had been utilized as a sacred place, where funeral ceremonies and interment—cremated or otherwise—

---

* Shetrone, H. C., 1926, p. 99.

were held. The entire space was carefully leveled and cleared of all obstructions and was covered by a stratum of coarse sand and gravel.

"A sort of wall or circumvallation, composed of stones and earth, enclosed the area, corral-like. This wall may have been supplemented by pickets, although no definite proof of this was evolved.

"Within this area, corresponding to its central portion, were erected, as needed, charnel-houses for the dead, their confines usually being marked by vertical posts set into the ground. An alternative of this procedure was the heaping of small mounds of earth over burials placed on the floor. A total of four or possibly five of these structures existed in Mound 25, two of which were of first importance. Three of the five were delimited by vertical posts and two of them— the two most important ones—had definite primary mounds erected over them."

To the present authors the evidence revealed by exploration of this great mound differs only in quantity not in kind from the evidence furnished by the smaller mounds of this great site. They prefer to believe that this mound covered two large and several other smaller house sites, in which at one time or another the rulers or chiefs of this village lived. Their life was not essentially different from that of the people of the village, but because they were held in high esteem they were assigned a home site in the center of the occupied area. About it an enclosure was built, and an interior wall of stone as described by Shetrone, probably marked the boundary of the "palace courtyard". Within this area each successive ruler had his dwelling, upon the floor of which, on his death he would be buried, surrounded by the other members of his family and former servants who had previously died and whose cremated remains had been retained for this purpose. It is, of course, possible that there may have been sacrifice of living persons, voluntary or otherwise, in order that they might accompany the Great One into the land of spirits. This is suggested by multiple burials in both Adena and Hopewell, but cannot, of course, be demonstrated. Sometimes small earth mounds were erected over such a group of burials. It is impossible to deduce all the details of such burial customs, but Shetrone* recog-

---

* Shetrone, H. C., 1926, p. 100.

nized the long history revealed by Mound 25, and the fact that the burials seemed to be in family groups when he wrote:

> "As has been assumed by others, Mound 25 must have been a process of growth through a considerable period of time. To account for the burials, apparently representing family groups, found in this and other mounds of the culture, it becomes a logical supposition that some form of temporary burial and reburial obtained with the Hopewell peoples, as with certain historic tribes."

As the result of this explanation by Shetrone, one comes to understand that burials were not made continually on the floor of such a house, but periodically on the death of a prominent person. He and many others would be buried at the same time, the others who had previously died having been cremated and the cremated remains saved for redeposit.

The fact that these smaller primary mounds were not all made at the same time but in themselves showed a development was noted by Shetrone[*] when he wrote of Burials 26, 27, 30, 31, and 32:

> "This group of five burials, all of which were cremated, represented a distinct departure from conditions obtaining in Mound Number 25 up to the time of their disclosure. They occupied a distinct small primary mound to the southeast of the large primary in which the preceding burials were found, and presented features strikingly different from those attending the typical burials of the structure.
>
> "In comparison with others of the main structure the primary mound covering this group of burials appears almost archaic in character.
>
> "With the exception of Burial Number 26, the graves within it showed but little preparation, only slight indication of small timbers being in evidence and the cremated remains being unaccompanied by artifacts."

This is a most significant observation by Shetrone. This small primary mound containing cremated burials appeared "archaic" because it *was archaic*. Cremation is very old in Hopewell, having its origin in the earliest known Adena. The description of this group of burials would apply equally well to any group of Adena burials in an Adena village midden area. This small primary mound may well be the first unit under the great Mound

---

[*] Shetrone, H. C., 1926, p. 84.

25, and it may be well to point out that in the study of relative chronology of Hopewell it is shown that while the Hopewell site is one of the latest occupied sites of Ohio Hopewell, it is also *one of the oldest*. That means that it has had a continuity of occupancy from the first to the last of the Ohio Hopewell Period. It is not, therefore, astonishing that in the early history of Mound 25 positive evidence of burial customs much like Adena should be found in the very area where their rulers lived and where, because the dead buried here were greatly venerated, they built over all of these former house sites of the great and the near great, each previously covered by its own individual primary mound, the largest mound in the entire Hopewell group.

In comparing burial customs of Hopewell and Adena, it seems unnecessary to consider in such detail the other great Hopewell sites. However, it may be well to point out that the interpretation of Turner Site is quite similar to the Hopewell Group. The group of mounds at Turner Site Numbers 3, 4, 5, 6, 7, 9, and 14 evidently corresponds to Mound 25 at Hopewell. That is, they together indicate the various house sites of the rulers or chiefs at Turner Site and like Mound 25 represent a long period of development at this site. The gravel walls of these and other mounds at Turner Site surely indicate the size of the houses. In such gravel walls it is believed there was once evidence of circular postmold patterns of dwelling houses. Such houses were the living quarters of family groups, and the fire basins on such house floors were primarily used in domestic economy. The four pottery vessels found in the fire basin in Mound 1 of the Turner Site* certainly suggest that the normal process of domestic life was continued on this house floor up to the time it was chosen as a place of burial. The same may be said of Mound 2 "Crematory Number 2" at Mound City**. Certainly pottery was not used as a burial offering by either Hopewell or Adena.

As pointed out in the early portion of the comparison of the burial traits of Adena and Ohio Hopewell, the Hopewell site was chosen for first consideration because of its great wealth of material culture, and its diversity in burial customs. It should now be pointed out that (see chapter on Chronology) this great

---

* Willoughby, Charles C., 1922, p. 31.
** Mills, Wm. C., 1922, p. 265.

site began very early in Hopewell history, and continued throughout the entire Hopewell span in Ohio, being one of the last Hopewell sites to be abandoned. Its trait complex has, therefore, been designated Late Hopewell. The same may be said of the Turner Site.

At the opposite end of the chronological scale is the Tremper site, which was one of the earliest of Ohio Hopewell sites. Evidence has been presented to show that Tremper site was the first Ohio Hopewell site abandoned. It closed so early that most of the indicators of high cultural development had not been developed at the time of its discontinuance. It had no copper breastplates, no copper headplates, no metal covered buttons, no cut bear teeth, no silver, and no obsidian.

It might be expected that this difference in chronology would also be expressed in burial traits, as well as in its material culture traits. This seems to be the case. At Tremper, there were no log tomb burials, but cremation was 100 per cent.

The Tremper site may have been so early that it was abandoned before they had adopted log tomb burial for persons held in high esteem, and so all were cremated. Nevertheless, they seemingly had adopted the custom of according *individual burial* to the cremated remains of some persons. At least the cremated remains of four individuals were buried separately, two on or above the mound floor and two below floor level. Two of these burials had artifacts placed with them and Mills recognized them as of unique importance.

Of these Mills* says:

"An individual cremated burial was found in the *room containing the great cache, ...* This burial appears to *have been of considerable importance,* as it was placed in the angle formed by the joining of two walls, and a row of small posts placed around it. A second individual cremated burial was found in *this room,* about two and one-half feet above the floor. With the charred remains was a flint spearpoint, six inches long.

Burials Beneath Floor Level

"A *feature peculiar* to the *Tremper Mound* was the finding of *cremated burials beneath* the *floor, ...* The two graves were three and one-half feet deep, the floors being

---

* Mills, W. C., 1916, p. 122.

the surface of the undisturbed sandstone strata underlying
the site. Their dimensions were seven feet long and three feet
wide, and seven feet long and five feet wide, respectively.
The first grave, No. 12, contained only a small amount of
ashes and charred remains, and no artifacts of any kind.
The second grave contained beside the cremated remains,
four copper ear ornaments, mica cut into the form of *crescents,* a *mica effigy* of the *bear,* and a small flint spear point.

PRIMITIVE MASONRY

"A special feature of this grave was a wall of thin slabs
of sandstone at the sides and ends of the grave, completely
lining it, and forming a vault-like receptacle, with perpendic-
ular walls. As far as recorded, this is the only instance of a
regularly laid up wall of stone, constructed by aboriginal man
in Ohio."

The italics are our own; done for the purpose of direct-
ing the attention of the reader to significant points.

The first burial was not only an *individual cremation,* but it
was placed in the "room containing the great cache", the most
important portion of the entire structure. It was in a corner, and
separately enclosed by a row of small posts.

The second individual in the same room did not have a special
enclosure, but had a flint spear point six inches long.

This situation is very much like that found in the (Adena)
Crigler Mound, Be 20, where the important personage (Burial 11)
was buried in a log tomb, accompanied by another cremated burial,
placed in a secondary position (a corner) in the tomb accompanied
by a flint spear about six inches long.

Further, two cremated burials were found in subfloor pits.
Mills recognizes this as unique in Hopewell, but it is a very common Adena trait. What is more, one of these burials was enclosed
in a well built stone vault, a further indication that this burial
demanded some special procedure. This burial had artifacts with
it, the other had no artifacts, and no stone vault, but each burial
had its own subfloor pit.

This individual who, although cremated, had an *individual
grave,* a pit *seven feet long* and *five feet wide* (about the size of
log tomb graves), and an individual stone vault built about the
grave, had very significant artifacts. Tremper Site was so early

that copper ear spools were still quite scarce. Although there were an estimated 400 individuals cremated at Tremper, there were only eight copper ear spools taken from the site, and of these, *four* of them were in *this* grave; two of these spools had flat discs, the least specialized of any known in Hopewell. In another part of the Tremper report Mills states that there were eight mica crescents and a mica bear effigy found in this grave. When one recalls that mica crescents are *numerous in Adena*, and that *this is the only* instance when mica crescents have been found in any Hopewell site; and the further facts that Tremper Mound yielded, in the great cache, reels of both copper and slate, not found in other Hopewell sites but frequently found in Adena, one is impressed with the evidence of the closeness of Adena contact with the Tremper site. Mills illustrates the cut mica image of a bear, and points out that the primate artistry was so realistic as to indicate "action". The bear is running. Could not the same be said for the cut shell image of the raccoon, taken from the Adena Mound? Thus, the separation of individual burials for separate treatment at a site where communal deposit of cremated remains was general, the use of subfloor pits for burial, as well as the type of artifacts placed with *this* most important personage, all point strongly to Adena influence. If Adena material culture had been discovered and its burial customs thoroughly understood *before* Tremper Mound was investigated, one wonders if Tremper would ever have been classified as Hopewell.

It has been shown that cremation is a very old custom in Adena*, and probably was the means used in the disposal of most of the Adena dead. The log tomb burial was in Adena the rarer form, reserved for specially selected persons. On such a basis, one is compelled to see in Hopewell and Adena such close similarity in log tomb construction, the use of cremation, the deposit of cremated remains and the building of primary mounds over such burials on the floors of houses; that one could not doubt that such customs had a common origin in the two groups. If from other evidence it can be shown that Adena in general preceded Hopewell, then it would be an easy transition to believe that Hopewell burial customs had their origin in Adena, and differed from them only because, being later, Hopewell had a greater wealth of material cul-

---

* Webb, Wm. S., 1942, p. 361.

ture to associate with the dead. It seems that this great wealth of Hopewell material culture has been one means, perhaps the most potent means, of obscuring the close relationship of these early peoples whose burial customs are so nearly identical. Thus, these authors are disposed for the reasons previously stated to attach much greater significance to this likeness in burial customs than they would attach to the difference in material wealth as shown by Adena and Ohio Hopewell, which last may be ascribed entirely to difference in chronology.

RELATIVE CHRONOLOGY IN OHIO HOPEWELL

If it could be demonstrated that the culture complex of Ohio Hopewell had its beginning in Adena and largely developed from it, it might be expected that continuing development would also be observable within the Hopewell Complex, such continuation manifesting itself by differentiating the cultural levels attained at the various sites. This differentiation would be the result of the chronological relation of each Hopewell site to the other members of the group. Cultural development of any kind requires time, in aboriginal society perhaps much time. If, therefore, it is demonstrated that developmental stages can be observed in Hopewell, resulting in cultural differentiation among the various sites, it might be argued that those sites showing highest development are those sites where this process has been longest at work. That is, those sites showing highest development either persisted for a long time and thus became beneficiaries of the developmental process, or else they began late in the history of the people and thus had the opportunity to acquire all the results of past development of their people elsewhere; and conversely, those sites which show less development are those sites where for reasons unknown, occupancy ceased at an early date. Their early discontinuance thus denied them an opportunity to acquire the result of the higher development attained by their people at sites which persisted into later times.

Among sites in a wide spread area, where intercommunication was difficult such conclusions as to the relative cultural development at different sites belonging to the same people might be quite at variance with the truth, but it should be remembered that the Ohio Hopewell area is relatively small (see Map I); and that all Hopewell sites lie along tributaries to the great Ohio River, which gave relatively easy intercommunication between these sites. This seems to guarantee that any development at one site would be communicated to all other contemporary sites rather quickly. No site would long lag behind the others in any particular element of cultural development so that one might expect the material culture of the whole group, at any one time, to be fairly homogenous. Thus one may assume that lack of development of any site discovered now, might thus be explained as evidence of its relative early discontinuance, whereas, high development would generally imply long continuity and probably more recent occupancy.

The danger of making such an assumption is fully appreciated since it is manifest that it is possible to point out both historic and prehistoric instances where it would seem that this assumption is not valid. However, the contention is that in a closely knit community such as Ohio Hopewell, for the reasons stated, it is *possible* that the assumption might be found to apply. The validity of the assumption would then rest on its ability to produce self consistent deductions which are in accordance with observation. It is recognized that no conclusion can claim any higher validity than the assumption on which it rests. Thus, in using the assumption as a *means* of *testing* for chronology in Ohio Hopewell, the authors accept the age old diction that "The proof of the pudding is in the eating." However, if the assumption leads to conclusions pointing to a self consisting chronological order of Ohio Hopewell sites, an order not at variance with any known facts of observations, and by which one is able to explain relationship, long suspected but not demonstrated, with other Hopewellian manifestations, the authors are prepared to attach relatively high validity to such assumption, until such time as positive disagreement with observed facts can be established.

The possibility of finding evidence of development in Hopewell, and thereby establishing a tentative relative chronology is not a new idea. In the report on the Seip Mound, Number 1, Shetrone and Greenman* say:

> "No intensive study of the relative chronology of the six groups has been made, and it is doubtful if the data made available by their excavations would reveal with any certainty the relative periods during which each group was erected."

The reference here is to the six great sites, Hopewell Group, Turner Group, Mound City, Seip Group, Edwin Harness Mound, and Tremper Mound.

After such a statement from able men who have had much experience in excavations of Ohio Hopewell, it might seem the height

---

* Shetrone, H. C., and Greenman, E. F., 1931, p. 491.

of presumption for one who has never excavated a Hopewell site, or even seen one during excavation, to undertake to develop a relative Hopewell chronology. However, Shetrone and Greenman suggest that the relative high development of various skills in Hopewell differ from site to site and might imply such development. This suggestion is at once an invitation, and a challenge to any other serious student of Hopewell to attempt to arrange the well known Hopewell sites in a developmental series, in the hope that this might yield a satisfactory chronological order. The development of a Hopewell chronology while important in itself, is for the purpose of this study, secondary to the study of Adena. The primary purpose is to establish a basis for chronology in Adena. The material wealth of Adena is so meagre as compared to Hopewell, and the typical Adena site shows, in material products, such a small percentage correlation with the total complex, it seems quite impossible to discover by simple inspection of artifacts in Adena any basis for chronological differentiation of sites. There is no basis for suspecting which, if any, Adena traits came early, or which, if any, may have come later in their history. Because of the great material wealth of Hopewell, its obvious highly developed skills, its approach in design toward artistic perfection, and wide range in the artifacts made, as well as materials used, it was felt that if material cultural development could ever be made a basis for relative chronology, certainly Ohio Hopewell should offer the best opportunity for such demonstration. Further because of the seeming close connection between Ohio Hopewell and Adena, as manifested by nonmaterial traits and the oft occurring suggestion of their contemporaneity, it was hoped that the establishment of a relative chronology in Hopewell might point the way to a relative chronology in Adena. In connection with development in Ohio Hopewell, Shetrone and Greenman[**] state:

> "On the other hand certain designs in copper from the Hopewell, Mound City, and Turner Group seem to indicate either greater skill in working copper or a greater demand for intricate effigy and geometric designs than prevailed among the builders of the Seip and Edwin Harness Mound of the Harness Group. All but one of the breastplates from Seip Mound, Number 1, were plain and only a single headplate

[**] Ibid., pp. 492-494.

with an open work pattern was found, whereas a great variety of effigy and geometrical forms, in open work and repousse patterns as well as in the round were taken from the mounds of the Hopewell, Mound City, and Turner Groups.

"A similar specialization is observable in the effigy platform pipes, mainly from the Tremper Mound and Mound City. Plain Platform pipes were found in mounds of the other groups, similar in all respects to certain plain types from the two last named groups. Only a single effigy platform pipe was taken from Seip Mound, Number 1."

* * * * * * *

"Neither elaborately cut copper pieces nor effigy platform pipes were found in the Harness Mound. For the criteria under consideration Mounds Numbers 1 and 2 of the Seip Group are similar. Two breastplates from the latter were cut at the ends in a simple scroll, and no effigy platform pipes were found."

Following this suggestion of artistic development as a possible criterion of age, data on artifacts which migh show progressive development in type or design have been taken from tabulation of the occurrence of Hopewell artifacts furnished by Shetrone and Greenman in the Seip Report.* These data as tabulated, report the total number of artifacts of a particular type found at each site. These sites varied in size and were of different kinds, and varied in the completeness of their exploration. Obviously absolute number of artifacts could mean little beyond the fact of their occurrence. Since most of these artifacts are assumed to occur definitely as burial offerings, the total number of artifacts from any site, as a first approximation should be proportional to the number of burials discovered at that site. If, therefore, the number of artifacts of a given kind per 100 burials could be determined, such ratios would constitute coefficients of occurrence density, which would permit a more exact comparison of two sites of different sizes, on a roughly quantitative basis.

Here some difficulty is encountered in determining exactly the number of burials which may have been associated with these artifact accumulations. In this analysis the actual number of burials, when reported, has been used and where (due to cremations) the number could not be known exactly, the reported

* Shetrone, H. C., and Greenman, E. F., 1931, p. 508

estimate has been used. On this basis the number of artifacts per 100 burials has been computed and tabulated for each of the six great Hopewell sites; however, Seip Group has been separated into Mounds No. 1 and No. 2. Where the number of artifacts per 100 burials was less than one, the fact of occurence has been indicated by X. Only artifacts were selected which seem capable of pointing to high artistic development. Finally near the foot of the tabulation, data on the total use of important or rare material has been tabulated in the belief that extensive use of foreign or rare material may be a measure of cultural development. The fundamental assumption then is that everything else being equal, that site is the latest which has the largest number of highly specialized artifacts per 100 burials, or uses the largest quantity of foreign material and conversely the earlier sites are those which show least artistic development, as indicated by a reduced number of highly specialized artifacts, and by the lack of foreign material, which is somewhat a measure of travel and communication with the outside world. While the comparisons drawn from this tabulation of data are not all that could be desired, yet the figures do seem to suggest the possibility that these six great Hopewell sites might be arranged in a sequence indicating quantitatively artistic advancement and progressive use of foreign or rare materials, and thus suggesting a relative chronology. As will be shown later, on the basis of this evidence, Hopewell and Turner while starting early, persisted longest and are thus called ''Late Hopewell''. Mound City and Seip constitute ''Middle Hopewell''; while Harness and Tremper are designated ''Early Hopewell'' because of their relatively early discontinuance.

While much of the data for this tabulation has been taken from the report on Seip Mound, Number 1, by Shetrone and Greenman, it was found by critical comparison that some numerical values given therein were at variance with the values given in the original reports. Much time has been spent in attempting to resolve these difficulties and thus make the tabulation as nearly correct as possible from available evidence. It is possible that some items are still in error, due in some cases to the vagueness of the language of the early original reports. Such general statements as ''more than 50'', or ''several score'', or ''half of all such

TABULATION OF ARTIFACT OCCURRENCE AT SEVEN HOPEWELL SITES

	Total Artifacts at Sites							Artifacts per 100 Burials						
	Hopewell Group	Turner Group	Mound City	Seip Md. No. 1	Seip Md. No. 2	Ed Harness Md.	Tremper Md.	Hopewell Group	Turner Group	Mound City	Seip Md. No. 1	Seip Md. No. 2	Ed Harness Md.	Tremper Md.
Estimated Total Burials	85	65	97	129	48	171	378	X = occurrence less than 1						
Animal, effigy, incised, cutout, round	15	24	48	29	4	14	3	18	37	50	23	8	8	X
Bear canines, cut, worked, drilled all types	114	42	10	65	31	52	0	133	64	10	50	62	18	0
Grizzly bear teeth only	32	X	0	14	0	0	0	38	X	0	10	0	0	0
Buttons, metal covered	289	10	23	48	20	15	0	340	15	24	37	40	8	0
Bracelets, copper	7	5	0	0	0	1	0	8	8	0	0	0	X	0
Breastplates, copper	64	3	4	46	16	10	0	74	5	4	35	32	6	0
Celts, copper	83	2	2	24	10	7	0	94	3	2	19	20	4	0
Conjoined tubes, copper	4	1	0	0	0	0	0	5	1	0	0	0	0	0
Crescents, copper	0	1	0	4	1	1	9	0	1	0	3	2	X	2
Earspools, copper	131	103	12	52	20	52	8	166	158	12	40	40	30	2
Head plates, copper	9	0	6	1	0	3	0	10	0	6	1	0	2	0
Designs, geometrical, cutout	219	427	14	200	66	70	0	257	650	15	160	132	40	0
Gold	0	15	0	0	0	0	0	0	23	0	0	0	0	0
Human effigy, incised, round, cutout	8	8	4	2	0	0	0	9	9	4	2	0	0	0
Iron, meteoric	9	35	0	8	2	15	0	10	41	0	6	4	8	0
Jaws of animals, cut, decorated	11	1	0	8	0	5	110	12	2	0	7	0	3	30
Obsidian	10044	11	57	24	0	X	0	11800	17	58	19	0	X	0
Pearls, by hundreds	127	160	7	150	0	41	0	150	245	7	117	0	24	0
Pipes, platform	47	3	226	3	0	4	142	56	4	232	3	0	2	36
Containers, shell	17	16	7	8	1	5	0	20	26	7	7	2	3	0
Silver	9	8	2	21	0	5	0	10	12	2	16	0	3	0
Total occurrence, copper	889	914	224	188	37	84	45	1046	1400	230	146	74	49	12
Total occurrence, mica	3279	77	173	207	60	74	112	3850	120	178	160	121	43	30
Cannel coal	2	29	0	0	0	0	0	3	44	0	0	0	0	0
Galena	16	7	100	3		30	4	18	10	100	2	0	19	1
Awls, drills, hairpins, copper	4	2	2	3	3	1	0	5	3	2	2	6	X	0
Shell by the 100	99	230	61	32	10	69	X	116	354	61	23	20	40	X
Canine teeth, small animal	30	2000	200	2000	0	400	0	35	3070	20	1550	0	230	0
Effigy animal teeth	12	10	40	10	0	0	0	14	15	40	8	0	0	0
Teeth, alligator and shark	13	12	105	16	5	30	0	15	18	106	12	10	17	0
Reels, copper	0	0	0	0	0	0	3	0	0	0	0	0	0	1
Reels, stone, calcite	0	25	0	0	0	0	3	0	38	0	0	0	0	1
Cones	11	1	0	0	0	0	8	13	2	0	0	0	0	2
Effigy atlatl weights	4	2		4			2	5	3		5			X
Expanded bar gorgets	7	2				2	4	8	3				3	1
Stone earrings	4	3					4	5	5					1

artifacts were,'' etc. make exact comparisons quite impossible, unless the serious student can get more exact information elsewhere.

In making comparison from the table, however, several items therein are of necessity misleading. For example, Mound City is reported to have yielded 211 effigy platform pipes and 15 plain platform pipes. This is a total of 226 platform pipes. It is believed that this number does not truly represent the facts since it is out of all proportion to the other sites. Actually only 9 plaform pipes were found with burials, and fragments of some 100 more were found mingled in the earth walls of a great depository covered by mica in Mound 13. The number of burials in this mound is much too small to have been associated with this great number of pipes, as individual burial offerings. These pipes seem to have been brought from elsewhere; the number of burials actually associted with them is thus unknown and indeterminate. Again, to this number of pipes has been added 117 other pipes found by Squier and Davis in Mound 8, thus obtaining the total of 211. Of these two great caches of broken pipes, Mills* says:

> "In the subsequent work of piecing these together to form entire specimens, it was found that only a few whole pipes were represented and that part of most of the entire number had not been included with the pieces found. It seems evident that fragments of a given specimen had been deposited in two or more places, and this belief was strengthened by the discovery that portions of a pipe found in Grave Number 1 completed a specimen, the parts of which were found in depository Number 5 some distance removed. It is known that a great many of the pipes found by Squier and Davis in Mound Number 8 could not be restored because portions thereof were not among the many fragments of their find. It seems very probable that many of their fragments correspond to unmatched fragments taken by our survey from Mound Number 13, and that the incompleted pipes from the two mounds would furnish a number of complete restorations."

Obviously this means that since the total pipes represented in each cache were added to obtain the tabulated figures, the number is much too large. Further, the number of burials found or destroyed by Squier and Davis is not known and now cannot be

---

* Mills, Wm. C., 1922, p. 344.

determined. Whatever it was, it is not included in the burial total from Mound City. Thus, the total of an estimate of 217 effigy platform pipes per 100 burials for Mound City is much too large. For the purpose of this tabulation it is statistically value-less for the reasons given. It is interesting to note how as an evidence of development this item alone, in this analysis is at vari-ance with the evidence shown by other artifacts, and materials.

Again in the item of bear canine teeth, cut and inset with pearls, it will be noted that none with pearls are reported from Mound City and Tremper Mound, although 10 drilled as pendants were found at Mound City. This artifact seems well adapted to be a measure of artistic achievement. Cutting through such teeth, the insertion of the pearls in cavities often cut from the inside of the tooth, and the reattachment of the severed tooth parts to make a complete ornament, required the high skill of a master crafts-man. Yet at these two sites otherwise showing high development, there were no cut bear teeth found. It will be noted that at these two sites the practice of cremation was 100 per cent. Can this mean that such artifacts were subjected to the fires of cremation and thus destroyed as at Seip Mound* Number 1 and that, there-fore, their failure to appear a these sites is not to be interpreted as an actual absence? Perhaps since, it is believed that bear teeth like pearl beads, were in general sewed on the garments of their owners and probably worn during life on proper occasions. Thus, at the death of the owner of such a garment, if the owner was to be cremated, the teeth might have been burned with the garment, as seemingly occurred at Seip Number 1. However, other artifacts were customarily not burned with the bodies. Further, these cut bear teeth were not found in other mounds with every extended burial, but in general, only in graves of important personages entitled to internment in very elaborate graves, and then such teeth were often found in great quantity. Thus, those individuals who were to be cremated may never have had such artifacts during life. The position of these ornaments in the grave of extended burials, may then be regarded as accidental, and the result of the decay of the robes and other vestments to which they were at-tached. Thus, cremation can hardly be offered as a reason for the absence of bear teeth at Mound City or at Tremper.

---

* Shetrone, H. C., and Greenman, E. F., 1931, p. 366.

These are only a few of the difficulties encountered if one attempts to statistically evaluate this evidence. Yet even with these admittedly uncorrected errors and uncertainties it does seem possible to see by an inspection of these tabulated values, a sequence in these sites which would place Hopewell and Turner at the highest development and, therefore, establish them as the latest sites. Mound City and Seip Mounds are almost as late as the Hopewell-Turner Group, but their art was not quite as high, and where type artifacts showed almost equal technique, the number of their specimens per 100 burials at Mound City and Seip were generally smaller than at Hopewell and Turner.

In attempting to compare Mound City with the Seip Mounds as a group, it will be noted that some artifact values make Mound City later than Seip Group, and some other artifact values point to Seip as having persisted longer, and hence, attained higher development. However, if the comparison be made on a basis of total material used, Mound City clearly has the higher development, having more copper, more mica, and more obsidian per 100 burials than the Seip Group, although Seip does show a much greater supply of pearls than Mound City. This seeming contradiction possibly may be explained as the result of destruction of pearls by cremation since cremation was 100 per cent at Mound City, and pearls were often attached to the clothing of the individuals. Individual garments have been found burned and deposited in piles or caches.

A comparison of Seip No. 1 with Seip No. 2 seems clearly to show that Seip No. 2 is older than Seip No. 1. Note how, in the major type artifacts, the number of artifacts per 100 burials is very nearly the same, for example, earspools per 100 burials show a ratio of 40/40; copper celts 19/20; and buttons, metal covered, 37/40. Thus, one may conclude that both sites existed in some part of the time band when these artifacts were plentiful. This means that both sites, Seip No. 1 and Seip No. 2, reached "saturation" for these types. Each had about the same number per 100 of the burial population. However, if one passes to the comparison of total quantity of material used for 100 population, Seip No. 2 was clearly discontinued earlier than Seip No. 1, having conspicuously less of copper in the ratio of 146/74 and less of mica in the ratio of 160/121, and Seip No. 2 had no obsidian at all, while Seip No. 1 had 19 per 100 burials. This is taken to mean that Seip Mound No. 2 was completed before obsidian was made available, at the Seip site. The same story is told by the occurrence of grizzly bear teeth at Seip No. 1 and by their absence at Seip No. 2. The report of Shetrone and Greenman on the excavation of Seip No. 1 shows that the primary mound at Seip No. 1 was trilobate and quite similar to Seip No. 2 which was never covered by a secondary mound. That is, Seip No. 1 may have begun so soon after the erection of the three primary sections of Seip No. 2, that interest shifted to the new Seip No. 1 and thus Seip No. 2 was left without a secondary mound erected over all.

Further, Harnesss and Tremper are clearly much the earliest of the group. Many of the high art forms are completely lacking. They had no human effigy forms, only a few animal effigy forms, and they possess many traits now known to appear in Adena, as for example copper crescents and expanded bar gorgets of stone.

Such evidence seems to suggest that Hopewell chronology might be considered to fall into a sequence of three major epochs, each characterized by the cultural level attained at certain sites as follows:

> Late Hopewell (Hopewell-Turner)
> Middle Hopewell (Mound City-Seip)
> Early Hopewell (Harness-Tremper)

While this seems, to a degree, to be certain, the complete solution of the problem is not so simple. Sites of different epochs, thus designated overlapped, in time. For example, while Hopewell and Turner had artifacts of the highest development, thus presumptively indicating the very latest times, they also had some artifacts, held in common with sites showing the least development. A more detailed interpretation will be presented later.

Doubtless much could be said in opposition to this suggested sequence because of the uncertainty attached to some items of the data. However, two important facts should be noted. This sequence places the Harness Mound and the Tremper Mound as the earliest of the group. They appear to be generally most like Adena, and if Hopewell grew out of Adena, that is their true position. Further, there may be objection to placing Tremper

Mound in this earliest group of Hopewell, by those who consider that the elaborate practices connected with cremation are to be considered evidence of high development.

This concept of cremation was held by all of the early excavators in the Ohio Valley. Cremation was diagnostic of Hopewell. Hopewell was the highest expression of prehistoric culture. Therefore, the more elaborate the practices in connection with cremation at any site, the more highly developed that site was considered to be. This idea is expressed by Mills[*] in the Tremper report when he says:

> "The mound marks the site of a sacred structure, wherein its builders cremated their dead, deposited the ashes in communal receptacles, made similar disposition of the personal artifacts of the dead, and observed the intricate ceremonies incident to funeral rites.

> "The builders of the Tremper Mounds had arrived at a culture stage where united or communal effort in great part replaced individual endeavor, and in so doing had reached a plane of efficiency probably not equalled by any other people in the Stone Age period of its development. This fact is attested most strongly by their burial customs, in which by the use of communal depositories for cremated remains and personal artifacts, they effected a plan for the disposal of the dead unhampered by the limitations of the Seip Mound and Harness Mound plans, the next highest noted in the Ohio Mounds."

In comparing Tremper Mound with other Hopewell sites relative to Mound City, Mills[**] states:

> "So similar indeed are the mounds and their contents, that it would not be surprising to find, if not already proven, that the builders of the Mound City group migrated southward through the Scioto Valley, and constructed the Tremper Mound and earthworks. Thus, are forged several important links in the chain of evidence as to the existance and career on this most advanced stone age peoples. We find them extending from Mound City, where their skill as builders and artists has been the wonder and admiration of archaeologists, southward to the Ohio River, where at the Tremper Mound Site, they reached the highest point of their development so far noted."

---

[*] Mills, Wm. C., 1916, p. 238.
[**] Mills, Wm. C., 1916, p. 240.

The conclusions thus reached by Mills were quite logical when based on the concept of cremation held by all early investigators, the importance of which, in their thinking is indicated by the terms used by Mills as "sacred structure," and "intricate ceremonies." One naturally hesitates to express an opinion or offer interpretations on Ohio Hopewell which run counter to the opinions of a man, who, because of his industry, ability, high scholarship, and close contact with the problem, probably had the best opportunity to understand Hopewell of any man past or present. However, the discovery that cremation was extensively used for those who might be called the "common people," in Adena, and that multiple deposit of cremated remains was practiced by Adena, greatly diminishes the value of cremation, and especially communal deposit of remains, as an evidence of high cultural development.

It is to be noted that at Tremper there is an almost complete absence of some artifacts usually considered as indicating high development. Such artifacts usually accompany extended burials. These burials seem, because of the elaborate tombs constructed for them and their accompanying artistic artifacts, to indicate personages held in high esteem. That persons of importance were often accorded inhumation in the flesh, and when so buried were often accompanied by material wealth in large quantity and of highest artistic quality is well illustrated by the great multiple burial in Seip Mound No. 1. This very characteristic Adena trait of elaborate extended inhumation for the chosen few may not have been adopted by Hopewell, before Tremper Site had been abandoned. While no extended burials were found at Mound City, the site was so thoroughly destroyed before being completely investigated, one cannot be sure that there were none such at Mound City.

Tremper Mound had no copper breastplates, no copper headdresses, no metal covered buttons, and no cut bear teeth, artifacts usually associated with elaborate extended burials in the flesh. At Tremper there were only eight copper earspools, only two per 100 burials. Of these eight (four pairs) one pair was made with flat disks on one side, a crude form not found in other more advanced Hopewell sites. This type may be considered a transition type leading to the double concave type developed later. This pair of flat disk ear ornaments (crude form) and one pair of the concave disk form were taken from one of the two very unusual, individual, sub-floor graves, which was walled up with sandstone slabs to form a "vault like receptacle." This burial seems to have been that of an important personage held in special esteem, if one may so interpret this unique form of grave. Further, Tremper Mound had two pairs of ring ear ornaments, one pair made of Ohio black slate and one pair of red pipe stone. These seem to be the identical form portrayed in the human effigy pipe from the Adena Mound.

Tremper had also a few tubular stone pipes, and one a "modified tubular pipe," so designated by Mills. This modified pipe is a transition between their own tubular pipes and straight base monitor pipes where the position of the stem and bowl became interchanged. Tremper was noted for its great number of pipes, which suggests that pipes were the personal property of many of the common people and perhaps the most treasured artifact that many of them had. This is also true of Mound City where pipes were the most numerous artifacts found. Tremper Mound was also outstanding for its copper and slate reels, which also are found in Adena, but not in other Hopewell mounds, although gypsum reels were found at Turner. It thus seems that Tremper Mound Site ceased to be occupied before Hopewell had developed the elaborate headdresses and carved copper breastplats, and being early, used cremation exclusively. Since this was the form of burial for all, the common people as well as the great, pipes and mica objects were found in great quantity. Since communal deposit of cremated remains began in Adena, and in sites like Kentucky, Jo. 9, cremation was the dominant burial practice, Tremper Mound was probably not much later than some Adena Sites. For further discussion of this point see chapter on Comparison of Burial Traits, Adena and Hopewell.

Thus while the accuracy of the tabulated values of occurrence of artifacts per 100 burials from the six great Ohio Hopewell Sites leaves much to be desired, it does seem possible to see therein evidence of development in the cultural complex, and to note significant differentiations between sites which might properly be regarded as due to a difference in chronology. In a study of chronology it is clear that the presence or absence of artifacts at any site

CHRONOLOGICAL BAR CHART

Selected Developmental Traits	Hopewell Sites — Numbers Indicate Artifacts per 100 Burials at Each Site							Adena Sites — Numbers Indicate Total Artifacts of Type at Site													Suggested Time Intervals
	Hopewell	Turner	Mound City	Seip No. 1	Seip No. 2	Harness	Tremper	Adena Md. (G1) Ohio	Metzger Md. (G13) Ohio	Cemetary Md. (G38) Ohio	Fortney Md. (G32) Ohio	Great Smith Md. (G59) W.Va.	Wright Md. (Mm 6) Ky	Beech Bottom Md. (G54) W.Va.	Glidwell Md. (G49) Ind.	Redman Md. 3 (G7) Ohio	C&O Md. (Jo 9) Ky.	Nowlin Md. Indiana	Ricketts Md. (Mm 3) Ky.	Robbins Md. (Be 3) Ky.	
Gold	5	23																			
Conjoined tubes		1																			
Cannel coal	3	44																			
Grizzly teeth set with pearls	38	X		10																	
Human effigies	9	9	4	2																	
Effigy animal teeth	14	15	40	8																	
Headplates, copper	10	0	6	1		2															
Pearls by the 100	150	45	7	117		24															
Silver	10	12	2	16		3															
Obsidian	10000	11	57	24		X															
Canines, small animal	35	3070	200	550		230															
Designs, geometric	257	650	15	160	132	40															
Buttons, metal covered	340	15	24	37	40	8															
Containers, shell	20	26	7	7	2	3															
Teeth, alligator shark	15	18	106	17	12	17															

← Artifacts of Late Hopewell →

Artifacts of Middle Hopew…	Awls, drills, hairpins, copper	5	3	2	2	6	X															
	Mica, total use	3850	120	178	160	121	43	30														
	Copper, total use	1046	1400	230	146	74	49	12														
	Shell by the 100	116	354	61	23	20	40	X														
	Animal effigies, all forms	18	37	50	23	8	8	X		1												
	Earspools, copper	166	158	12	40	40	30	2			1											
	Crescents, copper	0	1	0	3	2	X	2				1			1							
	Galena, use of	18	10	100	2		19	1														
	Pipes, platform	56	4	232	8		2	36						1		1						
	Animal jaws worked	12	2		7		3	30							1							
	Effigy atlatl weights	5	3		5		0	1														
	Adena Traits Rare above this Line																					
Artifacts of Early Hopewell and Adena	*Hopewell Traits Rare below this Line*																					
	Bracelets, copper	8	8				X	0		18	4			16	26		1		10	1	3	12
	Expanded bar gorgets	8	3				3	X		1					1	2		1	9		1	2
	Cones	13	2					2						2	2				6			
	Earrings, stone	5	5					1														
	Reels, stone or calcite		38					1					1		2		1		2			
	Reels, copper							1						1								
	Crescents, mica							2		2				3	2							2
Artifacts of Early Adena	*Only Adena Traits Below this Line*																					
	Finger rings, copper									4			1				1	2			5	1
	Grooved stones									1						2		1				
	Celts, stone, flat, sub-rectangular												1	8	5	8	1	2	3	3	3	5
	Handle, bone or antler, flat, cut to form															2				1	5	1
	Combs, bone									2					2						2	
	Pipes, tubular, constricted mouth									3					3			1	1		1	1

must be much more significant as determining the *time of closing* of a site than as indicating its *beginning*. That is, all sites begun after the culture complex was well established might be expected to receive all artifact types which the people had ever developed up to that time, even if some of the types were archaic at the time of beginning the new site. However, if a site was abandoned, it is highly improbable that it would have received any material or artifact forms, procured or developed after its abandonment.

In order to present visually the possible chronological relation of the seven Hopewell sites (Seip Nos. 1 and 2 separated), as revealed by the tabulated data of the occurrence of certain traits chosen as most likely to reveal cultural development, there has been prepared the following bar chart.

An arbitrary vertical line represents by its length the time extension of each Hopewell site. Traits on which data were available from the tabulation are arranged in a vertical column. Each trait is assumed to occur at a certain time interval, and a horizontal line drawn from its position in the column at the left should cut every vertical line to the right, representing the extension in time of that site if the particular site had that trait. Obviously, if the site did not have that trait, then one may assume as a first approximation that that trait came, in the history of the complex, either before or after the occupancy of that site. To illustrate, as the bar chart shows, the obsidian line cuts Hopewell, Turner, Mound City, Seip No. 1, and Harness, but does not cut Seip No. 2 and Tremper. Therefore, obsidian came so late in Ohio Hopewell it was not available to Seip No. 2 and Tremper; and the Harness Mound almost missed it, since Harness had only one piece in 171 burials. Again stone cones appear early in the complex so that while Hopewell, Turner, and Tremper had them, Mound City, Seip Nos. 1 and 2 were later and did not receive them.

Thus, in order to arrange such a bar chart the individual traits are *juggled into vertical positions* so that every trait line crosses all site lines which had that trait and *ideally does not* cross a site line which did not have that trait. *Final positions* of the traits in the vertical column are then reached by the *juggling process*, when each trait line crosses the *minimum number* of site lines which *do not have that trait*. In the bar chart, at the intersection of the site line and the trait line, the number of occurrences of the trait per 100 burials, at that site, is indicated. Theoretically there should thus be no "0" indicated. It was found possible to so arrange the traits that in 171 intersections only five zeros were left, or less than 3 per cent of the total. Such zeros may be taken as a measure of the inexactness of the method, because actual occurrence data may be expected to deviate from the ideal. However, when one considers all the elements of chance involved in the inclusion of an artifact in a site, the variability of human conduct of the occupants of any site, and the imperfection of available information on actual occurrence, the results indicated by this bar chart are all the more surprising. If one inspects these zeros as they occur in this chart, their relative significance or insignificance becomes apparent. For example, under Hopewell there is a zero for copper crescents. If the tabulation is valid, it indicated that statistically there should have been found at least one copper crescent at Hopewell. In the same way Turner Site should have yielded at least one headplate. Expressed in another way these zeros indicate that certain artifacts should have been found at the sites as indicated by the associated artifacts.

If this method of analysis has any value in portraying origins, continuations, and terminations of sites, then it appears that Hopewell and Turner began early in Ohio Hopewell History and continued longest, and finally reached the highest Late Hopewell development. Mound City and Seip Nos. 1 and 2 started somewhat later (Middle Hopewell), and the first two continued into the Late Hopewell period. However, there is a decrease in the number of artifacts in Middle Hopewell times possessed by Mound City and Seip No. 1, when compared to Hopewell and Turner, which continued longer in the Late Hopewell period. It is also obvious that Seip No. 2 reached its termination long before Seip No. 1. In fact, as explained, it may have been terminated before Seip No. 1 was begun, but still Seip No. 1 would show the earlier traits, since the people had these artifacts, and they were carried over.

Early Hopewell, consisting of the Harness and Tremper as well as Hopewell and Turner Sites seemingly started *much* earlier than Seip and Mound City. In fact these sites, particularly Tremper, may have been in part contemporary with some Adena Sites, since they have many Adena traits. Tremper seems, as shown, to have been terminated much earlier than Harness. While Harness seems to have continued beyond the end of the Middle Hopewell period, it is apparent that it was very little effected by Late Hopewell. For example, while Middle Hopewell (Mound City and Seip No. 1) had considerable obsidian (57 and 24 per 100 burials, respectively), Harness had only one piece for 171 burials or .58 pieces per 100 burials.

In drawing conclusions from such a chart, one must keep in mind that the horizontal trait line cuts the site history line in only one point, representing only an instant of time. Actually the trait was to be found at the site for a very considerable span of time which should be truly represented by a band of finite width. What is more important, many traits were coexistent at the site, that is, the broad time bands of variable width of many different traits were superposed. One can see a measure of the breadth of the time band of any artifact by the numbers of that artifact occurring at the site. For example, copper ear spools occurred at all seven Hopewell sites. There were as many available during the period of Seip No. 2 as during the period of Seip No. 1 (40 per 100 Burials). The band width was, therefore, represented by 40. Harness only had 30 per 100 burials. Thus, Harness may have been terminated so early it never attained a density equal to that at Seip Nos. 1 and 2. The time band at Tremper was very narrow (only 2 ear spools per 100 burials) because of its very early termination. In like manner, Mound City's time band for copper ear spools is relatively narrow (measured by 12 per 100 burials) because Mound City did not start till after ear spools had been in existance at Hopewell and Turner for some time. At Hopewell and Turner the ear spool appeared early and remained late, i.e., its time band was broad because both sites started relatively early and were seemingly the last to terminate. This long span of time for these two sites thus broadened the time band for earspools (and, it may be noted, generally for all other artifacts also), yet the artifact density at the two sites kept well together, in most cases so much so as to be remarkable.

To the list of traits, the data for which was obtained largely from the tabulation in the report of Seip No. 1 by Shetrone and Greenman, there have been added three additional traits which seem capable of measuring cultural development and hence possibly demonstrating chronology. These are stone earrings, expanded bar gorgets, and effigy atlatl weights.

Stone rings are believed to have been used in Early Hopewell as a substitute for similar rings of perishable material, possibly wood, the trait arising in Adena. They were in turn displaced by copper ear spools in Middle Hopewell.

Expanded bar gorgets, drilled with two holes, and also undrilled forms are believed probably to have been used in Adena as weights for atlatls or throwing sticks. They also occur in Early Hopewell. These are modifications of early forms of the ''boat stone'' used for the same purpose. Both of their forms are reported by Willoughby* as belonging to the ''Old Algonquian Group'' of the Northeastern United States. The significance of this fact will be discussed later.

In Early Hopewell such atlatl weights began to be carved into animal effigy forms, hollowed out like boat stones but still leaving one side flat for contact with the atlatl shaft. Some were drilled as an aid in attachment to the atlatl shaft. These forms in the ''round,'' were very artistically carved. An early example from Tremper was in the form of a beaver. The maker drilled two holes in the back of the beaver as is usual in boatstones. The same technique was used in the effigy of the eagle, and the effigy of the otter from Hopewell. However, the hollow bird effigy at Hopewell was drilled at the edges, and the ''Horned Serpent Monster'' at Turner is not drilled at all. All of these are believed to be an indication of development in artistic decoration of weights for the atlatl. As in the case of the ''Horned Serpent Monster,'' some of these atlatl weights may have been chiefly valuable as symbols, or ceremonial representations and were thus made of material and of sizes unsuitable for practical use.

The possible inexactness of the occurrence data in Ohio Hopewell as the result of obvious errors of unknown magnitude make it undesirable to draw too exact conclusions from such data. However, because straws can be used to show the direction of the wind, so here this bar chart does suggest a relative chronology among the various Hopewell sites as indicated by the order of their beginnings and terminations; and as a corollary suggests a relative sequence of occurrence and development of traits in Hopewell.

---

* Willoughby, Charles C., 1935, Fig. 53.

It is important to remember that this sequence is determined quite independently of any relation of Hopewell to Adena.

It is to be noted that some of these Hopewell traits also occur in Adena. More significantly those Hopewell traits which *occur in considerable numbers in Adena* are the traits which are found in "Early Hopewell." If Adena generally is antecedent to Hopewell, yet if in any part of their cultural span they were contemporary, these traits in "early Hopewell" should indicate the "late traits" in Adena. This seems to be precisely what is observed. The later a trait is in Hopewell, if it appears at all in Adena, the fewer sites show it, and the number of occurrences at any site is always small, usually only a single occurrence.

Returning to the Chronological Bar Chart, there has been indicated on the left hand margin the artifacts which are deemed to belong to Late, Middle and Early Hopewell periods.

Obviously, the boundaries between these groups, shown on the chart by horizontal lines, cannot be fixed exactly, because of their very nature.

The whole purpose of the chart is to obtain a "spread of artifact traits," which it is hoped and believed more or less closely represents their occurrence in time. Since the division of Hopewell Chronology into three major divisions is purely arbitrary and is done only as a matter of convenience, the location of the boundaries between these divisions, as shown on the Bar Chart can be only suggestive and as such is subject to revision.

Thus, while this bar chart was developed to seek for evidence of chronology in Hopewell, if any such existed; it does seem possible that it might give some indication of chronology of trait-occurrence in Adena, in so far as Adena had any Hopewell material traits.

For this reason the bar chart for Hopewell has been extended to include a number of the most productive Adena sites. For each Adena site a vertical site line has been drawn to cross all trait lines which the site manifested. Obviously it must cut many lines of other traits which did not occur at that site. This fact can have no great or exact significance beyond demonstrating the low correlation of any Adena site with the total complex, previously discussed. On the Adena site line, the trait occurrence has been indicated by *total* numbers at the site, and not occurrence per 100 burials as in Hopewell; this again, because of the relative poverty of Adena material culture. Not all of the material traits of these Adena sites have been plotted since only those traits which also occur in Hopewell are here significant. Data on the occurrence of a few selected Adena traits are shown *below* the horizontal line which separates Hopewell from Adena traits in the bar chart, merely to demonstrate that the site selected had other well known Adena traits, which do not occur in Hopewell, i.e., to demonstrate that the site was properly to be regarded as an Adena site.

An inspection of such Adena site lines reveals that while some sites had rare occurrences of artifacts which appeared in some cases as late as Middle Hopewell," there were many Adena sites which showed no Hopewell traits earlier than the period represented by the use of "copper bracelets." Obviously most Adena sites had many traits not known to occur in Hopewell. These traits by implication would be "Early Adena traits," and truly diagnostic of Adena.

On such a basis, one may, with some propriety differentiate Late Adena from Early Adena. Thus one may regard the occurrence of copper breastplates, copper celts, copper crescents, copper earspools, and platform pipes as indicating "Late Adena" which was possibly contemporary with Hopewell. Where these traits were absent, the occurrence of copper finger rings, worked handles of bone or antler, and tubular pipes with constricted mouth, would indicate Early Adena, which by all evidence so far available, preceded Hopewell. Mica crescents seem to be of Adena origin, and maybe the prototype of copper crescents which occur most frequently in Hopewell.

Early Adena sites are represented by The Glidwell Mound (G 49) and Nowlin Mound, Indiana; the Redman Mound 3 (G 7), Ohio; The Ricketts Mound, Mm 3, The Robbins Mound Be 3, and the C & O Mound, Jo 9, Kentucky.

Late Adena is illustrated by The Adena Mound, (G 1), The Metzger Mound (G 13), The Mt. Vernon Cemetery Mound (G 38), and The Fortney Mound (G 32), Ohio; Beech Bottom Mound (G 54), and The Great Smith Mound (G 59), West Virginia; and The Wright Mound, Mm 6, Kentucky.

Again the inexactness of the occurrence data makes it undesirable to draw too exact conclusions concerning the chronology of any particular site, however, there does seem to be a chronological spread among the Adena sites so far excavated; and notwithstanding the relative poverty of Adena material culture as compared to Hopewell, and the low correlation of any Adena site with the total Complex, it does seem possible to justify the separation of Adena sites into Early Adena and Late Adena on the basis indicated. It is to be noted that there appears to be sites of both ages in Ohio, and in Kentucky, but West Virginia sites seem to belong to Late Adena and Indiana sites to Early Adena. This might come to be quite significant if future investigations are found to confirm such chronological placement.

THE CERAMIC AFFILIATIONS OF THE OHIO VALLEY ADENA CULTURE

By James B. Griffin*

This discussion of the pottery from Adena sites is intended to complement similar treatment of other Adena traits by Webb and of the physical type of the Adena culture bearers of Snow. In the individual numbers of Volume V of the University of Kentucky Reports in Anthropology and Archaeology William G. Haag has presented in some detail the ceramic characteristics from some of the sites recently excavated. In the same volume I have a short report on the pottery from the Mt. Horeb site. Many of the pottery characters to be discussed in this section are illustrated in the above mentioned volume. At the end of the numerical list of Adena traits the pottery traits are given along with the number of the site at which each trait is found, and, where possible, the number of specimens at each site. In the section in which each Adena trait is defined or described the pottery traits are also listed with a brief reference to the original type description or to a discussion of the item.

The characteristics of Adena pottery and their connections with other cultural units will be presented in the following order:

1. The pottery complexes found at Adena sites in the Ohio Valley and the relationship of the Adena sites to each other in so far as it is indicated by the available material.
2. The ceramic connections of Ohio Valley Adena sites with other early pottery using cultures in the eastern United States.
3. The ceramic relationship between the Adena culture and Hopewell.
4. The temporal and cultural relationship of Adena.

Each of these major groups will be further divided according to the pottery types or traits in order to present in sufficient detail the objective data which can be obtained from a study of the pottery and which can be used to suggest the position of Adena culture in the growth and development of aboriginal life in the Eastern United States.

THE POTTERY FROM ADENA SITES

Some of the pottery traits from Adena sites occur so sparingly that they afford little evidence for comparison with other sites

---

* Curator, Museum of Anthropology, University of Michigan, Ann Arbor, Michigan.

or with other culture groups. The presence of the check stamp on a limestone tempered ware is noted by Haag for the large mound at the Wright site (Mm6) where it was found on one sherd.[1] It is not reported for any other Adena site and helps to indicate the temporal position of the large Wright mound. This is also true of the check stamp on a sand tempered ware, for it also is found only at the large Wright mound and in relatively small numbers (somewhere between 3 and 16). Three or four sand tempered plain surface sherds were found at the large Wright site and one is listed for the Mt. Horeb site. It is possible that this indicates a connection between the two sites on this basis for the presence of mica particles in the paste of the Mt. Horeb specimen suggests an imported vessel and the same feature was observed in the sherds from the Wright site. Both sites may have obtained this type from the same source.

A single grit tempered check stamp sherd was found at one of the C & O mounds and a single grit tempered fabric marked sherd was listed for the other C & O mound. No other such examples are known for Adena sites, although the fabric marked surface is present on some of the sherds called Fayette Thick at the Mt. Horeb site. It is possible that the fabric impressed and cord marked pottery from the Madisonville area is associated with the nearby Adena mounds as has been suggested.[2] This probability has been strengthened by the recent study of Turner pottery which indicates that these types are not common in Hopewell sites in southwestern Ohio. It is evident that the check stamp either on grit, limestone, or sand tempered paste is not a common feature of Ohio Valley Adena sites. It appears at one site in the Licking drainage and at one site in the Big Sandy drainage. It is not found in Adena sites north of the Ohio River.

One of the most interesting pottery types associated with the Kentucky Adena sites is Fayette Thick which so far has a limited distribution with its major appearance at the Mt. Horeb site in Fayette County, and a few sherds are also recorded for the small mound at the Wright site (Mm7). The only other Kentucky Adena site with this type was the Hartman site in Boone County. There is a significant difference however between Fayette Thick

---

[1] Haag, 1940, p. 81.
[2] Griffin, 1943, pp. 119-20; 142-3; Pl. LXXVI-LXXVII.

as a cultural feature and the check stamp discussed above. At the Mt. Horeb village sites it is the dominant pottery while Adena Plain is found in a minor role. At the Hartman mound in Boone County, Fayette Thick is the sole type recorded. At the small mound at the Wright site, Adena Plain is the majority type with a few cord marked specimens of Fayette Thick. One of the features of this pottery type is a large solid bulbous knob or lug which is placed on the outer body and almost certainly served as a handle. This feature is not found on any of the other pottery types from the Kentucky Adena sites nor has it been observed on pottery from Adena mound sites north of the Ohio. The small nodes on the lower rim which serve to identify Adena Plain may be a lineal descendant of this functional handle. Some of the other characteristics of Fayette Thick such as the pinched and finger punctate surface also are not found on other Adena pottery types. The only Ohio Adena sites which can be considered to have pottery which might be called Fayette Thick are the Hahn mound[3] and the Schwartz and Orr sites excavated by G. O. Dorsey in Licking County in 1895.[4]

The most eastern Kentucky Adena site, the C & O site, has a number of pottery types which are distinctive. Paintsville Simple Stamped as Haag[5] has pointed out is found only at this site and does not occur at any other Kentucky or Ohio Adena site. This is then an item which connects the C & O occupants with other groups rather than with the recognized Adena sites. Levissa Cord Marked is simply the local and temporal variant of Woodland Cord Marked. The exterior cord marked surface of this type is a link with the Mt. Horeb and Wright sites in Kentucky and with the Coon, Whitehead, and Serpent Mound sites north of the Ohio. At none of these sites is the cord marked surface found on a majority of the pottery and cord marked pottery is also not reported from a majority of the Adena sites both north and south of the Ohio River. Johnson Plain is the local and temporal variant of Woodland Plain as has been suggested by Haag.[6] Its closest connections are of course with the Adena Plain limestone tempered

---

[3] Griffin, 1942, p. 351.
[4] The collection from these two sites has been loaned to me by the American Museum of Natural History for the preparation of a report. They were excavated by G. O. Dorsey in 1895.
[5] Haag, 1942, p. 344.
[6] Ibid., p. 342.

pottery which is the dominant type at the Adena sites in north central Kentucky and with the grit tempered counterpart which is much more common in the Adena sites north of the Ohio. Features of Adena Plain pottery such as the thickened rim strip, the flaring rim, the small rim nodes, and flat to rounded bases are all present. One decidedly unusual vessel is illustrated from the C & O site.[7] This is a six lobed flat based jar which has no counterpart from any other Adena site.

The limestone tempered Adena Plain type is the dominant pottery at the majority of the Kentucky sites. Its features are quite constant from site to site. With more excavations, and particularly in village sites, some temporal significance may be attributed to the increasing or decreasing percentages of such features as the thickened rim, the use of rim nodes, and the presence of tetrapodal supports. So far only the large mound at the Wright site has had tetrapodal supports on Adena Plain. The barrel shaped body and rounded shallow base with a sharp angle with the body are distinctive features uniting the plain pottery of the Adena period on both sides of the Ohio. The sub-conical base and flaring rim have more wide spread connections.

North of the Ohio River, however, as has already been suggested, the Adena Plain pottery is predominantly grit tempered. This is also true of the cord marked pottery on Adena sites in Ohio and Indiana. Haag's suggestion regarding the relationship between the tempering material of the Kentucky Adena sites and the available rock material is well taken.[8] In the blue grass country it would be somewhat difficult to obtain any form of crushed rock except limestone. In the Adena sites along the southern border of the glacial deposits and down to the Ohio River it would be easier to obtain limestone than in the glaciated area of Ohio to the north. Within the plain surfaced and cord marked surfaced pottery associated with the Adena culture the specific type of granular temper in the majority of cases reflects the physiographic conditions in the area and is not an indication in itself of any close cultural connection with other groups. The most significant factor in the consideration of the tempering material used in the indigenous Adena pottery is that it is granular

---

[7] Webb, 1942, Fig. 7, No. 4.
[8] Op. cit., p. 342.

tempered and the use of the limestone, flint, glacial material, or sandstone is of considerably less significance. This interpretation will also be utilized in the Hopewell comparative section.

In the consideration of the ceramic features which are found at, and which connect Adena sites, the pottery type called Montgomery Incised has been left until near the end because it is the only type with decoration so far recognized from Adena sites. It was recovered from the large Wright mound, the Morgan Stone mound and from the C & O site. It will be remembered that this type is limestone tempered and as such has not been obtained north of the Ohio River[8a]. In fact it is not known from any other area. At the Mound Camp site in southeastern Indiana Setzler obtained a vessel which he described as having a "five-line diamond" design which was tempered with "quartz."[9] This would indicate a close connection with Montgomery Incised. Setzler mentions the presence of small conical feet and in all probability the vessel originally was a tetrapod. The rim sherds in the illustration of this vessel suggest a close connection to the Hopewell rim shape. This fact coupled with the design and the tetrapodal support would suggest that this vessel was more Hopewell than Adena. The implication is clear that incised pottery is not as important a factor in the Adena culture as the plain or even the cord marked surface treatment. See Figure 2, p. 104, this volume.

If the ceramic complex found at Adena sites is considered as a culture trait which serves to show the degree of relationship between the various sites in a taxonomic sense one might reach erroneous conclusions because of a number of factors which serve to obscure the actual aboriginal relationship. These have already been mentioned but will bear repeating. Of the total number of excavated Adena mound sites included in the comparative statement of this report a relatively large proportion were dug in a period where little or no attention was paid to observing, preserving, or reporting broken pottery fragments. The Adena people, with a very few possible exceptions, did not place pottery vessels with their dead. At some sites the village area was denuded of top soil and used to form the mound over a house site. In this way

---

[8a] In July, 1945, during a visit to the Peabody Museum—Harvard University, I came across grit-tempered Adena pottery including vessels with an incised diamond design from the Spruce Run Mound in Delaware County, Ohio, excavated by John T. Short in August, 1879.

[9] Setzler, 1930, pp. 447-48.

pottery fragments were incorporated from the village site and contained in the soil of the mound or are on the mound floor. They are thus of the same age or earlier than the mound construction. This is also true of much of the Ohio Hopewell Woodland pottery. With the exception of the Drake Mound (Fa 11) all of the Adena sites recently excavated in Kentucky have produced pottery. The amount of pottery recovered depending more on whether the soil of the mound was obtained from a village area than on any other consideration. The same may be said for the two Adena sites recently excavated by Morgan in Ohio. Thus, the presence or absence of pottery at some Adena sites does not indicate that the builders of the mound lived before the introduction of pottery into the area or that they were a backward or marginal group who did not want to make pottery. Another element which must be considered is that until Webb's preliminary explorations of the village areas in and near the Mt. Horeb site very little was known about the material from Adena village sites.

The distinguishing features of Adena pottery which serve to group it into a recognizable unit are the predominant plain and sometimes cord marked surface, the characteristic vessel shapes, the rim treatment, and the small rim nodes. These markers are found on almost all of the Adena sites both north and south of the Ohio from which pottery has been recovered. They do not occur in combination in any other earlier or contemporary cultural units, and hence could hardly have been derived directly from any one source.

If the ceramic complex at Adena sites in the Ohio Valley is used in an attempt to recognize temporal changes within the culture one again runs into difficulties. Before attempting any chronological interpretation of sites within the Adena culture or even of the place of Adena in the general ceramic scheme in the Mississippi Valley it is necessary to examine the distribution of the features found on the various pottery types and of the various ceramic elements not yet recognized as representing a specific type.

ADENA POTTERY AND OTHER EARLY CERAMIC GROUPS IN THE NORTH

Pottery of the specific Fayette Thick type in its peculiar combination of features does not seem to occur in Indiana, Ohio, or

West Virginia. Related Woodland types do of course appear in these areas as well as in Kentucky. In general, the coarser, cruder, and simple Woodland pottery found in relatively small villages, caves, and rock shelters in this area is the variety which is most closely connected to this type.

The Baumer period pottery of the southern Illinois area is rather closely related to Fayette Thick.[10] It has the same plain, cord marked, and fabric impressed with the latter by far the most common. It is characteristically limestone tempered although otherwise identical specimens are clay tempered. The ware has a greater range of thickness than Fayette Thick but a high proportion of the specimens are over 10 mm. Some of the sherds also have the cord marked or fabric impressed interior surfaces. Baumer vessels usually have flat, circular bases, with a characteristic "heel" where the base turns upward into the side wall. Baumer pottery and its associated culture complex has a considerable distribution in southern Illinois, southwestern Indiana and western Kentucky. There are a number of marked regional and undoubtedly chronological variations but it is at present believed to be the oldest Woodland pottery in the above mentioned area[11] and seems to represent the addition of pottery to the late hunting and fishing cultures of the Central Mississippi Valley. Part of the pottery complex continues on into the Hopewellian period and it was perhaps this fact which led some students to assign the entire culture to a later date or period than seems reasonable.[12] The available pottery from sites of the "Red Ochre Phase" in Central Illinois[13] are related to the Fayette Thick. This group seems to be a counterpart in the Illinois Valley of early Adena.

Black has briefly described a site in southwestern Indiana which has affinities with the Indian Knoll Aspect, Baumer, and with Adena-Hopewell.[14] At this site there are sherds with finger pinched decoration and flint temper which suggest part of the complex of Fayette Thick. At least one of the Green River Focus Components had a pottery complex resembling Fayette Thick near the surface although no other artifacts from the site were

---

[10] Willis, 1941.
[11] Cole, 1943, p. 301.
[12] Bennett, 1944, p. 14 and Fig. 2. See also his footnote 5.
[13] Cole and Deuel, 1937, pp. 48-49, 69.
[14] Black, 1941, pp. 33-34.

considered to have been associated with the pottery.[15] Another
site in western Kentucky with a related thick cord marked pottery
is a small early (?) Woodland mound in Muhlenbergh County,
Kentucky.[16]

In Ohio with the exception of the Schwartz and Orr mounds
the pottery obtained from Adena sites is not as thick and crude
as Fayette Thick. Comparable Woodland pottery has however been
found in various cave and rock shelters from southern Ohio. A
considerable amount of material still awaits publication by the
Ohio State Museum. In Mill's excavation of the area in front of
the Boone Rock shelter he obtained pottery which belonged to the
Fort Ancient and Hopewell cultures as well as another type which
he referred to as "historic Indian". His illustration of the pottery
which he called "probably modern Indian" shows a coarse thick
granular tempered ware which has the same type of solid cylindrical lug[17] found on Fayette Thick and which is also present on
pottery from other comparable cave and rock shelters in southern
Ohio mentioned above. In northern Ohio there are a number of
known sites with analagous pottery. One of these is a rock shelter
in Mohawk Park, Geauga County[18]. The pottery from this site is
a heavy thick cord marked type and one of the sherds has a large
lug 4 cm. in diameter. This lug projects 2 cm. from the exterior
wall of the sherd. Through the courtesy of R. G. Morgan, I have
recently studied another collection from the Chagrin drainage
where this heavy Woodland pottery has associated objects of
Adena type.

In the U. S. National Museum there is a collection from near
Boston, in Summit County (Cat. No. 32828), that was obtained
from a rock shelter. The outer surfaces are either plain or cord
marked with a wide cord. Of five rim sherds in the collection four
are vertical and have flattened lips. The lips of three of these
sherds are cord marked. The fifth rim curves inward to a slightly
restricted mouth. The lip is narrowed and rounded. The sherds
in this collection show that they were constructed by coiling and

---

[15] Webb and Haag, 1940, p. 100.

[16] Pre-publication information by courtesy of the Department of Anthopology
of the University of Kentucky.

[17] Mills, 1917, Fig. 7.

[18] Collection in the Ceramic Repository, University of Michigan through
the courtesy of Bertram S. Kraus of Cleveland.

one of the pieces has three perforations 2 cm. below the lip suggestive of crack lacing.

Another northern Ohio site where the large heavy lug has been found is the Each mound in Erie County, a Woodland site with strong Hopewell connections.[19]

In a recent paper on the pottery from the Sugar Run Mound site, Warren County, Pennsylvania, very similar early Woodland pottery to that from northern Ohio and New York was described.[20] This local variant of Woodland pottern has thick side-walls, coarse texture, large tempering fragments, cord marked exteriors and interiors. There are no plain surface sherds. In the above mentioned paper attention was paid to the cord marked interiors found in other sites and areas and the suggestion was made that this practice is fairly common in the northeast in an early Woodland context and that it is apparently absent in the southeast and Lower Mississippi Valleys.

The pottery from the lower levels at the Vinette site, called Type I by Ritchie, has both cord and fabric impressed surfaces on the exterior and interior.[21] This type of pottery is comparable to the description of Fayette Thick. It does not have any indication of finger punctates nor are there any large lugs. This is probably the earliest ware in New York and seems to come in during the transition between Lamoka and Brewerton foci and the succeeding Point Peninsula and Middlesex cultural groups. In the New York area as in the Ohio Valley the dentate and rocker stamped pottery is definitely later than this early Woodland ware.

Adena Relations in the Tennessee Valley

In the Tennessee Valley to the south there is no ceramic complex with the characteristics of Fayette Thick but a number of the elements of which it is composed can be found. In northwestern Alabama the finger pinching and punctating is present on Alexander Pinched, one of the types of the Alexander Series.[22] In this

---

[19] A manuscript describing the pottery from this site has been submitted to the Ohio State Museum. It will accompany Dr. E. F. Greenman's report on the site.

[20] To be published by the Pennsylvania Historical Commission as a part of the report on this mound group.

[21] Ritchie, 1944, pp. 164-166.

[22] The term "series" is used to apply to a group of pottery types which occur on the same ware and which are the product of a cultural group at a particular period of time. Thus the Alexander Series would be composed of O'Neal Plain, Alexander Incised, Alexander Pinched, and Smithsonia Zone Stamped.

group however the application of the finger marks is highly stylized and the ware is much finer. The closest approach to the rather haphazard and slipshod use of the finger punctates is more closely matched by the sherds classed by Haag as semilunar punctations of the Bluff Creek Punctated type found on the fiber tempered Wheeler Series.[23]

The use of the plaited or twined fabric impressions on a Woodland ware in northwestern Alabama was discussed in the comparative statement on the pottery from the Wheeler Basin.[24] Since then, Haag has described the same type of impressions on a sand tempered ware from the adjacent Pickwick Basin site of Luv65. At this site which is a Copena village, Haag lists a total of 62 (1.5%) sand tempered sherds out of a total recovered of 4094.[25] Fabric impressed sherds were 13 (21%) of this total of sand tempered sherds. Even more significant is the fact that only two other sand tempered fabric impressed sherds were found in the 19 sites listed in the Pickwick. Nine other sherds (15%) of the sand tempered ware are described as "cords impressed in designs", but only 3 other sherds with similar designs are listed for the entire basin and these three were from a shell mound, Ct° 27, the Mulberry Creek site. In his conclusions Haag made the following pertinent observation:

> "As in Wheeler Basin, the sand-tempered ware is most abundant on sites with fiber-tempered ware, yet it does occur sparingly on earth mounds and certain Copena sites. A few of the sherds found on the Copena sites are similar to those occurring on the shell heaps, *but most types are different.*[26] For instance, sand-tempered sherds bearing a textile impression and having other characteristics of form and technique similar to Long Branch Fabric Marked type (crushed limestone tempered) were found (site Luv65). On the same site was found a type characterized by cords impressed into the rim to form designs."[27]

This particular combination is not common in northern Alabama but has been found around Tupelo in northern Mississippi by Jennings [28] and farther to the west in the Mississippi flood plain

[23] Haag, 1942, p. 525, Pl. 99, Fig. 1; Pl. 155, Fig. 2.
[24] Griffin, 1939.
[25] Haag, 1942, p. 525.
[26] Italics mine.
[27] Op. cit., p. 521.
[28] Jennings, 1941, pp. 196-199.

by the Central Mississippi Valley Survey. In these areas the fabric impressed and cord impressed designs are found in an early Woodland horizon. Their significance at Lu∇65 is not too clear for these types are not at all characteristic of Copena, nor are the few other sand tempered sherds which might be part of the Alexander Series. Both around Tupelo and in the Delta area of western Mississippi the Alexander Series is found sparingly on sites with a small proportion of fiber tempered pottery and with a high proportion of the early sand tempered fabric impressed and cord marked pottery. One other minority type at Lu∇65, McKelvey Plain, was represented by 48 sherds or 1.1% of the total.

The dominant ware at the Copena Village site Lu∇65 is limestone tempered—3984 or 97.4% of the total. This ware in northwestern Alabama has a rather long history and there are significant variations which are not yet fully appreciated in the proportions of the different types of surface finish from one site to another. These ceramic changes I presume reflect chronological changes. At this site Mulberry Creek Plain comprised 50.2% of the limestone tempered pottery; Wright Check Stamp 33.4%; Pickwick Complicated Stamped 5.8%; Long Branch Fabric Marked 5.4%; and Bluff Check Simple Stamped 5.2%. At the nearby Copena Mound Lu°63, a total of 143 limestone tempered sherds were found; 64 of them in the old village midden beneath the mound. Of these 41% were Mulberry Creek Plain and 59% were Wright Check Stamp.

In the other mound of this Copena group, Lu°64, only two sherds were picked up with the earth comprising the structure. They are identified as limestone tempered in the report[29] but the illustration cited suggests that the sherds are actually sand tempered.[30]

At the time of the preparation of this report Webb and DeJarnette were loathe to assign the limestone tempered pottery complex at these sites to the Copena culture. The presence of this ware on the site *before* the erection of the mounds was admitted.

"The presence of these sherds in the mound does not, therefore, of itself, demonstrate that this pottery belongs to the Copena complex. That this type of pottery is precedent

[29] Webb and DeJarnette, 1944, p. 169; also Haag, op. cit., p. 525.
[30] Ibid., Pl. 195, Fig. 1.

to the mound (Lu°63), seems demonstrated by its occurrence
in greatest amount below the old humus line which seems to
indicate that the mound was erected on the site of a village.''[31]

The association of pottery with Copena sites so far recorded
in the literature is not particularly satisfying. At the Colbert
Creek Mound Lu°54 only two sherds of Mulberry Creek Plain were
recovered.[32] The Fisher Mound, Hn°4, only contained 6 sherds.
One of these is a sand tempered pinched or ''pineapple'' type of
the Alexander Series; while of the other five, four are Wright
Check Stamped and one is Mulberry Creek Plain. Three of these
sherds have conical legs attached.[33]

At the Boyd's Landing Mound, Hn°49, which, in spite of the
paucity of evidence ''we must conclude . . . was a Copena site'',[34]
four sherds are listed. Only one of these is illustrated, a Wright
Check Stamped rim, and it is called ''the Copena limestone-
tempered ware''.[35]

In the Wheeler Basin report a number of other Copena
mounds were examined. At La°37 no pottery or other village
debris was found.[36] At site La°14, however, there were a number
of intrusive late Middle Mississippi burials with shell-tempered
pottery. Webb refers to a collection of pottery from the site some
of which was cord marked and some with fabric impressions. The
sherd illustrated on Plate 52a is Long Branch Fabric Impressed.[37]
Whether any other specimens from the site were also limestone
tempered is not known.

At the Alexander Mound Fowke reported:

> ''There was no entire pottery in this mound, and none
> that seems to have been deposited intentionally. Scattered
> throughout the earth, however, were quantities of fragments
> carried in with the earth. They presented a great diversity of
> markings and decorations.''[38]

The pottery illustrated shows two specimens of Wheeler
Dentate Stamp of the fiber tempered ware, 15 examples of the
Alexander Series, 4 sherds of Long Branch Fabric Marked and

---

[31] Ibid., p. 156.
[32] Ibid., p. 93.
[33] Ibid., pp. 38-9.
[34] Ibid., p. 40.
[35] Ibid., p. 41.
[36] Webb, 1939, p. 52.
[37] Ibid., p. 57 and Pl. 52a.
[38] Fowke, 1928, p. 462.

1 example of Wright Check Stamped. On the basis of other Copena sites it is unlikely that this pottery is coeval with the Copena occupation. There was no mention of pottery at the Hog Island site also excavated by Fowke or at the Perkins Spring Mounds, Slaughter Place excavated by Moore.[39] At the Roden Mound A however, Moore refers to "fragments of an undecorated vessel of earthenware" which were near a Copena burial.[40] This was however the only mound of the six investigated at the Roden site in which pottery was recovered.

This discussion of the possible ceramic associations of Copena has been made because it has considerable bearing upon the relationships between Adena, Hopewell, and Copena. Like the Adena and Tchefuncte people the Copena group did not place pottery vessels with the dead. They often erected their mounds in an area where there was no village debris as was also a practice of the Adena culture. However, in the only good instance in which Copena mounds were placed on a village site and where village debris was included in the mound fill, namely, at the Wright Mounds and Village Site, the pottery is limestone tempered and bears distinctive surface finishes. Furthermore, most of the included sherds in the other Copena mounds have been sherds of this same complex. On the basis of that evidence I am strongly inclined to view this complex as found at the Wright site as Copena. This conclusion has a corollary, namely, that the similar limestone tempered complex of a high proportion of Mulberry Creek Plain, and Wright Check Stamp, with a small proportion of Long Branch Fabric Marked, a Bluff Creek Simple Stamped, and Pickwick Complicated Stamped when found at other sites and shell mounds will also belong to the Copena culture group and time period.

At some of the shell mounds and village sites in the Pickwick Basin the proportions of the various type of surface on limestone tempered ware is significantly different. At the Mulberry Creek site, Ct°27, there were roughly 3% each of the Wheeler and Alexander Series and almost 20% of the limestone tempered ware.[41] Within this ware Long Branch Fabric Impressed was 64%, Mulberry Creek Plain 32% while check stamp and other types of surfacing made up the other four percent. At Lu°5 the shell mound

---

[39] Moore, 1915.
[40] Ibid., p. 296.
[41] Haag, 1942, p. 525.

immediately across the Tennessee River from Ct°27 the incomplete excavations recovered only a small number of sherds (only 163), but they have the following proportions: Wheeler Series 18.5%; Alexander Series 3.6%; limestone tempered ware 67.5%; and clay tempered ware 10.4%.[42] There were no shell tempered pieces at the site. Within the limestone tempered group Long Branch Fabric Marked is 52%, Mulberry Check Plain 31.6%, and Wright Check Stamp is 16.4%. The proportions of the various kinds of surface treatment on the limestone tempered ware is thus roughly the same at the two sites. In each case there are a very few sherds of the Wheeler and Alexander Series associated with a high percentage of fabric impressed pottery on limestone temper. If this association is considered in connection with the complex in the adjacent area of northern Mississippi described above, it is possible to postulate that during the cultural development in northern Alabama after the pre-ceramic cultures there was a period when a small proportion of fiber and sand tempered types were produced along with the dominant early limestone tempered wares. There are also indications that Wright Check Stamp appeared in the area of northwestern Alabama before Pickwick Complicated Stamp and that as its percentage increased that of the fabric impressed type decreased. Accompanying this change was an increase in the proportion of plain surface limestone ware and the introduction of tetrapodal vessels with plain and check stamp surfaces. The Pickwick Complicated Stamp is at the close of the limestone tempered types in the Pickwick Basin. Following this we can recognize the ascendancy of clay tempered pottery in this area.

In the Guntersville Basin area to the east clay tempered pottery is of much less importance so that the limestone form of the granular tempered Woodland tradition continues on until the dominance of the full blown Mississippi shell tempered wares. It is expected that the early limestone tempered ware in the Guntersville Basin will have a high proportion of fabric impressed pottery.

In eastern Tennessee a comparable situation is recognized. I have already commented at some length on the early Woodland pottery in the Norris Basin area.[43] Farther down the Tennessee

---

[42] Ibid.
[43] Griffin, 1938, pp. 255-266.

the sites of the "Round Grave Culture" of Harrington produced a high proportion of fabric impressed pottery on markedly conoidal bases.[44] This pottery in its general character resembles Baumer but the shapes in use by the two groups are very distinct. There are other cultural differences and genetic descent of one group from the other is not probable. In the southeastern Tennessee area, if I interpret Lewis and Kneberg correctly, there is a different and perhaps somewhat later cultural group which they call the Candy Creek Focus.[45] In this cultural group there is a strong proportion of fabric impressed vessels along with plain and cord marked surfaces on limestone tempered vessels. Tetrapodal supports are found on this ware. There is also present a minority grit tempered ware which tends to decrease within the life span of Candy Creek. The first introduction of Swift Creek Complicated Stamp styles and other southeastern stamped techniques is found in this group.

The importance of this brief discussion of the ceramic sequence in the Tennessee Valley area lies in the association with the Copena culture of a limestone tempered series of pottery types which are related to the pottery of the Adena culture but which are apparently later. The suggestion can be further offered that artifacts bearing strong cultural relationships to Adena occur on sites and in cultural groups in the Tennessee Valley where a strong proportion of fabric impressed limestone pottery is found along with a small proportion of sand and fiber tempered pottery in the western Tennessee region and with cord marked, fabric impressed, and grit tempered Woodland pottery in eastern Tennessee.

ADENA AND TCHEFUNCTE POTTERY

In the Lower Mississippi Valley the recently defined Tchefuncte culture has many analogies to Adena in various items of the archaeological inventory.[46] A comparison of the ceramic traits is therefore in order. Even a casual glance at the illustrations of Tchefuncte pottery will be sufficient to demonstrate that there are fundamental differences between this lower Mississippi Valley representative of an early mound building period and the ceramics associated with Adena. There are also similarities. One of these

---

[44] Harrington, 1922, pp. 154-158. Harrington spoke of some of this pottery having shell temper. It is almost certainly limestone tempered.
[45] Lewis and Kneberg, 1941, pp. 29-35.
[46] Ford and Quimby, 1945.

similarities is that both Tchefuncte and Adena used a granular type of tempering material thus differentiating both from the presumably earlier fiber tempered wares in the southeast and from the later Mississippi shell tempered tradition. In contrast to the Adena use of crushed rock of varying types the Tchefuncte potters either used clay or sand. This may be a natural result of the types of material readily available in the lower valley. The origin of the clay particles may be ground potsherds but this has not been demonstrated, or they may be natural inclusions in the clay beds utilized. Sand would be readily available for use as temper and there is little evidence which would suggest that there is any direct connection between the employment of sand temper in pottery of the Alexander Series in the lower Valley and the sand tempered pottery which appears sparingly in some Adena sites in eastern Kentucky.

Tchefuncte pottery, both clay and sand tempered wares, was built by coiling or ring building and this is also true of Adena. With the possible exception of the fiber tempered wares this technique of vessel construction was consistently employed in the area east of the Rockies throughout most of the periods when pottery was manufactured. In the feature of vessel shape there are some marked differences between Tchefuncte and Adena. In their analysis of Tchefuncte shapes Ford and Quimby have emphasized the tetrapodal supports and flower pot shape, which form such a striking appearance in contrast to the almost universal bowl shape of the fiber tempered tradition and the conical based vessels of some of the Woodland pottery. My own examination of Tchefuncte ceramics leads me to wonder whether more of the sherds are not actually from bowls than would be suggested by the descriptions given for the Tchefuncte period types. The flower pot shape, or a roughly cylindrical or barrel shape body on a flattened base is associated with the fabric impressed Baumer and related pottery in the Central Mississippi Valley. Linton has recently commented upon the two types of bases associated with early Woodland and their old world connections.[47] For those whose views of ceramic origins are not limited to one direction a recent paper by De Laguna and her bibliographical references will also be of interest.[48] An-

[47] Linton, 1944.
[48] De Laguna, 1940.

other recently published paper by Gaul on the Upper Yenesei Valley in Siberia also furnishes data for speculation regarding the connections between the eastern Woodland cultures of the New World and those of northern Eurasia.[49] The one outstanding feature of pre-Middle Mississippi ceramics in the eastern area which does not have a remarkable analog in eastern and northeastern Asia is the tetrapodal vessel which appears in the Tchefuncte and Alexander Series. There are tripods in both the early Neolithic of northeast China and in the early ceramic levels of Middle America. In neither of these areas are there too close similarities to the Tchefuncte feet. It is highly probable that there are many undiscovered cultural and ceramic steps in the pre-Middle Cultures, pre-Mamom, pre-Tres Zapotes, and pre-Period I at Panuco of Middle America which will show similarities to some of the early ceramic types of the southeast. Almost all of the Middle American scholars recognize that the earliest horizons now described are ceramically sophisticated and are not near the stage of the theoretical origin of pottery south of the Rio Grande. As it is in Middle America so is it in the northern highlands of South America where the earliest pottery of the Chavin horizon appears on the scene as a full blown development with a crystalized and definitive style. This style has affinities in design and technique to early levels in Middle America and to the Hopewellian period in the Mississippi Valley.

In the Mississippi Valley and in the southeastern United States developmental sequences have been and can be presented which show ceramic changes from early simple pottery products up to the final aboriginal groups. Since this area does possess this sequence it is unnecessary to posit migrations of peoples or diffusion of ideas once the ceramic sequence was set in motion at the close of the Paleo-Indian cultures. However, this sequence may be but a marginal reflection of the undiscovered ''Early'' ceramic periods between the Tropics of Cancer and Capricorn. A considerable portion of the sequence may be the result of continuing diffusion from the Old World. On the basis of comparative typology and known developmental sequence (plus a bit of local pride) one might rationally propose that the southeastern United States development migrated southward.

---

[49] Gaul, 1943.

If one's inclinations lean toward developing traits within an area it would be possible to hypothesize on the basis of the data presented in the Tchefuncte report on the local origin of tetrapodal supports. This could be accomplished by progression in Fig. 18[50] from g, to c, to b or f, to e and a. The crucial point in this development would be from the semi-annular base which is well authenticated for Tchefuncte, and is also found on fiber tempered flat circular bases from site Lu°59 in northern Alabama.[51] Whatever the origin of the tetrapodal vessel in Tchefuncte it is highly probable that the Gulf area is the starting point for the spread of such vessels or of this idea to the north. Webb's comparative studies within the Adena culture and between Adena and Hopewell strongly suggest that the Adena site at which footed vessels were found belongs in the late Adena and early Hopewell period. This temporal allocation is substantiated by my own comparative ceramic studies.

Another point of comparison between Tchefuncte and Adena pottery is the Montgomery Incised pottery which also appears in late Adena. This not only has an analog in Tchefuncte Incised but also in Orange Incised[52] from the St. John's area. This latter type I personally believe is the prototype of many of the designs of Tchefuncte Incised. In the central Ohio Valley area such incised pottery has only been found on granular tempered ware which is almost certainly of local manufacture. It is probable that this decorative idea came into the area from the south.

THE ADENA CULTURE AND THE HOPEWELL BIRD DESIGN ON POTTERY

One of the most interesting ceramic questions of the later Hopewellian period is the combination of the zoned decoration and the use of a bird outline. Certain suggestions regarding this may not be out of place in this report. It is possible to see the derivation of rocker stamping, check stamping, and dentate stamping from the old linear-punctate technique of the Stallings Punctate style. In the Savannah river area both dentate and check stamping follow close on the heels of the linear punctate horizon. It would not have been difficult to have grasped the idea of produc-

[50] Ford and Quimby, 1945.
[51] Several excellent examples are in the Ceramic Repository.
[52] Griffin, 1945a.

ing such punctate impression by means of a single or multiple toothed implement rather than by multiple strokes with a single pointed implement. In the Gulf Coast area careless application of the linear punctate type of impression with a bar type tool would produce the prototype of Tchefuncte Stamped. The concept of a zoned decoration is at least as early as the engraved bone implements of the Bilbo site and the application of this to ceramics is present in such Tchefuncte types as Orleans Punctated. If we may then accept the merger of the zoned style of decoration which begins in the Tchefuncte culture with its locally contemporaneous rocker stamping, and with the later dentate stamping we are still without the bird.

Associated with the Adena culture in the Ohio valley are a series of plain and engraved tablets which can be considered a by-product of the northern emphasis of stone ceremonial and utility forms. In Webb's recent review of these tablets he suggests that the bird design on copper plates from some of the Ohio Hopewell sites had its prototype in Adena stone (and one might add bone) engraving.[53] The bird found on Hopewell and Marksville pottery is certainly related to that found on the Wright, Cincinnati, Berlin, and Wilmington tablets and on the bone disc from the Florence Mound. If the zoned and incised style of pottery decoration and the tetrapodal vessels are indeed southern some of the same mechanics of culture transmission which produced the similarities between the lower Mississippi and Ohio Valleys might have taken the bird design from the tablets to the south where they became part of the ceramic complex, or the introduction of this zoned style of decoration on pottery vessels into the Ohio Valley produced the merger in the northern Hopewellian center. It is also possible for someone to suggest that the Adena tablet birds were hatched from Marksville vessels. A possible objection to this theory is that there is no logical "egg" known from Louisiana which could have produced the Marksville bird. Clarence H. Webb has described and illustrated a fine bird on a steatite bowl from the pre-ceramic Poverty Point site in northeastern Louisiana[54] but this example is of a completely different style somewhat suggestive of the bird effigy mounds of the northern Mississippi

[53] Webb, 1940, p. 126.
[54] Webb, C. H., 1944, Fig. 31-1.

Valley and the "Eagle Effigy Mound" of Eatonton, Georgia. Webb also refers to stone beads carved in the form of birds but none are illustrated. It is not argued that these ornithological observations have answered the question raised in the preceding paragraph. They are intended as brakes to the ready acceptance of flat statements of the priority of the bird design in the Lower Valley.[55]

ADENA AND THE SOUTH APPALACHIAN AREA

Simple stamping as a type of surface finish is concentrated in the South Appalachian area. It runs from northern Florida to southwestern Ohio. Throughout much of this area it is associated in its earliest forms with the first granular tempered pottery. On the northwest coast of Florida it appears in the first recognized horizon which is equated culturally and temporally with the Deptford period of the Georgia-South Carolina coastal area.[56] In central Georgia Kelly has assigned Mossy Oak Simple Stamp to the early Swift Creek complex.[57] In the mountain areas of South Carolina and along the fall line simple stamping also appears in an early context.[58] In eastern Tennessee its associations are also with early Woodland pottery of the Candy Creek Focus.[59] Paintsville Simple Stamped of the eastern Adena sites is to be associated with these grit and sand tempered types. Of later date is a group of simple stamped or brushed surface on limestone in the Tennessee Valley of southeastern Tennessee where it is called Middle Valley Brushed and in northern Alabama where it is called Bluff Creek Simple Stamped. Haag correctly pointed out the connection between Bluff Creek and Paintsville[60] but his tendency to equate them temporally and include such features as tetrapodal supports is I believe in error. I do not know of any such supports on either Middle Valley or Bluff Creek Simple Stamp. In the Pickwick Basin it is a rare surface finish on limestone temper and the greatest number of sherds were found at the Copena village site Lu⁰65.[61] It is not associated with the early limestone tempered types and only begins to be used toward the end of the ap-

---

[55] Willey & Woodbury, 1942.
[56] Ford and Willey, 1940, pp. 137-143.
[57] Kelly, 1938, p. 59. Called Vining simple stamped at that time.
[58] Fewkes, 1928, Fig. 187-A; Griffin, 1945.
[59] Lewis and Kneberg, op. cit.
[60] Haag, 1942, p. 344.
[61] Haag, 1942, p. 525, type 3e.

plication of fabric impressions. It has its greatest development in northeastern Alabama and southeastern Tennessee in the period just preceding recognizable Middle Mississippi culture.

Another unusual ceramic feature of the C & O mound group at Paintsville is the presence of the lobed vessel on Johnson Plain. These are the only known examples from an Adena site. The lobing was accomplished by the use of rather broad, shallow vertical depressions running from the shoulder to the flat circular base. An apparently similar trait was in use in the northern part of the St. John's drainage in Florida at Racy Point,[62] a small sand mound, and at the base of the Tick Island mound.[63] These vessels are associated in this northeastern Florida area with small tetrapodal jars and other elements which indicate a cultural and probably chronological association with the Adena-Tchefuncte period.

Adena Pottery and Ohio Hopewell

In September, 1943, Richard G. Morgan and I classified and recorded all of the pottery from the Hopewell sites now in the Ohio State Museum. This collection was supplemented by the Turner pottery which was shipped to Columbus for study by the Peabody Museum of Harvard University and by my own notes on the Moorehead collection from the Hopewell site which was formerly in the Field Museum of Natural History. When circumstances permit it is our intention to publish a full statement on the ceramic complex of the six major Ohio Hopewell sites.

The most obvious difference between the Adena and Hopewell pottery is the much greater range of shape and decoration evidenced in the latter group. The quantity of the available pottery from the different Hopewell sites varies considerably and may not reflect the actual ceramic complex at some of them. However, on the basis of the available material some correspondences with Adena may be noted.

At the Tremper site a little less than half the pottery is limestone tempered and most of the remaining sherds are grit tempered. Almost 96% of the pottery is plain with small amounts of cord marked, simple stamped and miscellaneous incised comprising the remainder. Three of the simple stamp sherds are sand tem-

---

[62] Moore, 1894, p. 184-5 and Pl. XXIX, Fig. 2.
[63] Ibid., p. 156 and Pl. XXV, Fig. 1.

pered and are probably very closely related to Paintsville Simple
Stamp. None of the fragments now preserved are of the various
Hopewell zoned stamp types. Mills also commented upon this
feature of the site.[64]

Mound City has 38% limestone and 60% grit temper and the
remaining 2% is sand. Cord marking appears on half of the fragments and 38% are plain. This site has a fair representation of
the various zoned decorations as well as the famous vessels recovered by Squier and Davis and by Mills. There are also sand tempered simple stamped sherds.

At the Turner site which has not only the largest amount of
pottery but also shows the great variety, grit temper appears in
70%, limestone temper in 29%, and there is a small amount of
marked pottery comprises 67% of the sherds examined and 21%
had plain surfaces. The remaining 12% had different types of
decoration. Thus, from the only Hopewellian site with a large and
representative collection from both mound and village site excavation the proportion of decorated to "utility ware" is approximately the same as that reported from lower Mississippi Valley
Hopewellian sites.[65] It is not unreasonable to assume that the
ceramic complex at the Turner site exhibits a temporal range
somewhat greater than that shown from the other Ohio Hopewell
sites.

The Harness site collection at the Ohio State Museum is 96%
grit tempered and 4% limestone. The cord marked sherds comprise 46% and plain sherds 15%. An unusually high proportion
of the pottery is either stamped or Hopewell zoned stamped. The
total number of sherds is small and the proportions probably do
not accurately reflect the actual condition at the site. There are
no sand tempered sherds or simple stamping of any kind.

At the Hopewell site less than one per cent of the sherds are
sand tempered and the rest are crushed rock. Eighty-six per cent
of the pottery is cord marked, 10% is plain and the rest are
decorated or have the check or simple stamp. All six of the sand
tempered pieces are plain.

At the Seip mound almost the same proportion of grit temper
is found as at the Hopewell site. Seip does have 2% limestone

[64] Mills, 1917, p. 234.
[65] Ford and Quimby, 1945, p. 95.

and a very few sherds which are sand tempered. The sherds preserved from the Seip excavations indicate that 66% of them are cord marked, 20% plain and the remainder are either stamped or decorated after the well known Hopewellian fashions.

In summary we can say that out of a total of a little over 10,000 Ohio Hopewell sherds that almost two-thirds are cord marked and one-fifth are plain. Since the majority of the sherds from Adena sites are plain it might be argued that a Hopewell site which had a high proportion of plain utilitarian pottery was older than one which had a high proportion of cord-marked pottery. If this were true then the Tremper site would be by far the oldest Hopewell site, and it is interesting at least to recall that the Hopewellian zoned pottery is not recorded from the site. Mound City would be the next to appear, then Turner and Seip with almost identical proportions of Woodland Plain, followed by Harness and with the Hopewell site as most recent. However, such an arrangement of the sites will perhaps not be justified on the more thorough analysis which will be undertaken at a later date. It is, moreover, based on the assumption that plain ware preceeds cord-marking in the Ohio Valley and this does not appear to be the case.

There is, however, an undoubted connected between the plain Woodland pottery of the Adena sites and the same ware which appears in the Hopewell sites. The thickened upper rim which is a characteristic but not inevitable feature of the Adena rims is not often present on Hopewell pottery unless the rim shape associated with the cross-hatched incising is derived from the older Adena form. There is to be observed in the Adena vessels a tendency toward a flaring rim which preserves a rather gradual curve. Some specimens have almost an angle and at the Robbins site this feature is marked on most of the rims. This rim thickening on these sherds is at the base of the rim and not near the lip. This rim shape is a significant feature of many of the Ohio Hopewell rims and has not been illustrated in the literature. It will provide a vessel outline not too dissimilar from certain Mississippi jar shapes. None of the small lower rim nodes is to be found on the pottery from the Hopewell sites. This feature of the Adena period pottery may have been derived from the large and heavy lug which appears on Fayette Thick. This lug in turn has an analog on the large lugs which are associated with the stone bowls of the pre-pottery levels.

The cord marked Adena and Hopewell pottery are very much the same. The fabric impressed pottery of the Fayette Thick type is hardly balanced by the three fabric impressed sherds from the Turner site. There is a small proportion of both check stamp and simple in Adena and also in Hopewell. There are no complicated stamped sherds in Adena but there are a few such sherds in the Hopewell complex. Except for the appearance of Montgomery Incised and a similar vessel from Mound Camp there is no indication in Ohio Valley Adena of a development of the ornamented pottery which is associated with all of the Ohio Hopewell sites except Tremper. This is in contrast to the evident connection between some of the Tchefuncte techniques and styles and those of Marksville. There is some continuity then between Adena and Ohio Hopewell ceramics in the more utilitarian forms and surface finish but not in the most distinctive Hopewellian period ceramics which must then either have developed during the occupation of the Ohio sites or have been introduced from outside the area. This lack of distinctiveness of the Ohio Hopewell pottery complex has been recognized since 1938.[66]

The Illinois Valley Hopewell pottery development is another story, and I have seen only one good example of a trade sherd from that area in the Ohio Valley. It was found by a University of Kentucky field party during the excavation of site Group 1, the Old Fort Earthworks, in Greenup County, opposite Portsmouth, Ohio. This rim sherd was identical in all its features to specimens of the dentate variety of Naples Stamped pottery. It was also recognized as such by W. G. Haag and Henry Carey of the University of Kentucky staff. Unfortunately, it has been mislaid.[67] The Woodland pottery from this site has many close similarities both to Adena and to the pottery from the Tremper site across the river.

CONCLUSIONS

The pottery associated with the Adena sites in the Ohio Valley can be recognized as a significant unit of the widespread Woodland ceramic tradition. This tradition of pottery making has the

---

[66] Griffin, 1941, pp. 165; 211-213.
[67] It is not in the Ceramic Repository.

greatest areal extent in North America if not in the New World. Furthermore, many students of American archaeology admit the probability of its derivation from northern Eurasia. The regional variations and the chronological position of many of the Woodland types still awaits adequate definition and comparison but the preliminary work has been done and some tentative interpretations have been proposed.

We do not have any clear stratigraphic data available on the sequence of the pottery types found in association with the Adena culture so that our interpretations of the possible sequence and chronological connections are not entirely sound. It has been suggested that on a comparative basis both within and without the Adena Aspect that the pottery type known as Fayette Thick with its various types of surfacing treatment both on the interior and exterior has a relationship to Woodland pottery of an early period. The development of Adena would then appear to begin at a stage when this generally thick and coarse pottery was beginning to be abandoned for newer more advanced types. The early occupation of the Mt. Horeb site, the Hartman mound, and the small mound at the Wright site would be considered as belonging to an early Adena period on the basis of this hypothesis. The other pottery types or elements found in Adena pottery which have connections outside of the Ohio Valley are associated with sites which suggest a late period in the time span of the Adena culture. These features are the check stamp, simple stamp, the tetrapodal supports, and the incised pottery. This interpretation would allocate the large mound at the Wright site, Morgan Stone and at least part of the occupation of the C & O site to a late position in the life of the Adena culture. Cord marked pottery is not clearly enough connected with any one period for it to be reliable as a time indicator in this area. The dominant Adena Plain type extends throughout most of the life of the Adena culture. While its derivation is uncertain a closely similar type becomes one of the elements in the Hopewell ceramic complex in the Ohio Valley. Adena Plain is also close to Mulberry Creek Plain of the Copena period in northern Alabama. In some respects such as vessel shape, supports, rim shape, and modification the connection with Copena is even closer for the Kentucky limestone tempered Adena Plain as represented at the Wright site than is the connection of the same Adena unit with Hopewell pottery north of the Ohio. The absence of Adena material west of southeastern Indiana makes it unlikely that any movement of Adena took place down the Ohio and up the Tennessee. There is no Adena from southwestern Indiana, southern Illinois, western Kentucky or the contiguous areas of Missouri and northeastern Arkansas. I am at a loss to understand the statements of Ford and Willey that the "Burial Mound I complex provided the basis for the well-known Adena culture,"[68] on the assumption that Tchefuncte is the fountain of the early Woodland period in the Mississippi Valley. It might better be said that Adena provided the basis for "Burial Mound I." On the matter of priority of one area over the other as far as concrete data is concerned there is absolutely no evidence. It is simply a question of assuming the source of burial mounds and rationalizing from that point. Ford and Willey also refer to Adena sites near the mouth of the Ohio in which "are also found elbow pipes of both clay and stone which were used with separate stems."[69] I know of no such Adena sites. The reference may be to the Page site in Logan County, Kentucky. This can hardly be called Adena. Similar exception can be taken to calling four mound sites in eastern Tennessee "Attenuated Copena."[70] The assignment of Copena by the same authors to the early limestone tempered types in northern Alabama[71] I have also indicated by a comparative study is certainly in error. It should also be mentioned at this time that the vessel shape of some of the Mulberry Creek Plain of the Copena period is very close to the Mississippi Plain jars in its possession of a rounded bottom, wide mouth, and breadth-heighth proportion. There are also strap handles at Lu`65, the Copena village site, and at Lu`67, a shell mound with an occupation during the Copena period. Many of the triangular arrowpoints from Lu`65 look very much like the Mississippi type which appears in greater numbers at a slightly later period.

The reasons for regarding Ohio Hopewell as later than Adena on a comparative ceramic basis have already been given. It is unfortunate that no stratigraphic data is known on this point. Webb's seriation of certain significant Adena and Hopewell traits

---

[68] Ford and Willey, 1941; p. 335.
[69] Ibid., p. 336.
[70] Ibid., p. 337.
[71] Ibid., p. 341.

has afforded the same chronological and in large measure cultural interpretation which is provided by the pottery. The pottery does not provide evidence of a migration into the Ohio Valley from the south. The Hopewell pottery complex in Ohio cannot be derived en masse from Adena, nor from any other single source.

PHYSICAL ANTHROPOLOGY OF ADENA

This section deals with the Adena man himself as known from a study of the skeletal remains found in the elaborately prepared tomb graves either covered by or included in the large conical earth mounds.

The combined skeletal remains described in Volume V and the last number, Bulletin No. 6, of Volume III (the Adena site reports) form a group of 265 individuals. Of these burials, 51 are cremations, and consist of small fragments of thoroughly calcined bone. Further, of the burials of determinable sex there are twice as many males as females. This fact coupled with the apparently common practice of cremation, would indicate that these remains are those of a selected group, probably the important individuals of the community. However selected, they are the only known existing representatives of these early prehistoric Kentucky builders of earthworks.

Table I lists all the skeletons of the documented Kentucky Adena burials by age and sex.

TABLE I
POOLED ADENA SKELETAL DATA

Estimated Age Group	Total No.	%	Males No.	%	Females No.	%	Indeterminate Sex No.	%
Infant (x–3 years)	9	3.4	5	3.4	2	2.9	2	4.2
Child (4–12 years)	12	4.5	9	6.1	2	2.9	1	2.1
Adolescent (13–17 years)	14	5.3	4	2.7	10	14.3	....	0.0
Sub-Adult (18–20 years)	1	0.4	....	0.0	1	1.4	....	0.0
Young Adult (21–35 years)	143	54.0	93	63.3	39	55.7	11	22.9
Mid. Aged Adult (36–55 years)	15	5.7	14	9.5	1	1.4	....	0.0
Old Adult (56–x years)	3	1.1	3	2.0	....	0.0	....	0.0
Indeterminate Age	17	6.4	1	0.7	....	0.0	16	33.3
Cremations	51	19.2	18	12.3	15	21.4	18	37.5
TOTAL BURIALS	265	100.0	147	100.0	70	100.0	48	100.0
Males	147	55.5						
Females	70	26.4						
Indeterminate	48	18.1						
TOTAL BURIALS	265	100.0%						

As a whole, the Adena skeletons present well-marked sex differences. Whenever possible, the entire skeleton, skull, long and hip bones has been used to assess the sex and age of the individuals described in the site reports. The very fragmentary and cremated remains are most difficult to determine and largely constitute the "indeterminable" group. The aging of the skeletons is based upon the appearance of the deciduous and permanent teeth (Infants and Juveniles), the degrees of the union of the epiphyses of the long bones (Adolescents) and in the case of Adults, by the degrees of union of the skull sutures and by the age changes present in the pubic symphyses. It has been indicated elsewhere* that since growth patterns are very similar for the different racial stocks of mankind any small discrepancy which may exist in these data (based upon our knowledge of white people) will fall within the limits of the age groupings presented.

In order to describe the Adena Indian all known skeletal material was examined and studied. In reexamining the remains from the Kentucky Ricketts and Wright Mounds already reported,** several additional skulls were repaired yielding more measurements, and the estimated sex of several skeletons was changed,*** and in one case (Mm 6-1 op. cit.) the measurements of an adolescent female were removed from the adult series.

Further, the elimination of differences inherently due to personal equation in both metrical and morphological studies, was regarded as sufficently important to merit the remeasurement and observation of the skulls from the Ricketts and Wright Mounds; hence the entire skeletal content of these sites was reexamined, and studied. Thus all Kentucky material has been studied by one investigator and the description of these skeletons constitutes this section.

The total Kentucky series, some 78 adult skulls, 46 males and 32 females, and the postcranial bones of 38 males and 18 females has been measured and studied. These combined data are presented in Tables II, III, and IV. The individual measurements and indices are either included in Volume V, Numbers 3 through 7, or contained herein, Table VII.

---

* Snow, Charles E., 1942, p. 448.
** Hertzberg, H. T. E., 1940, pp. 233-257, Vol. III, No.6 and pp. 83-102, Vol. V, No. 1.
*** Long bones of Burials 27 and 28 from Mm 3 are regarded as females.

All new cranial data are included as a fold-in sheet, Table VII. No further postcranial studies of the Ricketts and Wright skeletons were deemed necessary, and the data are included with the total series. The measurements and observations obtained from the Adena Indian skeletons were made by the junior author, with the exception of the Ricketts and Wright postcranial,* in accordance with accepted techniques and by means of the usual sliding and spreading calipers, an improved craniophore, a goniometer, a flexible steel tape, an osteometric board, and a modified Bodel apparatus (for measurement of the angle formed at the elbow).

Every effort has been made to obtain all possible data. It is believed that all measurements, even approximate or affected by artificial deformation (in the case of most of the skulls), may be helpful in describing skeletal material which is rare and otherwise unobtainable. Therefore, approximate measurements and their derived indices make up the combined averages. More exact, but far fewer measurements may be had by averaging the undeformed, unparenthesized measurements in the tables of individual data included herein or in the separate numbers 3-7 of Volume V. Likewise the range of any measurement (skull or postcranial) may be quickly obtained from the tables of individual data in each site report or from Table VII herein.

In addition, each of the better Adena skulls is illustrated either in the separate site reports (Vol. V, Nos. 4-7) or appears herein, Figures 4-28, in the effort to portray the type of Indian with which this study deals.

As a final attempt to describe more effectively the Adena type, all of the available crania, an even one hundred of all ages, were critically reviewed. In the course of this examination, the presence of bifrontal flattening (both sides of the forehead) was noted for the first time. Since bifrontal deformation had been observed and noted before on Hopewell skulls** its presence has been carefully noted on the Ohio Hopewell material studied at this laboratory. This experience made possible the discovery of the same kind of deformation in the Adena skulls, a trait hereto-

---

* Hertzberg, H. T. E., 1940, pp. 233-257, Vol. III, No. 6 and pp. 83-102. Vol. V, No. 1.
** Moorehead Warren K., 1892, p. 240.
*** Stewart, T. Dale, 1940, p. 15.

fore undetected. This cultural feature is another important connecting link between Adena and Hopewell.

Unless acknowledged otherwise, all skeletal photographs were made by the junior author at the University Museum, Lexington.

CRANIAL MORPHOLOGY

The type of nearly all of the skulls present in the Adena Skeletal remains can be classified as centralid* (Hrdlicka's "gulf").** In looking at the Adena skulls (Figures 18 through 28 and in the other Reports in Volume V) one is impressed with the globular nature of most of the skull vaults, which are high and flattened on the back, the broad high foreheads, the massive flat faces, the prominent hooked nasal bones and the projection of the jaws. Usually the chins are of moderate prominence. These are the first broad headed peoples to come into Kentucky, and will be henceforth referred to as the "Adena" type.

Approximately 92% of the skulls (89% male, 95% female of all ages) are deformed at the back to moderate or pronounced degrees. In addition, nearly one-third show flattened areas also on each side of the forehead just above the frontal bosses. This deformation probably resulted from infant cradleboard practices.

There are a few skulls of both sexes which show little or no deformation and are regarded as unaffected by the small deformation when present. These appear somewhat different in their morphology. They are narrower with longer, less prominent faces. A few individual skulls resemble those common in the Hopewell graves. The possible mixing of these two types forms an intriguing subject which will be discussed more fully later on.

The typical Adena skull contrasts strongly with that found in the Shell Heap graves of Chiggerville and Indian Knoll.*** The Shell Heap people with their undeformed, long, narrow heads, their short broad faces, with flaring gonial angles, the more angular, less flat face, and in general less specialized mongoloid cast, are very different from the occupants of Adena tombs. A similar contrast exists between Hopewell and Adena skulls (see Figures 12 through 15).

---

* Neumann, Georg K., 1939-1941, p. 80, in accord with Von Eickstedt, E, 1934.
** Hrdlicka, A., 1940, pp. 452-458.
*** Skarland, Ivar, 1939, p. 36.
*** New data, Indian Knoll Oh 2, Kentucky, mean values for:

	MALES		FEMALES	
	No.	Mean	No.	Mean
Skull length	247	178.8 mm.	190	172.9 mm.
Skull breadth	249	135.5 mm.	192	131.0 mm.
Cranial Index	246	75.9	190	76.4

The detailed classification of these features is presented in Table II for 81 adult Adena skulls (the number in each group is enclosed with parentheses). The group with little or no deformation is treated apart. In addition, the skull morphology of four adolescent girls of about 15-16 years is included as a separate group to augment the description of these people in so far as is possible.

In each category of features described, the variation and number of cases are indicated.

One of the interesting facial features which occurs commonly among the male specimens, is the malar tuberosity. This bony eminence, providing muscular attachment, is often very large and prominent on rugged skulls, so much so as to suggest its utility as a minor sex criterion much like the browridges or mastoid processes. Figure 4 illustrates this unusual feature. This prominence on the cheek bones gives additional jut to the already outstanding malars of the Indian face and doubtless contributes to the "flat-faced" appearance which many of these Adena men had. Many Mongoloid peoples are noted further in this connection, for the thick, fatty, layer of skin tissue which lies over these structural features of the face (fatty polsters, malaris pedicularis).

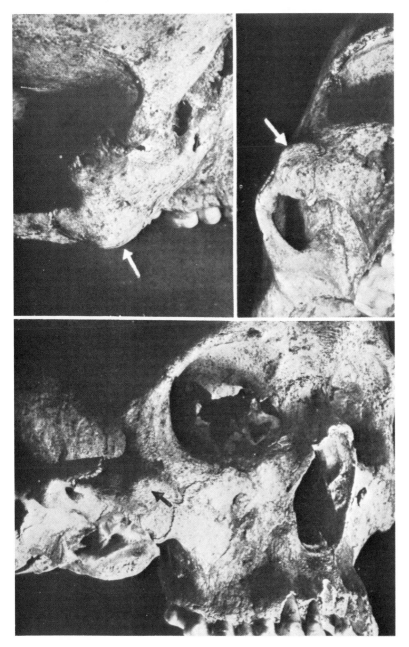

Fig. 4. The Malar Tuberosity. Views of the right cheekbone of Burial 7, a
young man, from Be 17, Landing Site, taken from above, below, and
in front. The tuberosity forms part of the structure which gives the
characteristic flatness to the face of the Indian.

CRANIAL MEASUREMENTS AND INDICES

The measurements and indices of 45 male and 28 female Adena skulls (the total Kentucky site series) divided into deformed and undeformed series are listed in Table III. It is to be noted that the averages are composed of approximations, and are often affected by different degrees of deformation; nevertheless, these are direct metric expressions of the size of the skulls of Kentucky Adena people. The "undeformed" group consist of undeformed skulls and a few with so little occipital flattening that it is regarded as not affecting appreciably the vault diameters.

Altogether, these measurements when compared with the range of human variation in size, indicate an Indian group with rather short, but broad and extremely high heads; with large, long, broad faces (both total and upper face); with long noses of medium width; with orbits of medium height and width (as measured from maxillo-frontale); with palates fairly large and the lower jaws big and robust. The arcs of the skull indicate the same characteristics; a small circumference, medium sagittal, and extremely large transverse measurements, head dimensions and proportions most directly affected by the pronounced degrees of occipital flattening. However, those skulls with slight or no deformation (undeformed) present similar proportions. The gross vault size is fairly large, with the module and capacity estimations high.

The most outstanding single dimension is that of height, undoubtedly increased by the pronounced deformation of the backhead. These deformed Adena skulls are the highest recorded in any human group.*

As a group, the indices or measurement ratios which express the proportions of the Adena skulls, define a type with very high, broad heads, with relatively narrow foreheads, with faces, orbits and nasal apertures of medium proportions and broad palates. The smaller group with relatively little deformation of the skull vault has the same general proportions with the exception that the vaults are narrower and two females have long faces and higher orbits.

---

* Collins, Henry B., 1941, p. 149, and Martin, Rudolf, 1928, p. 795, Vol. II.

TABLE II
ADENA CRANIAL MORPHOLOGY
MALES AND FEMALES

Morphological Observation	Deformed Males (35)	Slight or Undeformed Males (11
Muscularity	Medium 13, Large 22	Medium 6, Large 5
Weight	Light 1, Medium 24, Heavy 10	Light 3, Medium 5, Heavy 3
Form	Ovoid 22, Elliptical 1, Spheroid 7, Brisoid 3, Sphenoid 2	Ovoid 8, Spheroid 1, Pentagonoid 1,
Deformation	Occipital 22, Rt. Occipital 5, Left Occipital 8, Lambdoid 2, with Bifrontal 14, Frontal 4	Occipital 7, Rt. Occipital 1, Left Occ Lambdoid 1, with Bifrontal 1
Degree of Deformation	Small 2, Medium 12, Pronounced 21	None 1, Trace to Small 8, Medium 2
Transverse Form	Pentagonoid 12, Round 1, Rounded Pentagonoid 3	Pentagonoid 5, Rounded Pentagonoi
FRONTAL REGION		
Height	Medium 14, High 19, Very High 2	Medium 5, High 3
Breadth	Small 2, Medium 8, Large 16	Small 4, Medium 5, Large 2
Slope	None 3, Slight 12, Medium 19, Pronounced 1	Slight 3, Medium 7, Pronounced 1
Brow Ridges: Type	Median 7, Divided 11, Continuous 18	Median 3, Divided 4, Continuous 3
Size	Small 8, Medium 13, Large 12, Very Large 2	Small 1, Medium 5, Large 4
Glabellar Eminence	Small 14, Medium 11, Large 9, Very Large 1	Small 5, Medium 3, Large 1
Metopism	None 1, Traces 18	None 4, Traces 5
Bosses	Small 4, Medium 17, Large 12	Small 2, Medium 6, Large 2
Median Crest	Small 17, Large 1	Small 9
Post-orbital Constriction	Medium 18, Large 17	Medium 7, Large 4
PARIETAL REGION		
Sagittal Elevation	Small 22, Medium 10, Large 3	Small 7, Medium 4
Post-coronal Depression	Small 32, Medium 1	Small 11
Bosses	Small 9, Medium 17, Large 5	Small 3, Medium 7, Large 1
Size of Foramina	None 12, Small 6, Medium 10, Large 2	None 2, Small 6, Medium 3
Lambdoid Flattening	None 6, Small 17, Medium 6, Pronounced 2	Small 7, Medium 4
TEMPORAL REGION		
Fullness	Flat 4, Small 10, Medium 18, Large 2	Flat 2, Small 5, Medium 4
Mastoid Processes	Medium 2, Large 30	Medium 1, Large 10
Supramastoid crest	Small 4, Medium 6, Large 23	Medium 5, Large 6
Sphenoid Depression	Small 19, Medium 5, Large 2	Small 4, Medium 2, ?5
Pterion Form	H 6, K 9	K 4, ?7
Styloid Size	Small 2, Medium 5, Large 6	Medium 1, Large 2, ?8
Mandibular Fossa Depth	Small 4, Medium 18, Large 10	Medium 9, Large 2
Post-glenoid Process	Small 10, Medium 13, Large 10	Small 3, Medium 4, Large 4
Tympanic Plate Thickness	Thin 5, Medium 18, Thick 9, Very Thick 2	Thin 3, Medium 6, Thick 2
Auditory Meatus Shape	Oval 8, Ellipse 14, Slit 2	Oval 8, Ellipse 3
Petrous Depression	Small 8, Medium 13	Small 1, Medium 4, ?6
Exostoses in Auditory Meati	Both 2	None
Dehiscences in Auditory Floor	None 25, Left 3, Right 1, Both 6	Left 2, Right 1, Both 2
OCCIPITAL REGION		
Curvature	None 2, Small 13, Medium 5	Small 1, Medium 8, Pronounced 1
Position of Apex at Lamboa	Low 1, Medium 9, High 20	Medium 3, High 8
Form	Medium 10, Broad 19	Pinched 3, Medium 7, Broad 1
Torus: Size	Absent 1, Small 11, Medium 15, Large 4	Absent 1, Small 5, Medium 3, Large
Form	Ridge 13, Mound 18	Ridge 5, Mound 4
Wormian Bones	Few 12, (4-6), 5 (7-x) 12	None 2, Few 3, (4-6) 3, Many 2
Serration: Coronal	Submedium 6, Medium 16, Pronounced 10, Very Pronounced 1, ?2	Medium 8, Pronounced 3
Sagittal	Submedium 10, Medium 9, Pronounced 12, ?2	Submedium 1, Medium 8, Pronounce
Lambdoidal	Submedium 5, Medium 11, Pronounced 15, ?3	Submedium 1, Medium 7, Pronounce
FACE		
Size	Large 22, Very Large 5	Medium 2, Large 5, ?4
Orbits Shape	Oblong 9, Rhomboid 18, Square 1	Oblong 1, Rhomboid 5, Ellipse 1
Orbits Inclination	Small 1, Medium 20, Pronounced 6	Medium 5, Pronounced 2, ?4
Infra-orbital Suture	None 10, Facial 2, Orbital 2	None 3, Facial 1, Orbital 1
Suborbital Fossae	Absent 8, Slight 12, Medium 5, Deep 1	Absent 1, Slight 4, Medium 2
Malar Size	Medium 2, Large 17, Very Large 12	Medium 2, Large 5, Very Large 2
Anterior Projection	Small 2, Medium 5, Large 15	Large 7, ?4
Lateral Projection	Medium 2, Large 21	Medium 1, Large 6, ?4
Malar Tuberosity	None 9, Small 5, Medium 8, Large 4, Very Large 1	Small 2, Medium 2, Large 5
Marginal Process of Malar	Absent 1, Submedium 11, Medium 13, Large 1	Submedium 4, Medium 2, Large 1
Zygomatic Process, Thickness	Medium 15, Pronounced 6	Small 1, Medium 4, Pronounced 2
Infra-maxillary Notch	None 1, Slight 5, Medium 14, Deep 5	Medium 4, Small 2, ?4
Nasion Depression	Small 13, Medium 9, Deep 4	Small 4, Medium 2, Deep 1, ?4
Nasal Root Height	Low 13, Medium 8	Low 3, Medium 2, High 1, ?5
Nasal Root Breadth	Very Small 1, Small 11, Medium 8, Large 1	Small 4, Medium 3, ?4
Nasal Bridge Height	Low 1, Medium 6, High 4	Medium 2, High 1, ?8
Nasal Bridge Depth	Medium 10	Medium 4, ?7
Nasal Profile	Concavo-Convex 9	Concavo-Convex 3, ?8
Nasal Sills	Dull 6, Medium 15, Sharp 4	Dull 4, Medium 1, Sharp 2, ?4
Nasal Spine	Small 13, Medium 7, Large 1	Small 3, Medium 2, Large 1
Sub-Nasal Grooves	Absent 11, Small 8, Medium 5, Pronounced 1	Absent 2, Small 2, Medium 3
Total Facial Prognathism	Absent 1, Slight 3, Medium 7, Pronounced 12	Slight 2, Medium 3, ?6
Mid Facial Prognathism	Absent 4, Slight 9, Medium 10	Slight 5, Medium 1, ?5
Alveolar Prognathism	Slight 1, Medium 7, Pronounced 19	Medium 1, Pronounced 5, ?5
Alveolar Border, Preservation	Poor 3, Fair 8, Good 13, Perfect 4	Fair 2, Good 3, Perfect 2
Palate Shape	Parabolic 8, Hyperbolic 18, Elliptical 1, Large "U" 1	Parabolic 5, Hyperbolic 2, Elliptical
Palate Height	Low 2, Medium 17, High 10	Low 2, Medium 2, High 2, ?5
Palatine Torus: Shape	Ridge 17, Mound 5, Lump 3	Ridge 5, Mound 1, Lump 3
Size	Small 11, Medium 11, Large 3	Small 4, Medium 3, Large 1
Palatine Suture Direction	Transverse 3, Anterior 27, Posterior 4	Anterior 5, Posterior 1
Post-Nasal Spine	Absent 1, Small 2, Medium 4, Large 2	Small 1, Medium 2, Large 1
MANDIBLE		
Size	Medium 6, Large 16, Very Large 8	Medium 5, Large 5
Chin Form	Median 8, Bilateral 13, Medio-Bilateral 8	Median 5, Bilateral 3, ?3
Chin Projection	Negative 8, Neutral 3, Small 10, Medium 6, Large 3	Negative 2, Small 4, Medium 1, Larg
Alveolar Prognathism	None 3, Slight 14, Medium 10, Pronounced 3	Slight 5, Medium 2, Pronounced 1
Genial Tubercles Size	Small 6, Medium 11, Large 12	Small 2, Medium 4, Large 4
Mylo-Hyoid Ridge	Slight 3, Medium 24, Pronounced 2	Slight 3, Medium 6, Pronounced 1
Ptery-goid Attachment	Small 1, Medium 23, Pronounced 5	Medium 9, Pronounced 1
Gonial Angle, Eversion	None 5, Small 9, Medium 12, Pronounced 2	None 1, Small 6, Medium 2
Mandibular Torus	None 10, Small 16, Medium 3	None 4, Small 6
Ante-mortem Tooth Loss	(0) 13, (1-4) 11, (5-8) 2, (9-12) 2	(0) 2, (1-4) 2, (9-12) 1, (25-28) 1
Tooth Wear	Slight 2, Medium 10, Pronounced 20, Very Pronounced 1	Medium 2, Pronounced 3, Very Pron
Tooth Quality	Good 7, Excellent 21	Excellent 7

eformed Females (28)	Slight or Undeformed Females (7)	Deformed Adolescent Females (4) 15.5 Years

10, Medium 18
2, Medium 14, Heavy 4, ?8
13, Spheroid 6, Sphenoid 3, ?6
tal 15, Rt. Occiptal 6, Left Occipital 2,
ontal 12, Frontal ?2
m 11, Pronounced 12
gonoid 19, Round 1, Rounded Pentagonoid 5

Small 1, Medium 6
Light 1, Medium 5, Heavy 1
Ellipsoid 2, Ovoid 4, Spheroid 1

Occiptal 5, Rt. Occipital 1
None 1, Trace 1, Small 5
Pentagonoid 5, ?2

Small 4
Medium 4
Ovoid 3, Rhomboid 1

Occipital 2, Left Occipital 2, with Bifrontal 4
Medium 2, Pronounced 2
Square 1, Pentagonoid 3

, Medium 10, High 9, Very High 1
1, Medium 12, Large 10
1, Bulging 5, Slight 10, Medium 4
2, Median 10, Divided 9, Continuous 1, ?6
2, Trace 6, Small 14, Medium 1, ?5
2, Small 20, Medium 1, ?5
18, Traces 7, ?3
2, Medium 10, Large 10
20, Medium 1
3, Medium 14, Large 1

Medium 4, High 3
Small 2, Medium 3, Large 2
Bulging 1, Slight 3, Medium 3
Median 4, Divided 3
Trace 6, Small 1
None 2, Small 4, Medium 1
None 2, Traces 5
Small 1, Medium 4, Large 2
Small 5, Medium 2
Small 2, Medium 5

Medium 2, High 2
Medium 3, Large 1
Bulging 1, Slight 3
None 2, Median 2
None 2, Trace 1, Small 1
None 2, Small 2
None 4
Medium 1, Large 3
Small 4
Small 1, Medium 3

3, Small 12, Medium 4
23, ?5
3, Small 4, Medium 10, Large 4
11, Small 7, Medium 3
7, Small 7, Medium 5, Pronounced 3

Small 5, Medium 2
Small 7
Small 4, Medium 2, Large 1
None 1, Small 3, Large 3
None 1, Small 6

Small 4
Small 3, Medium 1
Small 1, Medium 3
None 2, Small 1, Medium 1
None 2, Small 1, Medium 1

9, Medium 9, Large 1
7, Medium 12, Large 4
3, Medium 12, Large 4
3, Medium 4, Large 2, ?18
K 4, ?22
m 3, Large 1, ?24
5, Medium 11, Large 3, ?9
7, Medium 13, ?8
a, Medium 10, Thick 10, Very Thick 1
), Ellipse 10, Slit 1, ?8
t 1, Small 5, Medium 2, ?20

Right 2, Both 3

Flat 2, Small 2, Medium 3
Medium 5, Large 1
Small 1, Medium 4, Large 2
Small 2, Medium 4, ?1
H 1, K 1, X 1, ?4
Small 1, Medium 1, ?5
Small 2, Medium 4, Large 1
Small 3, Medium 3, Large 1
Thin 2, Medium 3, Thick 1, Very Thick 1
Oval 5, Ellipse 2
Small 4, ?3
None
Both 2

Flat 2, Small 2
Small 1, Medium 3
Small 3, Medium 1
Small 2, ?2
H 1, ?3
Small 2, Medium 1, ?1
Medium 4
Small 2, Medium 2
Medium 2, Thick 1, Very Thick 1
Ellipse 4
Small 2, Medium 2
None
None 3, Large, Both 1

1, Small 15, Medium 3, ?9
m 8, High 19

m 11, Broad 11, ?6
t 1, Small 12, Medium 4, Large 1, ?9
2, Mound 18, ?8
2, (1-3) 6, (4-6) 7, (7-x) 3, ?10
e 1, Submedium 3, Medium 11, Pronounced 8, ?5
e 1, Submedium 7, Medium 8, Pronounced 5, ?7
e 1, Submedium 5, Medium 6, Pronnounced 9, ?7

Small 4, Medium 2, Pronounced 1
Medium 2, High 5
Pinched 1, Medium 2, Broad 4
Small 3, Medium 4
Mound 7
Few 3, (4-6) 3, (7-x) 1
Submedium 2, Medium 4, ?1
Medium 4, Pronounced 3
Medium 5, Pronounced 1, Very Pronounced 1

Small 4
High 4
Broad 4
Absent 1, Small 3
None 1, Ridge 1, Mound 2
Few 3, Many 1
Medium 3, Pronounced 1
Submedium 1, Medium 2, Obliterated 1
Submedium 1, Medium 2, Very Pronounced 1

m 5, Large 8, ?15
, Round 1, Ellipse 1, Square 3, Oblong 4,
mboid 5, ?13
4, Medium 8, Pronounced 2, ?14
3, Facial 2, Orbital 2, ?21
t 1, Slight 9, Medium 3, ?15
m 8, Large 8, Very Large 1, ?11
m 7, Large 8, ?13
m 10, Large 5, ?13
4, Small 1, ?13
e 1, Submedium 4, Medium 3, Large 2, ?18
2, Medium 10, ?16
3, Medium 7, Deep 1, ?16
t 1, Small 16, ?11
, Medium 4, ?18
Small 1, Small 7, Medium 2, Large 1, ?17
m 8, High 1, ?19
n 6, Large 1, ?11
vo-Convex 6, ?22
, Medium 10, Sharp 2, ?13
t 1, Small 5, Medium 2, Large 1, ?19
t 8, Small 6, Medium 1 ?13
m 2, Pronounced 8, ?18
3, Medium 6, Pronounced 1, ?18
unced 14, ?14
Good 7, Perfect 2, ?11
olic 2, Hyperbolic 13, Elliptical 2,
e "U" 1, ?10
Medium 14, High 3, ?9
4, Mound 1, Lump 2, ?18
t 4, Small 3, Medium 5, Large 1, ?15
erse 3, Anterior 6, Posterior 3, ?16
3, Medium 3, ?22

Medium 3, Large 1, ?3

Rhomboid 2, Square 1, ?4
Small 1, Medium 3, ?3
None 1, Facial 2, Orbital 2, ?2
Absent 1, Slight 1, Medium 4, ?1
Medium 2, Large 2, ?3
Medium 3, ?4
Small 1, Medium 3, ?3
None 1, Small 1, ?5
Submedium 2, Medium 1, ?4
Medium 3, ?4
Medium 2, ?5
Absent 1, Small 2, Medium 1, ?3
Low 1, ?6
Medium 1, ?6
Medium 1, ?6
Medium 1, ?6
Concavo-Convex 1, ?6
Medium 2, Sharp 1, ?4
Medium 2, ?5
Medium 1, ?6
Medium 1, Pronounced 2, ?4
Medium 2, ?5
Pronounced 2, ?4
Good 1, Perfect 2, ?4

Medium 2, Large 2

Rhomboid 2, Ellipse 1, Square 1
Small 1, Medium 3
Facial 1, Orbital 1, ?2
Slight 2, Medium 2
Medium 2, Large 2
Medium 2, Large 2
Medium 3, ?1
None 4
Absent 1, Submedium 2, Medium 1
Small 1, Medium 3
Medium 3, Deep 1
Absent 2, Small 2
Low 1, ?3
Small 1, ?3
Medium 1, ?3
Medium 1, ?3
Concavo-Convex 1, ?3
Dull 1, Medium 1, Sharp 2
Small 2, Medium 1, Large 1
Absent 2, Small 2
Medium 1, Pronounced 2, ?1
Medium 3, ?1
Medium 1, Pronounced 3
Good 3, Perfect 1

1, Medium 15, Large 1, ?11
n 10, Bilateral 3, ?15
ve 6, Neutral 8, Small 2, ?12
6, Medium 6, Pronounced 4, ?
9, Medium 6, Large 2, ?11
9, Medium 8, Pronounced 1, ?10
6, Medium 8, ?14
5, Small 7, Medium 3, ?13
5, Small 10, Medium 2, ?11
(5-8) 2, (9-12) 1

Medium 4, ?3
Median 3, ?4
Negative 2, ?5
Slight 1, Medium 1, ?5
Small 2, Medium 1, ?4
Absent 1, Slight 1, Medium 2, Pronounced 1, ?2
Small 2, Medium 2, ?3
None 2, Small 2, Medium 1, ?2
None 5, Small 2
(0) 3, (25-28) 1

Medium 3
Medium 3
Negative 1, Neutral 1, Small 1
Medium 2, Slight 1
Small 3
Medium 3
Small 3
Small 2, None 1
None 3
None 3

7, Medium 6, Pronounced 9, ?6
m 3, Good 4, Excellent 14, ?7

Slight 1, Medium 3, Pronounced 1, ?2
Excellent 4, ?3

Slight 2, Medium 1
Excellent 2, Good 1

TABLE III
COMPARATIVE SERIES OF ADENA, HOPEWELL AND COPENA SKULLS

MEASUREMENTS in millimeters†	Total Ky. ADENA No.	Average	Deformed Ky. ADENA No.	Average	Undeformed Ky. ADENA No.	Average	Ohio ADENA Deformed Chillicothe	Undeformed McAlla.	Deformed W. Va. ADENA	Total HOPE No.
Glab.-Occip. L.	38	166.2	28	164.0	10	172.4	163	184	168	60
Max. Br.	41	148.3	30	151.3	11	140.0	152	145	152	66
Bas. Breg. Ht.	20	151.0	15	151.7	5	149.0	154	....		24
Auric. Ht.	28	129.0	21	130.3	7	125.1	127		127	23
Mean Thick. L. Par.	44	5.6	34	5.6	10	5.5	6.7	6.3	....	59
Min. Fron. Diam.	41	91.6	30	92.8	11	88.5	97	100	....	56
Max. Fron. Diam.	28	121.6	19	124.5	9	115.6	123	123		33
Fron. Chord	42	114.5	33	115.0	9	112.8	116	113	....	48
Circumference	34	498.4	24	497.9	10	499.6	492	525		49
Nas.-Opis. Arc.	28	364.6	20	364.2	8	365.5	348			32
Transverse Arc.	38	335.5	27	341.2	11	321.5	339	....		30
Sagittal Arc.	41	117.8	31	117.7	10	118.0	110	125		31
Sagittal Chord	41	102.3	31	101.6	10	104.5	96	114		31
Cal. Capacity in cc.	27	1495.4	20	1510.8	7	1451.6	1485.4	....		22
Meas. Capacity in cc.	3	1405.0	2	1455.0	1	1350.0	....	....		....
Basion Nasion	19	104.2	14	101.5	5	111.8	115			20
Basion Prosthion	18	99.4	13	96.5	5	107.0	104			16
Bizygo. Diam.	30	141.0	21	143.1	9	136.1	147			34
Mid. Face Br.	23	101.9	16	102.6	7	100.3	103			21
Tot. Face Ht.	32	124.9ᵗ	26	125.5ᵃ	6	122.2ᵗ				33
Up. Face Ht.	33	73.8	26	74.6	7	70.8	81			35
Tot. Face Angle in degrees	20	84.4°	15	84.9°	5	83.4°	89°		78°	18
Mid. Face Angle in degrees	21	90.6°	15	91.1°	6	89.7°	96°			18
Alveolar Angle in degrees	20	66.8°	15	68.3°	5	62.2°	72°			18
Nasal Ht.	33	52.9	26	53.4	7	51.0	58			35
Nasal Br.	34	24.7	26	24.6	8	25.1	25			40
Up. Nasalia Br.	33	12.9	25	12.9	8	12.9	11			19
Low. Nasalia Br.	17	17.3	13	17.5	4	16.5	16			8
Mean Orb. Ht.	20	33.7	22	34.0	6	33.0	36			30
Mean Orb. Br. Max. Fr.	27	41.7	21	42.0	6	40.9	45.5			30
Interorb. Br.	29	20.9	21	20.7	8	21.0	18	24		30
Biorbital Br.	29	99.6	22	100.4	7	97.0	100			20
Ext. Alveo. L.	31	53.9	24	53.9	7	54.1	59			38
Ext. Alveo. Br.	30	67.5	26	68.1	4	63.5	70			38
Condy. Sym. L.	37	107.9	27	108.1	10	107.5	....			27
Bicondy. Br.	20	127.4	16	128.9	4	121.2	....			22
Bigonial Br.	31	108.1	22	110.4	9	102.4	....			41
Ht. of Sym.	32	36.1	23	36.7	9	34.6	....			41
Mandib. Ht.	33	59.0	24	59.8	9	56.9	....			27
Min. Br. L. Ramus	37	35.9	27	36.2	10	35.2	....			32
Mandib. Angle in degrees	28	120.2°	20	118.9°	8	123.5°	....			36
INDICES†										
Cranial	35	89.3	25	92.5	10	81.1	93.2	78.8	90.9	59
Leng. Ht.	19	92.1	15	93.5	4	86.9	94.5			22
Brd. Ht.	19	101.9	14	100.1	5	107.2	101.3			24
Leng.-Auric. Ht.	26	78.1	19	80.2	7	72.3	77.9		75.8*	22
Mean Ht.	19	96.7	14	97.0	5	96.0	97.8			21
Cranial Module	19	155.3	14	156.0	5	153.3	156.3			21
Frontal* (Min. F.-F. C.)	39	82.2*	30	80.7*	9	78.5	83.6	88.5		48
Frontal (Max. F.-F. C.)	26	106.9	18	108.5	8	103.5	106.0	108.9		30
Fronto-Par.	36	62.8	25	62.6	11	63.3	63.8	69.0		54
Tot. Facial	26	88.2	20	88.3	6	87.8	....			26
Up. Facial	27	52.2	20	52.4	7	51.8	55.1			28
Mid Facial	23	71.9	16	72.3	7	71.0	78.6			19
Cranio-Facial	28	95.7	19	94.8	9	97.5	96.7			34
Zygo-Frontal	27	65.1	19	65.1	8	64.0	66.0			32
Zygo-Gonial	26	76.9	18	77.6	8	75.2	....			31
Fronto-Gonial	30	117.3	21	117.5	9	116.7	....			35
Mean Orbital	25	80.7	19	80.7	6	80.7	79.3			30
Interorbital	22	21.4	15	21.2	7	21.7	18.0			20
Nasalia	17	71.3	13	70.6	4	73.7	68.8			7
Nasal	31	47.1	24	46.4	7	49.4	43.1	....		35
Ext. Palatal	25	124.5	22	126.2	3	113.7	118.7			36
Mandibular	20	84.5	16	83.9	4	87.0	....	....	....	21

† All measurements and indices approximate.
* Index calculated from averages above.

MALES														
f. H_1 io WELL	Def. H_1 Ohio HOPEWELL		H_2 Ohio HOPEWELL		Total Trophies Ohio HOPEWELL		Undef. H_1 Trophies Ohio HOPEWELL		Def. H_1 Trophies Ohio HOPEWELL		H_2 Trophies Ohio HOPEWELL		Total Ala. COPENA	
Avearge	No.	Avearge	No.	Avearge	No.	Avearge	No.	Avearge	No.	Avearge	No.	Avearge	No.	Avearge
184.4	7	180.4	6	177.5	17	182.8	13	185.6	2	174.5	2	172.5	7	179.1
136.9	7	139.9	9	148.4	18	137.6	13	136.7	3	136.7	2	144.5	7	143.3
143.3	4	146.2	3	146.7	6	144.3	2	139.0	3	151.0	1	141.0	3	142.7
122.0	1	122.0	5	122.8	7	124.4	3	123.3	2	131.0	2	119.5	....	....
5.5	6	6.1	5	5.3	17	5.1	12	4.9	3	5.0	2	5.6	....	....
93.2	7	93.5	6	94.2	17	93.5	12	92.6	3	93.0	2	100.0	7	95.1
112.8	4	113.5	7	120.2	8	114.9	4	114.0	2	112.5	2	119.0	....	....
113.9	5	117.0	6	113.5	8	112.6	4	113.8	2	112.5	2	110.5	8	111.0
513.3	4	516.2	6	512.1	15	515.1	11	515.5	2	517.0	2	507.0	3	505.3
374.6	3	382.9	4	367.8	10	368.6	7	366.8	2	387.5	1	343.0	7	364.0
309.8	4	314.2	6	318.8	7	309.4	3	318.7	2	311.0	2	309.0	5	324.2
124.6	4	126.2	9	124.2	6	125.2	4	120.7	....	....	2	119.0	....	....
111.4	4	109.8	9	110.3	6	111.8	4	115.2	....	....	2	105.0	....	....
451.7	1	1442.4	5	1520.9	6	1510.4	3	1531.6	1	1618.2	2	1424.4	....	....
420	....	....	....	....	....	....	....	....	....	....	....	....	....	....
103.8	3	106.3	2	105.0	6	104.7	2	106.5	3	103.3	1	104.0	3	109.7
102.0	1	100.0	2	101.0	5	101.0	2	106.5	2	96.0	1	100.0	3	101.7
136.7	2	137.0	5	141.8	12	141.5	7	138.4	3	143.7	2	149.0	5	144.4
104.8	....	....	5	104.4	4	103.5	2	103.0	....	....	2	104.0	1	103.0
129.5	2	127.5	5	128.4	10	126.2	6	127.8	2	128.0	2	119.5	3	124.7
77.6	1	82.0	5	75.6	12	74.7	7	75.0	3	77.0	2	70.0	3	74.3
82.5°	....	....	5	83.0°	5	84.2°	2	83.5°	1	82.0°	2	86.0°	....	....
88.1°	....	....	5	87.4°	5	90.6°	2	89.0°	1	91.0°	2	92.0°	....	....
67.8°	....	....	5	69.4°	5	66.6°	2	67.5°	1	65.0°	2	66.5°	....	....
54.4	1	59.0	5	52.4	11	57.0	7	52.6	2	53.0	2	51.0	3	50.8
26.6	1	24.8	5	25.0	12	25.8	7	26.6	3	26.0	2	23.0	4	25.0
12.3	1	14	2	13.5	3	14.0	2	13.5	....	....	1	15.0	....	....
18.2	....	....	....	....	2	17.0	1	17.0	....	....	1	17.0	....	....
34.9	2	34.2	5	33.9	11	34.6	8	34.8	1	36.7	2	33.5	4	34.0L
42.4	2	41.5	5	42.0	10	42.1	7	41.4	1	41.0	2	43.7	4	43.2L
20.1	3	23.6	5	22.0	6	22.0	3	23.3	1	19.0	2	21.5	3	20.7
99.1	....	....	5	100.6	4	101.0	2	101.0	....	....	2	101.0	1	101.0
57.2	2	55.0	5	54.6	11	55.0	8	56.1	1	51.0	2	52.5	3	55.0
68.3	2	64.0	5	69.2	12	67.6	8	67.2	2	67.5	2	68.5	3	68.7
109.5	3	112.3	4	104.0	3	102.5	1	105.0	....	....	2	101.0	4	104.0
126.0	2	121.5	3	127.7	4	127.5	1	125.0	1	129.0	2	128.0	1	127.0
103.8	3	98.3	5	111.4	12	107.0	8	106.2	2	105.5	2	111.5	3	112.3
37.9	4	38.5	5	37.6	11	36.6	9	37.1	....	....	2	34.0	3	34.3
60.6	3	60.7	4	65.8	4	58.2	1	59.0	1	54.0	2	60.0	5	58.6
36.2	3	33.3	5	36.2	5	35.6	2	36.5	1	33.0	2	36.0	5	35.8
121.2°	4	122.0°	4	115.2°	11	122.3°	7	123.6°	2	123.5°	2	116.5°	5	116.4°
74.2	6	78.5	6	83.2	17	75.7	13	73.8	2	80.4	2	83.8	7	80.2
77.8	4	81.5	2	80.2	5	81.0	2	71.8	2	88.5	1	84.4	3	78.1
103.1	4	102.9	3	98.7	6	103.2	2	101.0	3	110.6	1	99.2	3	98.9
66.8	1	67.8	5	68.9	6	68.3	3	64.3	1	79.4	2	68.8	....	....
89.0	4	91.0	2	88.5	5	91.1	2	83.9	2	98.2	1	91.4	3	87.2
155.0	4	156.0	2	158.2	5	155.4	2	156.8	2	156.6	1	150.0	3	156.8
82.3*	5	79.9*	6	83.0*	8	83.0*	4	81.5*	2	83.0*	2	90.5*	7	88.5
99.4	3	97.2	6	106.9	8	102.2	4	100.2	2	100.2	2	107.9	....	....
67.9	6	66.2	6	63.8	18	68.1	13	68.0	3	68.1	2	69.2	6	67.8
93.1	1	87.5	5	90.5	9	88.4	5	91.8	2	87.8	2	80.2	2	89.7
55.7	....	....	5	53.3	11	52.6	6	54.4	2	52.2	2	47.0	2	54.2
74.7	....	....	5	72.5	4	69.8	2	72.4	....	....	2	67.4	1	70.4
100.2	2	99.6	5	95.7	12	102.8	7	101.7	3	105.2	2	103.2	4	96.4
67.2	2	68.6	5	67.2	12	67.1	7	68.0	3	64.9	2	67.1	3	66.7
76.1	2	71.2	5	78.6	9	75.1	5	75.1	2	73.5	2	74.8	3	79.6
112.3	3	104.9	5	117.3	12	113.9	8	114.5	2	113.4	2	111.7	3	119.5
81.9	2	82.8	5	80.8	10	83.9	6	83.7	2	91.5	2	76.7	3	79.0L
19.6	....	....	5	21.9	4	22.6	2	23.8	....	....	2	21.4	....	....
64.2	....	....	....	....	1	85.5	1	85.5	....	....	....	....	....	....
48.9	1	44.9	5	47.7	11	49.6	7	50.5	2	51.0	2	45.1	3	47.7
119.8	2	116.4	5	127.0	11	122.4	8	120.0	1	125.5	2	130.4	3	124.9
87.9	2	92.2	3	81.6	3	80.6	1	84.0	....	....	2	79.0	1	82.0*

TABLE III (Continued)
COMPARATIVE SERIES OF ADENA, HOPEWELL AND COPENA SKULLS

MEASUREMENTS in millimeters†	H_2 Ala. COPENA No.	Avearge	H_1 Ala. COPENA No.	Avearge	Total Ky. ADENA No.	Avearge	Deformed Ky. ADENA No.	Avearge	Undeformed Ky. ADENA No.	Avearge	Total C HOPEW No.	
Glab.-Occip. L.	3	170.3	4	(185.0)	24	160.0	18	157.9	6	166.5	37	1'
Max. Br.	3	149.7	4	(138.5)	28	144.4	21	145.9	7	139.8	37	1?
Bas. Breg. Ht.	1	145.0	2	(141.5)	17	145.0	12	145.9	5	143.0	14	1?
Auric. Ht.					11	126.3	10	127.0	1	119.0	17	1?
Mean Thick. L. Par.					27	5.4	21	5.6	6	4.8	31	
Min. Fron. Diam.	3	94.7	4	(95.5)	21	88.4	18	88.4	3	88.3	37	?
Max. Fron. Diam.					14	118.2	12	119.2	2	112.5	30	1?
Fron. Chord	4	109.5	4	1112.0	24	109.3	19	109.5	5	108.4	38	1(
Circumference	2	507.0	1	502	18	481.0	15	480.5	3	483.7	30	4?
Nas.-Opis. Arc.	4	353.2	3	378.3	19	351.8	16	350.8	3	357.0	20	3?
Transverse Arc.	3	323.3	2	(326.5)	22	324.5	17	329.2	5	308.4	21	3?
Sagittal Arc.					20	115.6	14	115.8	6	115.2	24	1?
Sagittal Chord					22	100.3	16	99.6	6	102.3	24	1(
Cal. Capacity in cc.					10	1395.0	9	1405.1	1	1303.9	15	137
Meas. Capacity in cc.					2	1280.0	2	1280.0				
Basion Nasion	1	108.0	2	110.5	14	103.6	11	103.2	3	105.0	12	1(
Basion Prosthion	1	98.0	2	99.5	8	97.0	6	96.7	2	98.0	12	1(
Bizygo. Diam.	3	143.3	2	145.5	12	134.1	10	135.7	2	126.0	23	1?
Mid. Face Br.	1	103.0			10	97.8	8	99.2	2	92.0	19	?
Tot. Face Ht.	1	128.0	2	123.0	13	116.8[2]	11	117.7[3]	2	112.0[2]	21	12
Up. Face Ht.	1	76.0	2	73.5	16	70.3	13	70.3	3	70.3	26	7
Tot. Face Angle in degrees					9	82.0°	9	82.0°			13	8
Mid. Face Angle in degrees					9	88.8°	9	88.8°			13	8
Alveolar Angle in degrees					9	62.2°	9	62.2°			13	7
Nasal Ht.	1	50.0	2	51.5	18	50.5	14	50.6	4	50.0	25	5
Nasal Br.	2	26.0	2	24.0	17	24.7	14	24.6	3	25.0	26	2
Up. Nasalia Br.					12	12.4	11	12.6	1	11.0	10	1
Low. Nasalia Br.					8	17.2	8	17.2			6	1
Mean Orb. Ht.	1	34 L	3	34.0	10	33.1	9	33.1	1	36.2	22	3
Mean Orb. Br. Max. Fr.	1	42 L	3	43.7	11	40.1	9	40.3	2	39.0	19	4
Interorb. Br.			3	20.7	12	20.1	11	20.4	1	17.0	20	2
Biorbital Br.	1	101.0			12	94.8	11	95.4	1	88.0	16	9
Ext. Alveo. L.	1	54	2	55.5	17	53.4	15	53.3	2	55.5	28	5
Ext. Alveo. Br.	1	73	2	66.5	17	64.9	15	65.1	2	63.5	27	6
Condy. Sym. L.	2	103.5	2	104.0	14	104.7	12	105.3	2	101.5	15	10
Bicondy. Br.	1	127			11	120.4	10	120.9	1	116.0	11	11
Bigonial Br.	2	117.0	1	103.0	15	98.2	13	99.1	2	92.0	16	9
Ht. of Sym.			3	34.3	17	34.7	15	35.0	2	32.5	23	3
Mandib. Ht.	2	55.5	3	60.7	12	52.8	11	52.8	1	52.0	13	5
Min. Br. L. Ramus	2	36.0	3	35.7	16	35.2	14	35.1	2	35.5	18	3
Mandib. Angle in degrees	2	120.0°	3	114.0°	14	124.6°	12	124.8°	2	120.5°	18	12
INDICES†												
Cranial	3	87.3	4	74.9	24	89.9	18	91.7	6	84.6	36	7
Leng. Ht.	1	83.3	2	75.4	16	90.9	12	92.7	4	85.5	14	7
Brd. Ht.	1	96.7	2	99.9	17	101.5	12	101.0	5	102.6	14	10
Leng.-Auric. Ht.					10	80.2	9	80.8	1	74.8	16	6
Mean Ht.	1	89.5	2	86.0	16	95.9	12	96.8	4	93.4	14	8
Cranial Module	1	156.3	2	157.0	16	149.8	12	149.4	4	151.1	14	14
Frontal* (Min. F.-F. C.)	3	86.3	4	89.9	21	80.7*	18	80.4*	3	81.4*	36	8
Frontal (Max. F.-F. C.)					12	108.5	10	108.9	2	106.8	28	10
Fronto-Par.	2	64.2	4	69.6	19	61.2	16	60.9	3	62.5	33	6
Tot. Facial	1	89.5	1	89.9	7	89.6	6	89.4	1	91.2	18	9
Up. Facial	1	53.1	1	55.4	9	54.1	7	52.0	2	56.8	19	5
Mid Facial	1	70.4			9	72.9	7	70.6	2	80.5	18	7
Cranio-Facial	3	96.0	1	97.9	11	93.2	9	94.3	2	88.2	22	9
Zygo-Frontal	2	66.9	1	66.2	9	64.6	8	65.2	1	68.8	21	6
Zygo-Gonial	2	82.4	1	74.1	9	74.9	8	74.8	1	75.8	14	7
Fronto-Gonial	2	122.2	1	112.0	10	111.6	9	112.7	1	102.3	14	10
Mean Orbital	1	81.0L	2	78.1L	9	80.2	8	79.8	1	87.2	22	8
Interorbital					8	20.3	7	20.5	1	19.3	13	2
Nasalia					8	70.5	8	70.5			10	6
Nasal	1	50.0	2	46.6	16	48.9	13	48.5	3	50.3	23	4
Ext. Palatal	1	135.0	2	119.8	16	121.6	14	122.6	2	114.4	27	11
Mandibular			1	82.0	10	87.8	9	88.2	1	84.5	12	8

† All measurements and indices approximate.
* Index calculated from averages above.

FEMALES

f. H_1 io WELL	Defo. H_1 Ohio HOPEWELL		H_2 Ohio HOPEWELL		Undef. H_1 Trophy Ohio Hopewell	Def. Trophy Ohio Hopewell	Total Ala. COPENA		H_2 Ala. COPENA		H_1 Ala. COPENA	
Average	No.	Average	No.	Average	No. 192 Md. 24 Subadult	Marriett, Md. Subadult	No.	Average	No.	Average	No.	Average
178.3	9	175.4	4	170.5	164	166	7	161.0	6	159.0	1	173.0
135.7	10	136.9	4	143.5	134	139	7	147.7	6	151.6	1	124.0
139.8	5	142.8	1	143.0	....	143	2	134.5	1	138.0	1	131.0
120.4	6	123.3	1	120.0	114	125	....	....	....	....	....	....
5.3	10	4.9	3	5.1	5.6	4.6	....	....	....	....	....	....
89.5	10	90.4	4	92.2	88	87	4	91.2	3	92.3	1	88.0
112.3	7	111.7	4	115.2	110	112	....	....	....	....	....	....
109.2†	6	115.0	4	107.8	105	115	6	104.7	5	104.4	1	106.0
499.0	9	500.4	2	491.0	475	492	6	485.8	5	486.2	1	484.0
361.2	5	372.8	3	327.3	....	362	4	341.0	3	340.7	1	342.0
317.6	7	303.4	2	308.5	294	335	6	309.8	5	312.8	1	295.0
123.5	6	123.8	2	107.5	116	123	....	....	....	....	....	....
109.8	6	109.8	2	100.0	105	106	....	....	....	....	....	....
376.2	5	1392.5	1	1346.4	1236.0	1376.4	....	....	....	....	....	....
102.1	4	102.3	1	103.0	....	98	1	94.0	1	94.0	....	....
100.7	4	100.7	1	95.0	....	94	1	84.0	1	84.0	....	....
129.9	9	133.6	2	131.5	129	128	4	132.7	3	135.3	1	125.0
97.5	5	101.6	1	96.0	102	95	3	95.0	2	96.0	1	93.0
120.3	8	120.0	1	119.0	114[1]	121[1]	3	111.3	2	110.5	1	113.0
73.2	8	74.4	1	70.0	68	71	3	65.7	2	64.5	1	68.0
82.6°	5	83.0°	1	83.0°	84°	90°	....	....	....	....	....	....
87.9°	5	88.2°	1	88.0°	93°	93°	....	....	....	....	....	....
67.9°	5	74.0°	1	65.0°	67°	73°	....	....	....	....	....	....
51.6	7	53.7	1	50.0	47	52	3	46.3	2	46.5	1	46.0
25.4	8	26.0	1	24.0	25	22	3	23.0	2	22.5	1	24.0
11.6	....	....	2	14.5	8	11	....	....	....	....	....	....
18.6	....	....	1	(20.0)	18	14	....	....	....	....	....	....
34.4	7	34.4	1	35.0	31.5	33.0	3	35.0L	2	36.0L	1	33.0L
41.7	6	41.4	1	41.0	43.5	42.0	3	41.7L	2	40.5L	1	44.0L
20.5	5	21.0	2	21.0	18	16	3	20.7	2	21.5	1	19.0
97.2	4	98.5	1	94.0	98	92	3	96.0	2	95.5	1	97.0
54.9	9	55.1	1	52.0	54	49	3	52.3	2	50.5	1	56.0
64.8	9	65.3	1	64.0	66	67	2	62.0	2	62.0	....	....
103.9	4	108.7	2	102.0	98	108	2	95.5	1	91.0	1	100.0
117.3	4	120.0	1	129.0	....	117	....	....	....	....	....	....
94.9	5	99.4	1	92.0	99	96	1	90.0	1	90.0	....	....
33.9	7	34.8	2	32.0	37	34	1	30.0	1	30.0	....	....
53.9	4	55.5	2	61.5	48	56	2	47.5	1	53.0	1	42.0
35.2	6	35.3	2	37.5	37	36	3	33.0	2	35.0	1	29.0
120.9°	6	123.5°	2	112.0°	122°	119°	2	134.0°	1	135.0°	1	133.0°
75.4	9	78.5	4	84.2	81.7	83.7	7	92.2	6	95.6	1	71.6
76.4	5	80.3	1	85.1	....	86.2	2	83.8	1	92.0	1	75.7
99.7	5	104.0	1	102.5	....	97.2	1	105.6	....	....	1	105.6
68.0	5	68.8	1	71.4	69.5	75.3	....	....	....	....	1	88.2
87.9	5	90.6	1	93.2	....	94.1	1	88.2	....	....	1	88.2
147.3	5	152.7	1	150.0	....	149.3	1	142.7	....	....	1	142.7
82.1*	6	78.5*	4	85.6*	83.8	75.6	4	87.1*	3	88.5*	1	83.0
103.4	6	97.7	4	106.4	104.6	97.5	....	....	....	....	....	....
66.2	10	66.1	4	64.3	65.7	62.6	5	73.9	4	74.6	1	70.9
92.4	7	90.0	1	88.2	88.4	94.5	3	86.8	2	85.5	1	88.2
56.6	7	55.8	1	51.8	52.7	55.5	3	51.2	2	49.6	1	54.4
75.6	4	73.8	1	73.0	66.6	74.7	3	69.3	2	67.3	1	73.2
96.2	9	98.3	2	93.6	96.3	92.1	3	89.7	2	84.1	1	100.9
68.8	9	68.0	2	71.2	68.2	68.0	2	70.0	1	69.5	1	70.4
72.5	5	73.9	1	68.2	76.7	75.0	1	68.7	1	68.7	....	....
104.2	5	107.8	1	99.0	112.3	110.4	1	98.9	1	98.9	....	....
83.0	7	84.9	1	85.4	72.4	78.6	3	84.3	2	88.9	1	75.0
20.7	2	20.8	1	21.2	18.4	17.4	2	20.0	1	20.4	1	19.6
67.4	5	67.3	1	75.0	44.4	78.6	....	....	....	....	....	....
49.4	7	48.9	1	48.0	53.2	42.3	3	49.9	2	48.7	1	52.2
118.5	9	118.6	1	123.0	122.2	136.8	2	122.8	2	122.8	....	....
90.4	4	90.6	2	78.3	....	92.4	....	....	....	....	....	....

The palates are less broad. These differences are possibly all associated with deformation of the vault. The size of the sample, however, must be considered as a limiting factor.

When the more common indices of the skulls are considered under the usual classification, the following description by sex and deformation obtains:

ADENA SKULL CLASSIFICATIONS BY PROPORTIONS

	MALES		FEMALES	
INDEX	Deformed (25)	Undeformed and Slightly Deformed (10)	Deformed (18)	Undeformed and Slightly Deformed (6)
Length-breadth	Ultrabrachycranic	Brachycranic	Ultrabrachycranic	Brachycranic
Length-height	Hypsicranic	Same	Same	Same
Length-ear height	Hypsicranic	Same	Same	Same
Breadth-height	Acrocranic	Same	Same	Same
Fronto-parietal	Stenometopic	Same	Same	Same
Total facial	Mesoprosopic	Same	Same	Leptoprosopic (1)
Upper facial	Mesene	Same	Same	Leptene (2)
Orbital (mean)	Mesoconch	Same	Same	Hypsiconch (1)
Nasal	Mesorrhine	Same	Same	Same
Palatal	Brachyuranic	Mesouranic	Brachyuranic	Mesouranic

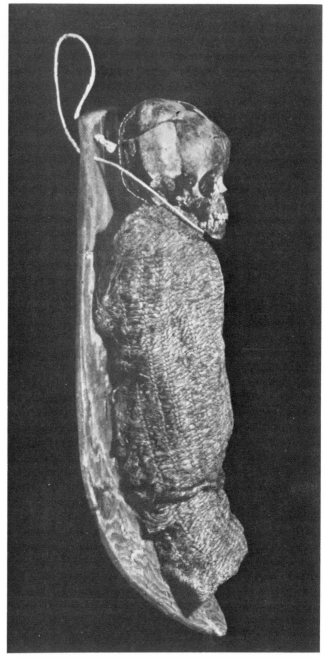

Figure 5. The use of the cradleboard.
This infant skull, Burial 66 from Robbins Mound,
Kentucky Be 3, is placed with a cradleboard and
textile from a rockshelter simply to i.lustrate the
trait.

HEAD DEFORMATION

The presence of so many Adena skulls with deformation leads to a discussion of the custom. It is surmised that a cradleboard custom of infant care prevailed (as it still does among many Indians). Here the skulls of infants and young children are particularly instructive since they retain most strongly the flattening effects of the deformation. Figures 27 and 28 portray deformed skulls of children with remarkably sharp angles of the back and top of the vault. Figure 5 is an attempt to illustrate the use of such a cradleboard with Adena materials recovered from the Rock Shelters* of Eastern Kentucky. It is supposed that in order to help hold the ungainly head, a binding of some sort was bound across the forehead. The soft bones of the infant head were thus brought against the flat surface of the cradleboard producing in time, the characteristic flat occiput observed. At the same time, in some cases due to the stresses of the binding on each side of the forehead the bifrontal flat areas were produced. Perhaps, as has been suggested by Hrdlicka and quoted by Steward** the use of small pads or possibly boards placed on each side of the forehead under the binding would produce this effect. Such pads would certainly increase the friction between head and binding and thus aid in immobilizing the head. In the horizontal position, it is obvious that gravity alone would tend to flatten the back of the head. After the child was released from the restrictions of the cradleboard, there must have been a tendency for the head to regain somewhat its natural shape. The head, however, would still retain to varying degrees, the deformation brought about by the cradleboard. It is possible, further, that some form of head binding was employed during childhood with the express intention of attaining a desired head form.

It would appear that the natural head shape would influence the ease with which deformation is brought about. The flattening of the head of a long headed infant would be a more difficult process than that of a round headed baby. It is an easily corroborated fact that babies with long heads lie naturally with the head

---

* Webb, Wm. S., and Funkhouser, W. D., 1936, p. 126.
** Stewart, T. Dale, 1943, p. 250.

on the sides, whereas babies with round heads lie with the head usually on the back. Thus a round head could be more easily kept in place against the cradleboard than a long head. This fact appears to be supported by the more frequent occurrence of occipital flattening among Indian groups of round headed ancestry than those of long headed stock.

The occipital deformation which occurs in 92% of both sexes of the Adena skulls appears as a flat plane above the line of the neck musculature and extends in pronounced degrees up on the parietals to obelion. Nearly one third of the adult Adena skulls show some bifrontal flattening in association with occipital. The flat areas are on each side above the frontal bosses and often meet to form a median crest. Usually the deformation disappears near the frontal side of the coronal suture although the adjoining parietals may share the sloping "roof like" flattening. In many instances this flat area may be palpated more easily than seen.

Figures 6 and 7 illustrate Adena deformation.

Deformation is present in Adena skulls from other localities outside Kentucky. The Chillicothe, Ohio, and Grave Creek, Wheeling, West Virginia specimens are excellent examples. See Figure 8.

MacLean[*] (Greenman's Mound 28) says: "A peculiarity of six or eight of the crania consisted in having the occipital bone flattened."

Thomas[**] (Greenman Mound 59) states "the skulls showed very plainly the flattening of the front." The two skulls (top Fig. 7) appear to have plane frontal deformation possibly like that just described.

When the skulls from the Hopewell sites in Ohio are observed, it is significant to find these same types of deformation on a fundamentally different skull type.

---

[*] MacLean, J. P., 1879, p. 193.
[**] Thomas, Cyrus, 1894, p. 426.

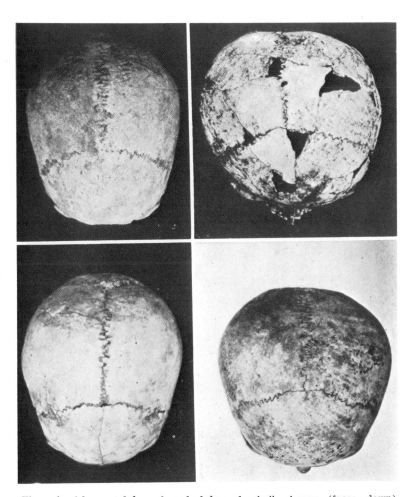

Figure 6. Adena undeformed and deformed skull shapes (faces down).
Upper left: Male skull, Burial 6, Be 17, undeformed.

Upper right: Top view of the skull of Burial 25, a young man,
Mm 3, with pronounced bifronto-occipital flattening.

Lower left: Skull of a young woman, Burial 31, Mm 3, with a
small amount of occipital flattening.

Lower right: The skull of Burial 13, also a young woman, from
the Wright Site, Mm 6, with a pronounced degree of occipital
flattening.

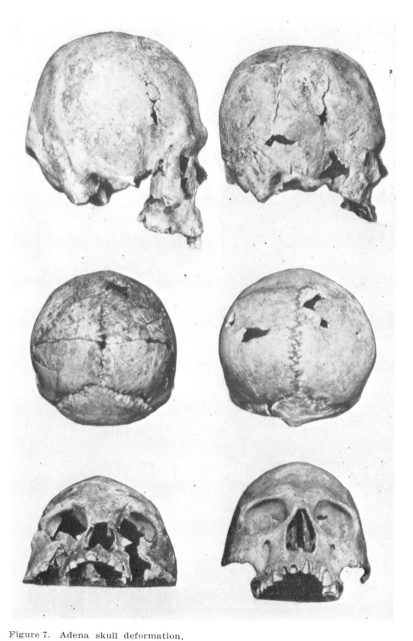

Figure 7. Adena skull deformation.

Top left: Burial 61, Right Burial 39 both males from Kentucky Robbins Mound Be 3, showing frontal? deformation along with occiptal.
Center left: Oblique view of back of Burial 23F. Kentucky Ricketts site Mm 3, and right, similar view of Burial 16M from Kentucky Wright Site Mm 6, showing bifronto-occipital deformation.
Lower left: Oblique view of Burial 21A, Male, Kentucky, Ricketts Mound, Mm 3, showing bifrontal flattening. Right: Similar view of Burial 1, Male, Ohio, Mound 2, Hopewell, showing typical Hopeweilian bifrontal deformation.

COMPARISON WITH OTHER ADENA SKULLS

Only a very few skulls from Adena mounds other than Kentucky are available for study. However the descriptions of many well preserved "Mound Builder" skulls are to be found in Morton's *Crania Americana* and in various other publications dealing with the "Mound Builders" and the excavations of their earthworks. Some of these "Mound Builder" skulls are preserved in the Academy of Natural Sciences, Philadelphia.

In Ohio, the skeletal material from the Westenhaver, Coon and McAlla Mounds can be studied, as well as an intact calvarium from a mound four miles below Chillicothe now at the Academy of Natural Sciences, Philadelphia.

Only one skull, illustrated in Morton's *Crania* plate 53, which was measured in the early days, exists from West Virginia. This small number however offers much satisfying confirmation of the Kentucky evidence.

The Chillicothe skull (Phil. Acad. Sc. No. 1512), Figure 8 center, is a deformed, aged male without the lower jaw and has been described in Morton's Catalogue* as follows:

> "This is, perhaps, the most admirably-formed head of the American race hitherto discovered. It possesses the national characteristics in perfection, as seen in the elevated vertex, flattened occiput, great interparietal diameter, ponderous bony structure, salient nose, large jaws and broad face. It is the perfect type of Indian conformation, to which the skulls of all the tribes from Cape Horn to Canada more or less approximate. Similar forms are common in the peruvian tombs, and have the occiput, as in this instance, so flattened and vertical as to give the idea of artificial compression; yet this is only an exaggeration of the natural form, caused by the pressure of the cradleboard in common use among the American nations. F.A. 81⁰ I.C. 90. Dr. E. H. Davis and E. G. Squier, Esq., A.D. 1849."

Possibly no other single Adena skull could be selected which approaches in so many instances, the average dimensions and proportions of the deformed Kentucky male series. The metric data of this excellent specimen (obtained by the junior author) are arranged in Table III where the similarities mentioned may be noted. (p. 255).

---

* Morton, Samuel George, 1849, Third Edition.

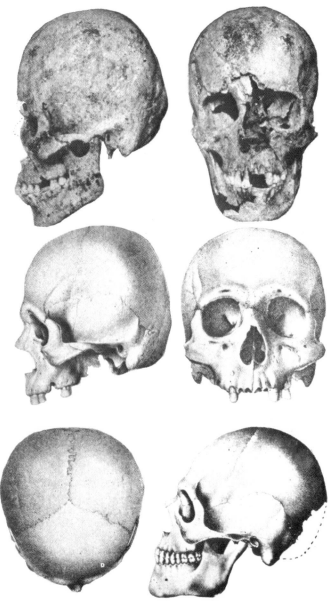

Figure 8. Kentucky and other Adena Skulls.
Upper: The deformed skull of a young man with typical Kentucky Adena features, Burial 49, Robbins Mound, Be 3.
Center and lower left: Views of the Adena male skull from Mound near Chillicothe, Ohio, early noted for its remarkable appearance.
Lower right: Male skull from the Adena Grave Creek Mound, Wheeling, now West Virginia, with typical Adena traits. Dotted line author's. Pictures center and lower, by courtesy of the Philadelphia Academy of Science.

The Westenhaver, Coon and McAlla material is either very fragmentary, and/or warped.

Skeleton 6, Westenhaver Mound, probably that of a young woman, is virtually crushed flat, and is characterized by the peculiar nature of the different bones which when handled ring like well-fired china. Apparently the bones have been heavily mineralized, and are covered with black ferric iron pigment. The skull appears to have been fairly short and broad, probably deformed (bifrontal-occipital), and high. The few approximate measurements obtained are as follows:

```
Minimum Frontal Diameter .............................. 81 mm
Maximum Frontal Diameter ............................. 113
Frontal Chord ............................................... 114
Minimum Diameter Nasal Bone ......................    6
Frontal Index, Minimum Frontal/Chord ..........  71.0
Frontal Index, Maximum Frontal/Chord ........  99.2
Anterior Interorbital Diameter ...........................  20
```

The McAlla calvaria appears to be undeformed but possesses a broad forehead which commonly characterizes the average Adena type. The measurements and indices appear in Table III.

The Grave Creek (Wheeling, now West Virginia) skull, No. 217, Figure 8, appears to be typically Adena and the description[*] of the specimen follows:

> "A glance at the drawing reveals the characteristic traits of the American skull, as seen in the full superciliary ridge, the salient nose, the rounded head, the flattened occiput, and the broad and ponderous lower jaw. Every tooth in this head is perfect; but a part of the occipital bone is deficient, and the dotted line is probably an approximation to the original outline."

This documented specimen is not available but measurements made by Squier and Davis[**] are listed in Table III, (p. 254).

---

[*] Meigs, J. Aitken, 1857, p. 222, quoting Clemens, James W., 'M. D., of Wheeling, Va.
[**] Squier, E. G., and Davis, E. H., 1848, p. 291.

POSTCRANIAL SKELETON

The Adena adult population, taken as a whole, possessed a medium to heavy lateral type of body build and were medium in stature; 168.0 cm (66.2 inches) an average of 20 individual males; 158.8 cm (62.5 inches) an average of 6 individual females. These stature estimates are calculated from data on all measureable bones of the same individual. The differences here indicated (9.2 cm) 3.7 inches are slightly less than those commonly observed in an average modern population.* However the predominate male proportion of these Adena burials and their selection remain unassessable factors.

The different long bones, compared with one another and in combination (intermembral indices) indicate the general size relationship of one body segment with another. These segments indicate that compared with those of European and American Whites the Adena Indians had long arms, broad torsos (broad shoulders, chests and hips) and fairly long legs (males particularly).

Specifically, the lower leg and arm bones are proportionately long. According to Hooton** this occurs frequently in the taller groups of American Indians.

These average proportions are portrayed in Figure 9. These schematic outlines were constructed upon average data from a congeries of any bones sufficiently preserved to be measured. They are intended only to give a general impression and are admittedly only approximations.

The bones of the Adena postcranial skeleton, on the average, indicate a more rugged muscularity than is commonly found on those of civilized White people. These Indian bones are marked further by an accompanying greater bowing of the shafts (front to back) and several functional features which are noteworthy.

In Table IV the classified morphology of the postcranial bones are presented, listing the occurrence by number and percentage. It will be remembered that these are a series of miscellaneous bones—simply all that were preserved.

* Martin, Rudolf, 1928, pp. 319 and 246.
** Hooton, Earnest A., 1932, p. 362.

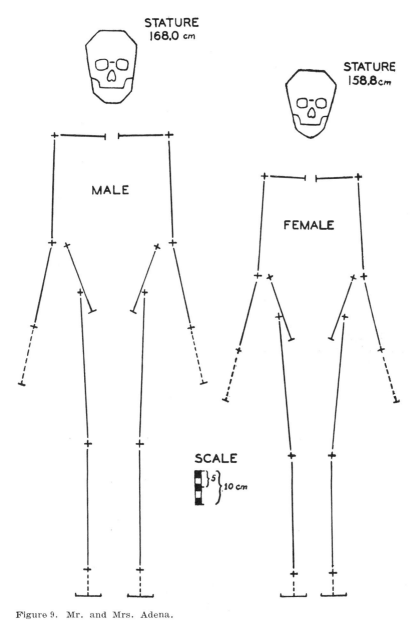

STATURE
168.0 cm

STATURE
158.8cm

MALE

FEMALE

SCALE

5
10 cm

Figure 9. Mr. and Mrs. Adena.
A schematic representation of the proportions of the Adena male and female based upon the average size of the different bones of the same skeleton of 20 males, 6 females.

Four male upper arm bones were found with indications of the rare supracondyloid processes.

The two main leg bones, the femur or thigh and the tibia or shin, of most of the Adena series, male and female alike indicate that the Adena people walked with a bent-knee gait and habitually squatted, sitting upon their heels. The surfaces of the tibial head slope backwards in most of the shin bones and the functional joint extensions (squatting facets) appear commonly on the neck of the femoral heads and at the ankle end of the shin bones. It is commonly known that many historic Indians sat cross-legged or squatted with their feet flat upon the ground.

In Table V are listed the long bone measurements and indices for the Adena series and for comparison, the Hopewell of Ohio and Copena of Alabama are appended. In general it appears from these series that the Hopewell people were somewhat larger than the Adena and that the Copena group were smaller. The very limited size of the Copena series is a factor to be considered before accepting this indication as valid.

TABLE IV

POOLED ADENA SERIES

Postcranial Morphology

	MALES				FEMALES			
	Left		Right		Left		Right	
	No.	%	No.	%	No.	%	No.	%
HUMERUS								
Shape of Shaft								
Oblong	13	36.1	11	29.0	4	36.3	3	37.5
Plano-convex	13	36.1	19	50.0	3	27.3	4	50.0
Prismatic	2	5.6	3	7.9	1	9.1	1	12.5
Irregular	....	....	1	2.6	....	....	....	....
Trapezoid	8	22.2	4	10.5	3	27.3	....	....
Total	36	100.0	38	100.0	11	100.0	8	100.0
Perforations of Olecranon								
Fossa								
Present	9	27.3	6	17.6	5	62.5	5	71.4
Absent	24	72.7	28	82.4	3	37.5	2	28.6
Total	33	100.0	34	100.0	8	100.0	7	100.0
Supracondyloid Process								
Absent	28	87.5	31	94.0	9	100.0	8	100.0
Traces	1	3.1	1	3.0	....	....	....	....
Present	3	9.4	1	3.0	....	....	....	....
Total	32	100.0	33	100.0	9	100.0	8	100.0
RADIUS								
Bowing								
Slight	10	34.5	8	26.7	1	16.7	....	....
Medium	13	44.8	17	56.7	3	50.0	4	100.0
Pronounced	6	20.7	5	16.6	2	33.3	....	....
Total	29	100.0	30	100.0	6	100.0	4	100.0
Shape of Shaft								
Prism	19	63.3	19	65.5	3	42.8	3	50.0
Oval	11	36.7	10	34.5	4	57.2	3	50.0
Total	30	100.0	29	100.0	7	100.0	6	100.0
Interosseous Crest								
Submedium	....	....	1	3.4	1	16.7	....	....
Medium	19	63.3	14	48.3	2	33.3	3	50.0
Pronounced	11	36.7	14	48.3	3	50.0	3	50.0
Total	30	100.0	29	100.0	6	100.0	6	100.0

TABLE IV
POOLED ADENA SERIES—Continued

	MALES		FEMALES	
	No.	%	No.	%
STERNUM				
Fusion				
None	....	....	2	33.3
Corpus	1	100.0	3	50.0
Complete	....	....	1	16.7
Total	1	100.0	6	100.0
Foramen				
Absent	1	100.0	3	100.0
Suprasternal Ossification				
Absent	....	....	2	100.0
Sternal Ribs				
Seven	....	....	1	100.0

	Left		Right		Left		Right	
	No.	%	No.	%	No.	%	No.	%
SCAPULA								
Superior Border								
Oblique	2	66.7	....	....	1	100.0	....	....
Wavy	....	....	1	100.0	....	....	....	....
Concave	1	33.3	....	....	....	....	2	100.0
Total	3	100.0	1	100.0	1	100.0	2	100.0
Notch								
Medium	11	61.1	1	20.0	2	100.0	1	100.0
Deep	7	38.9	4	80.0	....	....	....	....
Total	18	100.0	5	100.0	2	100.0	1	100.0
Vertebrae Border								
Concave	1	100.0	....	....	....	....	....	....
Teres Insertion								
Medium	....	....	3	18.7	1	100.0	2	100.0
Pronounced	16	100.0	13	81.3	....	....	....	....
Total	16	100.0	16	100.0	1	100.0	2	100.0
Shape of Acromion								
Sickle	2	16.7	1	9.1	....	....	....	....
Triangular	3	25.0	....	....	....	....	....	....
Intermediate	....	....	6	54.5	1	100.0	....	....
Quadrangular	7	58.3	4	36.4	....	....	1	100.0
Total	12	100.0	11	100.0	1	100.0	1	100.0

TABLE IV
POOLED ADENA SERIES—Continued

	MALES				FEMALES			
	Left		Right		Left		Right	
	No.	%	No.	%	No.	%	No.	%
Clavicular Facet								
Unlipped	6	60.0	6	66.7	2	100.0	....	....
Lipped	4	40.0	3	33.3	....	....	1	100.0
Total	10	100.0	9	100.0	2	100.0	1	100.0
Age Plaque								
Absent	3	50.0	3	37.5	1	100.0	1	100.0
Medium	3	50.0	5	62.5	....	....	....	....
Total	6	100.0	8	100.0	1	100.0	1	100.0
Glenoid Shape								
Oval	21	95.5	19	90.5	4	100.0	3	100.0
Elliptical	1	4.5	2	9.5	....	....	....	....
Total	22	100.0	21	100.0	4	100.0	3	100.0
Glenoid Lipping								
Absent	5	23.8	9	39.1	3	60.0	2	50.0
Beginning	11	52.4	11	47.8	2	40.0	2	50.0
Pronounced	5	23.8	3	13.1	....	....	....	....
Total	21	100.0	23	100.0	5	100.0	4	100.0
Pleating								
Absent	1	50.0	1	100.0	....	....	....	....
Slight	1	50.0	....	....	....	....	....	....
Total	2	100.0	1	100.0	....	....	....	....
Buckling								
Absent	1	100.0	1	100.0	....	....	....	....
FEMUR								
Third Trochanter								
Absent	14	40.0	15	42.9	7	63.5	4	33.3
Submedium	7	20.0	6	17.1	2	18.3	5	41.7
Medium	5	14.3	5	14.3	1	9.1	2	16.7
Pronounced	9	25.7	9	25.7	1	9.1	1	8.3
Total	35	100.0	35	100.0	11	100.0	12	100.0
Crista								
Absent	1	2.6	1	2.4	4	28.6	5	33.3
Submedium	19	50.0	19	46.3	7	50.0	8	53.3
Medium	12	31.6	14	34.2	2	14.3	1	6.7
Pronounced	6	15.8	7	17.1	1	7.1	1	6.7
Total	38	100.0	41	100.0	14	100.0	15	100.0

TABLE IV

POOLED ADENA SERIES—Continued

| | MALES | | | | FEMALES | | | |
| | Left | | Right | | Left | | Right | |
	No.	%	No.	%	No.	%	No.	%
Fossa								
Absent	11	29.0	9	23.7	4	28.6	6	40.0
Submedium	14	36.8	18	47.4	5	35.7	5	33.3
Medium	7	18.4	11	38.9	5	35.7	3	20.0
Pronounced	6	15.8	....	....	....	....	1	6.7
Total	38	100.0	38	100.0	14	100.0	15	100.0
Torsion								
Absent	1	3.0	....		....		....	
Negative	2	6.1	2	6.2	....	....	2	25.0
Submedium	12	36.4	16	50.0	1	50.0	5	62.5
Medium	15	45.4	11	34.4	....	....	1	12.5
Pronounced	3	9.1	3	9.4	1	50.0	....	....
Total	33	100.0	32	100.0	2	100.0	8	100.0
Poirier's Facet								
Absent	6	21.4	6	25.0	1	25.0	1	20.0
Present	22	78.6	18	75.0	3	75.0	4	80.0
Total	28	100.0	24	100.0	4	100.0	5	100.0
Bowing								
None	3	7.7	....	....	....	....	....	....
Submedium	9	23.1	9	21.9	4	40.0	4	28.6
Medium	14	35.9	12	29.3	5	50.0	7	50.0
Pronounced	13	33.3	20	48.8	1	10.0	3	21.4
Total	39	100.0	41	100.0	10	100.0	14	100.0
Shaft Section								
Triangular	2	4.9	2	4.8	....	....	....	....
Prismatic	16	39.0	17	40.5	6	40.0	8	50.0
Plano-convex	4	9.8	1	2.4	....	....		
Quadrangular	....	....	5	11.8	2	13.3	1	6.3
Oval	19	46.3	17	40.5	7	46.7	7	43.7
Total	41	100.0	42	100.0	15	100.0	16	100.0
TIBIA								
Proximal Retroversion								
None	1	3.5	2	5.3	1	16.7	....	....
Slight	6	20.7	7	18.4	....	....	2	33.3
Medium	10	34.5	10	26.3	1	16.7	1	16.7
Pronounced	12	41.3	19	50.0	4	66.6	3	50.0
Total	29	100.0	38	100.0	6	100.0	6	100.0

TABLE IV
POOLED ADENA SERIES—Continued

| | MALES | | | | FEMALES | | | |
| | Left | | Right | | Left | | Right | |
	No.	%	No.	%	No.	%	No.	%
Shape of Shaft (Hrdlicka)								
Type I	9	23.1	10	28.6	1	11.1	1	12.5
Type II	2	5.1	....	....	1	11.1	1	12.5
Type III	9	23.1	9	25.6	4	44.5	3	37.5
Type IV	7	17.9	6	17.2	....	....	....	....
Type V	12	30.8	10	28.6	3	33.3	3	37.5
Total	39	100.0	35	100.0	9	100.0	8	100.0
Squatting Facets								
Absent	5	18.5	5	16.7	3	42.8	1	12.5
Present	22	81.5	25	83.3	4	57.2	7	87.5
Total	27	100.0	30	100.0	7	100.0	8	100.0

	No.	%	No.	%
SACRUM				
Segments				
Five	10	100.0	2	100.0
Sacral Curve				
Slight	4	33.3	....	....
Medium	7	58.3	2	100.0
Pronounced	1	8.4	....	....
Total	12	100.0	2	100.0
Curve Begins				
4	6	42.8	....	....
3	8	57.2	2	100.0
Total	14	100.0	2	100.0
Simian Notch				
Absent	18	90.0	1	33.3
Present	2	10.0	2	66.7
Total	20	100.0	3	100.0
Sacral Type				
Homobasal	6	27.3	4	66.7
Hypobasal	12	54.5	2	33.3
Hyperbasal	4	18.2	....	....
Total	22	100.0	6	100.0

TABLE IV

POOLED ADENA SERIES—Continued

	MALES		FEMALES	
	No.	%	No.	%
Spinal Closure Begins				
6	1	10.0	....	....
4	9	90.0	2	66.7
2	....	....	1	33.3
Total	10	100.0	3	100.0
Arthritic Changes				
Absent	14	63.6	5	83.3
Present	8	36.4	1	16.7
Total	22	100.0	6	100.0
PELVIS				
Subpubic Angle				
Narrow	2	100.0	....	....
Wide	....	....	3	100.0
Total	2	100.0	3	100.0
Brim Shape				
Narrow Oval	3	75.0	....	....
Broad Oval	1	25.0	3	100.0
Total	4	100.0	3	100.0
Pubic Rami (internal edge)				
Lipped	1	25.0	2	100.0
Flat	3	75.0	....	....
Total	4	100.0	2	100.0
Rami Constriction				
Medium	3	100.0	3	100.0

TABLE IV
POOLED ADENA SERIES—Continued

	MALES				FEMALES			
	Left		Right		Left		Right	
	No.	%	No.	%	No.	%	No.	%
INNOMINATE								
Bony Outgrowths								
Absent	8	57.2	15	75.0	1	100.0	1	100.0
Present	6	42.8	5	25.0	....	....	....	....
Total	14	100.0	20	100.0	1	100.0	1	100.0
Ischiatic Notch								
Narrow	21	75.0	19	65.6	....	....	....	....
Medium	5	17.8	9	31.0	....	....	....	....
Wide	2	7.2	1	3.4	7	100.0	9	100.0
Total	28	100.0	29	100.0	7	100.0	9	100.0
Preauricular Sulcus								
Submedium	22	88.0	24	80.0	1	12.5	....	....
Medium	2	8.0	6	20.0	5	62.5	5	62.5
Deep	1	4.0	....	....	2	25.0	3	37.5
Total	25	100.0	30	100.0	8	100.0	8	100.0
Ilium								
Erect	9	45.08	8	30.8	2	33.3	1	25.0
Medium	4	20.0	7	26.9	1	16.7	2	50.0
Flaring	7	35.0	11	42.3	3	50.0	1	25.0
Total	20	100.0	26	100.0	6	100.0	4	100.0
Ischiatic Spine								
Broken	13	50.0	17	54.8	6	100.0	5	100.0
Medium	5	19.2	3	9.7	....	....	....	....
Pronounced	8	30.8	11	35.5	....	....	....	....
Total	26	100.0	31	100.0	6	100.0	5	100.0

ADENA PATHOLOGY

Dental abscesses, arthritis, osteoporosis symmetrica?, ostitis, dental decay (caries), and rickets, and combinations of some or all, have been diagnosed from diseased bones of these Adena Indians.

In Table VI, the occurrence of these forms of pathology by sex and age is compared with the total number of burials examined. This probably represents the minimum frequency of identifiable bone pathology inasmuch as it is limited to the better preserved skeletons or those afflicted parts which are preserved.

It is often thought that arthritis often arises from sources of infection such as abscessed teeth. If this is so the rather high incidence of dental abscesses may be indicative of the source of the infection which brought about the arthritic conditions. Often just the simple lipping of the lumbar vertebrae or of the elbow and knee joints is present. More complicated cases are present too, most notable is that of the crippled man, Burial 30, Site Be 3, Kentucky*.

The curious pinhole-like appearance of the outer surfaces of the brain case, the parietal and occipital bones in particular, is interpreted as evidence of osteoporosis symmetrica, a disease indicating diet deficiency. This porosity of the outer table of the skull bones, occurs symmetrically, most often on the back portions of the parietals bordering the sagittal suture, and frequently on the occipital and frontal bones as well but always on those surfaces not covered by the neck, temporal or frontal muscles. In the case of immature individuals the disease appears as perforations in the orbital roof accompanied by a boney thickening identified as cribra orbitalia.**

Generalized bone inflammation or ostitis is fairly common and appears as areas of swollen spongy tissue most conspicuous on the shafts of the shins and the thigh bones but also is found on the bones of the upper extremity.

Wm. McKee German, M. D., pathologist at Good Samaritan Hospital in Cincinnati, who has kindly examined and diagnosed

---

* Snow, Charles E., 1942, pp. 463-66.
** Snow, Charles E., 1943, p. 625.

TABLE V
POSTCRANIAL MEASUREMENTS (MM) AND INDICES*

	MALES							
	Total KY. ADENA				Total OHIO HOPEWELL			
	Left		Right		Left		Rig	
	No.	Average	No.	Average	No.	Average	No.	Av
HUMERUS								
Maximum Length	20	325.8	19	322.0	3	337.0	5	3
Physiological Length	9	320.6	8	334.8	3	333.0	4	3
Max. Diam. Head	25	44.4	20	45.3	3	48.0	6	
Max. Middle Diam.	34	22.7	35	22.4	6	22.6	5	
Min. Middle Diam.	34	16.0	35	22.4	6	17.0	5	
Middle Circumference	11	63.6	10	67.0	5	65.4	4	
Condylo-Diaphs. Angle	13	82.9°	11	80.6°	4	83.6°	2	
Middle INDEX	34	73.3	35	73.0	6	75.0	5	
Robust. INDEX	8	19.6	8	21.0	3	18.6	4	
ULNA								
Maximum Length	14	268.0	17	267.4	2	280.0	3	2
Middle Circumference	8	45.1	10	46.1	2	48.0	3	
Robust. INDEX	8	16.7	9	17.8	2	17.2	3	
RADIUS								
Maximum Length	16	254.3	16	254.4	....	....	2	2
Middle Circumference	9	42.7	7	44.3	....	....	2	
Robust. INDEX	8	16.7†	5	17.5	....	....	2	
CLAVICLE								
Maximum Length	12	150.9	14	149.0	2	155.0	4	1
Middle Circumference	8	35.6	8	34.7	2	34.0	4	
Robust. INDEX	7	23.6	9	21.7	2	22.0	4	
SCAPULA								
Total Height	....		....	....	....	....	1	]
Inferior Height	1	125.0	....	....	....	....	1	]
Breadth	2	103.5	....	....	....	....	1	]
Total INDEX	....	....	....	....	....	....	1	
Inferior INDEX	1	82.8	....	....	....	....	1	
LUMBAR VERTEBRAE								
Anterior Heights	20			28.2	1			31
Posterior Heights	15			28.3	1			31
Lumbar INDEX	7			100.4	3			99
SACRUM								
Height	8			112.0	1			114
Breadth	14			118.7	3			123
Sacral INDEX	7			104.6	1			103
PELVIS								
Total Br. (Bi-iliac)	11			273.0	4			285
Max. Br. (Sup. Strait)	10			125.8	6			126
A. P. Diam. (Sup. Strait)	8			111.9	4			116
Bi-ischiatic Br.	5			131.6	3			145
Ischiatic Interspin.	5			131.6	3			92
Ant.-sup. Interspin.	2			254.5	....			....
Brim INDEX	8			87.8	4			90
Total Pelvic INDEX	7			77.6	4			76

* All measurements and indices, approximate.
** Manouvrier, L., 1892, p. 169-244

FEMALES

ALA. COPENA			Total KY. ADENA				Total OHIO HOPEWELL				Total ALA. COPENA			
(Left)	Right		Left		Right		Left		Right		Left		Right	
Average	No.	Average	No.	Average	No.	Average	No.	Average	No.	Average	No.	Average	No.	Average
			6	300.9	3	296.3	3	310.0	2	306.0	2	288.0	3	297.0
			3	303.7	1	298.0	3	307.0	2	305.0	1	275.0	3	296.3
			8	39.0	8	41.5	3	43.0	3	40.0	2	39.5	3	39.0
			12	20.3	10	20.7	3	18.0	4	20.0	5	19.2	8	19.7
			12	14.7	10	14.6	3	13.0	4	13.0	5	13.8	8	13.7
			4	58.2	3	59.0	3	54.0	3	55.0	5	53.4	8	55.4
			3	80.7	3	81.0	3	84.0°	3	86.0°	4	84.9°	4	83.5°
			12	72.7	10	70.6	3	73.0	4	66.2	5	71.9	8	70.3
			3	19.1	1	19.5	3	17.5	2	18.1	2	18.8	3	19.0
60.0			1	262.0	3	254.7	2	245.0	2	250.0	2	236.5	5	240.0
41.5	3	42.0			1	51.0	2	39.0	2	41.0	5	40.0	5	39.6
16.9					1	20.1	2	16.0	2	16.2	2	16.3	5	16.9
40.5			4	222.0	3	233.0	3	227.0	4	234.0	2	220.0	2	216.0
38.5	1	38.0					3	38.0	4	37.0	4	35.2	5	37.2
16.0							3	16.6	4	15.9	2	15.3	2	17.1
			3	144.3	2	153.0	3	149.0	4	146.0	3	140.7	4	136.1
			2	31.0	1	37.0	3	32.0	4	31.0	5	31.4	4	31.5
			2	23.0	1	26.6	3	21.7	4	21.4	3	22.1	4	23.1
	1	154.0			1	144.0								
	1	125.0			1	105.0			1	109.0				
	1	107.0			1	108.0	1	95.0						
	1	69.5			1	75.0								
	1	85.6			1	102.8								
					3	28.0			2	29.2			1	22.6
					3	28.0			2	29.0			1	25.0
					3	100.1			2	98.8			1	94.0
					2	97.5			1	116.0			2	92.5
					3	117.7			4	123.0			2	113.0
					1	116.3			1	104.4			2	122.0
					2	252.5			5	279.4			2	259.0
					2	129.0			6	136.5			2	131.5
					2	120.5			3	125.0			2	93.0
									4	173.0			1	147.0
									1	112.0				
					2	89.4			3	89.4			1	71.0
									5	73.0			1	70.8

TABLE V *(Continued)*
POSTCRANIAL MEASUREMENTS (MM) AND INDICES*

	MALES						
	Total KY. ADENA				Total OHIO HOPEWELL		
	Left		Right		Left		R
	No.	Average	No.	Average	No.	Average	No.
INNOMINATE	Left		Right		Left		R
Height	15	211.8	14	210.4	5	219.4	7
Breadth	11	149.1	9	154.0	2	163.0	4
INDEX	9	70.2	8	72.5	1	76.0	4
FEMUR							
Maximum Length	29	456.6	29	451.6	16	463.5	9
Bicondylar Length	28	452.2	27	446.9	17	458.3	20
Max. Diam. Head	35	45.3	34	46.3	27	43.8	28
Subtroch. A. P. Diam.	37	26.2	38	26.4	23	26.4	22
Subtroch. Lat. Diam.	37	31.1	38	30.5	23	34.4	22
Middle A. P. Diam.	37	29.7	38	30.0	24	31.5	22
Middle Lat. Diam.	37	26.0	38	25.7	24	27.0	22
Middle Circumference	16	85.9	16	85.0	14	93.0	11
Platymeric INDEX	34	85.2	38	87.3	23	77.5	22
Middle INDEX	36	83.3	36	85.6	24	85.8	22
Robust. INDEX	11	19.7	11	19.5	6	20.5	9
TIBIA							
Maximum Length	22	373.4	22	377.5	10	381.0	7
Physiological Length	12	361.5	13	366.2	6	376.0	4
Nut. For. A. P. Diam.	34	35.8	32	36.3	9	39.0	7
Nut. For. Lat. Diam.	32	25.1	30	25.4	9	25.0	7
Middle A. P. Diam.	34	31.4	31	31.3	13	34.1	11
Middle Lat. Diam.	34	23.0	31	23.2	13	23.0	11
Middle Circumference	10	86.0	11	85.3	7	94.0	5
Platycnemic INDEX	32	70.1	29	69.9	8	63.7	7
Middle INDEX	33	72.4	31	74.1	13	67.6	11
Robust INDEX	8	23.4	9	22.9	4	24.9	3
FIBULA							
Maximum Length	12	366.3	11	361.3	2	384.0	3
Middle Circumference	7	46.7	7	46.8	3	54.0	3
Robust. INDEX	6	12.1	7	13.1	2	14.0	3
INTERMEMBRAL INDICES							
Humero-radial	10	78.4	13	79.7	....	....	2
Humero-femoral	14	71.6	15	72.2	....	....	3
Claviculo-humeral	8	46.7	12	42.6	3	48.1	3
Tibio-femoral	18	83.6	17	84.4	7	84.3	6
Intermembral	3	69.0	4	69.2	....	....	1
STATURE ESTIMATIONS (cm.)							
Manouvrier**							
HUMERUS	20	165.9	19	164.9	3	168.9	5
ULNA	14	169.2	17	169.0	2	175.4	3
RADIUS	16	171.2	16	171.2	....	....	2
FEMUR	28	167.6	27	166.8	17	168.4	20
TIBIA	22	167.8	22	168.5	10	170.8	7
Average HEIGHT	201 bones	167.9 cm.			69 bones	169.0	

* All measurements and indices, approximate.
** Manouvrier. L., 1892, p. 169-244

	FEMALES												
ALA. COPENA		Total KY. ADENA				Total OHIO HOPEWELL				Total ALA. COPENA			
Right		Left		Right		Left		Right		Left		Right	
Average	No.	Average	No.	Average	No.	Average	No.	Average	No.	Average	No.	Average	No. Average
Right		**Left**		**Right**		**Left**		**Right**		**Left**		**Right**	
1 215.0		2 201.1		4 199.0		5 198.4		6 199.7		1 197.0		2 195.5	
....		1 143.0		1 148.0		3 151.0†		5 150.0		1 145.0		2 143.5	
....		1 70.1		....		1 75.5		4 78.5		1 73.6		2 73.4	
1.8	6 454.8	12 425.7		7 428.0		13 442.0		14 442.0		4 413.2		2 414.5	
5.8	4 444.2	11 417.3		7 421.4		13 435.0		13 426.3		4 407.7		2 408.0	
5.7	6 46.0	13 40.9		14 42.1		19 42.1		19 41.8		4 40.5		5 40.2	
4.4	11 25.6	18 23.4		18 23.5		16 23.3		16 23.1		9 20.7		9 21.2	
1.4	11 31.2	18 28.4		18 28.3		16 30.4		16 30.2		9 29.8		9 29.6	
9.2	11 29.2	16 26.0		16 25.5		17 27.8		17 27.1		9 24.4		9 25.1	
4.8	11 25.2	16 23.8		16 23.6		17 24.2		17 24.1		9 24.6		9 23.9	
3.3	11 83.5	7 77.0		4 75.5		11 81.0		10 78.0		9 75.1		9 75.6	
8.5	11 76.4	17 82.8		18 83.9		16 76.3		16 77.1		9 69.5		9 72.1	
5.2	11 86.8	16 92.2		16 93.1		17 88.6		17 88.3		9 95.2		9 91.8	
8.6	6 18.8	6 18.2		1 17.1		7 18.2		8 17.6		5 17.9		2 17.6	
......	2 361.5	6 354.0		6 345.0		9 363.8		4 365.0		2 340.0		2 342.5	
......	1 345.0	1 358.0		1 336.0		6 356.0		5 352.0		1 318.0		4 325.2	
35.4	4 36.2	9 30.8		7 30.1		7 33.0		6 33.0		5 31.6		8 31.5	
21.6	4 24.0	9 23.0		9 23.2		7 22.0		6 21.0		5 19.8		8 21.6	
32.0	7 31.0	10 27.5		9 26.9		10 29.2		9 29.8		5 28.4		8 28.1	
20.7	8 20.9	10 21.2		9 21.1		10 19.9		9 20.0		5 17.8		8 18.7	
34.7	7 80.0	2 77.0		2 76.5		6 76.0		6 78.0		4 72.8		7 74.1	
31.3	4 67.2	10 75.6		7 75.9		7 66.1		6 64.1		5 62.5		8 68.5	
34.8	7 68.4	9 76.4		9 78.5		10 68.3		9 67.7		5 62.7		8 65.5	
......	1 24.4	....		....		5 20.8		3 21.0		2 21.6		2 21.2	
......	1 355.0	....		1 334.0		2 344.0		3 347.0		1 329.0		....	
43.7	4 43.8	....		1 46.0		2 39.0		3 42.0		2 39.5		2 43.0	
......	1 15.2	....		1 13.8		1 11.3		4 11.9		....		....	
......	....	2 77.9		....		2 75.6		2 77.5		....		....	
......	....	4 73.5		2 71.2		2 70.9		2 69.6		1 68.7		1 71.0	
......	....	2 45.3		1 43.6		1 50.9		....		....		....	
......	....	4 82.7		3 82.8		8 83.2		7 83.2		....		....	
......	....	....		1 70.0		2 66.8		2 67.4		....		....	
......	....	6 156.5		3 155.4		3 158.8		2 157.9		2 152.4		3 155.6	
66.6	....	....		3 165.4		2 160.4		2 162.6		2 157.2		5 158.5	
65.9	....	4 158.2		3 162.6		3 159.9		4 163.0		2 157.5		2 147.8	
66.5	4 166.2	11 156.0		7 156.7		13 159.3		13 157.6		4 154.0		2 154.3	
......	2 165.2	6 159.6		6 158.0		9 162.7		4 163.3		2 156.8		2 157.3	
bones 164.0 cm.		49 bones 158.0 cm.				55 bones 160.1 cm.				26 bones 155.5 cm.			

much of the Kentucky Adena bone specimens, impressed with the spectacular form of rarefying ostitis* stated the following:**

"I am struck with the increasing volume of lesions which could be explained by syphilis—the numerous sabre shin bones—the numerous bones which show periostitis and osteosclerosis. . . May not the increasing volume of such lesions be adding up to a point where we might consider them evidence of syphilis?"

Dental decay (caries) occurs but is not very common, Figure 10. Occasionally the wear on the teeth has been of such a degree

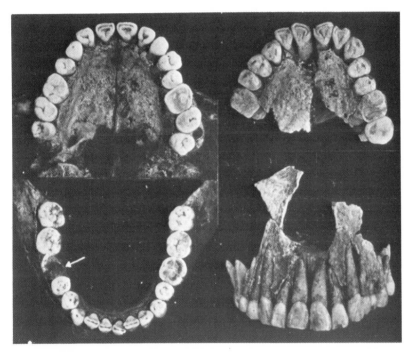

Fig. 10. Dental Variations
  Left: The upper and lower dental arcades (the palate and lower jaws) of Burial 13, Mm 6, Wright site, (a young woman) with shovel-shaped incisors. Note the absence of the upper right pre-molar and the socket of a supernumerary tooth between the upper left 2nd and 3rd molars. An arrow indicates the dental decay (caries) which has virtually destroyed the lower right 1st molar.
  Right: Inferior and front views of the fragmentary upper jaw of Burial 2, Mm 3, Ricketts site, a young man with large, long-rooted teeth. Note the shovel-shaped incisors and the inward torsion (mesiolinqual rotation) which characterizes most of the skulls, juvenile and adult.

* Snow, Charles E., 1942, p. 461, Vol. V, No. 5.
** German, Wm. McKee, 1944, letter of February 3rd.

that secondary deposition of dentine has taken place thus sealing off the pulp chamber saving the nerve and the tooth

Only four fractures (all healed) were found, two of the right collar bones of young men. Healed lesions of the bones of the skull are also rarely found.

Gaps or dehiscences in the anterior surface of the floor of the bony auditory canal near its medical boundary are frequent. The occurrences presented in Table VI list left, right, and both. When these gaps were present on both sides, they were also tabulated under the side, i.e. if both were perforated, they were counted also as left and right.

TABLE VI
ADENA PATHOLOGY
Arthritis

Age Group		Jaw Joint L.	Jaw Joint R.	Neck	Thorax	Lumbar	Pelvis	Upper Ex-tremity L.	Upper Ex-tremity R.	Shoulder Joint L.	Shoulder Joint R.	Lower Ex-tremity L.	Lower Ex-tremity R.	Total Examined
Y. Adult	M	4	4	4	3	8	2	1	0	2	2	3	1	93
	F	2	2	2	2	2	0	0	0	1	1	0	1	39
Mid-Adult	M	0	0	5	2	4	2	0	0	1	1	0	1	14
	F	0	0	1	1	0	0	0	0	0	0	0	0	1
Old Adult	M	0	0	2	2	2	0	0	0	0	0	0	0	3
	F	0	0	0	0	0	0	0	0	0	0	0	0	0
Cremations	M	0	0	2	1	1	0	0	0	0	0	0	0	18
	F	0	0	0	0	0	0	0	0	0	0	0	0	15
	?	0	0	1	1	1	0	0	0	0	0	0	0	18

Dental Decay (caries)

Age Group		Upper In-cisors L.	Upper In-cisors R.	Upper Pre-molars L.	Upper Pre-molars R.	Upper Molars L.	Upper Molars R.	Lower In-cisors L.	Lower In-cisors R.	Lower Pre-molars L.	Lower Pre-molars R.	Lower Molars L.	Lower Molars R.	Total Examined
Adolescent	M	0	0	0	0	0	0	0	0	0	0	0	0	4
	F	0	0	0	0	0	0	0	0	0	0	1	0	10
Y. Adult	M	0	1	0	1	0	2	0	0	0	1	1	4	93
	F	0	0	0	0	0	0	0	0	0	2	2	3	39

TABLE VI—Continued
Dental Abscesses

Age Group		Upper						Lower						Total Examined
		In-cisors		Pre-molars		Molars		In-cisors		Pre-molars		Molars		
		L.	R.	L.	R.	L.	R.	L.	R.	L.	R.	L.	R.	
Y. Adult	M	0	0	0	0	7	13	0	0	3	3	20	21	93
	F	0	0	1	1	3	3	0	0	3	3	4	4	39
Mid-Adult	M	0	0	1	1	1	1	0	0	1	1	1	1	14
	F	0	0	0	0	0	0	0	0	0	0	0	0	1
Old Adult	M	1	1	0	0	1	1	0	0	1	1	1	1	3
	F	0	0	0	0	0	0	0	0	0	0	0	0	0

Ostitis or Periostitis

Age Group		Body Region														Total Examined
		Hu-merus		Ulna		Radius		Clavicle		Femur		Tibia		Fibula		
		L.	R.	L.	R.	L.	R.	L.	R.	L.	R.	L.	R.	L.	R.	
Adolescent	M	0	0	0	0	0	0	0	0	0	0	0	0	0	0	4
	F	1	1	1	1	1	1	1	1	1	1	1	1	1	1	10
Y. Adult	M	2	2	0	0	0	0	1	1	6	5	8	8	3	3	93
	F	0	0	0	0	0	0	0	0	0	0	2	1	1	1	39
Mid-Adult	M	1	1	1	1	1	1	1	1	1	1	1	1	1	1	14
	F	0	0	0	0	0	0	0	0	0	0	0	0	0	0	1

Healed Lesions on Skull

Age Group		Frontal	Parietal		Occipital	Total Examined
			L.	R.		
Adolescent	M	0	0	0	0	4
	F	1	0	0	0	10
Young Adult	M	2	0	0	1	93
	F	1	0	0	0	39
Cremation Sex?		0	1	0	0	18

TABLE VI—Continued
Osteoporosis Symmetrica?

Age Group		Orbital Roofs L.	Orbital Roofs R.	Frontal	Parietals	Occipital	Palate, Pterygoid Bases	Total Examined
Infant	M	2	2	0	1	1	0	5
	F	0	0	0	0	0	0	2
Child	M	0	0	0	0	0	0	9
	F	0	0	0	1	0	0	2
Adolescent	M	0	0	0	0	1	0	4
	F	4	4	4	5	5	2	10
Young Adult	M	3	3	11	21	18	2	93
	F	4	4	4	11	7	0	39
Mid-Adult	M	0	0	0	2	2	0	14
	F	0	0	0	0	0	0	1
Old Adult	M	0	0	1	1	1	0	3
	F	0	0	0	0	0	0	0
Cremations	M	0	0	0	1	0	0	18
	F	0	0	1	1	1	0	15

Column header note: "Skull Region" spans Orbital Roofs, Frontal, Parietals, Occipital, Palate/Pterygoid Bases.

Healed Fractures

Age Group		Radius L.	Radius R.	Clavicle L.	Clavicle R.	Pelvis L.	Pelvis R.	Total Examined
Young Adult	M	0	0	0	2	0	1	93
	F	1	0	0	0	0	0	39

Dehiscences in Auditory Floor

Age Group		Left	Right	Both	Total Examined
Adolescent	M	0	0	0	4
	F	2	2	2	10
Young Adult	M	13	10	9	93
	F	3	6	3	39

THE USE OF PIGMENTS ON SKELETONS

Skeletons with different members stained or coated with either black or red pigment have been noted at several different Adena mound sites (Riley, Landing, Hartman, Crigler) in Kentucky.

The Kentucky Adena skeletal remains have recently been re-examined with this particular feature in mind, and the evidence seems to indicate that some of the bones of nearly all of the skeletons regardless of age or sex, show either black and/or red stains.

In Ohio skeletons from the Adena Westenhaver, Coon and Florence Mounds show smiliar pigmented surfaces. The Westenhaver (Burial 6) in particular is coated with a dull black pigment, inside and out of the skull onto roots of the teeth and over the outsides of all of the bones of the skeleton; the lower leg bones show red ochre on them also. The Coon Mound fragments are stained black and on top of that frequently are gaudy gobs of red ochre. The Florence Mound infant is similarly stained and traces of red ocher are visible in the surrounding earth about the skeleton as it lies on exhibit at the Ohio State Museum at Columbus.

The same conditions are present among the Hopewell skeletons with the additional green staining of the bones from the numerous copper objects which so often accompanied the burials.

Many careful chemical tests have been made of samples of these bones stained with dull black. All show very strong positive reactions indicating a ferric iron compound. This substance, we are informed, could conceivably be formed by the contact of the decomposing tissues of the corpse with some source of iron such as red ochre (hematite).[*] In some well preserved Adena and Hopewell tombs, red ochre as stains, coating or lumps has been noted.

All of this evidence is taken to indicate that the Adena and Hopewell peoples used red ochre to adorn their dead as part of the ceremonial ritual which undoubtedly accompanied the placement of the body of the deceased in its prepared tomb. The placement of this sort of coloring material on special regions of the body seems apparent, too. Very frequently parts of the head, the

---

[*] Maxson, Ralph N., 1943, p. 618, Vol. V, No. 7.

face and lower jaw in particular, were selected. At other times the pigment seems to have been spread over the entire body.

There are instances in many of the tombs of Adena, Hopewell, and Copena burials which indicate that red ochre, a black iron compound and/or graphite was applied directly to the bones involved.

In one case, Burial 8, Mm 6, Wright site (Figure 11) the pigment is in so regular a design that it would seem almost certainly to have been applied to the bone and not the flesh. A graphite streak one-half inch wide extends down the center of the forehead across the nasal bones and over the upper jaw coating even the exposed roots of the teeth. This streak lay on top of red ochre which covered most of the vault with an ''open'' area across the center of the forehead. Burial 11, Crigler Mound Be 20 shows graphite on the forehead, cheekbones and clavicles. The lower extremities, including the hip region were covered with lumps of red ochre, some of which had stained the surrounding earth. See traits 85–88.

Hrdlicka* quotes from Moorehead concerning Hopewell Painted bones as follows:

''In Ohio painted bones were found by Prof. E. W. Putnam (Turner group mounds) and by Mr. W. K. Moorehead. The latter writes me on the subject as follows:

'Painted bones have been found in a mound at Omega, Ross County, Ohio; in Jackson County mound, Ohio, and in two mounds within the corporate limits of Chillicothe. One of the latter was discovered by Mr. Clarence Loveberry, assistant curator of the above (Ohio Archaeological and Historical) society. The others were found by myself. Near Green Camp, Marion County, Ohio, in a stone grave 6 feet below the surface, Mr. Loveberry discovered a skeleton entirely painted.

'All of these were coated with red pigment or ochre, including in nearly every case all of the larger bones. There are other instances in which just the hands, or the feet, or perhaps the skull were coated. These are usually from mounds, either large or small. Bones on which the pigment was simply heaped were clearly distinguished by the surrounding soil being also stained.

'I have never observed instances in which skeletons

---

* Hrdlicka, Ales, 1904, p. 612.

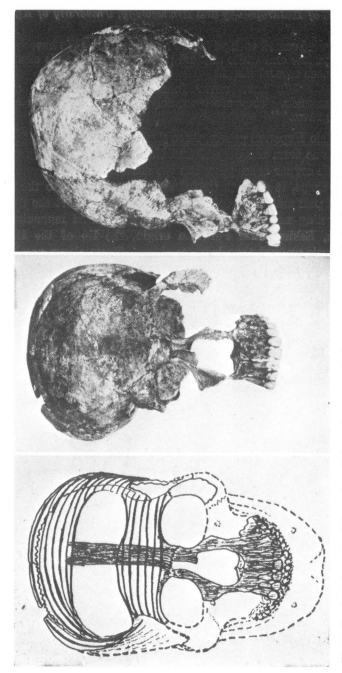

Figure 11. Drawing and photographs of the deformed skull of a young woman. Burial 8, Wright Site, Mm 6, showing a dark, vertical streak of graphite applied over an area covered by red ochre (horizontal lines), and down over the nose and face.

were coated with yellow or black paints. (We have found yellow and white mineral paints near the hands of skeletons several times.)

'We have never found painted bones in stone mounds. They are invariably in earth mounds or stone graves.' ''

In Ohio Hopewell graves, three skulls, two from the Hopewell Site and one from the Seip Mound No. 1, were found with carefully made copper cones placed in the nasal apertures. From the size and shape, it appears that these were inserted into the nostrils as a post mortem preparation in order to support the tip of the shriveling nose. As can be observed in dried mummies of Egyptian, Eskimo, and Peruvian origin, the tip of the fleshy nose shrivels up and thus loses its shape. These clever nasals of copper would have delayed this mark of death.

In summation, it may be said that the Adena, Hopewell and Copena peoples took great pains to decorate their dead, both in the cases of interment in the flesh and the bones of defleshed skeletons. This custom appears to have been followed by many different historic groups described by Hrdlicka.*

---

* Hrdlicka, Ales, 1904, pp. 610-611.

THE PROBLEM OF THE TROPHY SKULL

It has been shown (see Trait 92) that, among the varied burial customs used by Adena, infrequently an isolated skull was placed in a mound or village midden, without any evidence of a prepared grave, and with no artifacts in association. Such isolated skulls usually have the axis and atlas vertebrae in association. This has been taken to mean that the individual was decapitated and the head thus buried. The disposition of the remainder of the body in such cases is unknown. Such isolated skull burials seem to have no connection with the problem of the "Trophy" skulls.

Again it has been shown that, rarely, in cases of decapitation, the skull is buried with the body, being placed between the femora (see Trait 93). This bizarre custom, reported from four burials in two sites seems again to show no connection with the "trophy" skull complex.

The term "Trophy" in connection with detached Adena skulls found in the graves of other individuals, was first used by Greenman* (Table C) in reference to a separate skull found on the abdomen of an extended burial in the Fudge Mound**, Randolph County, Indiana. In his report on this mound, Setzler says,

> "Since such human skulls are quite common among burials of the Hopewell culture in Ohio, anthropologists have looked upon them as ceremonial offerings."

Thus, it is evident that the term "Trophy" was borrowed by Greenman, to describe in Adena a condition which occurred more frequently in Ohio Hopewell, and which he regarded as similar. The first reported instance of this trait which directed attention to it was the contents of the intrusive pit in Mound 3 of the Turner Group***. Here sixteen separate crania were found arranged about two extended burials in a pit intruded into Mound 3. Of these Willoughby says,

> "The sixteen skulls were unaccompanied by other bones. They were probably family relics, connected with or belonging to the man whose skeleton occupied the center of the grave. Thirteen of them have superficial scratches or cuts

* Greenman, E. F., 1932, p. 445.
** Setzler, Frank M., 1931, p. 31.
*** Willoughby, Charles C., 1922, p. 60.

on their surface, apparently made with flint knives in the process of removing the flesh. Some of the skulls had been painted red, the red ochre still adheres to the surface of six. It is more common on the forehead, facial bones, and jaw, but in one skull it occurs about the base as well, and in this and one other on the temporal fossa. Five of the skulls have one to four perforations, about 1/8 inch in diameter, in the vault of the cranium. The sixth example has eleven perforations, and another apparently started. . . . The position of the holes seem to indicate that at least a part of them were intended for the passage of a suspending cord. Others may have been used for the insertion of feathers or other decorations.''

The excavation of the Marriott Mound No. 1*, a portion of the Turner Group, yielded another skull buried separately in a small stone lined grave. In reporting on the graves in this mound, Putnam says the smallest contained a complete skull with under jaw.

"A hole ¼ inch in diameter had been bored through the occipital bone, near the margin of the foramen magnum. The position of the hole suggests that a cord, for purpose of suspension, may have been passed through it and out of the great foramen."

It thus appears that while instances of detached skulls accompanying extended burials in graves, had been found, the term ''Trophy'' had not been applied until excavation of the Hopewell Group. In his report on Burial 5 of Mound Number 2, Shetrone** says,

"Ten inches to the right of the skull lay a detached human skull—that of a young male upon which rested a curved helmet-like copper plate. This separate skull, apparently a trophy, shows distinctly the marks of the flint knife employed in detaching the scalp and tissues.

"While the skeleton proper of this burial was badly decomposed its skull, as well as the trophy skull, was in an excellent state of preservation. * * * * *''

The use of the term Trophy by Shetrone seems to imply all that is properly comprehended in the term. Funk and Wagnalls Standard Dictionary defines trophy as,

"Anything taken from an enemy and displayed or treasured up in proof of victory; hence, a memento of victory or success.''

---

* Putnam, F. W., 1884, p. 455.
** Shetrone, H. C., 1926, p. 26.

Again, in speaking of this same burial with its accompanying separate skull Shetrone says,*

"With the skeleton of a venerable male, accompanied by many implements and ornaments, there was found the separate skull of a young male wearing a copper head plate. The latter probably was a trophy skull, either that of an enemy captured in battle or that of a relative retained as a family relic."

In this language is posed the problem of the so called "Trophy" skull. Are they (1) trophies according to the usual definition, or are they (2) ceremonial offerings (Setzler) or (3) family relics (Willoughby)?

While separate skulls found in the graves of other burials are relatively few in Adena they seem to indicate a practice similar to that in Ohio Hopewell. Such skulls are much more numerous in Ohio Hopewell than was at first supposed. In fact the Hopewell site has yielded many skulls, (11 known) drilled, cut, scraped, polished, or otherwise altered, before final burial. The solution of this problem, that is, the evaluation of the archaeological significance of this trait, and its interpretation can best be understood by a study of the physical or morphological characteristics of these skulls. If they were all of adult males one might be disposed to consider favorably the suggestion that they might be enemies, taken in battle. If it could be shown that they were physically different from the population with which they were associated, such evidence might be offered as partial confirmation of the true trophy concept. This might be further strengthened if any of them showed evidence of physical violence during life. None of these assumptions seem to coincide with the facts in any degree.

In Kentucky Adena, there are several instances where detached skulls were found: Burial 10, Mm 6, Wright Site; Burial 3, Be 15, Riley Site; Burial 1, 10, and 12, Be 17, Landing Site. Of these only the first is well enough preserved for study. It is clearly the skull of a young man, deeply stained with a black ferric iron compound, and is of a peculiar, light, friable bone. Fig. 25, top, shows this interesting specimen. The vault has been slightly deformed (bifronto-occipital) and is rather narrow for

---

* Shetrone, H. C., 1930, p. 199.

the Adena type. It appears to approach the Hopewell type, although the skull form is high mesocranic (C. I. 79.9). It could conceivably represent Hopewell or some blend therewith.

Only two trophy skulls have been found in the Kentucky mounds; Burial 7, Mm 6, Wright Site, and Burial 38, Be 3, Robbins Site. Only Burial 7 is worthy of discussion since it alone is well preserved and measurable. The skull is that of a young male, with medium frontal-occipital deformation. It is illustrated in Fig. 24, top, and is in every respect Adena in character. We have not been able to detect any evidence of cut marks, drill holes or of any other type of preparation as a trophy such as characterizes the Hopewell trophy skulls. We conclude therefore on the basis of two trophy skulls, one of rather fragmentary nature, the other well preserved, that they were of the same physical type as the skeletons buried in the flesh.

There are 29 trophy Hopewell skulls, all of which apparently show definite marks of some type of preparation. Of this number, 25 are males, and four females. Of the 16 male skulls from the Turner site, 11 have been measured. Eleven others come from the Hopewell mounds No. 24 and 25, one each from the Marriott and Seip Mounds.

The Ohio Hopewell trophies reflect precisely the same physical types which constitute the Hopewell burials, themselves. The four females and all but three of the males are of either the H_1 undeformed (50%) or the H_1 deformed (about 35%) type, clearly of the same basic, long headed stock as Hopewell. Three of the males (15%) are of the H_2 (Adena-like) type. See the two skulls at right of Figure 16. These designations are defined on page 288.

All of these skulls show signs of some sort of preparation either as cut marks, scraping and polishing striae especially along the periphery of muscular attachments, or as gouging, sectioning, and drilling; one, some, or all in combination. The use of a hand lens is very helpful in the observation of these signs.

Usually, the trophy skull occupies a definite place in relation to the burial which it accompanies. In at least one instance, Burials 34, Mound 25, Hopewell Site, where a female trophy skull was found in association with an elaborate grave of a typical Hopewell male, it could be inferred that the female had some relation to or with the male.

On the basis of these numerous specimens, it may be said that the trophy skulls show the same range of physical types as do the Hopewell burials which they accompany; both sexes are clearly represented. If they represent enemies they are of the same or similar kind of physical type; and there is evidence that females were intentionally captured, and the "trophy" thus secured.

We speculate that possibly these trophies found in Ohio Hopewell graves were Hopewellians themselves, who for reasons of honor, memory, love, or other motives for particular consideration, were accorded this special preparation. If burial exposure was practiced, then the cut-marks and other signs are evidence of the cutting and scraping off of dried ligaments and other clinging tissue. Holes were drilled usually in the vault, and also through both jaws possibly for suspension, articulation, or decoration as suggested by Willoughby and others.

One thing is certain, all skulls found separately in Hopewell graves need to be scrutinized carefully with a hand lens to detect this evidence of preparation.

COMPARISON WITH HOPEWELL AND COPENA SKULLS

All of the available skulls from Hopewell mounds (the Hopewell site itself, Harness, Seip, Esch, and Marietta) have been measured and studied by the junior author.* These data when combined with the Turner Mound series described by Hooton** and with the Porter Mound skulls reported by Neumann*** from a total Ohio Hopewell series numbering 104 measurable adults; 66 males, and 38 females, including 24 (recognized) trophy skulls. Table III presents the approximate measurements and indices of these male and female series.

On the basis of morphology, these total series, excluding the trophy skulls, have been divided into subseries designated as (H_1) undeformed, (H_1) deformed and (H_2). The (H_1)s are long headed types which constitute about 80% of the total and are regarded as typical Hopewell. The H_2 type is remarkably similar to and indistinguishable from the Adena type. The trophy skulls have been separated into corresponding groups.

For comparative purposes, the much smaller but total Copena series has been divided similarly.

Type skulls of these three mound building peoples have been selected and are illustrated below in Figures 12, 13, 14, and 15.

The average measurements and indices of these Hopewell and Copena skulls listed in Table III appear to justify their selection. For example, the undeformed H_1 group appear to have longer, narrower and less high skull vaults than those of the same type which are deformed occipitally (H_1 deformed). These are dimensions and proportions which are most directly affected by the forces of deformation. The H_2 type, a broadhead, is strikingly similar to the Adena type. The illustrations, Figures 16 and 17 show this resemblance. The "A" indicates the Adena skulls and the others are all of known Hopewell origin. The two skulls at the right of the male group, are Hopewell trophies. In the female group the two skulls on the right, one Adena, the other Hopewell appear quite similar.

* Snow, Charles E., manuscript on Ohio Hopewell crania in preparation.
** Hooton, Earnest A., 1922, pp. 99-132.
*** Neumann, Georg K., 1941, pp. 479-488.

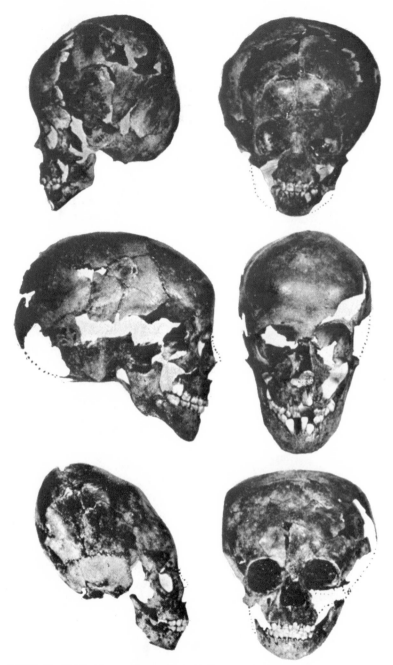

Figure 12. Child Adena, Hopewell, and Copena Skulls.

Upper: Burial 66, Be 3, Robbins Mound, Kentucky. Adena, Age 1½ years, male?, pronounced occipital deformation.
Center: Burial 48, Seip Mound, Ohio, Hopewell, Age 7 years, male, Bifrontal deformation.

Lower: Burial 96, Mg ᵛ64, Alabama, Copena, Age 2 years, male?, Parallelo-fronto-occipital deformation.

(Courtesy Alabama Museum of Natural History.)

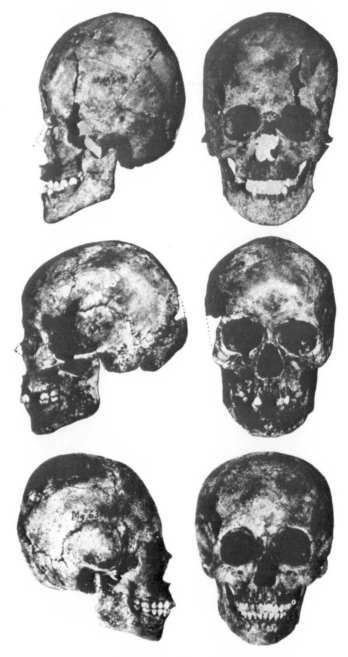

Figure 13. Adolescent Adena, Hopewell, and Copena Skulls.

Upper: Burial 1, Mm 6, Wright Mound, Kentucky, Adena, Age 15 years, female, Bifronto-occiptal deformation.

Center: 41606, Hopewell Site, Ohio, Hopewell, Age 17 years, female, Bifrontal deformation.

Lower: Burial 77, Mg °63., Alabama, Copena, Age 14 years, female, Fronto-occipital deformation.

(Courtesy Alabama Museum of Natural History.)

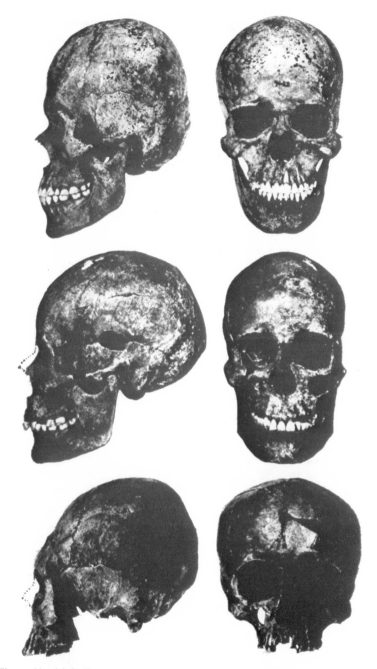

Figure 14. Adult Female Adena, Hopewell, and Copena Skulls.

Upper: Burial 13, Mm 6, Wright Site, Kentucky, Adena Age 22 years, pronounced occipital deformation.

Center: Burial 15, Mound 25, Hopewell Site, Ohio. Hopewell, Age 22 years, bifrontal deformation.

Lower: Burial 89, Mg °63, Alabama, Copena, Age 22 years, fronto-occipital deformation.

(Courtesy Alabama Museum of Natural History.)

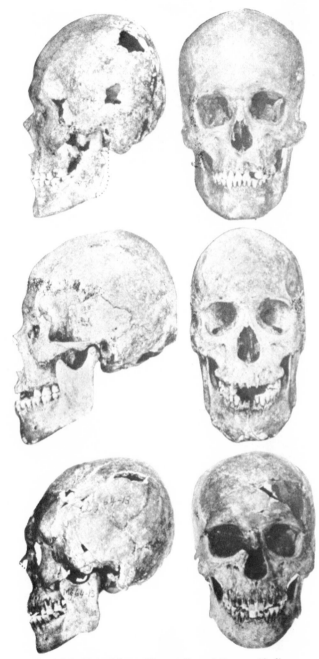

Figure 15. Adult Male Adena, Hopewell, and Copena Skulls.
Upper: Burial 14, Mm 6, Wright Site, Kentucky. Adena, Age 35 years, pronounced bifrontal-occipital deformation.
Center: Burial 1, Mound 2, Hopewell Site, Ohio. Hopewell, Age 37 years, bifrontal deformation.
Lower: Burial 13, Mg v64, Alabama, Copena, Age 28 years, fronto-occipital deformation.
(Courtesy Alamaba Museum of Natural History.)

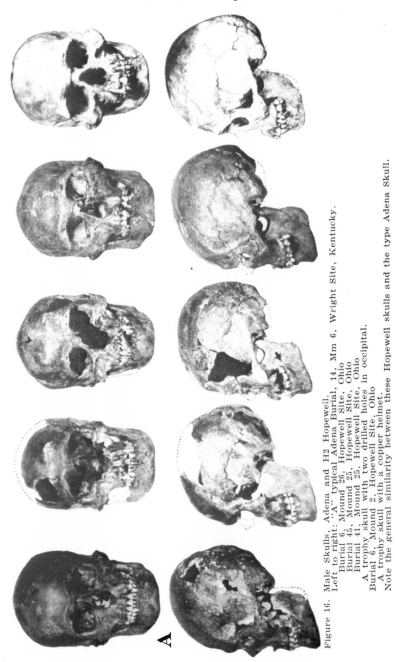

Figure 16. Male Skulls, Adena and H2 Hopewell.
Left to right: "A" typical Adena Burial, 14, Mm 6, Wright Site, Kentucky.
Burial 6, Mound 26, Hopewell Site, Ohio
Burial 45, Mound 25, Hopewell Site, Ohio
Burial 41, Mound 25, Hopewell Site, Ohio
A trophy skull with two drilled holes in occipital.
Burial 6, Mound 2, Hopewell Site, Ohio
A trophy skull with a copper helmet.
Note the general similarity between these Hopewell skulls and the type Adena Skull.

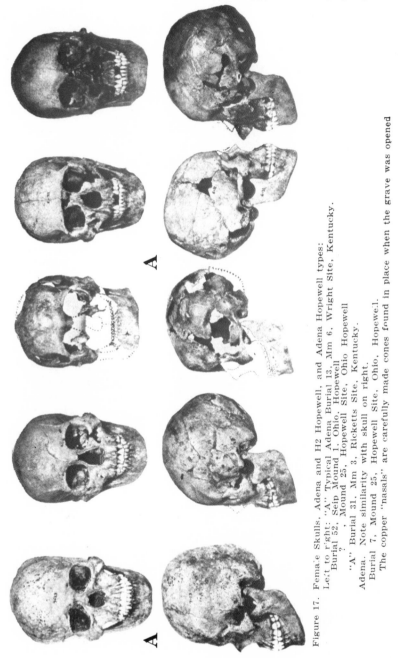

Figure 17. Female Skulls, Adena and H2 Hopewell, and Adena Hopewell types:
Left to right: "A" Typical Adena Burial 13, Mm 6, Wright Site, Kentucky.
Burial 52, Seip Mound 1, Ohio, Hopewell
?, Mound 25, Hopewell Site, Ohio Hopewell
"A" Burial 31, Mm 3, Ricketts Site, Kentucky.
Adena. Note similarity with skull on right.
Burial 7, Mound 25, Hopewell Site, Ohio, Hopewell.
The copper "nasals" are carefully made cones found in place when the grave was opened

From these indications it is evident that the Hopewell skeletons buried in the mounds are of a mixed physical type made up approximately 80% long heads (H_1) and 10-15% broad heads (H_2 Adena-like) leaving a 5–10% unknown, or of mixed or otherwise unidentifiable nature.

If Adena grew into Hopewell and the members of these two different peoples contacted, would not the apparent mingling of the two be expected? The probability of such an Adena-Hopewell admixture is strongly indicated by the archaeological data.

If the series thus presented are representative ones, a comparison of the predominate types found in Adena and Hopewell burial mounds should indicate some significant facts.

Accordingly the proportions of the predominant (92%) deformed Adena male and female series (Table III) have been tabulated and arranged in the following table in contrast to the main' undeformed long headed Hopewell series (H_1 undeformed). The figures within parentheses are the number of cases involved for each index considered.

Although in all but four instances these male and female series fall within the same technical category due to the arbitrary limits of the categories, unit differences between Adena and Hopewell proportions have been included. These unit differences are of such magnitude that they appear to be fundamental. It should be here noted, of course, that these vault proportions are affected by deformation in the case of the Adena series. However, if the total Adena (deformed and undeformed) and total Hopewell series (undeformed and deformed) are compared the same kind but smaller differences become apparent. Therefore, it seems that these series of skulls indicate that:

(1) Adena skeletons are of a broad headed stock which by cradleboard practices, deformed the heads of their infants, thus amplifying those vault diameters which characterize their skulls. The group appears relatively pure, and may be the first round headed group to enter the Ohio Valley from the South suggested by Neumann.*

(2) The Hopewell skeletons are of a long headed stock probably related to the dolichocephals (sylvid) of the eastern woodland

---

* Neumann, Georg K., 1941. pp. 481 and 488.

COMPARISON OF ADENA AND HOPEWELL SKULL PROPORTIONS

Proportion or Index	MALES — Adena Def.	MALES — Hopewell Undef.	FEMALES — Adena Def.	FEMALES — Hopewell Undef.
Length-breath	Ultrabrachycranic (25)	Dolichocranic (30)	Ultrabrachycranic (18)	Subdolichocranic (23)
Unit difference		—18.3		—16.3
Length-height	Hypsicranic (15)	Same	Same (12)	Same (8)
Unit difference		—15.7 (11)		—16.3
Length ear height	Hypsicranic (19)	Same (10)	Same (9)	Same (10)
Unit difference		—13.4		—12.8
Breadth-height	Acrocranic (14)	Same (11)	Same (12)	Same (8)
Unit difference		+3.0		—1.3
Mean Height	(14)	(10)	(12)	(8)
Unit difference		—8.0		—8.9
Frontal Bone (Max. Fr./Fron.-chord)	(18)	(13)	(10)	(18)
Unit difference		—9.1		—5.5
Fronto-parietal	Stenometopic (25)	Metriometopic (24)	Stenometopic (16)	Metriometopic (19)
Unit difference		+5.3		+5.3
Cranio-facial	(19)	(15)	(9)	(11)
Unit difference		+5.4		+1.9
Total Facial	Mesoprosopic (20)	Leptoprosopic (11)	Mesoprosopic (6)	Leptoprosopic (10)
Unit difference		+4.8		+3.0
Upper Facial	Mesene (20)	Leptene (12)	Mesene (7)	Leptene (11)
Unit difference		+3.3		+4.6
Orbital	Mesoconch (19)	Same (13)	Same (8)	Same (14)
Unit difference		+1.2		+3.2
Nasal	Mesorrhine (24)	Same (17)	Same (13)	Same 1 (15)
Unit difference		+2.4		+.9
Palatal	Brachyuranic (22)	Same (18)	Same (14)	Same (17)
Unit difference		—6.4		—4.1

region.** The presence of long headed skulls with greatly flattened occipital regions and others of Adena-like character would suggest a mixed group; long heads predominant.

(3) The small Copena series suggests, like Hopewell, that Copena was a mixture of different physical types, mainly broad headed like Adena. Their heads were deformed to extreme degrees of fronto-occipital (possibly pseudo-circular) flattening. A minor type, long headed by nature shows similarities to Ohio Hopewell long heads, including the bifronto-occipital type of deformation.

** Hooton, Earnest A., 1922, p. 132, and Neumann, Georg K., 1941, pp. 481 and 488.

COMPARISON OF ADENA AND HOPEWELL
POSTCRANIAL

The calculated stature estimations based on the average lengths of the separate long bones indicate that the Hopewell people, men and women were a little taller (about an inch) and possibly heavier than the Adena people. Although the numbers of each are small, the Hopewell and Adena series are nearly equally represented by the average statures of all the measurable bones of the same individual as listed below:

CALCULATED STATURE (Manouvier)*
Adena and Hopewell Series

	Males			Females		
	No.	Average in cm.	Inches	No.	Average in cm.	Inches
Adena	20	168.0	66.2	6	158.8	62.5
Hopewell	12	170.2	67.1	9	162.2	63.9

When the average sized Adena bone is compared with those of the Hopewell series, side by side, Table V, it is apparent that on the whole, the Hopewell series is larger in nearly each case. The small numbers involved, and the fact that the series are composed of unpaired bones, are factors which must be weighed and considered carefully. On the basis of these data it appears that the Hopewell people were larger, as a group, than the Adena Indians. It is possible, of course that some actual Adena skeletons (mechanical admixture) are included in the Hopewell graves and/or actual miscegenation of stocks took place, thus some of the Hopewellians may possess expressed Adena genes. The few Copena measurements seem to show that the Copena group was smaller than both the Adena and Hopewell Indians.

---

* Manouvier, L., 1893, p. 169-244.

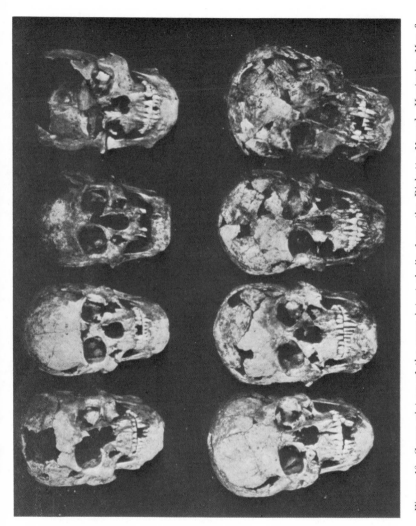

Figure 18. Group picture of the more intact skulls from the Ricketts Mound, Kentucky Mm 3. M=Male, F=Female.
Top left to right: Burials No. 17M, 31F, 12M, 1M.
Bottom: 16F?, 14M, 25M, 21BM.

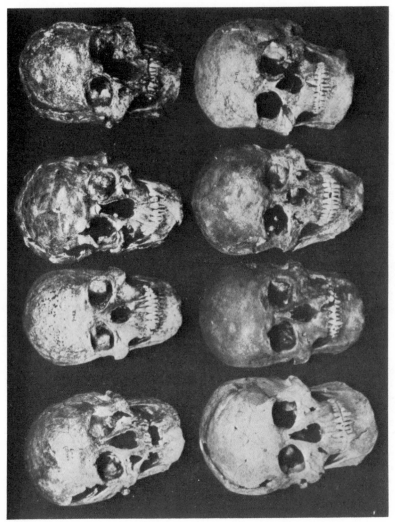

Figure 19. Group picture of the skulls from the Wright Mounds. Kentucky Mm 6 and Mm 7. Top left to right: Burials No. 7M (trophy), 13F, 5F, 10M. Bottom: 16M, 14M, 21M, 11M.

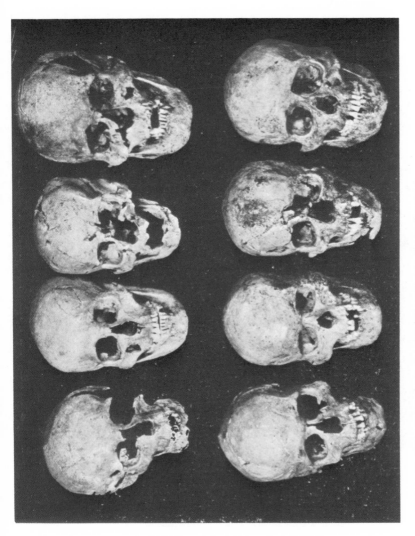

Figure 20. The skulls from the Robbins Mound, Kentucky Be 3.
Top left to right: Burials Nos. 46F, 59F, 48F, 39M.
Bottom: 79M, 36M, 49M, 30M.

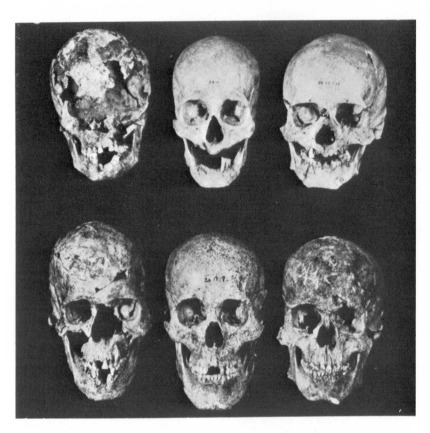

Figure 21. The skulls from the Landing site, Kentucky Be 17.
Top left to right: Burials Nos. 15F, 6M, 14M.
Bottom: 13M, 7M, 5M.

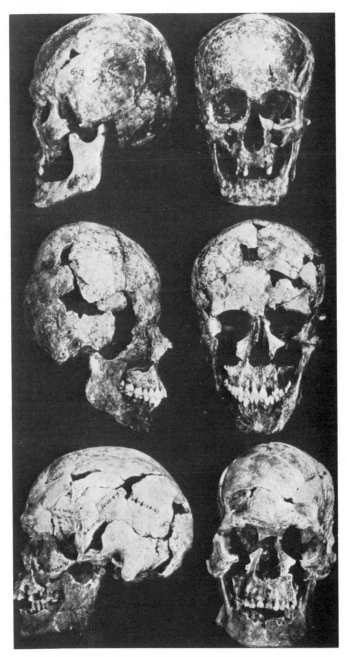

Figure 22. Side and front views, Adena male skulls from the Ricketts Site, Mm 3.

Upper: Burial 12, an old man with typical Adena features. Note healed lesion over left orbit indicated by arrow.

Middle: The skull of a young man, No. 25, with pronounced bifronto-occipital flattening and typical Adena facial profile.

Lower: The skull of a young man, No. 21, the only male Adena longhead (warped).

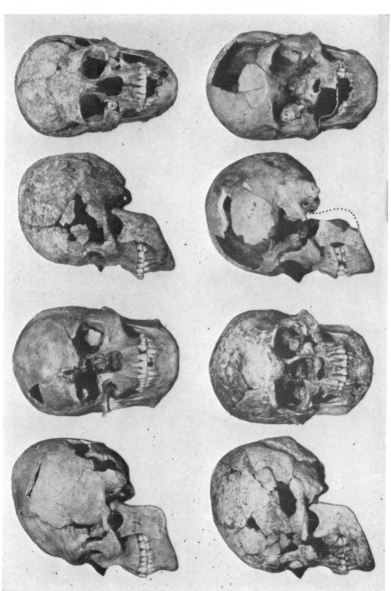

Figure 23. Adult skulls from the Ricketts Site Mm 3.
Upper left: No. 1, Young adult male with pronounced bifronto-occipital deformation.
Upper right: Number 16, a young woman? with medium occipital deformation and a long face.
Lower left: Number 23, a short faced young woman with a medium degree of bifronto-occipital flattening.
Lower right: Number 28, a globular vaulted young woman with a small amount of occipital deforma-

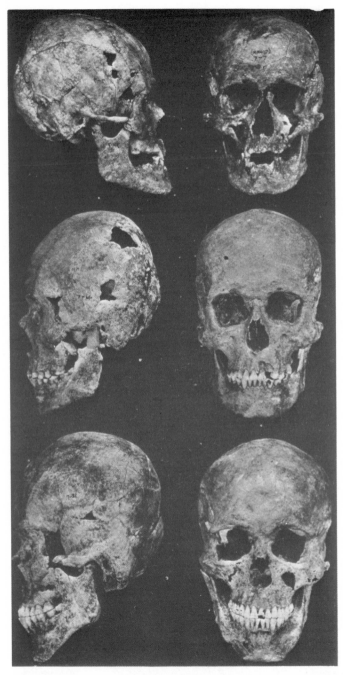

Figure 24. Side and front views of Adena male skulls from the Wright Site, Mm 6.
Upper: Burial 7, A trophy skull. A young man with a prominent chin and typical Adena features.
Middle: Burial 14, a young man with pronounced occipital deformation. Type Adena skull.
Lower: Burial 21, a young adult male with a large face and globular skull vault. Medium bifronto-occipital deformation.

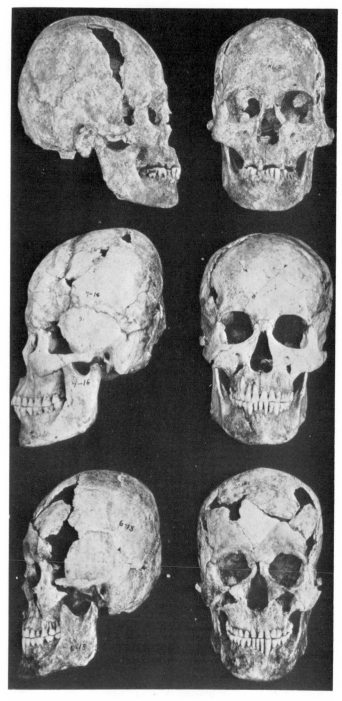

Figure 25. Adena Male Skulls.
Upper: Burial 10, age 37 years from the Wright Site, Mm 6, with slight deformation and prominent lateral flare of the cheek bones. The teeth have been worn down to the gum line. A detached skull.
Center: Burial 16, age 26 years with pronounced bifronto-occipital flattening and a large face, Wright Site, Mm 6.
Lower: Burial 13, age 26 years, from the Ricketts Site, Mm 3, with pronounced bifronto-occipital flattening. Note the edge to edge bite, the pronounced wear of the teeth and the very prominent chin.

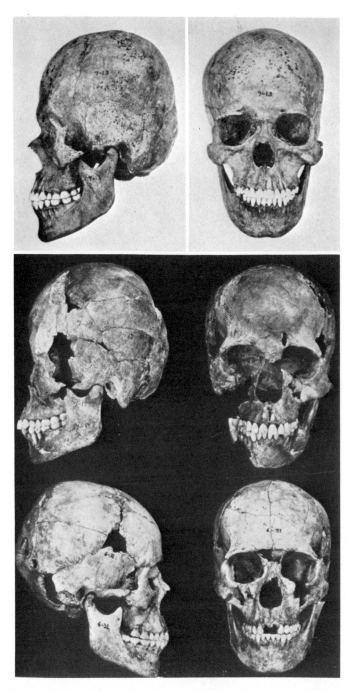

Figure 26. Side and front views of Female Adena skulls from the Wright and
Ricketts Sites.
Upper: Burial 13, Wright Site, Mm 6. a young woman with pronounced skull deformation. This is the best preserved female
specimen found in Kentucky. Type skull.
Middle: Burial 17, Wright Site, Mm 6, a young woman with pronounced skull flattening. Note the bulging forehead, protruding
jaws, and the flat face.
Lower: Burial 31, Ricketts Site, Mm 3. a young adult female with
a small amount of skull deformation.

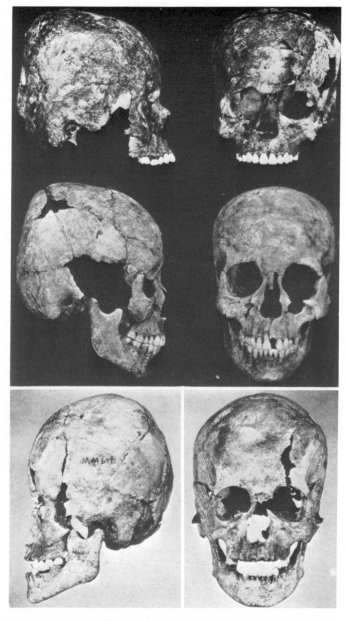

Figure 27. Skulls of Adena adolescents.
    Upper: Burial 20, Wright Site, a boy of 15 years with pronounced
    occipital flattening and other typical morphology.
    Center: Burial 30, Ricketts Site, a girl of 14 years also with pro-
    nounced bifronto-occipital deformation. Note the sharp curve at
    the top of the backhead.
    Lower: Burial 1, Mm 6, Wright Site, a girl of 15 years with typical
    Adena features including bifronto-occipital deformation.

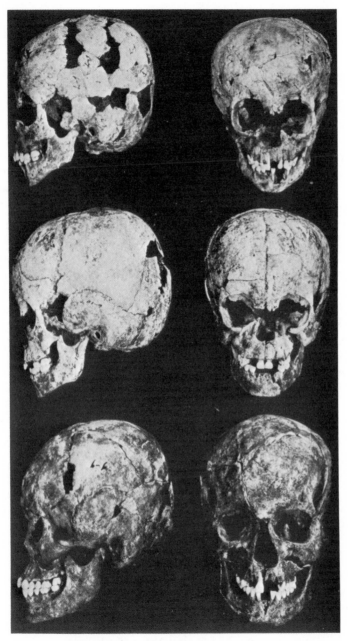

Figure 28. Adena children from the Ricketts Site.
    Upper: Burial 7, a girl? of 3 years with a medium amount of occipital flattening.
    Middle: Burial 10, a boy? of 4 years also with a medium amount of occipital deformation. Note the metopic suture which divides the forehead.
    Lower: Burial 6, a girl of 16 years with pronounced bifronto-occipital deformation.

CONCLUSIONS

In the preceding discussion, an attempt has been made to integrate a considerable body of information obtained by field and laboratory work and to present the basic data concerning the Adena People. In this summation, one is impressed by the close similarity of the total Adena cultural complex with that of Ohio Hopewell. Any conclusions, therefore, relative to the Adena People must necessarily include a consideration of their cultural relation to Ohio Hopewell in both time and space.

Further, for the first time there has been made available physical anthropological data from a considerable series of Adena skeletons. This permits a comparison of the man himself, Adena Man, with his cultural analogue and near contemporary, Ohio Hopewell Man.

Since in drawing conclusions it is always important to distinguish between fact and opinion, between objective data and subjective explanation, the discussion on conclusions will be presented under the following three sub-heads:

Important Basic Data

Interpretation of Data

Speculations

Under *Important Basic Data*, there is summarized factual information which seems, to these authors, valid beyond the point of question. Any solution of the Adena problem must include an explanation of these facts. Under *Interpretation of Basic Data*, the authors offer their analysis of the problem and an explanation of the observed relationships. While these authors believe their deductions from this summation of data to be sound, it is conceivable that another and different interpretation might possibly be found which would synthesize all available data. However, until such other interpretation is offered, they prefer to believe their explanation of these facts to be correct and to represent historic validity. Under *Speculations* are mentioned many possible relationships and suggested explanations which today seem to have a high degree of probability, but for which there can, at present, be offered no absolute demonstration.

TABLE VII.—INDIVIDUAL MEASUREMENTS AND INDICES OF SKULLS FROM THE RICKETTS AND WRIGHT SITES, KENTUCKY

Measurements in Millimeters / SKULL NUMBER	Glabello-Occipital Length	Maximum Breadth	Basion-Bregma Height	Mean Thickness Left Parietal	Minimum Frontal Diameter	Auricular Height	Calculated Capacity in cc.	Horizontal Circumference	Nasion—Opisthion Arc	
	a	b	c	d	e	♂				
Males										
1	[163]	[148]	[148]	5.9	89	[127]	[1452.2]	[(480)]	[350]	[3.
2	[(168)]	[(150)]	....	4.8	101	....	....	[(520)]	[361]	[(3:
12	[165]	[145]	[(148)]	6.7	87	[125]	[1427.7]	[483]	[349]	[3:
13	[(165)]	[(151)]	....	5.8	98	[(130)]	[(1519.6)]	[(490)]	....	[(3-
14	[157]	[152]	[(157)]	5.0	96	[133]	[1495.5]	[488]	[363]	[3-
15	[(180)]	[140]	....	5.3	93	....	....	[(527)]	[(376)]	[(3:
17	‡[(172)]	[(139)]	[(152)]	5.5	85	[(121)]	[(1391.5)]	[(502)]	[(352)]	[(3:
18	‡[170]	[137]	....	5.0	83	....	....	[488]	....	[2(
19	‡[(163)]	....	....	3.5	....					
20	[169]	[160]	[160]	6.7	95	[134]	[1661.8]	[(508)]	[371]	[(3:
21	[(197)]	[(136)]	[(154)]	6.7	(96)	....	....	[(535)]	[(388)]	[(3:
22	[166]	[154]	....	6.0	92	[(125)]	[(1503.5)]	[(500)]	[(370)]	[3:
25	[155]	[(155)]	[(153)]	6.0	101	[(134)]	[(1512.3)]	[491]	[355]	[3!
26B	....			5.0	....					
26C	....			4.0	....					
33	[(170)]	[(148)]	....	4.0						
36	[(170)]	[(145)]	....		(98)				[(365)]	[(3:
37	[(166)]	[(145)]	....	4.0						
38	....	[(168)]	....	5.5						[(3!
Number	13	13	6	18	13	7	7	10	9	
Average	[(165.6)]	[(149.5)]	[(153.0)]	5.3	(93.3)	[(129.1)]	[(1494.4)]	[(496.8)]	[(360.2)]	[(3:
Range	155–172	137–168	148–160	3.5–6.7	83–101	121–134	1391.5–1661.8	480–527	349–376	2(–3!
Females										
3	‡[(159)]	[142]	[(143)]	5.0	....	[(119)]	[(1303.9)]	[(469)]	[356]	[31
5	‡[(161)]	[(140)]	[(132)]	4.0	89	....	....	[(473)]	[(328)]	[3)
16	[160]	[150]	[155)]	5.1	92	[132]	[1484.4]	[490]	[366]	[34
23	[165]	[146]	[(139)]	6.3	86	[(118)]	[(1362.4)]	[489]	[350]	[31
26A	....			4.5						
28	[151]	[139]	[(137)]	7.0	89	....	....	[(458)]	[(340)]	[31
31	[(159)]	[138]	[138]	5.0	83	[(122)]	[(1300.2)]	[474]	[342]	[31
34	[(157)]	[141]	....	7.3	88	[(127)]	[(1350.7)]	[(476)]	....	[(3:
39	[(166)]	[(141)]	....	6.0	(90)	....	....	[(480)]	[(359)]	[(31
Number	8	8	6	9	7	5	5	8	7	
Average	159.8	142.1	140.7	5.6	88.1	123.6	1360.3	476.1	348.7	32
Range	151–166	138–146	132–155	4.0–7.3	83–92	118–132	1300.2–1484.4	458–490	328–366	31–34
Skull Number										
Males										
3	....			....	89					
7 Trophy	[169]	[(152)]	[(143)]	5.5	93	[(125)]	[(1509.2)]	[502]	[367]	[33
10	[172]	[(137)]	[(160)]	6.0	94	[129]	[(1445.9)]	[(486)]	[(355)]	[32
11	[(154)]	[(158)]	....	6.0	94	[(134)]	[(1526.5)]	[(502)]	[(373)]	[(35
14	[167]	[149]	[(152)]	7.0	96	[134]	[1510.5]	[488]	[(352)]	[34
15	[(191)]	....	....	(5.5)	....					
16	[162]	[163]	[(149)]	6.0	92	[131]	[1601.1]	[505]	[377]	[(34
18	....	[(155)]	....	(8.5)	90					
21	[160[	]156]	(165)	7.0	100	137	[1586.4]	[(500)]	[(374)]	[36
Number	6	6	5	7	7	5	5	5	6	
Average	[(169.2)]	[(152.0)]	[(153.8)]	6.1	93.5	[(131.2)]	[(1530.6)]	[(496.2)]	[(366.3)]	[(34
Range	160–191	137–163	143–165	5.5–7.0	89–100	125–137	1445.9–1601.1	486–505	352–377	32–36(
Females										
5	[159]	[(152)]	....	6.7	92	[(135)]	[(1519.9)]	[(483)]	[358]	[(35(
6	[(166)]	[(143)]	[(147)]	4.0	....	....	....	[(495)]	[(353)]	....
8	[(155)]	[(140)]	....	5.0	84	....	....	....	[(360)]	....
12	....			....	90					
13	[156]	[142]	[153]	6.0	86	[128]	[1359.7]	[470]	[359]	[33:
17	[147]	[146]	....	6.3	88	[125]	[1302.4]	[471]	[(341)]	[32
Number	5	5	2	5	5	3	3	4	5	
Average	[(156.6)]	[(144.6)]	[(150.0)]	5.6	88.0	[(129.3)]	[(1394.0)]	[(479.8)]	[(354.2)]	[(33(
Range	147–166	140–152	147–153	4–6.7	84–92	125–135	1302.4–1519.9	470–495	341–360	35(

Parentheses () enclose approximate measurements and indices.
Brackets [] enclose measurements and indices regarded as affected by deformation.
Superscript figures indicate increment included for tooth wear.
* Measurements and indices not included in averages, because of warping, pathology, etc.
‡ Skulls with little noticeable deformation.

	Sagittal Arc	Frontal Chord	Dacryal Chord	Total Facial Angle	Mid-Facial Angle	Alveolar Angle	Bizygomatic Diameter	Mid-Facial Breadth	Nasion-Menton Height	Nasion-Prosthion Height	Basion-Nasion Length
]	[117]	110	......	(83°)	(90°)	(63°)	[(144)]	......	(125³)	(74)	[108]
]	[130]	113									
]	[101]	110	......	(93°)	(97°)	(79°)	[(134)]	98	(120⁴)	(73)	[(108)]
]	[116]	(114)									
]	[118]	120	......	87°	92°	79°	[(143)]	102	129⁴	76	[(103)]
]	[124]	119									
]	[104]	107	......	(91°)	(98°)	(72°)	(138)	97	124⁴	75	[(120)]
]	[110]	108	(22)				(137)				
]	[109]	120	......				[(148)]		(121⁶)	(72)	
]	[123]	116	......	86°	91°	65°	[142]	(97)	125⁴	74	[111]
]	[121]	(118)	......				[(143)]	(100)	(120⁴)	(70)	[(127)]
]	[125]	114	......				[(147)]	100	132⁴	76	
]	[115]	117	......	(81°)	(87°)	(65°)	[(140)]		126²	77	[(106)]
....	....	......									
)]	[(122)]	113	......								
)]	[(140)]	110	19								
	[120]	110									
	[108]										
7]	17	16	2	6	6	6	10	6	9	9	6
	[117.8]	(113.7)	20.5	86.4°	92.3°	70.3°	[(141.6)]	(99.0)	(124.7)	(74.0)	[(109.3)]
	101	107	19	81	87	63	134	97	120²	70	103
	140	120	22	93	98	79	148	102	132⁴	77	120
	[123]	109	......				(124)	96	(113²)	(70)	[(93)]
	[105]	101									[(99)]
)]	[(126)]	(117)	......	(80°)	(88°)	(57°)	[135]	100	126⁴	70	[103]
]	[127]	105	......	(89°)	(97°)	(61°)	[(141)]	(99)	(108⁴)	(66)	[(102)]
	[115]	112	......				[(136)]				[(87)]
	[110]	105	......	86°	91°	69°	[(129)]	98	116⁴	67	[101]
]							[(143)]		(119⁴)	(71)	
	[125]	110	......								
1	7	7	......	3	3	3	6	4	5	5	6
	118.7	108.4	......	85°	92°	62.3°	134.7	98.2	116.4	68.8	97.5
	105	101	......	80°	88°	57°	124	96	108⁴	66	87
	127	117	......	89°	97°	69°	143	100	126⁴	71	103
		112									
)]	[(114)]	114	(24)	(78°)	(85°)	(52°)	(135)	100	(121⁸)	(73)	[(100)]
)]	[123]	113	(22)	82°	86°	64°	(145)	99	126⁶	(74)	[(128)]
)]	[(105)]	120	(23)	(86°)	(90°)	(73°)	(142)	106	126⁴	(69)	
	[119]	113	23	89°	93°	83°	[145]	102	128⁴	77	[(101)]
	[130]	118	24	76°	83°	54°	[(146)]	110	(135²)	(83)	[93]
									131⁴	78	
	[(121)]	124	27	92°	97°	75°	[(147)]	103	131²	75	[(108)]
	6	7	6	5	5	5	6	6	7	7	5
0)]	[(118.7)]	116.3	(23.8)	(83.4°)	(88.8°)	(65.6°)	[(143.3)]	103.3	(128.7⁴)	(75.6)	[(106.0)]
-	105–	112–	22–	76–	83–	52–	135–	99–	121–	69–	93–
	130	124	27	92	97	83	147	110	135	83	128
]	[(106)]	109	......	(76°)	(83°)	(53°)			(124²)	(75)	
	[(104)]	112	......								[(113)]
	[115]	111	......							(73)	
...		104									
	[122]	116	23	82°	91°	62°	130	101	121²	71	[99]
	[109]	106		82°	88°	67°			116²	72	
	5	6	1	3	3	3	1	1	3	4	2
4)]	[(111.2)]	109.7	23	(80°)	(87.3°)	(60.7°)	130	101	(120.3²)	(72.8)	[(106.0)]
	104–	104–		76–	83–	53–			116–	71–	99–
	122	116		82	91	67			124	75	113

Measurements in Millimeters	Basion-Prosthion Length	Nasal Height	Nasal Breadth	Left Orbital Height	Left Orbital Breadth	Right Orbital Height	Right Orbital Breadth	Upper Nasalia Breadth	Lower Nasalia Breadth	Interorbital Breadth
SKULL NUMBER	k	l	m	n	m'	n'	p	q	h	
Males										
1	[100]	(53)	25	33	(45)		(42)			21
2			(23)		(41)	(34)	(42)			22
12	[(91)]	57	23	34	41	35	42			(20)
13				(34)	(42)	34	43	(16)		(26)
14	[(41)]	53	23	34	(40)	35	42	12	19	(23)
15										
17	(107)	51	21	30	42			13		(19)
18								11		(20)
19		54	27	(34)	43					
20	[99]	54	(25)			(33)	42			
21		(50)	26	(35)	(42)	(32)	(41)	(14)	(20)	(23)
22		53	24	35	42	34		13	(19)	
25	[(105)]	53	(23)			(34)	(40)	(12)	(18)	20
26B										
26C										
33			(24)					14		
36								13		20
37										
38										
Number	6	9	11	8	9	8	7	9	4	10
Average	[(98.8)]	(53.1)	(24.1)	(33.5)	(41.9)	(33.9)	(41.7)	(13.1)	(19.0)	(21.3)
Range	91	50	21	30	40	32	40	11	18	18
	107	57	27	35	45	35	43	16	20	26
Females										
3	[(190)]	(47)	22					(11)		(17)
5										
16	[(99)]	50	26	(32)	(41)	33	(41)	15	(18)	(20)
23	[(96)]	50	27	(31)	(39)					
26A										
28	[(83)]									
31	[101]	48	24	(31)	(40)	32	41	12	17	(20)
34		(50)			(37)			(17)		(22)
39										
Number	5	5	4	3	4	2	2	4	2	4
Average	93.8	49	24.8	31.3	39.2	32.5	41	13.8	17.5	19.8
Range	83	47	22	31	37	32	41	11	17	17
	101	50	27	32	41	33	41	17	18	22
Skull Number										
Males										
3										
7 Trophy	[(101)]	53	25	(34)	(38)	33	42	(13)	18	22
10	126	53	24	36	43	37	43	15		21
11		53	(25)	(35)	43	(33)	42	13	(18)	20
14	[(93)]	53	25	34	40	35	40	10	18	23
15		(60)	23	(33)	(42)					
16	[99]	55	25	34	43	34	41	13	(14)	21
18										
21	[(99)]	53	25	33	41	34	42	18	17	25
Number	5	7	7	7	7	6	6	6	5	6
Average	[(103.6)]	(54.3)	(24.6)	(34.1)	(41.4)	(34.3)	41.7	(13.7)	(17.0)	22.0
Range	93–	53–	23–	33–	38–	33–	40–	10–	14–	20–
	126	60	25	36	43	37	43	18	18	25
Females										
5		(53)	(27)	35	(43)	(34)	(43)	(13)	(22)	(22)
6		(51)					(39)			
8		(52)	(28)		42			(11)	(22)	(21)
12										
13	[94]	49	23	33	42	32	42	10	16	18
17		49	27	32	42	(32)	42	14		19
Number	1	5	4	3	4	3	4	4	3	4
Average	[94]	(50.8)	(26.2)	33.3	(42.2)	(32.7)	(41.5)	(12.0)	(20.0)	(20.0)
Range		49–	23–	32–	42–43	32–	39–	10–	16–	18–
		53	28	35		34	43	14	22	22

Parentheses () enclose approximate measurements and indices.
Brackets [] enclose measurements and indices regarded as affected by deformation.
Superscript figures indicate increment included for tooth wear.
* Measurements and indices not included in averages, because of warping, pathology, etc.
‡ Skulls with little noticeable deformation.

External Length of Palate	External Width of Palate	Condylo-Symphyseal Length	Bicondylar Width	Height of Symphysis	Mandibular Height	Bigonial Diameter	Minimum Breadth of Ascending Ramus (Left)	Mean Angle of Mandible	Indices	Cranial	Length Height
t	u	v	w	x	mh	y				b/a	c/a

ICKETTS SITE
Mm 3

55	66	106	131	36	58	117	34	118°		[90.8]	[90.8]
(49)	(70)	(108)	(139)	(38)	(54)	107	37	(121°)		[(89.4)]	....
....	....	(105)	(125)	....	(54)	98	30	(122°)		[88.0]	[(89.8)]
(51)	(70)	(108)	(135)	36	(66)	105	35	....		[(91.5)]	....
....	....	(111)	....	(39)	(57)	114	38	(114°)		[96.9]	[(100.0)]
53	56	(104)	....	(30)	(54)	....	35	(120°)		[(77.8)]	....
....	....	(105)	....	(36)	108	31	(127°)		‡[(80.8)]	[(88.5)]
....	(56)	(113)	(120)	(33)		103	37	....		‡[80.6]	....
54	68	(110)	(124)	34	(61)	....	36	(120°)			
....	(68)	107		(32)	(53)	(105)	35	(120°)		[94.7]	[94.7]
(59)	(69)	(114)		(34)	69	(121)	37	116°		[(69.0)]	[(78.2)]
(55)	68	(104)		(39)		113	39	(127°)		[(92.7)]	....
....	....	....	....	37	(60)	108	37	(118°)		[(100.0)]	[(98.7)]
(52)	(63)	....	....	....	....	....	....	....			
....	....	....	....	....	....	....	....	....		[(87.2)]	
....	....	....	....	....	....	....	....	....		[(85.3)]	
....	....	(108)	....	....	....	114	38	....		[(87.5)]	
8	10	13	6	12	11	12	14	11		12	6
(53.5)	(65.4)	(107.9)	(129.2)	(35.2)	(50.6)	(109.4)	35.6	(120.3°)		[(89.4)]	[(93.8)]
49	56	104	120	30	53	98	30	114		80.6	88.5
59	70	114	139	39	69	121	39	127		100.0	100.0
58	(67)	(105)	....	(33)		94	35	(123°)		‡[(89.3)]	[(90.9)]
				(30)						‡[(87.0)]	[82.0]
(58)	(67)	(112)	(125)	(37)	(48)	103	36	130°		[93.9]	[(97.0)]
51	63	(105)	....	32	(48)	106	35	(125°)		[88.5]	[(84.2)]
....	....	(98)	....	(35)	(55)	(102)	(33) Rt.	(121°)		[92.2]	[(90.8)]
53	(60)	107	(123)	37	53	96	33	125°		[86.9]	[86.9]
....	....	(105)	(120)	36	(60)	(97)	39	(115°)		[(89.9)]	....
....	....	101	115	35	55	(92)	(34)	(120°)		[(85.0)]	....
4	4	7	4	8	5	7	6	7		8	6
55.0	64.2	104.7	120.8	34.4	51.2	98.6	35.3	122.7°		89.1	88.6
51	60	98	115	30	48	92	33	115°		85.0	82.0
58	67	112	125	37	60	106	39	130°		93.9	97.0

RIGHT MOUND
Mm 6

(53)	....	(110)	....	(35)	(58)	107	37	(120°)		[(89.9)]	[(84.6)]
(56)	65	(113)	(125)	40	(61)	(109)	39	(125°)		[(79.7)]	[(91.1)]
(50)	73	(101)	....	(40)	(67)	109	38	(107°)		[(102.6)]	....
(52)	74	(107)	....	37	(63)	(115)	34 Rt.	(113°)		[92.6]	[(94.5)]
(58)	(74)	(111)	....	41	....	....	38 Rt.	....		....	....
(56)	71	110	124	38	67	115	34	120°		[100.6]	[(92.0)]
(47)	(68)	....	....	....	....	....	....	....			
54	67	112	(136)	38	(50)	110	36	126°		[97.5]	[(103.1)]
8	6	7	3	7	6	6	5	6		5	5
(53.2)	(69.7)	(109.1)	(128.3)	(38.4)	(61.0)	(110.8)	36.8	(118.5°)		[(92.1)]	[(93.1)]
47–	65–	101–	124–	35–	50–	107–	34–	107–		79.7–	84.6–
58	74	113	136	41	67	115	39	126		100.6	103.1
54	70	108	124	(37)	57	(96)	33	125°		[(95.6)]	....
....	....	....	....	....	....	....	....	....		[86.2]	[(88.6)]
(51)	....	....	....	....	....	....	....	....		[(90.5)]	....
53	74	108	121	37	54	98	32	129°		[91.0]	[98.1]
57	64	....	....	36	....	....	35	....		[99.4]	....
4	3	2	2	3	2	2	3	2		5	2
(53.8)	69.3	108.0	122.5	(36.7)	55.5	(97.0)	33.3	127°		[(92.5)]	[(93.4)]
51–	64–	108.0	121–	36–	54–	96–	32–	125–		86.2–	88.6–
57	74		124	37	57	98	35	129		99.4	98.1

TABLE VII.—(Continued) INDIVIDUAL MEASUREMENTS AND INDICES OF SKULLS FROM THE RICKETTS AND WRIGHT SITES, KENTUCKY

Measurements in Millimeters / SKULL NUMBER	Breadth Height c/b	Length Auricular Height c/a	Mean Height $\frac{c}{(a+b)/2}$	Cranial Module $\frac{(a+b+c)}{3}$	Fronto-Parietal e/b	Total Facial g/f	Upper Facial h/f
Males							
1	[100.0]	[77.9]	[95.2]	[153.0]	[60.1]	(86.8)	(51.4)
2					[(67.4)]		
12	[(102.0)]	[75.8]	[(95.5)]	[(152.7)]	[60.0]	(89.6)	(54.5)
13		[(78.8)]			[(64.9)]		
14	[(103.2)]	[84.8]	[(101.6)]	[(155.3)]	[63.2]	(90.2)	(53.2)
15					[(66.4)]		
17	[(109.4)]	[(70.4)]	[(97.8)]	[(154.3)]	[61.2)]	(90.0)	(54.3)
18					[60.6]		
19						(81.9)	(48.7)
20	[100.0]	[79.3]	[97.3]	[163.0]	[59.4]	88.0	52.1
21	[(113.2)]		[92.5)]	[(162.3)]	[(70.6)]	(83.9)	(48.9)
22		[(75.3)]			[(59.7)]	(89.8)	(51.7)
25	[(98.7)]	[(86.4)]	[(98.7)]	[(154.3)]	[(65.2)]	(90.0)	(55.0)
26B							
26C							
33							
36					[(67.6)]		
37							
38							
Number	6	7	6	6	10	9	9
Average	[(102.2)]	[(79.0)]	[(97.7)]	[(155.4)]	[(63.0)]	[(87.8)]	[(52.2)]
Range	98.7 109.4	70.4 86.4	95.2 101.6	152.7 163.0	59.4 67.6	81.9 90.2	48.7 55.0
Females							
3	[(100.7)]	[(74.8)]	[(95.1)]	[(148.0)]		(91.2)	(56.5)
5	[(94.4)]		[(87.8)]	[(144.3)]	[(63.6)]		
16	[(103.2)]	[82.5]	[(100.0)]	[(155.0)]	[61.3]	93.4	51.8
23	[(95.2)]	[71.5)]	[(89.4)]	[(150.0)]	[58.9]	(76.6)	46.8
26A							
28	[(98.6)]		[(94.5)]	[(142.3)]	[64.0]		
31	[100.0]	[(76.7)]	[(93.0)]	[(145.0)]	[60.1]	(90.0)	(52.0)
34		[(80.9)]			[62.4]	(83.3)	(49.7)
39					[(63.8)]		
Number	6	5	6	6	7	5	5
Average	98.7	77.3	93.3	147.4	62.0	86.9	51.4
Range	94.4 103.2	71.5 82.5	87.8 100.0	142.3 155.0	58.9 64.0	76.6 93.4	46.8 56.5
Skull Number Males							
3							
7 Trophy	[(94.1)]	[(74.0)]	[(89.2)]	[(154.7)]	[(61.2)]	(89.7)	(54.1)
10	[(116.9)]	[75.0]	[(103.9)]	[(156.3)]	[(68.6)]	(87.0)	(51.0)
11		[(87.0)]			[(59.5)]	(88.9)	(48.6)
14	[(102.0)]	[83.2]	[(98.2)]	[(154.0)]	[64.4]	88.4	53.1
15							
16	[(91.5)]	[80.9]	[(91.7)]	[(158.0)]	[56.4]	(89.8)	(53.4)
18							
21	[(105.8)]	[85.6]	[(104.4)]	[(160.3)]	[(64.1)]	(89.2)	51.0
Number	5	5	5	5	5	6	6
Average	[(102.1)]	[(79.7)]	[(97.5)]	[(156.7)]	[(62.9)]	(88.8)	(51.9)
Range	91.5– 116.9	[74–87]	89.2– 104.4	154.0– 160.3	56.4– 68.6	87.0– 89.8	48.6– 54.1
Females							
5		[(84.9)]			[(60.5)]		
6	[(102.8)]		[(95.2)]	[(152.0)]			
8					[(60.0)]		
12							
13	[107.8]	[82.0]	[102.8]	[150.3]	[60.6]	93.2	54.6
17		[85.1]			[60.3]		
Number	2	3	2	2	4	1	1
Average	[(105.3)]	[(84.0)]	[(99.0)]	[(151.2)]	[(60.4)]	93.2	54.6
Range	102.8– 107.8	[82–85.1]	95.2– 102.8	150.3– 152.0	60.0– 60.6		

Parentheses () enclose approximate measurements and indices.
Brackets [] enclose measurements and indices regarded as affected by deformation.
Superscript figures indicate increment included for tooth wear.
* Measurements and indices not included in averages, because of warping, pathology, etc
‡ Skulls with little noticeable deformation.

	y/f Zygo-Gonial	y/e Fronto-Gonial	e/f Zygo-Frontal	m/n Left Orbital	m'/n' Right Orbital	r/s Interorbital	p/q Nasalia Transverse	l/k Nasal	u/t External Palatal	v/w Mandibular (1)	mh/v Mandibular (2)
.3)]	(80.5)	130.4	(61.8)	(73.3)	......	......	......	(47.2)	120.0	81.0	54.7
......	......	106.2	......	......	(81.0)	......	......	......	......	(77.7)	(50.0)
.5)]	(73.1)	112.5	(64.9)	(83.0)	83.3	(20.8)	......	40.4	......	(84.0)	(51.5)
......	......	107.1	......	(81.0)	(79.1)	(25.2)	......	......	......	......	......
.1)]	(79.7)	118.8	(67.1)	(85.0)	83.4	(23.2)	63.2	43.5	(137.2)	(80.0)	(61.2)
......	......	......	......	......	......	......	......	......	......	......	(51.3)
..4	(78.3)	127.0	(61.6)	71.5	......	(20.2)	......	41.2	105.6	......	(51.9)
..0	75.2	124.2	(60.6)	......	......	......	......	......	......	......	......
......	......	......	......	(79.1)	......	......	......	(50.0)	......	......	(54.0)
..8	(74.0)	(110.5)	66.9	......	78.6	......	......	(46.3)	126.0	(91.7)	(48.2)
..0	(84.6)	(126.0)	(67.2)	(83.4)	(78.2)	(23.0)	(70.0)	(52.0)	......	(87.1)	64.5
..6	(76.9)	122.9	(62.6)	83.4	......	......	(68.4)	45.3	(116.9)	......	......
..4	(77.2)	107.0	(72.2)	......	(85.1)	......	(66.7)	(43.3)	(123.6)	......	(57.8)
......	......	......	......	......	......	......	......	......	(121.1)	......	......
......	......	......	......	......	......	......	......	......	......	......	......
......	......	......	......	......	......	......	......	......	......	......	......
......	......	......	......	......	......	......	......	......	......	......	......
4.6)]	9	11	9	8	7	5	4	9	7	6	10
	[(77.7)]	(117.5)	[(65.0)]	(79.9)	(81.2)	(22.5)	(67.1)	(45.5)	(121.5)	(83.6)	(54.5)
3.8	73.1	106.2	60.6	71.5	78.2	20.2	63.2	40.4	105.6	77.7	48.2
).0	84.6	130.4	72.2	85.0	85.1	25.2	70.0	52.0	137.2	91.7	64.5
7.4)]	(75.8)	......	......	......	......	(19.3)	......	(46.8)	(115.5)	......	......
).0]	76.4	112.0	68.2	(78.1)	(80.5)	(20.2)	(83.4)	52.0	(115.5)	(89.6)	(42.8)
6.6)]	(75.2)	123.2	(61.0)	(79.5)	......	......	......	54.0	123.5	......	(45.7)
8.0)]	(75.0)	(114.6)	(65.5)	......	......	......	......	......	......	......	(56.2)
3.5)]	(74.5)	115.6	64.3	(77.5)	78.1	(20.8)	70.6	50.0	(113.1)	(87.0)	49.5
1.4)]	(67.8)	(110.2)	(61.5)	......	......	......	......	......	......	(87.5)	(57.1)
		(102.1)	......	......	......	......	......	......	......	87.9	54.4
6	6	6	5	3	2	3	2	4	4	4	5
4.5	74.1	113.0	64.1	78.4	79.3	20.1	77.0	50.7	116.9	88.0	52.0
7.4	67.8	102.1	61.0	77.5	78.1	19.3	70.6	46.8	113.1	87.0	42.8
1.4	76.4	123.2	68.2	79.5	80.5	20.8	83.4	54.0	123.5	89.6	57.1
8.9)]	(79.3)	115.0	(68.9)	(89.5)	78.6	22.7	(72.3)	47.2	......	......	(52.7)
5.9)]	(75.2)	(116.0)	(64.8)	83.7	86.1	20.8	......	45.3	......	(90.5)	(59.2)
0.0)]	(76.8)	116.0	(66.2)	(81.4)	(78.6)	20.2	(72.2)	(47.2)	(130.0)	......	(66.3)
7.4	(79.3)	(119.8)	66.2	85.0	87.5	23.2	55.5	47.2	(140.3)	......	(58.8)
......	......	......	......	(78.6)	......	......	......	(38.4)	(127.5)	......	......
9.6)]	(78.8)	125.0	(63.0)	79.1	83.0	21.0	(92.9)	45.4	(126.8)	88.8	60.9
......	......	......	......	......	......	......	......	......	(144.6)	......	......
4.3)]	(74.8)	110.0	68.0	80.5	81.0	24.2	105.9	47.2	124.0	(82.4)	(44.7)
5	6	6	6	7	6	6	5	7	6	3	6
5.2)]	(77.4)	(117.0)	(66.2)	(82.5)	(82.5)	22.0	(79.3)	(45.4)	(132.2)	(87.2)	(57.1)
8.9-	74.8-	110.0-	63.0-	78.6-	78.6-	20.2-	55.5-	38.4-	124-	82.4-	44.7-
5.9	79.3	125.0	68.9	89.5	87.5	24.2	105.9	47.2	144.6	90.5	66.3
......	......	(104.3)	......	(81.4)	(79.2)	(22.0)	(59.2)	(50.9)	129.5	87.2	52.8
......	......	......	......	......	......	......	......	(53.8)	......	......	......
1.6)]	75.4	113.9	66.2	78.6	76.3	18.5	62.5	46.9	139.5	89.3	50.0
......	......	......	......	76.2	76.2	19.2	......	55.1	(112.2)	......	......
1	1	2	1	3	3	2	2	3	3	2	2
1.6]	75.4	(109.1)	66.2	(78.7)	(77.2)	(19.9)	(60.3)	(51.7)	(127.1)	88.2	51.4
......	......	104.3-	......	76.2-	76.2-	18.5-	59.2-	46.9-	112.2-	87.2-	50—52.8
......	......	113.9	......	81.4	79.2	22	62.5	55.1	139.5	89.3	......

Important Basic Data

(1) Adena man was a builder of mounds over the dead, beside Hopewell of Ohio, the only mound builder antedating Middle Mississippi times in the Ohio River Valley, who constructed earthworks other than mounds.

(2) Adena man built earthworks other than mounds of two kinds:

(a) He enclosed large areas of varied form (25 acres or more) with earth embankments.

(b) In the vicinity of such earthworks or attached to them, he constructed embankments about circular areas. These so-called "sacred circles" have diameters of the order of 250 feet and an area of about one acre. They are similar in size and construction to the circles associated with, or attached to, the geometric earthworks of Ohio Hopewell.

(3) Extended burials in the flesh in log tombs were inclusive in, intrusive into, or precedent to earth mounds erected over prepared floors, in general, quite similar to such occurrence in Ohio Hopewell.

(4) Such floors at the base of burial mounds usually show by post-molds in the sub-soil that a house structure once had been erected thereon.

(5) Adena man practiced cremation of the dead, the redeposit of cremated remains and the communal deposit of such remains.

(6) Adena burials show abundant evidence that the individuals accorded log tomb burial in mounds constituted a selected minority of the population, the remainder, the majority probably being cremated. The basis of selection is unknown, but such evidence suggests a complex society wherein those selected for log tomb burial represent an honored group, perhaps members of the ruling or chieftan class. The same process of selection seems observable in Ohio Hopewell.

(7) Log tomb burial and deposit of cremated remains frequently took place on the *floor* of a house. On the house floor a small earth mound was built over the burial; the house was then burned and a larger mound erected over all.

(8)   The burial complex of Adena is strikingly similar to Ohio
       Hopewell, such minor differences as appear being attrib-
       uted to chronology and the resulting difference in material
       wealth.

(9)   Based on the assumption that the more highly specialized
       artifact types indicate later development, it has been shown
       that early Adena is chronologically precedent to Ohio Hope-
       well and culturally ancestral to it.

(10)   The rare occurrence of Hopewell artifacts on some Adena
       sites seems to indicate that such sites were contemporary
       with early Ohio Hopewell.

(11)   The known area of Adena occupancy, so far proven by ex-
       cavation, in the Ohio River drainage is about 300 miles E–W
       and about 200 miles N–S. This area is nearly centered about
       Chillicothe, Ohio, a point of concentration of Ohio Hopewell.
       That is, Ohio Hopewell manifested itself in greatest density
       and highest development in a somewhat restricted region ly-
       ing practically at the center of the known Adena area.

(12)   Adena man built in this region the earliest known wooden
       houses, and by building successive structures on the same
       house site, accumulated small village middens. These village
       sites are often preserved by being covered by mounds.

(13)   Such house sites, while distant from each other several hun-
       dred feet, so that no deep village midden ever accumulated,
       nevertheless were arranged in groups to constitute large
       communities. This arrangement would make possible a con-
       siderable population in a relatively limited area, but would
       leave no midden extensive enough to persist to the present
       time unless it was covered by a mound or otherwise pro-
       tected.

(14)   Adena man presents the earliest known evidence of the use
       of corn, sunflower seed and squash as food in this area.

(15)   The earliest known *townhouse?*, ceremonial lodge?, or coun-
       cil house?, which shows internal evidence of having been
       used by an organized group, has been found in Adena.

(16)   Adena man presents the earliest evidence of the smoking
       custom in the region.

(17) Adena man probably made the first pottery in the Ohio Valley, and with the possible exception of Ohio Hopewell man, was the only pottery maker in this area who did not make a practice of placing pottery with the dead.

(18) The cultural development of Adena man had reached a stage where his artistic motifs were beginning to show by symbolism the existence of a social, religious, and ceremonial complex of traits. He had the hand-eye design and the "feathered serpent." The Great Serpent Mound of Ohio is believed to be of Adena origin. He had the head, beak and talons of the raptorial bird, quite similar in form and artistic motif to the copper eagles of Ohio Hopewell, as well as the human mask or death symbol engraved on stone tablets.

(19) Adena man wove and used textiles employing many techniques, and various vegetal fibers.

(20) Adena man worked and used copper very rarely, mostly for personal adornment.

(21) Adena man appears as the first brachycephal in Kentucky, burying the selected dead in the apparent sex ratio of two males to one female. The calculated body size is medium; the torso, heavy.

(22) Adena man is basically of broad headed ancestry. Of the total group, 92% are deformed usually to a pronounced degree at the back of the head (occipital). Possibly, this flattening was the unintentional, practical result of cradleboard binding—a technique of infant care.

(23) One-third of the Adena skulls show evidence of bifrontal flattening accompanying that of the occipital—again possibly due to cradleboard practices of infant care.

Interpretation of Data—Explanation

In attempting to understand the significance of the foregoing data, which the authors regard as valid, the following interpretation seems to them to constitute a satisfactory explanation of all known facts.

Adena man, long before Middle Mississippi times, occupied a portion of the Ohio River drainage, in Southeastern Indiana, Central and Eastern Kentucky, and Southern Ohio. In this area, this broad headed people with head deformation, sufficiently developed agricultural husbandry, to permit their sedentary occupation of large tracts of land. The rock shelters* of Eastern Kentucky have yielded, in association with Adena artifacts, evidences of corn, squash, pumpkins, gourds, tobacco, sunflower and other edible seeds. The extent of development of their agricultural economy is at present unknown, but it was certainly sufficient to encourage the formation of large centers of population and to guarantee them a continuity of occupancy. Only by these means could the trait of mound building with its important aspect of earthwork construction have been developed and used so extensively. Except for these minor rock shelter evidences of Adena man's occupancy, and a few small areas known to show sparcely scattered stone artifacts and Adena potsherds, there remain today only earth mounds, often in groups, frequently in the vicinity of earthworks and so called "sacred circles." Such clustered evidence of Adena man's mound building activity seems to demonstrate a considerable concentration of population in a relatively limited area, yet there remains today no extensive or deep village middens such as are commonly observed on the sites of the shell mound dwellers of earlier times, or such as are easily found on sites of the later Fort Ancient peoples. Only very recently has it been recognized that many Adena mounds were erected on their small undisturbed village middens. Only thus by being covered by a mound, have such village middens been preserved. The absence of large village middens and at the same time the presence of massive earthworks arguing a considerable population density, together present something of a paradox; however, it may be easily explained on the supposition that each family or unit of society had its habitation site located several hundred feet from its nearest neighbor, so far from it that no deep midden could ever accumulate, yet close enough to permit a considerable population to occupy an area of a few hundred acres. By this means a closely knit community could be established with sufficient man-power and unity of purpose successfully to undertake the large tasks accomplished by these mound builders.

When one views the extensive earthworks on some Adena sites,

---

* Webb, W. S., and Funkhouser, W. D., 1936, p. 147, and Funkhouser, W. D., and Webb, W. S., 1930, pp. 246, 267, 291.

where embankments may be a mile or more long, and where earth
mounds may be of the order of 200 feet in maximum diameter at
the base and up to at least thirty-one feet in height, one is necessarily impressed with the large amount of earth, dug, transported,
and elevated into place. This means a large expenditure of human labor. When one remembers that Adena man, the earliest
of the earth-work builders in this region, had no metal tools, not
even copper, as utility implements, the prodigious engineering
construction under the circumstances is even more astounding.
Granted a sufficient population to perform such an amount of
labor and a community so well organized and disciplined as to
guarantee the completion of such a task, which evidently was carefully planned before being initiated, one naturally seeks the master motive which must lie back of such obvious planning and laborious execution. Perhaps it was a natural reaction which led some
of the early writers when describing some of these Adena earthworks to refer to them as forts and fortifications. Even these very
numerous so-called "sacred circles" so similar in form and size
were described by implication as forts, the depression being referred to as a "moat," thus implying it may have once held water.

While it is impossible today to know for certain the purpose
of such construction, these authors have reached the conclusion
that all things considered, there is no evidence that any of this
construction served any military purpose of either offense or defense. There has been found no evidence that Adena man individ-
ually or collectively engaged in violence. This is in striking contrast to the peoples who preceded him and also to those who followed him. In Shell-Mound graves, skeletons are frequently found
with flint or antler projectile points imbedded in the bones, offering positive evidence of violent death. Frequently, such skeletons
are found buried in groups in the same grave, indicating mass violence. No suggestion of such evidence has been found in any
Adena skeleton material. In later Middle Mississippi times, whenever the occupation of a village site became permanent, a stockade
was constructed enclosing the village. Such stockades show evidence that they were sometimes destroyed by fire and were rebuilt.
Always they had gateways, screened from the outside by secondary
palisades. Often the gateways were protected by "towers" built

astride the stockade. Bastions were built on the outward face of the stockade at regular intervals. Such constructions about villages in Middle Mississippi times were clearly a form of military engineering for the purpose of community defense. Their rebuilding after destruction by fire is further evidence of their necessity. In Adena there is an entire absence of such evidence. If one may draw any valid conclusions from such negative evidence, it would seem to indicate that when Adena man occupied this portion of the Ohio River Valley he had no enemies, or at least left no proof of them. Perhaps for most of his period of occupancy in this region, his was the *only* people sufficiently numerous and adequately organized to have waged war on a large scale.

Thus, if we may conclude that he had mastered his environment by controlling his food supply through rudimentary agriculture and that he was not forced to waste his substance or his time in military adventure, it is easy to understand how he could have devoted his energies to the construction of earthworks, and other cultural objectives. While the purpose of such earthwork construction cannot be fully demonstrated, there are evidences pointing toward the existence of a basic, fundamental congeries of social, religious, or ceremonial concepts which powerfully motivated Adena man, and which seems to be widespread among Adena communities throughout the whole area of their occupancy. The larger earthworks are fundamentally quite similar on all sites where they are found. Particularly is this true of the ''sacred circles,'' which are generally similar in size and construction. Since we know they were usually constructed in pairs and that they were the seat of circular wooden structures or stockades, the inference is plain that their purpose was identical. They are so numerous that one may infer that every large Adena community had at least two, and often more. The point is that such construction would seem to indicate an identical need in every Adena community which was met in practically an identical way. The fact that widely separated communities in Indiana, Kentucky, and Ohio engaged in such nearly identical construction would argue that all communities had the same ideal plans, that such plans were deeply significant, and the ideas represented, firmly rooted in their community life.

Thus, in the major trait of earthwork construction, as well as minor trait of house construction and the varied and important burial traits manifested in Adena, Adena man shows that much of his activity in life, as well as the disposition of his body at death was controlled by custom or regulation. This suggests that his was a complex and rather highly organized society compelling the assent of the individual to its dictates. It is possible that much of his earthwork construction had at bottom a religious ceremonial significance, which dominated the social organization. In some such way the community acted as a unit in its earthwork, mound-building activities. It was in this way that all communities constructed earthworks of much the same pattern.

The point of origin of Adena man with his mound-building traits cannot yet be demonstrated, but it is certain that he was the *first builder of earthworks* in this region, and thus could not have derived these traits from any earlier occupants of the region. As a broad headed individual, with head deformation, one would suspect a southern origin, and his mound-building traits would point to the Middle American Area as a possible source.

As has been pointed out in the body of this report, the major problem of Adena aside from its description, presented herein, is its relation to Ohio Hopewell. It now appears that the mound-building, earthwork traits, and burial customs of these two great prehistoric manifestations, are fundamentally identical and since they arose in the same area and are so very different from all other cultural manifestations in that area, one finds it impossible to believe in a separate origin for them. Their fundamental identity has long been obscured by several factors. Among these are: (a) the vastly greater material wealth of Ohio Hopewell; (b) the somewhat higher cultural development of Ohio Hopewell due to its later chronological position; and (c) to the fact that the Adena complex of traits has been only very imperfectly known up to the present time.

The problem of origins would be greatly simplified if it could be shown that Hopewell man himself had the same physical characteristics as Adena man. It would then be easy to understand Ohio Hopewell as a simple chronological development of Adena. Suspecting that this cultural development of Adena into Ohio Hopewell would be indicated by similar physical characteristics, it was something of a surprise to observe in the early stages of this investigation that early Ohio Hopewell man was basically an undeformed long headed individual. A careful study of all available documented Hopewell crania shows that while most of them were basically long headed, *a considerable portion of them were deformed by apparently the same method as that used by Adena.* This has been described in the chapter on the physical anthropology of Adena. Further there are some crania in Ohio Hopewell which are very similar to Adena crania. It appears that Ohio Hopewell might be described as basically a long headed people who took over the Adena technique of infant care which led to a similar type of head deformation, and who may have also adopted a certain number of Adena individuals into its community. If, therefore, Ohio Hopewell shows evidence, as it seems to do, of a mixture of broad and long headed peoples, as well as unmistakable evidence of having adopted the Adena form of head deformation, it is easy to understand the apparent identity of their burial customs, and the high development of mound building and earthwork construction in Ohio Hopewell, the basic and earlier forms of which are found in Adena.

The solution of the problem of the origin of Hopewell was not seriously considered by the early excavators of Hopewell sites in Ohio, partly because the physical anthropological evidence was considered of no great importance and because of a lack of knowledge of the prehistory of adjoining regions. The problem has been attacked only in comparatively recent times, particularly within the last decade.

The few physical anthropologists who have studied Hopewellian skeletal remains have all associated the people with the dolichocephals of the eastern Woodlands area. (Hooton[*], Neumann[**], Stewart[***]).

After the McKern classification had been presented, Deuel[****] some ten years ago proposed a classification of the known manifestations in the Mississippi Valley by describing two basic cultures; these he called "Mississippi" and "Woodland". During the past decade refinements in classification methodology have led

---

[*] Hooton, Earnest A., 1922, p. 132.
[**] Neumann, Georg K., 1941, p. 488.
[***] Stewart T. D., 1943, p. 252.
[****] Deuel, Thorne, 1935, pp. 429-430.

to a definition of the "Woodland Pattern" which is made to
include the manifestation of a population spread over a large portion of the area in the North Central United States, some groups
of which seemingly were widely separated in time. Because of this
separation in time and space, opportunity existed for a great
diversity of traits so that the presence or absence of any trait at a
particular site is not an insurmountable barrier to the inclusion
of the site within the pattern. Interest here attaches not so
much to a definition of the Woodland Pattern, but to its use in
connection with Hopewell and Adena. Deuel[*] recognized certain "apparent exceptions" (Adena and Hopewell) to the Woodland Basic Culture and thus explained his classification:

> "For this discussion, I shall term the one more generally
> familiar in the Southeastern United States as the Mississippi
> Basic Culture; that better known in the upper valley as the
> Woodland Basic Culture. This paper is an attempt to outline
> our knowledge of these basic cultures in the light of a four
> year survey of the region for the University of Chicago. It
> is to be remembered that the classification is in no sense de-
> pendent upon genetic relationship or spatial distribution;
> the units are classified as suggested by McKern on "trait
> complexes" alone.
>
> "For convenience in handling certain apparent excep-
> tions, it may be well to indicate a further subdivision of the
> basic cultures into phases. The details by which the smaller
> units are determined are omitted here for lack of space. The
> Woodland may be separated provisionally into (1) the Red
> Ochre phase (including the Adena of Ohio and West Virginia
> as well as the more widely spread and simpler components of
> Wisconsin, Illinois, Indiana, Michigan, and New York); (2)
> the Central Basin phase (comprising the richly developed
> Hopewell of Ohio and the so-called Hopewell variants of Iowa,
> Wisconsin, Michigan, Indiana, and Illinois; and (3) the
> Tampico (less spectacular and less well-known than the two
> preceding)."

Two years later when Cole and Deuel[**] came to describe the
prehistory of Fulton County, Illinois, they presented a sequence
of manifestations, which by placing the most recent first, was as
follows:

(1) Middle Mississippi   (3) Central Basin   (5) Black Sand
(2) Hopewellian   (4) Red Ochre

---

[*] Deuel, Thorne, op. cit.
[**] Cole, Fay-Cooper, and Deuel, Thorne, 1937, pp. 16-20.

Relative to Illinois Hopewell in this sequence they say:

"Judging primarily by the pottery types and projectile points, there seems to be a cultural continuity running from Black Sand through the Central Basin to the Hopewellian. This leads us, for the present, to class the latter as a specialized phase of the Woodland pattern. The change in physical type between the Black Sand and later peoples is more apparent than real, for occasional individuals recalling the early longheaded population appear even in the late Mississippi burials." (P. 16.)

"The types of cultural manifestations in Fulton County suggest that the earlier groups had their cultural connections with the people of the north and northeast. Latter influences, from the south and southeast, either profoundly affected the generalized Woodland and led to the specialization known as Hopewellian or indicate the appearance of a new cultural phase conforming in many ways to the Wodland pattern. Still later we have the appearance of people with the Middle Mississippi culture." (P. 20.)

In recent years, the term Basic Woodland has come to be applied to manifestations occurring in an enlarged area embracing most of the Southeast, by archaeologists whose early training and experience has been largely in the North-Central States. The term seemingly is used to include most, if not all manifestations not assignable to Middle Mississippi. The extension of this idea is illustrated by Jennings* when in discussing early cultural manifestations in Northeastern Mississippi he says:

"In the Miller horizon, delineated from those sites deliberately dug in an attempt to find a proto-Chickasaw horizon, many significant facts and implications have appeared. We find ourselves injected forcibly into the theatre of speculation where the problems of Hopewellian-Copena-Adena-Marksville relationships, both chronological and developmental, are being threshed out. This matter of the Hopewellian pattern and its many variants is one of considerable importance. (Page 214.)

*   *   *   *   *

"It might be well to point out that the generalized Copena traits, repeatedly mentioned in this report, are probably no more than the generalized Woodland basic pattern traits which spread over the Southeast at an early period. Griffin (1939, p. 162ff) points out that all the cultures of the South-

---

* Jennings, Jesse D., 1941, pp. 214, 218.

east, prior to the Middle Mississippi levels, reflect these same basically Woodland characteristics.

"Basic Woodland is, of course, used advisedly in the face of wide professional disagreement as to what traits comprise the basic Woodland pattern. Whatever traits are ultimately accepted as defining this elusive stratum, there is little doubt that the artifacts from early levels in the Southeast resemble eastern Woodland more than they do the Middle Mississippi horizons." (P. 218.)

By 1941 it was plain to everyone that the term "Woodland" as then in use needed clarification. Thus in May of that year at the University of Chicago, there was called the First Woodland Conference. The delegates represented the New England and the North-Central states as far west as Minnesota and Nebraska. In the report of this conference* its purpose was explained as follows:

"The term 'Woodland', is employed in the American archaeological field, has come to be used by local students to serve a variety of dissimilar cultural purposes, and to lack clear definition to general students and instructors. To the regional specialist 'Woodland' may be interpreted in terms of his own local manifestations; to the ceramic analyst, in terms of a variety of pottery; and to the ethno-historian, in terms of tribes or migratory bands. There is little wonder that the uninitiated general student, in utter bewilderment, has demanded a definition for 'Woodland', or has refused to recognize it as a useful, valid term." (P. 393.)

As a result of this conference a tentative trait complex known as "The Woodland Pattern Complex" was set up, which contained 81 traits of which 25 traits were pottery traits.

The difficulty of defining the Woodland Pattern, as recognized by Jennings; into which Deuel had cast both Adena and Hopewell is explained by Griffin** as follows:

"Part of the difficulty of establishing satisfactorily comprehensive terms for such broad divisions as the Woodland Pattern is that this division, as it is now conceived, covered a very wide geographical area and persisted throughout a considerable period of time with continual modification of the specific traits. There are distinct indications that there is a genetic continuity, both in some of the cultural elements and

---

* The First Archaeological Conference on the Woodland Pattern, 1941, pp. 393-400.
** Griffin, James B., 1943, p. 239.

in the physical type, from a widespread and already somewhat diversified preceramic level into the various Woodland divisions in the United States.'' (P. 339.)

It is to be noted that this statement was made some years after, and with full knowledge of, the conference definition of Woodland Pattern.

With this definition in mind, in his chapter on ''Speculations'', Griffin proceeds to classify Adena as a subdivision of the Woodland pattern and to discuss Adena-Hopewell relationships as follows:

> ''The Adena culture not only has these connections with this early pottery and agricultural level in the Ohio Valley, but is related to the recently defined Copena Aspect in northern Alabama. It is highly probable that the Adena Aspect, or whatever cultural division it may eventually turn out to be, is a forerunner of the Hopewell culture as it is found in the Ohio area. Adena does not extend much farther west than eastern Indiana and has its strongest concentration in south central Ohio and the contiguous parts of Kentucky and West Virginia. It would appear to represent a more highly institutionalized burial complex of the first semisedentary agricultural populations of the area. (P. 306.)

*　　*　　*　　*　　*　　*

> It has been well known to Midwestern archaeologists that the developed Hopewellian culture groups in the west have as many burial traits in common with Adena as they do with Hopewell. The Adena-Hopewell considered as an archaeological unit equivalent to a phase has a basic Woodland background which was spread throughout the eastern United States, and many of the traits held in common in the phase are the result of this background and not the subsequent diffusion of these traits from an Ohio center. There is, however, in the Hopewell Aspect in Ohio a truly extraordinary cultural aggregate which has cultural associations with groups in the South, such as Copena, the Crystal River Focus in Florida, and with the Marksville Focus in the lower Mississippi Valley. The Hopewell culture in the North must then be the result of an amalgamation of cultural influences from virtually the whole eastern United States, unless it is conceived that these outlying ''trading-posts'' are the result of different groups of people emigrating from the Ohio area with little blocks of Hopewell culture and setting up a new division centered around these. The eventual untangling and sorting out of the cultural elements that go to make up

what is called Hopewell will make an extremely interesting but lengthy study. That the Hopewell culture was in a dominantly agricultural stage seems obvious, but little mention has been made of corn and other evidences of such an economy in the literature.'' (P. 307.)

This expression by Griffin probably satisfies a majority of those who are content to think of a widespread Woodland pattern as furnishing a background for Adena-Hopewell culture groups, where any positive or negative deviation from the Woodland pattern as defined, may be explained as a ''significant variation'' within some subordinate division of the pattern.

When Ritchie* came to classify the aboriginal culture of New York State, he recognized three distinct patterns, which he designated ''Archaic'', ''Woodland'', and ''Mississippi''. Also he recognized the existence of a separate manifestation which he designated as the Hopewellian phase. This phase he does not include in the Woodland pattern for the reason stated by him:

''The presence in the northeastern area of burial mounds, certain non-mound burials with associated grave goods, and artifacts from surface sites, all linked in some obscure way with the 'Mound Builders of Ohio', has long been recognized, and as already stated, has induced Parker to define a 'Mound-Builder occupation' for New York, Wintemberg to speak of 'a northeastern extension of the so-called mound-builder culture centering in Ohio', and Willoughby to conclude that what he terms the 'Old Algonquian' culture in New England, characterized by a substantial majority of the same artifact, forms found in the Vine Valley Aspect of the New York area, is a less specialized prolongation or peripheral survival of the Hopewellian culture.

''A detailed analysis of the contents of the numerous small burial mounds of western Pennsylvania, western New York, and lower Ontario, demonstrates the non-Hopewellian, and to a large degree non-deterministic, nature of much of their scanty contents, while the surface finds reported from the vicinity of the New York tumuli and the artifacts from the non-mound burials in New York and Ontario, attributed to the Hopewellian culture, are actually seldom or never recovered from true Hopewellian mounds.'' (P. 202.)

He suggests three hypotheses as possible explanations for

_____
* Ritchie, Wm. A., 1944, pp. 202-323.

this mixture of Hopewellian and non-Hopewellian traits. Of the first two of these he says:

> "In accounting for this complex several alternative hypotheses are possible. According to the first, it is totally the product of intrusive Hopewellian people, despite the inclusion of a relatively large amount of commonplace utilitarian material, not customarily thought of as Hopewellian, although generally similar to that found in mounds classified ás Hopewellian in Indiana, Illinois, and even Ohio, the Turner group in particular. On this assumption it would be more truly representative of the culture as a whole than is the case with the admittedly mortuary aspect presented by the great mound offerings, which may mask the essential Woodland foundation of the manifestation.

> "The numerous 'non-Hopewellian' traits susceptible of duplication in the Vine Valley Aspect suggest the second interpretation, namely a connection with this paradigm, or with a still undefined antecedent Woodland group partaking of the same fundamental widespread culture. Because a whole mortuary complex is involved, and not simply the presence of a few possibly diffusion-acquired elements, it is logical to postulate an actual migration of small detachments of Hopewellian people from the southern Ohio center, equipped with their characteristic artifacts wrought of Ohio materials, probably via both the Allegheny Valley and the south shore of Lake Erie, along which numerous evidences of their sojourn are found." (p. 218.)

However, another observation of Ritchie[*] is quite pertinent to the present problem. He finds in the Archaic Pattern three foci, the "Lamoka", "Frontenac" and "Brewerton", of which he says:

> "In the Frontenac Focus, the contact product of the Lamoka and Brewerton cultures, the chief features of both constituents are reproduced and the shell component, weak in the former and wanting from the latter, has an unexpected development.

> "A sharp cleavage in physical type distinguishes the Lamoka and Brewerton foci, the former being the product of a long-headed, long-faced, and narrow-nosed people, the latter being associated with folk broader in all these features, while in the composit Frontenac, as might be anticipated, both somatic strains exist." (P. 322.)

---

[*] Ritchie, Wm. A., op. cit.

In discussing the chronological phase of the Archaic occupation of the eastern United States as physiographically defined by Ford & Willey‡, Ritchie says:

"In all likelihood the area was thinly populated except in certain favorable, widely isolated localities, at a relatively early date. The stream of population doubtless flowed southward from the Canadian forests, its ultimate source being one or more Asiatic invasions with subsequent regional specilizations arising partly from ecological causes, hence the earliest sites should theoretically be found in the north, not in the south, as Ford and Willey have recently postulated. (p. 323.)

The present authors accept the statement of Ritchie as substantially correct, and thus see in the Frontenac focus of the Archaic period the result of a union of an early long-headed people, as represented by the Lamoka focus with a later broad-headed people as represented by the Brewerton focus. This fusion occurred in Central New York State probably in the Late Archaic period.

Recalling now the "cultural continuity" from "Black Sand" through "Central Basin" to Hopewellian for Illinois as expressed by Cole and Deuel, there is reason today to believe that this continuity can be observed extending backward in time to reach the preceramic cultural level of the long-headed peoples such as the shell mound dwellers of Kentucky. This period in New York is designated by Ritchie as the Archaic. It may well be that these long-headed people of the shell mounds, after long development formed one of the cultural streams which, after being profoundly affected by later influences from the South and Southeast, as suggested by Cole and Deuel, developed through various levels of culture finally to produce the Hopewellian manifestation.

Griffin, as previously quoted, seems to express the same idea when he speaks of "distinct indication" of a "genetic continuity" in cultural elements and in physical type from a widespread preceramic level into various Woodland divisions.

It thus appears that in the Northcentral and Eastern States there has already been recognized an occupancy, extended in time and space, of a basically long-headed people, whose long development shows an observable continuity in cultural expression,

‡ Ford, J. A., and Willey, Gordon R., 1941, p. 326.

and whose physical type persists without essential modification from the Archaic preceramic levels through various cultural strata to the more advanced subordinate divisions of the Woodland Pattern terminating in the Hopewellian manifestation.

It may well be that some day when Hopewell development comes to be studied, the details of its cultural evolution in part may be found to follow some such course as suggested. Such a study would be a major contribution to the prehistory of Central North America, and might now seem to be long over due.

However, it is not the purpose of the present authors to present a study of Hopewell development or attempt to solve all of the problems of Hopewell origin. They would be quite content to confine their attention solely to Adena which presents in itself a problem of large complexity. This they might have done, except for the fact that they have become convinced that Hopewell material culture is in large part rooted in that of Adena, and many of its most important burial and earthwork traits find their prototypes in Adena. Because of these facts they are convinced that Adena is culturally ancestral to Ohio Hopewell. That is to say, Ohio Hopewell not only is a product of this "genetic continuity" above referred to, the cultural stream possibly arising in the Archaic, and flowing by way of various cultural manifestations, all of which are parts of the Woodland pattern; but Ohio Hopewell also is a recipient and beneficiary of another cultural stream flowing to it by way of Adena. This last stream is far too important to be neglected as it has been in the past.

This concept of the problem of the Adena-Hopewell relations at once raises the question of the origin of Adena. The outstanding fact now possible to demonstrate with the largest series of Adena crania so far available is that Adena man and his progenitors were broadheaded and were occipitally deformed. These diagnostic characteristics he could not have "inherited" from any known "Woodland" ancestor, neither could he have possibly "developed" them here after arrival. He must have brought them when he first came to the Ohio Valley. The characteristics of broadheadness and head deformation are only two of a group of other important traits which are associated in Adena, namely, mound building over the dead, cremation, earth work construction, some form of agriculture, pottery making, and some concept of house construction. One must see in this change in head form, the introduction of a new type of man into the Ohio Valley.

The long continuity of occupancy of long-headed people in the region may well be explained by early migrations from Asia via the Bering Sea route. But it would be difficult to understand a second and later such migration of a new type of man, a broad-head, with the new complex of traits *one of which involves the use of corn as food.*

While the source of the ancestors of Adena man are quite unknown, it seems to these authors to be quite reasonable to look upon Middle America or Mexico as a source of origin. This idea is further discussed under "Speculations".

Further, one may briefly summarize the evidence for the belief that Ohio Hopewell developed out of Adena as the result of contact with an early long-headed stock as follows:

(1) Ohio Hopewell developed its highest manifestation at the center of the area of Adena occupancy.

(2) Their burial customs are practically identical with Adena, making allowance for the greater material wealth of Ohio Hopewell due to its later place in the chronological scale.

(3) The mound-building and earthwork traits of Ohio Hopewell find their earlier prototypes in Adena earthworks and burial mounds.

(4) Together, their cultural development is wholly unlike that of any other peoples, either earlier or later, in this region.

(5) Many artifacts in Late Adena sites show contact with Early Hopewell.

(6) Many art motifs show identical symbolization of ceremonial concepts.

(7) The fact of symmetry in certain Adena designs as well as in many designs of Ohio Hopewell suggests a common technique in the production of symmetry which may have had its origin in an Algonquian custom as reported by Quimby, see Trait 148.

(8) Adena man, a broad-headed individual, had occipital deformation nearly universally, and bifrontal flattening was frequent, while Hopewell man was basically a long-headed individual, originally undeformed.

(9)   Ohio Hopewell adopted the same form of head deformation
as Adena and Adena physical types are found constituting
a minority of the total Hopewell population at their important sites.

SPECULATIONS

Speculations may be regarded by some scientists as having no
place in a chapter on conclusions, since speculations are beyond
the limits of positive demonstration. These authors feel that speculations may have considerable value as suggesting the direction
which future investigations might take, with profit, when opportunity offers. However, they should not be regarded or quoted
as the fixed opinion of the authors.

Adena man, as it has been shown, appears as the first brachycephal in the Ohio Valley region. Further, it appears that he introduced the cultural custom of head deformation (cradleboard).
The authors identify the Adena physical type as the first representatives of the "Gulf" type defined by Hrdlicka[*], and associated with later prehistoric cultures by Collins[**], Neumann[***]
(Centralid) Newman & Snow[****], Stewart[*****], Hulse.[******]
It is probable that the source of this brachycephalic group lay
somewhere in Middle America. The associated custom of head
deformation appears likewise to have come from this same area
where it appears to have had a long history of practice. The more
simple forms of vertical occipital, and bifronto-occipital deformation, and possibly some frontal in combination with the first
named, all appear in the Adena skulls.

These ideas are likewise expressed by Collins[†] as follows:

"The affinities of the later brachycranic type in the
Southeast seem to lie in the opposite direction, probably in
eastern Mexico, as Hrdlicka (1922), pp. 117, 131) has suggested. Though the paucity of comparative data for Mexico
prevents demonstration of this point, it appears not unlikely
that herein may lie the explanation of the process of brachy-
cephalization that seems to have occurred generally throughout the Southeast. The brachycranic Gulf type would seem

* Hrdlicka, Ales, 1940, p. 453.
** Collins, Henry B., Jr., 1941, p. 154.
*** Neumann, Georg K., 1941(a), p. 488; 1941(b), p. 81.
**** Newman, Marshall T., and Snow, Charles E., 1942, pp. 460-461.
***** Stewart, T. D., 1943, p. 264.
****** Hulse, F. S., 1941, pp. 65-68.
† Collins, Henry B., Jr., 1941, p. 154.

best explained as a blend between the earlier coastal population, of Northeastern origin, and a later broad-headed strain which probably entered the Southeast from Mexico. Such a hypothesis finds support in the evidence of strong cultural influences from Mexico, most of which, as Phillips (1940) shows, have been received in relatively late prehistoric times. Artificial cranial deformation was doubtless one of the culture traits thus introduced from Mexico. The custom was not practiced in the Northeast nor by the early southern groups which we have been considering (Stewart, 1940; Snow, 1940). It was, however, present in Mexico, Middle America, and Peru from the earliest known times, and it was evidently from this direction that it later spread to the Southeast and Mississippi Valley.''†

These authors venture to believe that this ''process of brachycephalization'' began with the advent of the ancestors of ADENA as they traveled up the Mississippi Valley.

The inference from this cultural trait of head deformation alone is significant, and when emphasized by its association with a radically different physical type, along with an interesting combination of other traits of a material nature, it appears that there is evidence of a migration here of a new group of people from some new source, probably Middle America.

Of late, anthropologists have indicated (Vaillant*, Phillips**, Stewart***) agreement toward the ever-accumulating evidence of late prehistoric Mexican influence in the Southeast. The question is when did it begin?

The authors speculate that it began with the immediate ancestors of the Adena people as the authors understand Adena.

In the late Archaic period, this ''influence'' is assumed to have taken the form of a migration up the Mississippi Valley of a new people with a different cultural heritage and a new economic pattern to finally reach and establish a homeland in the Ohio River Valley. Here they began a long period of development and growth which produced the cultural complex described herein as Adena. Through its contact and fusion with the long-headed

---

† The fact that cranial deformity is so rarely encountered in peninsular Florida would seem to preclude the possibility that the custom had reached the Southeast by way of the Antilles.
* Vaillant, George C., 1932, pp. 10-19.
** Phillips, Philip, 1940, pp. 366-367.
*** Stewart, T. D., 1944, p. 320.

indigenous population of the region they laid the foundation for Ohio Hopewell.

Possibly, as has been said of other accomplished and well recognized ancient cultures, this mixing and blending of two different peoples brought about a hybrid vigor, genetically and culturally, which combination produced those leaders, gifted ingenious individuals, responsible for the notable achievements which characterize Ohio Hopewell. It is not unlikely that the high cultural level attained by Ohio Hopewell may have resulted from the social stimulation incident to this contact with an agricultural economy. Thus, we may assume that earlier Adena-Hopewell descendants took the basic Adena culture and added significantly to it to achieve the peak of Hopewell development as it appeared in Ohio in Middle and Late Hopewell times. This high development was unique in North America, north of the Rio Grande.

This supposition of the fusion of the (southern) deforming Adena broad-headed people with the (northeastern) long-headed people of the late Archaic period can account for the characteristic head deformation of the long-headed Ohio Hopewell; the near identical burial customs of Adena and Hopewell; the presence of Adena type skulls in Hopewell sites; and the presence of scattered Hopewell artifacts on some Late Adena sites.

Obviously, if the concept of the development of Ohio Hopewell is substantially correct, there was a period of Adena occupancy and development in the Ohio Valley prior to the contact. This period, designated Early Adena, is one which shows no Hopewell artifacts. Sites of this period have been found in Kentucky, Indiana, and Ohio. The contact period, before the complete merging of Adena with the early Hopewell, is designated as Late Adena. This period, characterized by the presence in Adena sites of a few scattered, unique, and obviously Hopewellian artifacts, has been found in Kentucky, Ohio, West Virginia, and northwestern Pennsylvania. A case in point is the original Adena Mound in Ross County, Ohio. The magnificent anthropomorphic tubular pipe in its art motif is certainly Hopewell; it is unique in Adena. Nothing like it has ever been recorded from any other Adena site. So far as the authors are aware, no one has heretofore reported a belief that this pipe is of Hopewell origin, but in the beautifully executed life size figure of the "Mound-Builder" in the Ohio State Museum, designed to represent "The Prehistoric Sculptor", the individual portrays an Ohio Hopewell man, with typical Hopewell artifacts. He is shown in the act of carving a pipe, a replica of the Adena mound tubular pipe. This figure, in natural color, was chosen by Shetrone as the frontispiece for "The Mound-Builders".

Returning to the basic postulate that the ancestors of Adena came into the Ohio Valley by way of a migration from Middle America, it is recognized that this idea will be received with much skepticism by some to whom diffusion and development are the only proper methods of explaining cultural changes. It is easy to understand the diffusion of a particular trait or group of associated traits or the development of an artifact from a simple to a more complex form, but the present authors find it impossible to see how a fundamental change in head form accompanied by a characteristic form of deformation could be either diffused or developed without the introduction of a new type of man. In this particular case, the assumption is made easy by the fact that this new man also introduced a complex of new traits.

The same forms of cranial deformation* fronto-occipital and parallelo-fronto-occipital which are found on Hopewellian skulls appear among Maya skulls of the Old Empire city of Copan.

Some anthropologists** have recognized evidence of Mexican influence in Middle Mississippi times. This idea seems to be suggested by Phillips*** when he says,

"(1) that Middle Mississippi, as now defined, shows among other 'outside influences' a considerable number of characteristics that can only be interpreted as the result of more or less direct contact with Middle America; and (2) that although some of these features may have been inherited from earlier cultures in the Mississippi Valley (and therefore may be regarded as only remotely Middle American in origin) the more unequivocal ones, and those that give the culture its special flavor, seem to have been introduced directly into the Southeast at a comparatively late time."

---

* Longyear, John M., 1940, p. 151, and Stewart, T. D., 1943, p. 114; and quoting Vivchow, R., 1897, pp. 324-328.
** Stewart, T. D., 1944, pp. 317-332.
*** Phillips, Philip, 1940, pp. 366 and 367.

Earlier Mexican influence in the Southern United States is suggested by Ekholm*. Why should it be unthinkable that such "influence" might not have occurred before Middle Mississippi times and might not have been in part due to a migration?

Some may object to the suggestion of a migration from Middle America unless intermediate sites showing effects of the migration can be demonstrated. It should be remembered that large areas in the Mississippi Valley remain as yet unexplored. Future excavations may present such evidence. However, these authors believe that it is not necessary to assume that any intermediate sites ever existed in such magnitude as to leave an archaeological trace to the present time.

In this connection the possibility that Tchefuncte may represent such evidence is at once apparent.

Recently Ford and Quimby** have reported on "The Tchefuncte Culture, An Early Occupation of the Lower Mississippi Valley". In this report they compare Tchefuncte and Adena. In this discussion they say, in part:

"The comparison of Tchefuncte and Adena traits indicates a typological similarity which suggests a cultural relationship between the two cultures."

After listing some twenty traits which they affirm are held in common by Tchefuncte and Adena, they say:

"Tchefuncte and Adena are easily distinguishable by a majority of traits which they do not hold in common just as are Marksville and Ohio Hopewell. Indeed, it is surprising that there are any similarities between Tchefuncte and Adena, considering their spatial separation and environmental differencies. We believe, however, that there is a fundamental similarity between the two cultures. While both Tchefuncte and Adena, in their respective areas, seem to have derived a large part of their cultural heritage from the Archaic, these new traits which they hold in common have been added . . . .

"If this small collection of traits—burial mounds, pottery features, and pipes—are new in the East at this stage, a question immediately arises as to the direction in which they are moving. To suppose them to have appeared simultaneously in the lower Mississippi and Ohio Valleys is not reasonable.

---

* Ekholm, Gordon F., 1940, p. 330.
** Ford, J. A., and Quimby, George I., Jr., 1945, p. 93.

This involves the question of the relative ages of Tchefuncte and Adena; a question which we do not have the evidence to answer fully.''

While Ford and Quimby are not at all dogmatic in their statements, and all conclusions are drawn with proper scientific reserve, yet the effect of this comparison appears to these present authors as misleading. Ford and Quimby state a belief in a fundamental similarity between Tchefuncte and Adena. They point out that it is unreasonable to assume these traits, held in common, appeared simultaneously in two widely separated areas, thus, suggesting that these traits moved from one area to the other. They raise the question of the direction of motion and state that it is a question of relative age, thus implying that these traits moved from the earlier to the later culture. Since Tchefuncte had many traits belonging to the Archaic pattern of culture and is, therefore, presumptively older, the inference is plain that Tchefuncte first had these Adena-like traits and from this source they were passed on to Adena. That is, so far as these traits are concerned, Tchefuncte might be considered culturally ancestral to Adena. To such conclusions or implications, the present authors must definitely dissent. The reasons therefore which constitute a large part of this paper may be better understood by a study of the list of traits which are said to suggest a cultural relationship with Adena. There is offered as evidence of this cultural relationship a list of twenty traits, three of which are pottery traits. The remaining seventeen traits are listed herein in a vertical column with comments in a parallel column.

Traits as Listed	Comments
Conical burial mounds	This trait found in Adena is not diagnostic of it. Many mounds in Middle Mississippi times were of the same form. Many Adena mounds are not conical.
Circular post-mold patterns beneath mound	At Tchefuncte this trait seems to rest on only one partial pattern at one site. This pattern, less than a quadrant of a circle, has only some thirteen molds. They do **not** appear to possess the diagnostic quality of being "paired" or show outward sloping. Such patterns as the one figured are common in Middle Mississippi sites.

Traits as Listed	Comments
Leaf shaped, chipped flint projectile points. Stemmed projectile points	These two traits as stated are too general to be diagnostic of Adena. They are found on all Archaic sites in deep shell mounds from bottom to top.
Tubular pipes with flattened mouth pieces	These tubular pipes are of clay, none such are known in Adena. The Adena tubular pipe made of stone differs considerably in form, being more exactly cylindrical, and less conical, than the Tchefuncte type, and is **not** decorated. Adena tubular pipes are believed to be Shaman "medicine" tubes, used ceremonially, not for smoking.
Chipped flint ovate scrapers and chipped flint drills	These traits are too general to be diagnostic of Adena. Both are very numerous on all Archaic sites and are found from top to bottom of the deepest shell middens.
Quartz crystals	This is not an Adena trait. In one Adena site, one such crystal was reported because it had been worked. No other occurrence in Adena is known.
Boat stones	This is not an Adena trait. Adena did have triangular bars of galena, but they were not hollowed out. They are not true boat stones. True boat stones are often found in shell mounds, but not in Adena sites.
Sub-rectangular bars	In Adena, some so-called "bars" are triangular, diamond shaped, or elliptical, but not sub-rectangular. Sub-rectangular bars are found by the score in shell mounds and probably were atlatl weights.
Bone awls Bone chisels	These traits are found in all types of village sites in the southeast. They do not prove Adena association.
Antler flaking tools Antler projectile points	These two traits are found in Adena, the first, rarely, and the last, very rarely. Both traits are found in shell mounds from top to bottom even when debris is 25 feet deep. They cannot be regarded as proof of Adena connection.
Flakers of deer ulna	This is not an Adena trait, but it is often found in later sites such as Ft. Ancient and also in the Archaic.
Worked animal jaws	This trait is very rare in Adena, but much more frequent in the Archaic, and also frequent in Fort Ancient.
Perforated or cut animal teeth	This trait not found in Adena.
Containers made of conch shells	This trait not found in Adena. They are frequent in Ohio Hopewell and are also found rarely in Copena, but not in Adena.

Thus the evidence of cultural relationship of Tchefuncte with Adena, as presented by this list of traits is not impressive and appears to these authors as quite tenuous, especially if it is coupled with the suggestion that Tchefuncte was the source of Adena culture. These authors have suggested that Adena, a broad-headed people, practicing occipital deformation, may have had their early origin in Middle America or Mexico. One might speculate that if such a migration of the early ancestor of Adena came into the Ohio Valley from the southland about the close of the Archaic period, their route of travel might well have led them by way of the Delta Country, and Tchefuncte may thus represent an incidental contact between a people migrating up the Mississippi Valley in the late Archaic and the long-headed peoples native to the region. This might conceivably account for Tchefuncte cultural manifestation without the necessity of any implication that Tchefuncte was ancestral to Adena, which to these authors does not seem probable on the basis of the evidence submitted. This contact might account for the brachycephalic element present in some of the Tchefuncte skulls and the evidence of possible frontal deformation recently noted and not heretofore reported.*

If Adena, a deforming broad-headed people with the concept of a complex social organization, by contact with representatives of the eastern long-headed people, having a somewhat less highly developed society, stimulated them to a development of Ohio Hopewell which seems to have reached a higher level of cultural development than that attained by Adena, one naturally wonders what became of Adena after the contact. Physical anthropology seems to show that some Adena-like individuals became, to all intent and purpose, Hopewell people. Whether this is the result of a mingling of blood or a mixing of peoples cannot as yet be demonstrated. It may be assumed that some Adena sites continued to be occupied while Early Hopewell was developing, but the archaeological record would seem to indicate that all Adena sites had ceased to be occupied before Late Hopewell had acquired any alligator teeth, grizzly bear teeth, obsidian, silver, or conjoined tubes of copper, since not a single Late Hopewell artifact has ever been found in any Adena site. One may

---

* Skull, S. T., No. 15496, a male, Skull S. M., No. 17, a female.

assume, therefore, that as Ohio Hopewell rose in strength and importance and developed further the same mound-building traits which they had adopted from Adena, for reasons unknown, some of them may have moved southward. The Lower Ohio and Tennessee Rivers provided both an excellent means and a route of travel. These authors speculate that this may have been the means by which Copena in Northern Alabama became established. In making such an assumption, it is not necessary to conceive that a chain of occupational sites should have been established along the Ohio in South Indiana and Illinois and along the lower Tennessee in Western Kentucky. The extent of occupancy of Copena in the southwest is as yet not fully known, but excavations along the Tennessee River in Alabama show that that area is a region of concentration of a mixed group of broad-headed (68%) and long-headed (32%) people who had many Adena traits, but whose material culture was largely that of Hopewell. This group contains individuals which show extreme forms of head deformation which occur in Ohio Hopewell, but are not found in Adena. The Copena people followed in time the riparian people of the Shell Mounds in this region, but were definitely earlier than the Middle Mississippi peoples of the Southeast. Their artifacts which are clearly of Hopewell origin; copper breast-plates, copper ear spools, copper reels, copper celts, galena masses, all point to Middle Hopewell. There are no *Late Hopewell artifacts in Copena*. The Copena people are predominantly *broad headed* with pronounced fronto-occipital deformation. Some resemble the deformed Ohio Hopewell long heads with bifronto-occipital deformation. They are thus distinct and possess a material culture unlike any other cultural complex in the Tennessee Valley.

The copper reels which were used by Copena seem to show internal evidence* that they were later than Ohio Hopewell copper reels, which in turn are later than copper or stone reels in Adena. This analysis of the chronological development of the copper reels seems to be quite objective. One may speculate, therefore, that Adena sites never show any contact with Late Hopewell in Ohio because such Adena as had not been completely fused with Hopewell by Middle Hopewell times and had not become indis-

---

* Webb, Wm. S., 1941, p. 192.

tinguishable from it, had, before Late Hopewell times, migrated down the Ohio and up the Tennessee Rivers, taking with them the joint cultures of the two parent stocks. Thus, we may speculate on the disappearance of Adena as such from the Ohio River Valley and the rise of Copena in northern Alabama along the Tennessee River Valley. Thus, we may see the possibility of Copena in Alabama being in part contemporary with Middle Hopewell in Ohio and, although widely separated from it, still maintaining some communication with it.

This is a very intriguing speculation which calls for much careful field work along the Tennessee River and throughout the Southeastern United States, particularly in Alabama. Such communication between Copena of Alabama and Hopewell of Ohio in Middle Hopewell times is definitely suggested by the five large steatite pipes taken from Seip Mound No. 1. After describing these pipes, Shetrone and Greenman* compared them to illustrations presented by Thruston**, as a result of which they say:

> "It is very evident that the five effigy pipes from the Seip Mound do not pertain to the Hopewell culture, and that they are typical of the Tennessee-Cumberland region."

This statement is quite correct so far as it goes. It needs only to be added that it is the *Copena* people of the Tennessee-Cumberland region who possessed these pipes to make plain the cultural and chronological significance of the occurrence of these steatite pipes in an Ohio Hopewell Mound. Such magnificent pipes as those taken from Seip Mound No. 1 were perhaps never very numerous anywhere. That is, their number certainly was limited, and their possession restricted by scarcity and value to only those persons of wealth or distinction who were able to possess them. The significance of these pipes may be illustrated by their placement just above the great multiple burial of extended remains at Seip Mound No. 1. This burial was notable for its great wealth of accompanying material, surely indicating the importance of the individuals. These dog pipes from the Seip Mound No. 1 in material, form, and method of manufacture find their nearest prototypes in Copena of Alabama as illustrated by specimen from Site La° 37***.

---

* Shetrone, H. C., and Greenman, E. F. 1931 p. 432
** Thruston, Gates P., 1897, p. 203.
*** Webb, Wm. S., 1939, Plate 41-b.

Another evidence of contact between Copena of Alabama and Ohio Hopewell is the copper reel taken by Mills* from the Hazlett Mound in Ohio. This reel shows not only internal evidence of its Copena origin, as has been previously pointed out**, but it was associated with other Copena artifacts and burial traits.

Turning now to consider the possible influence of Adena in the Southeastern United States particularly in the central part, where Copena occurs in Alabama along the Tennessee River, one might speculate on what became of the Copena people and their culture complex, which in many ways was so different from that which preceded and that which followed it in that area. If straws may be depended on to show the direction of the wind, many of the highly developed social groups of the proto-historic and the historic periods in that region left abundant evidence that their society was organized about activities which centered about a large building in their village, commonly called a "Townhouse." The townhouse seems to have been the place where the rulers of the community assembled for all ceremonies of a social, religious, or governmental nature. Certain it is that the townhouse or council house was an important institution in both Cherokee and Muskogee social organizations in Middle Mississippi times.

Evidence of the use of the townhouse in Adena has been presented.*** The house was circular, had a raised clay platform for use of the presiding officer and possibly also for his near associates in authority, while the members of the council occupied places against the circular wall of the structure about the central fire. The single doorway or entrance to the house was symmetrically placed opposite the raised platform or "dais" of the presiding officer. This is important as demonstrating that Adena society shows the earliest evidence of the town house or council house concept. One may speculate on the possible connection between the circular stockades built inside the so-called "sacred circles" of Adena and Hopewell. They may have been used for the same purpose, but at least one complete town house floor pattern has been found to have been the base of a large Adena mound, the mound having been erected *over the town house site*

---

* Mills, Wm. C., 1921, Figure 30.
** Webb, Wm. S., 1941, p. 199.
*** Webb, Wm. S., 1943, p. 518.

after the house was burned. This took place after the construction of an especially elaborate log tomb exactly over the raised clay platform on the town house floor.

It seems significant that when the town house appears in later times in the Southeast, it, too, should be so much like the Adena structure. At Macon, Georgia, on the Ocmulgee Old Fields,* there has been found the remains of a ceremonial earth lodge or town house. It is perhaps one of the best preserved sites of its kind in the Southeast. This structure had a circular wall and a single entrance. Opposite the entrance and against the wall was an elevated platform of clay upon which several officials might have been seated. Against the wall on both sides of the structure, clay seats for many individuals were arranged. The roof had been supported by four large posts, and the house had been burned before a mound had been erected over it. All of these characteristics are quite like Adena. The most significant fact of all, however, was to be found in the elevated clay platform. This platform had its front edge and surface carved in the form of an eagle, showing the great head, eyes, and beak characteristic of the raptorial bird. This image is between the central fireplace and the seats on the rostrum or ''dais'' and is part of it. Certainly it is in the most conspicuous place in the town house. Surely one may conclude that this eagle image had for those who met in this town house some deep and significant meaning. It has already been pointed out in the Adena trait list that the raptorial bird, shown by beak, head, and talons, frequently appeared in Adena as an art motiff. Can this be the same bird? Is it possible that these symbols had the same ceremonial significance with the Adena and Muskhogean peoples?

Recently a very able article by Waring and Holder** has appeared dealing with ''A Prehistoric Ceremonial Complex in the Southeastern United States.'' This paper is well written and their general conclusions seem amply justified. Only in one particular do the present authors feel justified in offering a contrary opinion, and that, by way of an extension of the ideas of Waring and Holder rather than by way of contradiction. In discussing

---

* Kelly, A. R., 1938, Plates 2b-3a.
** Waring, A. J., Jr., and Holder, Preston, 1945, p. 28.

the chronological development of this ceremonial complex, they state:

> "To summarize the chronological aspect of the complex; these elements appear suddenly and late. When they appear, Macon excepted, they appear fully elaborated. No developmental sequences of the elements are traceable. Such Hopewellian traits as the serpent representations, the cermonial celt and the omnipresent conch bowl might be regarded as suggesting a background of ceremonialism upon which the complex proper might develop. The gap between the two is wide, none the less."

In general, the present authors do not take kindly to the idea that the elements of this complex appear "suddenly," or that they appear "fully elaborated." In any case where the occurrence of an element offers the suggestion of suddenness, there may be two reasons for such manifestations; first, it may mean that the elements of the developmental sequences have simply *not yet been found* because they lie elsewhere in other cultural horizons; or second, these elemental prototypes may have been found, but not recognized for what they were.

It is very satisfying to have Waring and Holder suggest that such Hopewellian traits, as they mention, might be regarded as suggesting a background upon which the complex might develop. The gap between Hopewellian and late Middle Mississippi ceremonials may be wide, but it certainly has been growing less and less as the result of excavation in the last decade. It cannot be expected that, in the early stages of any development sequence of such an element, one would find great numbers of artifacts showing the element, or that the element would appear in great elaboration. Thus, when looking for evidences of the early stages of development, one must be content with relatively few examples and must expect them in general to be relatively crude in form. Thus, if we search in Hopewellian sites for evidence of this ceremonial complex, we cannot expect to find it in such magnificent quantity and quality as a much later site, such as Spiro Mound, would show. Elements of this Southeastern ceremonial complex appearing in Hopewell-Adena may be listed briefly as:

> (1) Raptorial bird (eagle?), shown engraved on bone and cut in copper in Hopewell; on engraved stone tablets and on human bone gorgets in Adena.

(2)   Serpent, engraved on stone tablets in Adena.   The great Serpent Mount of Ohio is now believed to be of Adena origin.   Serpent image cut in mica from Turner Site in Ohio Hopewell.

(3)   Hand-eye design, engraved on clay tablet in Adena.

(4)   Human mask or death motif, cut in stone tablet in Adena and represented in head dresses in Hopewell, and possibly by the pottery head* from Seip Mound No. 1.

(5)   Metal covered buttons and beads, a common trait in Hopewell; found in later horizons having the ceremonial complex.

(6)   Circular town house, in Adena, similar to the ceremonial lodge of later peoples having the ceremonial complex.

(7)   Use of conch shell vessels common in Hopewell and Copena.

Can it be that in the use of the eagle symbol on the floor of the circular town house of the later peoples at Ocmulgee we see a continuing Adena influence brought to the Muskhogean people by the much earlier Copena people of northern Alabama? Can it be that the use of the hand-eye design, the design of the "feathered serpent," as well as the human face or death mask are also parts of the inheritance of the Muskhogean peoples derived from the Copena peoples whose material culture was Early to Middle Hopewell, but whose basic social, religious, and ceremonial concepts were definitely Adena?

In speaking of the Macon Plateau manifestation of Mound C at Ocmulgee, Fairbanks** says:

"The presence of elaborate sub-mound log-tombs, cremations, bundle burials, and the one instance of sheet copper ornaments and copper covered canine jaws is suggestive of Adena influences, or perhaps Hopewellian."

"From the list of Adena traits given by Black*** (after Greenman), it appears that thirteen traits are present, namely log tombs, subfloor graves, skeletons with beads, important central graves, stemmed projectile points, bark prepared graves, disc shell beads, cremation, red ochre on skeletons (?), marginella beads, notched projectile points of flint, thumb-nail flint scrapers, extended burials, reburials.   While the stemmed and notched projectile points illustrated by Black show a high degree of similarity to type found on the Macon

---

* Morgan, Richard G., 1941, p. 384.
** Fairbanks, Charles H., unpublished manuscript.
*** Black, Glenn A., 1936, pp. 298-299.

Plateau, these most probably are generalized traits, since they, as well as the thumbnail scrapers, occur widely throughout Georgia. The sub-mound burial tombs containing bundle and extended burials associated with red paint and olivella and disc shell beads constitute a complex that definitely suggests relationship. In view of the fact that the majority of traits are Middle Mississippi in character the burial complex must be regarded as a survival from an older and not necessarily ancestral culture.''

* * * * * *

"These traits form an integral part of the Macon Plateau component at Mound C but it is not certain that they occur in other components of the focus. They seem to be the only link traits with either Elementary Hopewell or Adena that are present at Mound C. As the Macon Plateau component represents an earlier invasion of the southeast by a Middle Mississippi people it can be assumed that they at some time were in a region where these traits existed. The alternative explanations, that Adena or Hopewell remains extended into the Georgia region, cannot be supported on the basis of present data.''

These authors believe that this complex of traits, as described by Fairbanks, plus two additional traits, namely, large greenstone celts with rounded poll, circular cross-section and flared bit, and large marine conch shell dipper with columella removed such as was found in Pit 54 containing group burial 69 within it, at Mound C, are all diagnostic of Copena as it is manifested in northern Alabama along the Tennessee River. These authors speculate that, contrary to the conclusion of Fairbanks, the alternative explanation might be possible; namely, that this Hopewellian manifestation as represented in Copena might well have extended into the Georgia region about Macon, and even further south, and thus been the means of passing on these traits to later Middle Mississippi peoples.

On such a basis, one may speculate that in some way at present unknown the Hopewellian cultural manifestation on the Tennessee River in northern Alabama known as Copena may have fused with the Early Muskhogean peoples of that region and thus contributed the Adena concepts of governmental, ceremonial, and religious rites as evidence in the use of the town house and many detailed art motifs.

How far extended and how potent Adena influences by way of Hopewell and Copena may have been on later peoples of Middle Mississippi times in the Southeastern United States, particularly the possessors of the ceremonial cult complex so well described recently by Waring and Holder, cannot in the present state of our knowledge or lack of knowledge be evaluated. One may be tempted to wonder if Adena influence may not have been far greater than heretofore suspected. It should be remembered that at Spiro, the great wealth of ceremonial cult material came from a series of vaults having log roofs all in a conical earth mound. Certain it is that in the Ohio Valley *Adena man made the first log tombs and closed them with a roof of logs.*

BIBLIOGRAPHY

ANDREWS, E. B.
1877 "Exploration of Mounds in Southwestern Ohio," Peabody Museum, Harvard University, Tenth Annual Report, Volume II, No. 1, Cambridge, Massachusetts.

BACHE, CHARLES AND LINTON SATTERTHWAITE, JR.
1930 "Excavation of a Mound at Beech Bottom, West Virginia," The Museum Journal, University of Pennsylvania, Volume XXI, Nos. 3 and 4, Philadelphia, Pennsylvania, pp. 133–136.

BENNETT, JOHN W.
1944 "Archaeological Horizons in the Southern Illinois Region," American Antiquity, Volume X, No. 1, pp. 12–22.

1944 "Hopewellian in Minneosta," American Antiquity, Volume IX, No. 3, p. 336.

BLACK, GLENN A.
1933 "The Archaeology of Green County," Indiana History Bulletin, Volume X, No. 5, Indianapolis, Indiana.

1936 "Excavation of the Nowlin Mound," Indiana History Bulletin, Volume XIII, No. 7, Indianapolis, Indiana

1941 "Cultural Complexities of Southwestern Indiana," Proceedings of Indiana Academy of Science, Volume 50, pp. 33–35.

BUCHNELL, DAVID I., JR.
1920 "Native Cemeteries and Forms of Burial East of the Mississippi," Bureau of American Ethnology, Bulletin 71, Washington, D. C.

COFFINBERRY, W. L.
1875 Proceedings of the American Association for the Advancement of Science, p. 293.

COLE, FAY-COOPER
1943 "Chronology in the Middle West," Proceedings of the American Philosophical Society, Volume 86, No. 2, pp. 299–304.

COLE, FAY-COOPER AND THORNE DEUEL
1937 "Rediscovering Illinois," Archaeological Explorations in and Around Fulton County, The University of Chicago Press, Chicago, Illinois.

Collins, Henry B., Jr.
1941   "Relationships of an Early Indian Cranial Series from Louisiana," Journal of the Washington Academy of Sciences, Vol. 31, No. 4, pp. 145–155.

DeLaguna, Frederica
1940   "Eskimo Lamps and Pots," Journal Royal Anthropological Institution, Volume 70, pp. 53–76.

Dun, Walter A.
1884   Journal of the Cincinnati Society of Natural History, Volume VII, pp. 104–203.

Deuel, Thorn
1935   "Basic Cultures of the Mississippi Valley," American Anthropologist, Vol. 37, No. 3, pp. 429–446.

Ekholm, Gordon F.
1940   "The Archaeology of Northern and Western Mexico," The Maya and Their Neighbors, D. Appleton, Century Co., New York, pp. 320–330.

Ellis, H. Holmes
1944   "Two New Specimens from Ohio", American Antiquity, Volume IX, No. 4, p. 449.

Fairbanks, Charles H.
        "The Excavation of Mound C, Macon Group," unpublished manuscript deposited with Ocmulgee National Monument.

Fewkes, J. Walter
1928   "The Archaeology of the Piedmont Region of South Carolina," Exploration and Field Work, Smithsonian Institution, 1927, pp. 157–164.

Ford, James A. and George I. Quimby, Jr.
1945   "The Tchefuncte Culture, An Early Occupation of the Lower Mississippi Valley," Memoirs of the Society of American Archaeology, No. 2, American Antiquity, Supplement to Volume X, No. 3.

Ford, James A. and Gordon R. Willey
1940   "Crooks Site, A Marksville Period Burial Mound in LaSalle Parrish, Louisiana," Department of Conservation, Louisiana Geological Survey, Anthropological Study, No. 3.

1941   "An Interpretation of the Prehistory of the Eastern United States," American Anthropologist, Volume 43, No. 3, Part 1, p. 325.

Fowke, Gerard
1888   News item in the Cincinnati Commercial Gazette, July 23, 1888.

1895 "Archaeological Work in Ohio, Excavation of a Mound in Pike County, Ohio," Proceedings of the Academy of Natural Sciences of Philadelphia.

1902 "Archaeological History of Ohio," Ohio State Archaeological and Historical Society, Columbus, Ohio.

1905 "The McEvers Mounds, Montezuma, Pike County, Illinois," Missouri Historical Society Collections, Volume II, No. 5, St. Louis, Missouri.

1928 "Archaeological Investigations—II," Bureau of American Ethnology, Forty-Fourth Anuual Report.

FUNKHOUSER, W. D. AND W. S. WEBB

1930 "Rock Shelters in Wolfe and Powell Counties, Kentucky," University of Kentucky Reports in Anthropology and Archaeology, Volume I, No. 4.

1935 "The Ricketts Site in Montgomery County, Kentucky," University of Kentucky Reports in Anthropology and Archaeology, Volume III, No. 6.

GAUL, JAMES H.

1943 "Observations on the Bronze Age in the Yenisei Valley, Siberia," Papers, Peabody Museum American Archaeology and Ethnology, Volume XX, pp. 149–187.

GERMAN, WILLIAM MCKEE

1944 Personal Communication, February 3, 1944, with report on diseased bone specimens.

GREENMAN, E. F.

1932 "Excavation of the Coon Mound and an Analysis of the Adena Culture," Ohio Archaeological and Historical Quarterly, Volume XLI, No. 3, Columbus, Ohio.

1938 "Hopewellian Traits in Florida," American Antiquity, Society for American Archaeology, Volume III, No. 4.

GRIFFIN, JAMES B.

1938 "The Ceramic Remains from Norris Basin, Tennessee," Bureau of American Ethnology, Bulletin No. 118, pp. 253-358.

1939 "Report on the Ceramics of Wheeler Basin," Bureau of American Ethnology, Bulletin No. 122, pp. 127–165

1941 "Additional Hopewell Material from Illinois," Prehistoric Research Series, Volume II, No. 3, Indiana Historical Society.

1942   "Adena Pottery," American Antiquity, Volume VII, No. 4, pp. 344–358.

1943   "The Fort Ancient Aspect, Its Cultural and Chronological Position in Mississippi Valley Archaeology," University of Michigan Press, Ann Arbor, Michigan.

1945   "Ceramic Collections from Two South Carolina Sites," Papers Michigan Academy Science, Arts, and Letters, Volume XXX.

1945a   "The Significance of The Fiber Tempered Pottery of The St. Johns Area in Florida," Journal Washington Academy of Sciences, Volume 35, No. 7, pp. 218-223.

HAAG, WILLIAM G.
1940   "A Description of the Wright Site Pottery," University of Kentucky Reports in Anthropology and Archaeology, Volume V, No. 1, pp. 75–82.

1942   "A Description and Analysis of the Pickwick Pottery," Bureau of American Ethnology, Bulletin No. 129, pp. 509–527.

1942   "The Pottery from the C. & O. Mounds at Paintsville," University of Kentucky Report in Anthropology and Archaeology, Volume V, No. 4, pp. 341–349.

HARRINGTON, MARK R.
1922   "Cherokee and Earlier Remains on Upper Tennessee River," Indian Notes and Monographs, Volume XII, No. 24.

HERTZBERG, H. T. E.
1940   "The Skeletal Material from Ricketts Mound," The University of Kentucky, Reports in Anthropology and Archaeology, Vol. III, No. 6.

1940   "Skeletal Material from the Wright Site, Montgomery County," The University of Kentucky, Reports in Anthropology and Archaeology, Vol. V, No. 1.

HOOTON, EARNEST A.
1922   "The Skeletal Remains in the Turner Group of Earthworks, Hamilton County, Ohio," Charles C. Willoughby, Papers of the Peabody Museum of American Archaeology and Ethnology, Vol. VIII, No. 3.

1932   "Up from the Ape," The MacMillan Co., New York, N. Y.

HRDLICKA, ALES

1940   "The Painting of Human Bones Among the Indians," Smithsonian Institution, Annual Report, Washington, D. C.

1922   "The Anthropology of Florida," Publications of the Florida Historical Society, No. 1, De Land, p. 23.

1940   "Indians of the Gulf States," Catalog of Human Crania in the U. S. National Museum Collections, Smithsonian Institution, Vol. 87, No. 3076, pp. 315–464.

HULSE, F. S.

1941   "The People Who Lived at Irene," Physical Anthropology in Irene Mound Site, Chatham County, Georgia, by Joseph Caldwell and Catherine McCann, The University of Georgia Press, Athens.

JENNINGS, JESSE D.

1941   "Chickasaw and Earlier Indian Cultures of Northeast Mississippi," Journal of Mississippi History, Jackson, Miss., Volume III, No. 3, pp. 155–227.

JONES, CHARLES C.

1873   Antiquities of the Southern Indians, New York.

KELLY, ARTHUR R.

1938   "A Preliminary Report of Archaeological Explorations at Macon, Georgia," Bureau of American Ethnology, Anthropological Paper No. 1, Bulletin 119, pp. 1–69.

KROGMAN, WILTON M.

1939   "A Guide to the Identification of Human Skeletal Material," Federal Bureau of Investigation, The Law Enforcement Bulletin, Volume 8, No. 8, August, 1939, Washington, D. C.

LEWIS, THOMAS M. N. AND MADELINE KNEBERG

1941   "The Prehistory of the Chickamauga Basin in Tennessee," University of Tennessee Anthropological Papers, No. 1.

LILLY, ELI

1937   "Prehistoric Antiquities of Indiana," Indiana Historical Society, Indianapolis, Indiana.

LINTON, RALPH

1944   "North American Cooking Pots," American Antiquities, Volume IX, No. 4, pp. 369–381.

LONGYEAR, JOHN M., III
>1940   "A Maya Old Empire Skeleton from Copan, Honduras," American Journal of Physical Anthropology, Vol. 27, No. 1, pp. 151–154.

MACLEAN, J. P.
>1879   "The Mound Builders with an Investigation Into the Archaeology of Butler County, Ohio," Robert Clarke and Company, Cincinnati, Ohio.

MANOUVRIER, L.
>1893   "Le determination de la taille apres les grands os des membres, Memoirs de la Soc. d'Anthropol de Paris," Series 2, Volume IV.

MARTIN, RUDOLF
>1928   "Lehrbuch der Anthropologie," Second Edition, Volume II.

MAXSON, RALPH N.
>1943   "Report referred to in Physical Anthropology," Section by Snow in Reports in Archaeology and Anthropology, University of Kentucky, Volume V, No. 7, p. 618.

McGUIRE, JOSEPH D.
>1897   "Pipes and Smoking Customs of the American Aborigines," based on material in the U. S. National Museum, Annual Report, U. S. National Museum.

McKERN, W. C.
>1931   "A Wisconsin Variant of the Hopewell Culture," Bulletin of the Public Museum of the City of Milwaukee, Volume X, No. 2, Milwaukee, Wisconsin.

MEIGS, J. RITKIN, M. D.
>1857   "Catalogue of Human Crania in the Collection of the Academy of Natural Science of Philadelphia," based on the Third Edition of Dr. Morton's Catalogue of Skulls, J. B. Lippincott Company, Philadelphia, Pennsylvania.

MILLS, WILLIAM C.
>1902   "Excavation of the Adena Mound," Ohio Archaeological and Historical Quarterly, Volume X, No. 4, Columbus, Ohio.
>
>1907   "Exploration of the Edwin Harness Mound," Ohio Archaeological and Historical Quarterly, Volume XVI, No. 2, Columbus, Ohio.
>
>1909   "Exploration of the Seip Mound No. 2, Certain Mounds and Village Sites in Ohio," Volume II, Part 1, Columbus, Ohio.

1916 "Exploration of the Tremper Mound, Certain Mounds and Village Sites in Ohio," Volume II, Part 3, Columbus, Ohio.

1917 "Archaeological Remains of Jackson County, Certain Mounds and Village Sites in Ohio," Volume II, No. 2, Columbus, Ohio.

1917 "Exploration of the Westenhaver Mound," Ohio Archaeological and Historical Quarterly, Volume XXVI, No. 2, Columbus, Ohio.

1921 "Flint Ridge, The Hazlett Mound, Certain Mounds and Village Sites in Ohio," Volume III, Part 3.

1922 "Exploration of the Mound City Group, Certain Mounds and Village Sites in Ohio," Volume III, Part 4, Columbus, Ohio.

MOORE, CLARENCE B.

1894 "Certain Sand Mounds of the St. John's River, Florida," Journal of Academy of Natural Science of Philadelphia, Volume X, Page 2.

1908 "Certain Mounds of Arkansas and Mississippi," Academy of Natural Science of Philadelphia, Volume XIII, Part 4, Philadelphia, Pennsylvania.

1915 "Aboriginal Sites on Tennessee River," Journal of Academy of Natural Science of Philadelphia, Volume XVI, Part 2.

MOOREHEAD, WARREN K.

1892 "Primitive Man in Ohio," G. P. Putnam's Sons.

1894 "The Metzger Mound," Proceedings of the Academy of Natural Science of Philadelphia, p. 314.

1897 "Field Work," Publication of the Ohio Archaeological and Historical Society, Volume V, Columbus, Ohio.

1899 "Field Work," Publication of the Ohio Archaeological and Historical Society, Volume VII, Columbus, Ohio.

1917 "Stone Ornaments of the American Indian," Andover Press, Andover, Massachusetts.

1922 "The Hopewell Mound Group of Ohio," Field Museum of Natural History, Publication No. 211, Volume VI, No. 5, Chicago, Illinois.

MORGAN, LEWIS H.

1881 "Houses and House Life of the American Aborigines," Contribution to North American Ethnology, U. S. Geographical and Geological Survey, Volume IV, Washington, D. C.

MORGAN, RICHARD G.

1941   "A Hopewell Sculptured Head," The Ohio State Archaeological and Historical Quarterly, Volume L, No. 4.

MORTON, SAMUEL GEORGE, M. D.

1839   "Crania Americana or a Comparative View of the Skulls of Various Aboriginal Nations of North and South America," J. Dobson, Chestnut Street, Philadelphia; Simpkins, Marshall and Company, London.

1849   Third Edition.

NEUMANN, GEORG K.

1939   "The Relationship between Archaeological Cultures and Physical Types in the Eastern United States," paper presented at annual meeting of the American Association of Physical Anthropologists, Chicago, Illinois.

1941a   "Crania from the Porter Mound, Ross County, Ohio," Papers of the Michigan Academy of Science, Arts, and Letters, Volume XXVI, 1940, pp. 479–488.

1941b   "The Crania from the Hagan Mound and their Relationship to Those of Two Late Prehistoric Populations of Central Illinois," Section in Contributions to the Archaeology of the Illinois River Valley, Transcations American Philosophical Society, Philadelphia, N. S., Vol. 32, Part 1, pp. 79–82.

NEWMAN, MARSHALL T. AND CHARLES E. SNOW

1942   "Preliminary Report on the Skeletal Material from Pickwick Basin, Alabama," An Archaeological Survey of Pickwick Basin in the Adjacent Portions of the States of Alabama, Mississippi, and Tennessee, Bureau of American Ethology, Bulletin 129.

PHILLIPS, PHILIP

1940   "Middle American Influences on the Archaeology of the Southeastern United States," The Maya and Their Neighbors, D. Appleton Century Co., New York, New York, pp, 349-367.

PUTNAM, FREDERICK W.

1882   "Notes on the Copper Objects from North and South Americas contained in the collection of the Peabody Museum," Fifteenth Annual Report of Peabody Museum, Harvard University, Volume III, No. 2.

1884 "The Marriott Mound and Its Contents," Eighteenth Annual Report, Peabody Museum of American Archaeology and Anthropology, pp. 450–466.

1887 "Twelfth Annual Report," Peabody Museum of Harvard University, Volume III, No. 7.

1890 "The Serpent Mound of Ohio," Century Magagine, Volume XXXIX.

PUTNAM, FREDERICK W. AND C. C. WILLOUGHBY

1896 "Symbolism in Ancient American Art," American Association for the Advancement of Science, Volume XLIV.

QUIMBY, GEORGE I., JR.

1943 "A Subjective Interpretation of Some Design Similarities between Hopewell and Northern Algonkian," American Anthropologist, Volume 45, No. 4, p. 633.

READ, M. C.

1879 "Stone Tubes, Suggestions as to Their Possible Use," American Antiquarian, Volume II, No. 1, Chicago, Illinois, p. 53.

RITCHIE, WILLIAM A.

1938 "A Perspective of Northeastern Archaeology," American Antiquity, Society for American Archaeology, Volume IV, No. 2.

1944 "The Pre-Iroquoian Occupations of New York State," Rochester Museum Memoir, No. 1, Rochester, New York.

ROMANS, BERNARD

1775 "A Concise Natural History of East and West Florida," New York, New York.

SCHOOLCRAFT, HENRY F.

1843 "Observations Respecting Grave Creek Mound," Transactions of the American Ethnological Society, Volume I, New York, New York.

SELTZER, FRANK M.

1930 "The Archaeology of the Whitewater Valley," Indiana History Bulletin, Volume 7, No. 12.

1931 "Archaeology of Randolph County and the Fudge Mound," Indiana History Bulletin, Volume IX, No. 1.

1933 "Pottery of the Hopewell Type of the U. S. National Museum," Publication No. 2963, Smithsonian Institution, Volume 82, Washington, D. C.

SHETRONE, H. C.
1920 "The Culture Problem in Ohio Archaeology," American Anthropologist, Volume XXII.

1926 "Exploration of the Hopewell Group of Prehistoric Earthworks," Ohio Archaeological and Historical Quarterly, Volume XXXV, No. 1, Columbus, Ohio.

1930 "The Mound Builders," D. Appleton and Company, New York.

SHETRONE, H. C. AND E. F. GREENMAN
1931 "Exploration of the Seip Group of Prehistoric Earthworks," Ohio Archaeological and Historical Quarterly, Volume XL, No. 3, Columbus, Ohio.

SNOW, CHARLES E.
1942 "The Skeletal Remains from the Robbins Mound," Reports in Anthropology and Archaeology, Volume V, No. 5.

1943 "The Skeletal Remains from the Landing Site," Reports in Anthropology and Archaeology, Volume V, No. 7.

SPECK, F. G.
1937 "Montagnais Art in Birch Bark, A Circumpolar Trait, Indian Notes and Monographs," Museum of the American Indian, Heye Foundation, Volume IX, No. 2, New York, Broadway at 155th Street.

SQUIER, E. G. AND E. H. DAVIS
1848 "Ancient Monuments of the Mississippi Valley," Smithsonian Contributions to Knowledge, Washington, D. C.

STEWART, T. D
1940 "New Evidence on the Physical Type of the Bearers of the Hopewellian Culture," American Association of Physical Anthropologists, Abtract presented in Proceedings of Eleventh Annual Meeting.

1943 "Skeleton Remains from Platte and Clay Counties, Missouri," Archaeological Investigations in Platte and Clay Counties, Missouri, by Waldo R. Wedel, Bulletin 183, U. S. National Museum.

1943   "Skeletal Remains from Tajumulco, Guatemala," Excavations at Tajumulco, Guatemala School of American Research, Santa Fe, N. M., Monograph No. 9.

STEWART, T. D. AND P. F. TITTERINGTON
1944   "Filed Indian Teeth from Illinois," Journal of the Washington Academy of Sciences, Vol. 34, No. 10, pp. 317–321.

SWANTON, JOHN R.
1911   "Indian Tribes of the Lower Mississippi Valley," Bureau of American Ethnology, Bulletin 43, Washington, D. C.

THOMAS, CYRUS
1894   "Mound Explorations," Bureau of American Ethnology, Twelfth Annual Report, Washington, D. C.

THRUSTON, GATES P.
1897   "Antiquities of Tennessee," Published at Cincinnati, Ohio.

TOMLINSON, A. B.
1838   "Grave Creek Mound," A Letter to J. S. Williams published in American Pioneer.

VAILLANT, GEORGE C.
1932   "Some Resemblances in the Ceramics of Central and North America," The Medallion Papers, Giia Pueblo, Globe Arizona, pp. 1–50.

VON EICKSTEDT, E.
1934   Rassenkunde und Rassengeschichte der Menschheit, Stuttgart.

WARING, A. J., JR. AND PRESTON HOLDER
1945   "A Prehistoric Ceremonial Complex in the Southeastern United States," American Anthropologist, Volume 47, No. 1.

WEBB, CLARENCE H.
1944   "Stone Vessels from a Northeast Louisiana Site," American Antiquities, Volume IX, No. 14, pp. 386–395.

WEBB, WILLIAM S.
1938   "An Archaeological Survey of the Norris Basin in Eastern Tennessee," Bureau of American Ethnology, Bulletin No. 118, Washington, D. C.

1939   "An Archaeological Survey of Wheeler Basin on the Tennessee River in Northern Alabama," Bureau of American Ethnology, Bulletin No. 122.

1940   "The Wright Mounds, Site 6 and 7, Montgomery County, Kentucky," University of Kentucky Reports in Anthropology and Archaeology, Volume V, No. 1.

1941   "Mt. Horeb Earthworks and the Drake Mound," The University of Kentucky Reports in Anthropology and Archaeology, Volume V, No. 2.

1941   "The Morgan Stone Mound," The University of Kentucky Reports in Anthropology and Archaeology, Volume V, No. 3.

1942   "The C. & O. Mounds at Paintsville, Kentucky," The University of Kentucky Reports in Anthropology and Archaeology, Volume V, No. 4.

1943   "The Crigler Mounds and The Hartman Mound," The University of Kentucky Reports in Anthropology and Archaeaology, Volume V, No. 6.

1943   "The Riley Mound and The Landing Mound," The University of Kentucky Reports in Anthropology and Archeaology, Volume V, No. 7.

WEBB, WILLIAM S. AND DAVID L. DEJARNETTE
1942   "An Archaeological Survey of Pickwick Basin in the Adjacent Portions of the States of Alabama, Mississippi, and Tennessee," Bureau of American Ethnology, Bulletin 129.

WEBB, WILLIAM S. AND JOHN B. ELLIOTT
1942   "The Robbins Mounds," The University of Kentucky Reports in Anthropology and Archaeology, Volume V, No. 5.

WEBB, WILLIAM S. AND W. D. FUNKHOUSER
1936   "Rock Shelters in Menifee County, Kentucky," University of Kentucky Reports in Anthropology and Archeaology, Volume III, No. 4.

WEBB, WILLIAM S. AND WILLIAM G. HAAG
1940   "Cypress Creek Villages, Sites 11 and 12, McLean County, Kentucky," University of Kentucky Reports in Anthropology and Archeaology, Volume IV, No. 2.

WEDEL, WALDO R.
1938   "Hopewellian Remains near Kansas City, Missouri," Proceedings of the National Museum, Volume 86, No. 3045, Washington, D. C.

WELCH, L. B. AND T. M. RICHARDSON
1879   "A Description of Prehistoric Relics Found Near Wilmington, Ohio," American Antiquarian and Oriental Journal, Volume I.

WILLEY, GORDON R. AND R. B. WOODBURY

    1942   "A Chronological Outline for the Northwest Florida Coast," American Antiquities, Volume VII, No. 3, pp. 232–254.

WILLIS, ROGER K.

    1941   "The Baumer Focus," Society for American Archaeologists Notebook, Volume II, No. 2, p. 28.

WILLOUGHBY, CHARLES C.

    1922   "The Turner Group of Earthworks, Hamilton County, Ohio," Papers of the Peabody Museum of Harvard University, Volume VIII, No. 3, Cambridge, Massachusetts.

    1935   "Antiquities of the New England Indians," Peabody Museum of American Archaeology and Entnology, Harvard University, Cambridge, Massachusetts.

INDEX

A

B

C

THE UNIVERSITY OF TENNESSEE PRESS
KNOXVILLE